IN SEARCH OF FREEDOM

IN SEARCH OF FREEDOM

BY

JOGESH CHANDRA CHATTERJI

GYAN

Published by

Gyan Publishing House
5, Ansari Road
Daryaganj, New Delhi-110002
Phone: 011-47034999, 9811692060
E-mail: books@gyanbooks.com

Distribution Network
gyanbooks.com
India, USA, Canada, UK, Australia

ISBN: 978-93-6280-503-4 (HB)
First Published, 1958

2nd Impression 2024

Printed at: Gyan Press, Delhi.

IN SEARCH OF FREEDOM
Author: JOGESH CHANDRA CHATTERJI

IN SEARCH OF FREEDOM

By

JOGESH CHANDRA CHATTERJI, M.P.

PREFACE

The year 1857 saw the first fight for freedom against British rule in India. The movement was suppressed but British became alarmed. After the Indian Association was formed in Calcutta as a political move, Mr. Hume, a British I.C.S., started the Indian National Congress in 1885, with the sole object of channelling nationalistic movements in a slow and moderate way.

The Congress till 1904 was an annual gathering of leaders for passing pious resolutions in a beggarly way. The year 1905 was a great turning point in our national history when the then Viceroy, Lord Curzon, partitioned Bengal against the wishes of the people. The fight against this started from Bengal and gradually spread over the whole country and India stood as a nation.

As a counter challenge the Britishers worked out a new device of 'Divide and Rule' and gave birth to the Muslim League in 1906. The Congress later gave recognition to this newly born babe of the British Empire. The revolutionaries did not recognise it. In fact they did not generally enlist Muslims in their underground guerilla organisation.

Britain held India by force. So the revolutionaries had to come forward to meet this armed adversary with bombs and pistols. The first burst of bomb at Muzaffarpur in 1908 was a new kind of noise which aroused people from their long slumber. The next bomb on the Viceroy in Delhi in 1912 shook the Empire for a pretty long time.

Then came World War I in 1914 and Indian revolutionaries made a grand effort to oust the British from India with the help of the Germans, when Mr. Gandhi and the Congress were vigorously helping Britishers in their war efforts just to gain some reforms. After this war the country could feel how futile it was to flatter the foreigners. Then Gandhiji propagated the non-violent non-cooperation movement. An armed guerilla fight against the British might was beset with great danger. But the Gandhian mass demonstration was much easier for a weak and meek people to adopt.

This new utopia of non-violent non-cooperation was a mere revival of the old Vaishnavite, Buddhist and Jain Philosophy (Non-violence is the supreme virtue). Naturally this was much to the liking of the traditional spirit of religiosity pervading throughout the old Hindu India, since the advent of the Buddha. The weak people had very quickly grasped this less risky method of non-violent non-cooperation.

The strong sundried bureaucracy of Great Britain was not to be intimidated by these harmless gestures of threats by an unarmed mass. Naturally therefore the movements of 1921, 1930 and 1932 could not achieve their ends. Thus while the Gandhians were busy whirling their non-violent charkhas, the lawyers with their constitutional agitations, the progressive Congressites striving to spread their socialist wings and the Communists acquainting themselves with the rules and methods of Moscow, the militant youths of the country carried on unceasingly with their secret activities for the emancipation of the country. The Government was ever ready to crush them with all possible oppressive methods at its command which began to make people appreciate their sufferings and sacrifices for the national cause.

Sir N. N. Sarkar, the then law member, Government of India, proved in 1935 by citing 56 court cases of Bengal that the Bengal Congress was mainly dominated by the revolutionaries for many years.

What was true about Bengal in early years, began to hold ground for the rest of India during World War II. Gandhiji gave only the slogan of "Quit India" and the motto "Do or Die", but after the arrest of Congress leaders the masses turned the movement into a violent revolution, the long desired end for which the secret revolutionaries were striving hard for decades at great sufferings and sacrifices. Some hints from Mr. Amery, the then Secretary of State for India in his B. B. C. radio speech and the radio speeches of the I. N. A. and Netaji Subhas Chandra Bose fanned the flame of revolution.

By the latter part of 1941 the Congress was politically dead. The Communists were with the Government. Only the underground revolutionaries were then active in a very limited way, as important members were in jail. With the Japanese attack in December 1941 a new hope was generated in India and the result was the violent uprising of August, 1942. The Congress leaders were in jail, but the revolutionary masses whom the Congress kept so long in suppression, were violently active in the field. This was the outcome of the activities of the secret revolutionary parties carried on for decades. The idea of an organised national fight was undoubtedly derived from the revolutionaries.

1942 movement proved that the country was quite ready for a mass revolutionary fight; but the Gandhian leadership failed to give proper guidance. So the immature and unprepared move failed to produce the desired result. It was crushed by inhuman brutality.

The organised armed march of the Indian National Army under the able leadership of Netaji Subhas Chandra Bose to capture India was checked. The I. N. A. march failed, because the revolutionary forces which could help and welcome them with open arms, were already crushed in 1942 movement. But even through their defeat in the front, they were successful, after the War, in giving the death blow to the British regime in India. For, the I. N. A. leaders' trial in Delhi Red Fort, gave rise to a renewed outburst of the revolutionary forces in the country; student unrest in Calcutta gradually engulfed the whole country. The open navy revolt in Bombay and Karachi ultimately proved to be a great revolt of the Indian elements of the armed forces; police also joined hands with them.

Transfer of power through compromise demoralised India.

It is then the shrewd Britishers could see that this vast country could no longer be kept under subjugation by the mercenary Indian soldiers and they quitted India through a compromise with the weak leadership of the Congress, who readily agreed to the proposal of communal division of the country without any transfer of population and keeping it under the British Commonwealth of Nations. The folly of their compromise is being felt by the common man through vast unemployment, constant rise of prices of essential commodities, disintegration, characterlessness, corruption and degradation. Propaganda of socialism under the firm grip of capitalism is self-evident. Day in and day out we are preaching peace and non-violence, but our next door neighbours are our worst enemies. This is painful to all lovers of the country. How can a corrupt and degraded people give proper resistance to the powerful foreign invaders ? By mere meetings and howlings we are only making ourselves a laughing stock.

A revolutionary change is the need of the hour.

Revolutionaries in general and Netaji Subhas in

particular were strongly against any sort of compromise, which inevitably brings weakness in national character which again brings about a general national degeneration. That is being realised now by every correct thinking person. Right thinking men feel that the degradation of national character is the biggest disaster facing the country today. Army is linked up with the general population. Naturally the infection is present there also. In this way the national security is in jeopardy.

This would not have been, had 1942 and the I. N. A. movements been simultaneous. In that case, the I. N. A. march to Delhi would have achieved its objective. The small Anglo-American forces in eastern India would have found themselves surrounded by Indian revolutionary masses on the one side and the armed I. N. A. forces on the other. The huge Indian elements of the British army would have certainly made common cause with their country men. In that event the I. N. A. march to Delhi would have been strengthened at every step having been joined by the revolutionary masses in Assam, Bengal, Bihar, Uttar Pradesh and the occupation of Delhi would have been an easy affair. A strong independent India would have thus been formed without any dismemberment by communal division. That India, naturally, would have been of high national character. Real socialist planning could have been possible and the spirit of co-operation would have unfolded itself in blossom. The country's progress would have been steady, unhampered by the evil spitefulness of our neighbours. Now even Pakistan is kicking at us. Today we find ourselves helpless in resisting the Chinese and Pakistani aggressions.

When a country is in danger only its patriotic youths of strong moral character can save it. When they raise their organised voice against the misdeeds of rulers, the people hear them and that saves a nation from all round degradation. They do not spare anybody who is in the wrong. They must remember that the sovereignty of the country lies with the people. They are only to stand boldly for the people and the people can be saved. If the youths can exhibit their character in this national crisis, the people will surely stand by them.

Calcutta
February 1967.

Jogesh Chandra Chatterji

FOREWORD

I convened a Conference of Indian Revolutionaries in Delhi in December in 1958. The main object was to compile a history of the contribution of the revolutionaries to the freedom movement. It seemed to be too big a task to be accomplished by anyone individually, but the Government attitude was clearly apathetic.

So, is this book, rather the personal experience of my life as a revolutionary fighter for freedom. I am, therefore, quite conscious of its various shortcomings including repetitions. I started this dangerous life as a school boy at Comilla (now in East Pakistan); and in the second stage, my secret party, the Anushilan Samiti, deputed me to northern India in 1923.

Between the 30 years from 1916 to 1946, I spent 24 years in prison, out of which nearly two years and a half I had been on hunger strike, the longest two being—one in Agra jail in 1934 for 142 days and the other next year in Lucknow jail for 111 days.

I am now 72 years old with my nerve system shattered and I could write this book somehow because Congress High Cammand have been generous to me to concede a seat in the Parliament since 1956.

A good number of my friends have helped me in writing this book. A few names I must mention. My friend Radha Swami was assisting me all along. Dr. A. K. Mazumdar, Dr. Halder, Prof. Nigam took much interest. When I was in Delhi Nursing Home, Prof. Devajyoti Burman took away the manuscript so that in case of my death the book will remain. But the tragedy is that he himself passed away just when, through his labour, the book was about to be out. The book will carry the sacred memory of his, my esteemed revolutionary associate, who was M. A. in a dozen subjects and was himself an institution. Shri P. C. Chatterjee has ever been a source of constant inspiration and guide and assisted in every way towards the fulfilment of my task. They all deserve my most heartfelt thanks.

I am grateful to Shri K. C. Ghosh for the supply of the photo of Sailesh Chandra Chatterjee.

To Dr. R. C. Majumdar, the eminent historian, who contributed an introduction, almost from his sick bed, I record by sincerest gratitude.

I fell ill soon after the MS went to press. Quite a few unfortunate errors went undetected for which I feel sorry. An errata is given at the end.

Calcutta

February 1967. Jogesh Chandra Chatterji

DEDICATION

In Memory of

Sailesh Chandra Chatterjee,

whom Doctor Khan's mortal injection laid at eternal rest in 1933 in Deoli Detention Camp where he was detained along with five hundred revolutionary fighters for India's freedom from Bengal.

You could not see India free. But I wonder whether you have been spared the pains through which I am going, as a result of what is happening in independent India to-day, the nineteenth year of our free existence. Was this the freedom for which you fought and died?

—Jogeshda

CONTENTS

THE APPENDIX

CHAPTER I

MY VILLAGE SURROUNDINGS

Home is sweet to all. But to me it is only a dream now. I shall never again see the place where I was born and spent my childhood with my friends and relatives, villagers and all others with whom I enjoyed living. My grandmother, mother and many others lived and breathed their last in our village.

I was born in the year 1895 in Gaodia, a village in the hinterlands of Bikrampur, noted as the birth-place of a number of scholars, humanists and political leaders, in the District of Dacca now in East Pakistan. My father, the late Babu Bipin Chandra Chatterji, was a businessman at Daulatkhan in the District of Barisal and one of my uncles was a Teshildar there in the Court of Wards. Another uncle of mine worked as an assistant in his brother-in-law's business at Gauhati in Assam. I remember how eagerly we waited for their home-coming during holidays. They always brought presents for us and the days they stayed with us took the colour of festivals. Good food, tolerance of our childish pranks and relaxation of the usual routine left memories of their visits, then as now.

The man who influenced my childhood most was a cousin of my father who lived with us in the village. He was a Naib in a Zemindary estate and his office was very near our village. He was a well-informed man and was fully conversant with new ideas and events. It was from him that I first heard of the Russo-Japanese war (1904) a year before the Bengal partition movement began. We heard with rapt attention when he narrated how Japan captured Port Arthur and how Japanese Admiral Togo destroyed the Russian Fleet. Japan's victory created a great enthusiasm in our minds. We felt that at last some Asian nation had shown that the Europeans were not invincible.

The intellectual alertness and zeal for social reform which my uncle evinced was, however, not a unique phenomenon in our village. Bikrampur had a cultural tradition of its own. It is believed that Dipankar Atish, the man who preached Buddhism in Tibet, was born in Bikrampur. In more recent times persons of hallowed memory like Dr J. C. Bose, C. R. Das, Dr Aghornath Chatterji (father of the late Sarojini Naidu) and many others came from this area. The area was known as a centre of learning from the earliest days of the history of Bengal. And despite the apathy of the Government towards the educational development of the region, even in 1922 Bikrampur could boast of at least 32 High schools affiliated to the University of Calcutta and 13 National Schools of high school standard. Besides these there were a number of primary and middle schools for children.

During my childhood the Government found that the schools of Bikrampur were the centres of what they used to call seditious activities. Because of this they looked askance at them. Police raids on the houses of teachers and students became more and more frequent. Even the women of our village evinced a type of social awareness unheard of in many parts of India of those days. I vividly remember an incident of how they stood against the superstitions of the time.

Rajani Nath Roy, a great son of Bikrampur, about whom Bipin Chandra Pal has written in his *My Life and Times* married a Kulin girl named Bidhumukhi and became a Brahmo. Roy topped the list in almost all the University Examinations, joined the Finance Department of the Government, rose to the rank of Accountant General of Bengal and died in 1906.

Bidhumukhi was a kulin girl from Bikrampur. To save the customs of the Kulins she was to be married to an old Kulin Brahmin who already had a number of wives. The kulin men believed that if they could marry a hundred times, they would go directly to heaven and the Kulin families had to marry their girls to another Kulin failing which they usually forced their girls to remain spinsters. For Bidhumukhi, however all this was too much to stand. She was secretly helped to get out of the clutches of her superstition ridden family by two brothers who were her distant relatives. One of the brothers was Barada Nath Haldar who later became the father-in-law of C. R. Das. Bidhumukhi was sheltered in Bharat Ashram in Calcutta. Soon she was enabled to get the help of Durga Mohan Das, father of C. R. Das, who brought her up with his own daughters.

Roy was initiated to Brahmo Samaj by Keshab Chandra Sen. He married Bidhumukhi in accordance with the Civil Marriage Act. This caused a consternation in our village as well as in the surrounding areas. Roy came with his wife to his village home. One day some people were invited to dine with the Roys. While the dinner was in progress, Bidhumukhi happened to come under the canopy where the dinner was being served. At once there was turmoil. Some village elders and other guests present asked everybody to leave their seats without eating any food. But there were others who objected to this type of unseemly behaviour. My mother and aunt were also present at this dinner. After having accepted the invitation they did not want to insult their hosts. They said that they were honoured by the invitation from Bidhumukhi, a lady of great learning and courage, hence they would continue their dinner. Thanks to their courageous stand, the dinner went on.

Such courage and clear-headedness were unheard of in those days when people could not differentiate between the Hindu reform movements and Christianity. Any one who wanted to reform the Hindu society was called a Christian and a heretic. To cross the seas was a travesty of religious and social morals. People suffered the village ostracism which even deprives a man of the barbar's and and washerman' services for such offences. But even so the essential humanism which is the heritage of Bikrampur triumphed. My mother and aunt and many other ladies of the village proved again that the vital humanistic current was not dead in Bikrampur.

Whenever I think of Bikrampur and its people one thing comes very vividly to my mind—the abundance of water in the area. I do not know what connection water has with progressive and humanistic ideas. Yet I feel that the soft and at the same time terrible nature surrounding us in Bikrampur has somehow or other influeneed the lives and aspirations of the people of the area.

Bikrampur is criss-crossed by rivers and canals and during the rainy season the entire area looks like a vast sea with innumerable islands. The nearest business centre from our village was Lohajang on the bank of the mighty Padma. At Lohajang there was also a steamer station which connected our area with the world outside. There were no roads, and boats were the only means of communication in those days. But in the winter when the canals dried up we could walk from village to village.

Each house of our village was a symbol of the peace and openness of village culture. There were no walls at that time round the houses. A middle-class or a rich family had a pond or two in the yard. During the rainy season even house-to-house contact had to be maintained by boats. And when market places were inundated during the rainy season, big boats were used as shops.

As a result of the yearly inundation the soil was fertile and every year there were rich crops of jute and rice. The people developed an aesthetic conception of living by being sensitive to the bounties and hazards of Nature. Living in such a place we had to learn swimming as soon as we stopped toddling. Boating came naturally to us. The abundance of fish in the rivers, canals and ponds allured us to fishing and many times we had narrow escapes when our boats were caught in storms.

The rains brought us plenty and the children heard the stories of the great classics of Ramayana and Mahabharata sitting round their grandmothers.

I wonder whether the children of the present generation hear the same set of stories or not. Possibly their grandmothers are too busy in other preoccupations and do not find time to tell them stories.

Every month there was a religious function and the chain of monthly celebrations was climaxed by the Durga Puja. During the Pujas we were treated with presents and sweets and the usual routine of attending to our studies was temporarily forgotten. Like all children we counted the days for the coming festivities. Going to school, interupting our games, was very often disliked by us. But coming from Bikrampur we could not avoid the school.

The school had also its own charm. By the time I went to school the nationalist movement fired the imagination of the people. And the school teachers of Bikrampur stood in the vanguard of that movement, spread the spirit of the movement for national freedom to their students, worked for the amelioration of the suffering people and were living examples of dedicated life before us.

I think it was in the year 1904 or 1905 that the sudden appearance of a big boat in our village surprised and perplexed us. The grey-haired Headmaster of the neighbouring village school was in it. He was clad in Khaddar. With him was a group of boys also clad in Khaddar. All of them got down in our village and proceeded towards our village school. I followed them with immense curiosity. They were singing "Bow to the coarse cloth as our poverty-striken unhappy Mother India cannot afford to give us anything better......". The Headmaster and other teachers of our village school received them. A meeting was held. The speakers preached swadeshi and boycott of British goods.

The meeting left a lasting impression on my childish mind. I could vaguely see the connection between the meeting and my father's refusal to send Manchester clothes during the next Puja which was held soon after the meeting. Many children, however, did receive new foreign-made clothes during the Pujas. But this did not distress me. I was so stirred by the speeches which I heard in that meeting, that I thought that I would be able to bring peace and tranquility to Mother India by refusing to put on foreign clothes. I even refused to join the Puja festivities as I thought that I had *no right to enjoy when Mother India was in* chains. The meeting was the beginning of my quest for the freedom of my country and of my people.

BARISAL CONFERENCE OF 1906

A political Conference was held at Barisal, in 1906. It was specially important because of the recent partition of Bengal and also because the

Lieut. Governor of Bengal had already started repression. The President of the Conference was Barrister A. Rasul. The Conference was broken up by the army, and men like Surendranath Bannerjee were grossly insulted. The heroic boy, Chittaranjan Guha Thukarta, was brutally assaulted for shouting "Bande Mataram". Sir Bamfylde Fuller, the Lieut. Governor, influenced the Nawab of Dacca to form the Muslim League in persuance of the policy of divide and rule. The consequences were the Hindu Muslim riots at Comilla and Jamalpur. These incidents gave a new turn to the Swadeshi Movement. The Dacca Anushilan Samiti gradually went underground.

There was no open police activity in our village but the Anushilan members were instructed to be alert. Any new comer entering the village was looked upon with suspicion. In this way an atmosphere of secrecy was created by our elders, who were members of the Samiti. This was perhaps an index to what was happening in the rest of East Bengal. I do not recollect anything associated with secret activities in our village. But I came to know later that one member of the Roy family of our village had joined the secret Anushilan Samiti. On his information the Gaodia dacoity was committed by the Anushilan Samiti in 1911, in which many important members of the Samiti participated. This decoity has been described by the late

Pratul Chandra Gangooli in his articles published in the Bengali monthly *Prabasi*.

AT DAULATKHAN IN BARISAL

I had to leave home and go to Daulatkhan in Bhola sub-division. The year was, possibly, 1907. Like the place of my birth this was also an interesting place. Bhola sub-division, like Bikrampur, was a low- lying area not far off from the sea. Daulatkhan was on the bank of the river Meghna. On the other side of the Meghna was Hatia Island in Noakhali. Even river water in this area was salty. People had to use water from the ponds. The vast majority of the population was Muslim. They had good relations with the Hindus in those days. The soil was very rich and rice of good quality grew in abundance. Some coconut also was produced, but betelnut was the main product. Betelnuts from this area and Noakhali almost monopolised the markets of Northern India. The rich soil made the economic condition of the people quite good.

I lived in Daulatkhan for nearly two years and was a student of the Middle English School there. Politically the place was very dull. The Muslims were not interested in the partition agitation. Though influential, the Hindus were very limited in number and they spent their time in their respective avocations. Most of the businessmen in the big bazar were Hindus from Bikrampur.

The only interesting things there for me were

the two weekly newspapers, the *Hitabadi* and the *Bangabasi*. Soon after my arrival, very interesting news came in these papers. The Muzaffarpur Bomb Case was a matter in which everybody became very interested. My father and uncle also read the news with great care. In fact these papers generated such a hunger for news that a group of people would rush to our big business house as soon as they noticed the paper being delivered by the postman.

The Muzaffarpur Case really shook the country from one corner to the other. It was followed by reports of arrests at Maniktola and the Court proceedings of the Alipore Bomb Conspiracy case. Thus mentally I was in touch with the sensational cases of the revolutionaries who even while in jail killed the approver Naren Gosain. The martyrdom of Kanailal Dutta and Satyendra Nath Bose, the two accused in the Gosain murder case, thrilled my boyish heart.

I also came in contact with a person in the bazar who was an expert lathi player. He took much interest in teaching me lathi and I used to go to him every afternoon. My father was very happy about this as lathi exercise improved my health.

As regards my education, I did not progress much from what I had learned in my village school. My father realized this and worried about my proper studies. That is why after about two years I had to leave Daulatkhan and come to Comilla.

CHAPTER II

AT COMILLA, NEAR ASSAM

My father accompanied me to Comilla in 1909 and left me there under the guardianship of my uncle, the late Bisweshwar Chatterjee. He was a pleader in the Comilla Court. I was fortunate to get the opportunity of living with him. He was by nature very generous and a man of strong moral character and intensely patriotic. People of the town had the highest respect for him. Any stranger to the town was sure to get food and shelter at his house. His house was something like a free students hostel, because even unknown students from different districts stayed in his house like intimates of the house-hold.

Had I not come here at this stage, I do not know what would have happened to the feelings I had gathered in my tender heart at Gaodia and Daulatkhan.

COMILLA ORGANISATION

Biren Chatterjee, the famous revolutionary, used to come to the house of my uncle often. I knew him from my childhood as a relative and it was also known to me that he was a revolutionary. He used to carry me on his bicycle to different places and used to sell clothes but I could not understand the object of his doing so except that it was his means of livelihood. Biren Chatterjee often visited the house of Ramesh Banerjee who was the agent of the Singer Sewing Machine. I could not understand the purpose of these frequent visits either.

Two years later things were crystal clear to me when one night Ramesh Banerjee and nine others were arrested in a midnight police raid, tried and sentenced to 7 years R. I. for attempted dacoity. Sarada Chakravarty was the first District organiser of Comilla Anushilan Samiti. By the time I came to the Committee Purna Chakravarty had replaced him. Sarada Chakravarty was later murdered by the Party because he betrayed the revolutionaries by his failure to stick to the ideals of the Samiti. One of the oldest members of Comilla Sàmiti was Pulin Gupta, who was later sent to Pabna as District organiser. But eventually he came back to Comilla and became Assistant to Purna Chakravarty.

Under Purna Chakravarty's leadership the district organisation of the Tippera district grew by leaps and bounds. Comilla, Brahmanbaria and Chandpur centres were strengthened. Organisation among students became very strong and consequently village units also developed.

ANUSHILAN SAMITI

Immediately after the Sepoy Mutiny of 1857 in which the English educated people of the country took scarcely any part, a new type of national consciousness came into being. The birth of this Indian Association and the formation of the Indian National Congress in 1885 brought into force an aspect of this new consciousness. But the other aspect of this consciousness which is to be found in Dinabondhu Mitra's *Nil Darpan* and other books some of which were even proscribed by the British Government had to wait 11 long years to find an organisational shape.

Anushilan Samiti, a secret revolutionary organisation, which played a very big part in the revolutionary movement of India of which I was a part and parcel throughout my revolutionary life, deserves a few words.

This organisation was started in Calcutta in 1902 with Barrister Pramatha Nath Mitra (generally known as P. Mitra) as its founder President, Aurobindo Ghose and C. R. Das as Vice presidents and Jatindra Nath Banerjee as Secretary. Many extremist leaders, including Sarala Devi, Bepin Pal and Sister Nivedita were its supporters.

In 1905, P. Mitra with Aurobindo and Bepin Pal toured some Bengal districts in order to establish branches of the Anushilan Samiti. On such an occasion, Pulin Behari Das was picked up as the fittest person to take up the charge of the Dacca Anushilan Samiti. P. Mitra was so much impressed by his new disciple that he ceremoniously gave him the initiation at his residence in Calcutta.

It was Pulin Behari Das, the iron man, who really organised the Dacca Anushilan Samiti in every district of East and North Bengal. According to the Sedition Committee Report of 1919, within a few years this dynamic personality established 500 branches of the Samiti.

The idea of Anushilan was taken from the book 'Anushilan' written by the great Bengali intellectual and author Bankim Chandra Chatterjee. The ideal was the attainment of perfection of life. For this purpose it was thought that the four stages of life, described in the Sanskrit texts of the Hindus, were to be gone through. Each stage had to be cultivated to its perfection. And for this the most necessary thing was believed to be self-development and self-fulfillment. The way to achieve these ends is called Anushilan. A member of the Anushilan Samiti had a mission for the fulfillment of which he was to lead his life. Bankim's ideas of rebellious sannyasins given in his book 'Ananda Math' were religiously translated into action by Pulin Behari Das and his trusted men. They gradually spread the organisation far and wide and in course of time it assumed the character of somewhat an All-India organisation. The organisation's activities spread even among the Indians living overseas.[1]

In the West Bengal branch of the Samiti, Barindra Kumar Ghose, the younger brother of Aurobindo, was too eager for speedy militant activities ; and it is likely that in this he was influenced bv his elder brother Aurobindo Ghose. But P. Mitra and the majority of the Samiti were not in favour of getting involved into immediate revolutionary activities. They were pleading for organisational strength and patience till the opportune moment came. This led to the separation of Barindra and his group from the Samiti. Barindra

1 Regarding the ramification of the organisation we may mention here a few facts. Dr. Charu Chandra Ghose went to the North West Frontier Province as a missionary of the Anushilan Samiti as early as 1908. He became not only one of the top public leaders of the province, but also inspired many youths to revolutionary activities.

Dr. V. V. Athalye of Satara was drawn into Anushilan Samiti when he was a student of the National Medical College in Calcutta. He started a secret revolutionary organisation in his state and was given a heavy sentence as a leader of the Satara Conspiracy Case in 1910.

Dr. Hedgeware of Nagpur became a member of the Samiti when, like Dr. Athalye, he was a student of the National Medical College in Calcutta. He led a life of mission and later started the Rastriya Swayang Sevak Sangha, a physical culture organisation.

In foreign countries, besides many others, two missionaries of the Anushilan Samiti became well-known figures One was Dr. Tarak Nath Das, who became well-known in international affairs. The other was Mr. Abani Mukherjee, who was sent to India from Japan by Rashbehari Bose with a notebook containing about 400 addresses of revolutionary sympathisers in India. He was arrested at Singapore with that notebook, but later escaped to Soviet Russia. He came back to India incognito in the 1920's and returned to Russia when he married. He is possibly dead now.

and his associates started a newspaper called *Jugantar* and also a bomb factory at Maniktola Garden in Calcutta. For some time the *Jugantar* played a significant role in rousing the people's interest in revolutionary activities. But Barindra and his associates thought that was not enough. In order to give an additional fillip to their activities and propaganda, a bomb was thrown at Muzaffarpur by Kshudiram Bose and Prafulla Chaki. This created a stir in the entire country. Soon even the village minstrels started singing about the heroic deeds of Kshudiram. In the sequel, the bomb factory was discovered by the police ; and Barindra, Aurobindo and others were arrested. They were tried in the Alipore Conspiracy Case (1908) and all the important persons, except Aurobindo, were sentenced. C. R. Das, the most promising barrister of the Calcutta Bar defended him. The court proceedings were published in the papers and the people read them eagerly.

From the name of their paper *Jugantar* Barindra's group came to be popularly known as the Jugantar group. The Jugantar group became practically defunct after the Alipore Conspiracy Case. But it soon came into prominence under the able leadership of Jatin Mukherjee, the immortal leader of the now famous Indo-German conspiracy of the first World War days. After Jatin Mukherjee's martyrdom, the Jugantar group disintegrated and different groups in different parts of Bengal, led by different individuals were popularly known as Jugantar. Between these different groups there was hardly any cohesion and there was no centralised leadership to control the activities of the different groups in Bengal which went by the name of Jugantar. Sometimes the top leaders of the different groups used to co-operate on the basis of some specific actions. Thus there was Jibanlal Chatterjee's group in Vikrampur, Surendramohan Ghosh's group in Mymensingh, Purna Das's group in Faridpur, Monoranjan Gupta and Arun Guha's group in Barisal, Bipin Ganguli's group in Howrah, besides many other local and localised groups of revolutionaries which used to call themselves as Jugantar. But Anushilan Samiti had a different history.

The Anushilan Samiti, led by Pulin Behari Das under the guidance of P. Mitra, maintained a steady progress and in the long run it developed into more or less a countrywide organisation for an armed revolution. Discipline and secrecy were strictly observed and consequently the police vigilance had hardly any information on the ramifications of the organisation. The Samiti felt the necessity of some propaganda organs. And for this purpose they used to publish and distribute secretly two papers—*Swadhin Bharat* in Bengali and *Liberty* in English.

Anushilan Samiti became a secret. centralised

organisation of iron-disciplined men of strong moral character. Its members were not after name or fame; they only worked for the good of the people and the country. Complete self-effacement *for the cause of the people and the* nation was what the Samiti demanded from its members.

The Anushilan Samiti very easily attracted the attention of a group of young men who were working at Chandannagore, a French possession near Calcutta, with similar ideas under the leadership of Matilal Roy and his associate Rashbehari Bose. The Dacca Samiti and the Chandannagore group merged together and soon Chandannagore became the virtual headquarter of the Anushilan Samiti. And it was because of this that Girija Babu, an important leader of the Dacca Anushilan Samiti, became a most trusted lieutenant of Rashbehari Bose in Northern India. Sachindra Nath Sanyal and Girija Babu bade adieu to Rashbehari Bose when he left Calcutta for Japan in a Japanese ship from the Outram Ghat in 1915. Rashbehari wrote very feelingly about Girija Babu from Japan, as he did about Sanyal. He also wrote that the expenses for his journey to Japan were borne by the Anushilan Samiti.

After Pulin Behari Das was sentenced and sent to the Andamans Jail, the real leadership of the Anushilan Samiti came to Narendra Mohan Sen and Pratul Chandra Ganguli. I had the privilege of working under them during the years I spent in Bengal and it was Pratul Chandra Ganguli who, as the leader of the Anushilan Samiti, sent me in 1923 to U. P. to work as the representative of the Samiti. But let me write about the Comilla organisation first.

The late Birendra Nath Chatterjee, veteran revolutionary of Bengal, was a relative and co-villager of my uncle, Bisweswar Chatterjee. He was one of the early followers of late Pulin Behari Das, the leader of the Dacca Anushilan Samiti, and was the first person to be sent to Comilla to organize a branch of the Anushilan Samiti. His first recruit was late Surendra Nath Maulick, one of my cousins. Maulick recruited the brothers, Ramesh Banerjee and Dr. Abinash Banerjee who figured during the Comilla riots of 1907.

My uncle's house played a very big part both in the revolutionary movement as well as in the Gandhian non-cooperation movement. I shall come to that later. Shri Janakinath Sarkar, the well known headmaster of the Iswar Pathshala, who, as a student, was living in the house of Bisweswar Chatterjee, was also a recruit to the Party. He was a classmate of Maulick. The great philanthropist of Comilla, late Mahesh Chandra Bhattacharya, established the Iswar Pathshala and chose Sarkar as the Headmaster of the institution. Sarkar was a brilliant scholar and had been a class-mate of the only son of Bhattacharya, who died when he was a student of the B. A. class.

DISCIPLINE IN COMILLA ORGANISATION

Our District organiser had the over-all charge of the three districts of Chittagong Division, namely, Tripura, Chittagong and Noakhali. He was appointed by the Central Organisation and was directly responsible to it. Every worker of the district acted according to his direction. In the district he was independent, but he had to be cooperative. Central representatives had no freedom to move with the members of the district without the knowledge and permission of the district-in-charge.

The District Organiser had an assistant who knew all about the district. When the D. O. was arrested by the police, his assistant used to take charge till some other D. O. was sent to the District from the centre.

The D. O. had no authority to organise any murder or dacoity in his district. These had to be sanctioned by the Centre. The D. O. had to keep himself informed of the places in his district from where money could be available. The Centre maintained a list of persons who were experts in certain types of actions like dacoity or murder and one person was in charge of the Violence Department. The leaders of the Violence Department could not move in a district without the permission of the D. O. of the district. He generally knew the experts personally. Before a decoity was committed for money, the person in charge of the Violence Department went to two or three districts, heard of the possible places from the D. O.s and then selected one place in one district. If it was a boat dacoity, expert boatmen were requisitioned. If an iron safe had to be broken open, the in-charge of the Violence Department requisitioned persons accordingly. If, say, 12 men were required in a dacoity, the leader of the Violence Department, would, in collaboration with the Centre and the D. O. of the district assembled these men from different places at a pre-arranged place after nightfall so that they were unable to recognise one another in the dark. They would then reach the place under the leader's direction and different persons would perform their assigned work and as soon as a bugle or a whistle would ring, they would stop their work, stand round the leader, who counted them and ordered them to march on. After reaching a specified place the booty and the arms would be handed over to new men, who in their turn would carry them to safer custody. Every individual was searched to ensure that nothing was left with any one of the group which committed the dacoity. And the actionists went back empty-handed to their own places. If they were somehow caught they could not be prosecuted for lack of evidence.

The same was the procedure for murder. If

three persons went for the action, one would actually shoot and two would be on guard. After the action the revolvers or pistols and cartridges would be handed over to another custodian and they themselves would go empty-handed.

When a member left a district and went to another, he was introduced to the new D. O. through the Centre. If there was any letter of introduction from the previous district, it was channelled through the Centre. He could not keep any contact with any member of his former district. *Correspondence also was not allowed.*

Arms were all under the Central Organisation and were kept in the custody of unsuspected persons.

The address of a person not known to many was used for correspondence. He had to hand over the letters unopened. And the letters were destroyed after they were read. Even burnt letters could be read out if not reduced to ashes. Blotting paper was not used, because this could be read out and deciphered. Persons who had committed a decoity or a murder together, were not to talk about it even amongst themselves.

The D. O. had to reveal all information to the Central Organiser or his Deputy who could meet any member even in private if deemed necessary. Once a D. O. left a district he could not maintain any more connection with that district.

As a part of discipline the members were

distributed into batches of not more than five persons including the Batch leader. Over a number of batches were the Circle Leaders, who had to submit daily reports to the D. O. or his Deputy every evening.

The batch leaders were responsible for the entire well being of the members of his batch.

Recruiting was another dificult task for the secret organisation. Before a member was recruited detailed information about him was collected. A man of character with strong partiotic feelings was recruited after due scrutiny.

Detailed information was sent to the Centre by the D. O. So the Centre knew, or was in possession of the necessary information about the district.

A secret semi-military organisation was not an easy task at a time when the country was under the mighty British imperial rule. Therefore Mantra-Gupti (secrecy) had to be observed very rigidly. That was really the life line of our organisation. A betrayal could easily make our life impossible. Hence the adherence to the Pratijnas (Vows) :

"I shall not disconnect myself from the Samiti."

"I shall always observe strictly the discipline of the Samiti."

"Wherever I may be, I shall present myself before the D. O. whenever asked for."

"Always I shall engage myself for the good of

the Samiti."

"I shall observe secrecy. Whatever I shall know or learn from the Samiti, shall not be given out to any outsider."

"I shall not discuss Samiti affairs unnecessarily. I shall keep aloof from argumentations and talkativeness."

"Whenever I come to know of any conspiracy against the Samiti, I would at onee try to suppress it and report it to the D. O."

"I shall always speak the truth to the D. O. and shall not keep anything secret from him."

"I shall keep my moral charecter spotless."

"I shall do good to my country and the world at large."

These were the essential points taught to the members. Every member knew them thoroughly well and observed them strictly. Our D. O., Purna Chakravarty, was a personification of these Vows. Every member had deep respect for him and loved him very dearly. As the basis of the Samiti had a religious orientation, every member looked upon himself as a servant of God. It may be mentioned here that Pulin Behari Das, the leader of the Dacca Anushilan Samiti, was intensely religious ; and so was Barrister P. Mitra, the Founder of the Anushilan Samiti.

We were Karmayogins. Our Karma (action) was a part of the Yoga (salvation). We would work as duty but were not to be perturbed if the result was not forthcoming. Our object was political. We thought that without making ourselves men of sterling character we could not achieve our political objective. To serve the country was the religious duty of the members of the samiti. Anushilan's main task was the formation of character of high order and this required a faith. It is not surprising that the founders and leaders of the Samiti found this faith in religion. For the Indian educated public did scarcely accept positivism as a faith to live by. Politics was infused with religion and the idea of a secular politics was still not attractive. It is not surprising that often independence was translated as " Mukti ", a term signifying blessedness.

We read and discussed the *Bhagavad Gita*, books of Swami Vivekananda, *Desher Katha* (Affairs of the country) of Sakharam Ganesh Deuskar, poems and writings of Rabindranath Tagore, writings on Nihilism of Russia, Carbonari Movement of Italy, Irish Rising, American War of Independence, besides French Revolution. We read books on the Sepoy Mutiny, and the lives of Shivaji, Guru Govinda Singh, Rana Pratap, etc. and the two *Jugantar* articles *Mukti kon Pathe* (Which) Way Salvation Lies) and *Bartaman Rananiti* (Tactics of Modern Warfare).

Before we went to commit a dacoity we used to make offerings to (Goddess) *Kali* and we carried the offered Prasad and flowers with us, so that the Mother's blessings be with us in our performance of the secred duty for the fulfilment of the great mission of our life, that is, to free the motherland from alien bondage. Because of all these rituals and our faith we became fearless and inspired as if possessed by the idea of the great mission to which we dedicated ourselves. And hence there was a great difference between us and the ordinary run of men.

A number of young men of character and education were attracted to the Anushilan Samiti. To give a random idea of the type of youth the Samiti att'acted to itself it may be stated that in the year 1915 alone six of its members secured scholarships in the Matriculation examination from the Comilla Zilla school. all the four divisional scholarships, one district scholarship and one special scholarship of standing first in the University in Additional Sanskrit.

Anushilan training produced iron men. The Anushilanites have proved through their activities that they were extra-ordinary men. Though many of them later left the Party, they were never ordinary men. Some have turned Sanyasins, but even there they have very earnestly taken up the work of social welfare. Some joined the Ramakrishna Mission. Even those who have not been able to attain anything outstanding in life, have maintained their high character, have not sudmitted to greed or bowed down before anything they thought to be wrong. It is a pity that after independence these men have only been ignored and pushed to the background.

The Samiti in Comilla was very important in many respects. In this district we had the two centres—Belonia and Udaipur Farms for training in shooting, etc. as well as for sheltering the leading absconders of the party. There were some very earnest members in the different villages of the district. Sometimes a whole family was our sympathiser. They suffered terribly. The Sarker family of village 'Korpai' was one such family. Their house and all other property were seized by the police because all three brothers of the family were absconding. The police drove out even the women and children from their ancestral home. Yet they never bowed before the oppressors.

Another house, the house of the District organiser, Purna Chakravarty, was like a fortress. The leaders from outside and prominent local members used to visit it but the police knew nothing of it although it was in the central part of the town. Another rendezvous of ours was a homœopathic dispensary in the Kandirpar centre of the town facing to Town Hall. Everybody visited this dispensary day and night but nobody, including the police informers, suspected anything. Se well-knit was our organisation.

The revolutionaries had their own open and secret literature also. The *Sandhya* and the

Jugantar, well-known open organs preached the ideas of revolution publicly and had wide reading clientele. Let me quote a few sentences from the *Sandhya* to show the trend of thought of the founder revolutionaries. "We want complete independence. The country cannot prosper so long as the last shred of the Firinghi's Supremacy over it is left. Swadeshi, boycott, are all meaningless to us, if they are not the means of retrieving our whole and complete independence. Rights granted by the Firinghies as favour, we shall spit at and reject, and we shall work out our own salvation." The *Jugantar's* articles, "Which Way Salvation Lies", were inspiring articles stating the object of the revolutionaries which was nothing short of independence. The revolutionary movement was the direct actton movement for independence and hence the organs preached that.

As I said before, the Anushilan Samiti had two secret organs: *Liberty* in English and *Swadhin Bharat* in Bengali. Thes secret papers were distributed dramatically on the same day throughout the country and even abroad. Of course *Swadhin Bharat*, was for Bengal only. The distribution of *Liberty* secretly on a certain day throughout India and abroad was a proof of the ramification of the organisation. This created a great impression on the public as a concrete proof that the organisation though secret was widespread. During the First World War an issue of the *Liberty* declared " Our object is not to gain a few privileges but to create a nation of men free and independent ". The very names *Liberty* and *Swadhin Bharat* indicate clearly that the revolutionaries wanted independence and nothing short of independence.

The British Government disliked the people of India reading revolutionary literature and they extensively proscribed such books, but the revolutionaries continued to print and circulate them.

Lokmanya Tilak, Surendra Nath Banerjee, Bipin Chandra Pal, Lala Lajpat Rai, Madan Mohan Malviya and Rabindra Nath Tagore, the giants of Indian nationalism, were also great admirers of the revolutionaries. These ,and a host of other public leaders preached nationalism but revolutionaries translated that into action. The mass and public leaders could not keep their eyes closed. They knew the nation was seething with discontent and that the tide of revolution would sweep them away if they failed to radicalise themselves. As a result the radicalisation of the Indian National Congress followed. From an organisation of mere professionals, the Congress became as it were, over night an organisation of the masses. Tilak came forward as the first leader of the masses. He was so much stirred by the activities of the revolutionaries that he courted six years of jail at a very advanced age admiring the Muzaffarpur bomb outrage by Khudiram Bose and Praphulla

Chaki. Indeed these were the first great inspiring events not only for Bengal but for the whole country. It was a turning point in our fight for Freedom, for we did a lot of preaching but it was a practical action by revolutionaries which came as a challenge to the alien rulers with a view to forcibly oust them from our land.

The next great event also followed in logical sequence. Because of the activities of the death-defying revolutionaries, the Bengal partition was annuled in 1911 and the capital was transferred from Calcutta to Delhi. The next year the Viceroy Lord Hardinge, was making his state entry into the new capital in a procession with much imperial pomp and grandeur. The revolutionaries were not idle onlookers. Basanta Biswas, disguised as a woman, was sitting there on the roof of the Punjab National Bank amidst women. When the procession reached Chandni Chowk all attention was on the Viceroy, seated on a big elephant. Biswas saw the opportunity and quietly dropped the bomb. All was smoke. Lord and Lady Hardinge were wounded and the Mahout died.

Silent jubilation was observed in the country. India and the world at large realised that the spirit of Khudiram was fully alive. Khudiram's was a feeble challenge but this was a mighty one.

To come back again to Comilla, the arrest and conviction of Ramesh Banerjee and 10 others in 1912 was due to the betrayal by the party member,

Deven Ghose, a well-known wrestler. Ghose had to pay heavily for this. One evening he was murdered by Biren Chatterjee. So the people of Comilla came to know that to betray the party was a serious affair. This was a good lesson for the party man as well, The revolutionary ferment in Comilla continued unabated.

The Bengal provincial political conference was held in 1913 at Comilla. Barrister B. Chakravarti was the President and among others was Surendra Nath Banerjee. We dragged Banerjee's carriage from the Railway Station to the house where he stayed. There was a general order from the Government that no student should participate in it. We did not care for this prohibitory order and did everything for the success of the conference. Basanta Kumar Mujumdar was the Captain of the volunteers, galloping all over the town, sitting on his white horse in military attire. Though we did everything, we were not allowed to enter the conference because of police vigilance. The ordinary students did not dare to enter the cenference, but we, the secret party men, entered through the back side of the pandal where Majumdar himself made an opening for us. The speech delivered by Banerjee at this conference was on of his best. I have never in my life heard a greater orator. This and many other such incidents show how the revolutionaries availed of every opportunity to further their cause—the freedom of the country.

The world war in 1914 offered the revolutionaries a grand opportunity for the fulfilment of a long cherished ambition, of making an end of the British Government in India. We were up and doing. Revolutionaries in India and abroad made a combined and vigorous effort to do away with the British rule in India. The Sedition Committee has given a comprehensive account as to how with the help of the Germans the Indian revolutionaries made a magnificent attempt to free India from the yoke of alien rule.

HOW THE BENGAL PARTITION AGITATION TOOK A SERIOUS TURN

Muslim rule did not exercise any centralised authority in India for various reasons which need not be traced here. Governors were semi-independent and revenue collectors wielded great influence as feudals. But self-contained villages were indidifferent to these things. They had neither the education nor the means of communication to think of things beyond their villages. They had their miseries of life but that was thought to be God-ordained.

When the Britishers came even then the villagers were indifferent. But when after the industrial revolution in Europe, the artisans of India lost their avocations, their life became extremely miserable. Millions of people died in famine in different parts of India. Alien rulers became harder in administation and extortions increased. " India must be bled " were the words of a Secretary of State for India. Oppressions and, at the same time, introduction of the railway system, mineral and jute industries, brought about a great change. Textile industries also grew in Bombay. But introduction of industries failed to bring about a revolution as it did in Europe.

The books of Dutta and Digby revealed that the Indian peasantry did not have a bellyful even once in a day and half of the Indians did not get two meals a day. But things continued as they were.

Bengal was very prosperous and consequently the exploitations also became greater. But at the same time a middle class population sprang up there. Britishers required English knowing men and Bengal supplied many. Britishers were acquiring new states and the Bengali Babus followed them. They were the Chhota Sahibs. Thus Bengali colonies sprang up in the different cities and towns outside Bengal. English education gave the Bengalies greater knowledge of Western civilization and of scientific developments. This aroused in them the idea of their rights as equals of the masters. Similar was the awakening in Maharastra. Bengal and Maharastra were the first two regions of India where the impact of the West stirred the intellectuals. Reformation movement after reformation movement followed and soon spread throughout the length and breadth of the country.

This was the process of awakening. This process worked through conscious efforts of some exceptionally gifted person. Raja Ram Mohan Rov was the man who gave the first shaking. There were also a galaxy of writers who contributed to the great awakening. With the turn of the century, Surendra Nath Banerjee came to focus the rising political consciousness of the people. His oratory was so powerful that the entire country felt that the Britishers were at the root of all our miseries. The picture of a United India—united in its suffering gradually took shape. An immotional togetherness emerged. India became a nation.

Revolution was in the air. The Boer War had ended. Japan came out victorious against the mighty Czarist Russia. In Russia itself there was the rising of the revolutionists against the Czarist Government. The Irishmen were fighting against the Britishers for their independence. Dr. Sun-yat Sen was making considerable headway in China against the ruling Manchu regime. There were risings in the Muslim countries. These things had natural repercussions on the thoughtful Indian leaders.

Phadke became a martyr by fighting against the British and Lokmanya B. G. Tilak and his followers clashed several times with the British high officials even by the end of the 19th century. The

Chapekar brothers were hanged on the charge of murdering two British officials ; the Natu brothers were given transportation for life. The tallest and most respected public leader of India till 1920, the year of his death, was Tilak. He was an extremist and a revolutionary. He was the first Indian to declare publicly "Swaraj (independence) is our birth-right".

Revolutionary ferver in India started from Bengal and gradually engulfed the entire country. A real fight for freedom began. Bengal Partition—a settled fact—was unsettled. The revolutionaries had their first real success.

Divide and rule is a common maxim and that became the objective of Lord Curzon ever since he became the Governor General of India and as early as 1903 he gave vent to his voice against it and next in 1904 in Bombay also emphatically advocated for the partition of Bengal. The announcement of the 3rd December, 1903, was condemned by the entire population of Bengal, Hindus and Muslims alike. In July 1905 it was announced that the partition was to take effect from the 16th October that year. Swadeshi and Boycott were decided upon in the public meeting of Calcutta on the 7th August, 1905.

This was the turning point in the history of the freedom movement in India. Three British observers of Indian affairs foresaw the activities which were brewing inside Bengal in particular and

India in general. Wrote Andrew Carnegie in June 1906 that the home rule sentiment was in recent years growing rapidly and commenting on Lord Kitchner's activities in strengthening the British military position in India, this shrewed observer of Indian affairs commented thus "If all were known, it is not Russian or any foreign attack that the militiary officials dread. It is the growing home rule sentiment they consider dangerous to British control. It is against the people of India not against the foreigner, that the legions are *to be moved. It is within, not without India, that* the wolf turns".

Sir Henry Cotton wrote, "There is now a party of Indian Nationalists who despair of constitutional agitation advocate the establishment of an absolutely free and independent form of national Government. These men are the shadow of a cloud which casts itself over the future. A few years ago there was no prospect of the rise of such a party. They are the product of a policy of reaction, which has led to discontent and unrest and impatience of the British connection with the country. Their numbers are increasing, but they are not yet in a position of popular leaders. The recognized leaders of Indian thought and the original pioneers of the national movement, are still unaffected by these symptoms of alienation from the British Government. They are men of moderate views."

Sir Valentine Chirol wrote, "The question of Partition itself receded into the background, and the issue until then successfully veiled and now openly raised, was not whether Bengal should be one unpartitioned province or two partitioned provinces under British rule, but whether British rule itself was to endure in Bengal or, for the matter of that anywhere in India."

The partition agitation was a unique expression of Bengal's disapproval to this act of dividing and disintegrating the province. Once the lead was given from Calcutta it was taken up by the entire population. It was confronted from every angle of public opinion and total condemnation was expressed through meetings, processions, writings and songs in every nook and corner of Bengal.

This was the occasion when the idea of composite nationalism came into being. As Dr. S. C. Roy observes. "In fact between Aurobindo, Bipin Chandra and Brahmabandhab, they created a new nationalist movement and philosophy in the country to which Rabindranath supplied the genius of his poetic muse. Before this there was certainly politics but there was no ideal of composite nationalism, and it is the one special contribution of the Bengal School of Political thinkers, who made their mark in 1905."

When the partition did not yield the desired result of dividing Hindus and Muslims, the

Governor of Bengal and the Nawab of Dacca tried to create artificial communal hatred, by provoking the Muslim masses against the Hindus. As a result there was communal riot in Comilla in 1907. The beginning of the riot is a sordid story. The Nawab of Dacca visited Comilla. One morning while the Nawab was passing through the market and a big number of Muslims were following him, a Hindu merchant's servant was sweeping the shop. The passing sight attracted the servant and he stood at the door of the shop with the broom in his hand. Some one of the Nawab's followers shouted that the Hindu was showing a broom to the Nawab to insult him (a customary insult in Bengal). At once the shop was attacked and it turned into a big communal riot. A Muslim was shot down and the riot subsided.

At Jamalpur, district Mymensingh, the agitated Muslim mob attacked the Hindu Goddess Basanti's image and broke it. Basanti Puja is one of the biggest ceremonies of the Hindus in Bengal and attack on the image extremely enraged the Hindus. And it resulted in a large scale communal riot. A Muslim was fired at and the riot stopped. Later it was known that this shooting was done by revolutionaries who came from Calcutta.

As the result of these communal riots and Government repressions the Hindu youths became very much excited and the more zealous among them added to the number and strength of the secret activities of the revolutionaries. These riots like the anti-Partition movement indirectly helped to accentuate the underground anti-British activities. Thus the motive behind the Partition as well as the riots miserably failed.

CHAPTER II

PREPARATION FOR THE REVOLUTION

Our Comilla organisation was not lagging behind. We were fully prepared under our able leader, Purna Chakravarty. Just as in 1912 Deben Ghosh was shot dead because he gave information to the police which led to the arrest and conviction to 7 years rigorous imprisonment of ten very active members of the Samiti for attempt at dacoity, so also, early in 1915, the Head Master of Zilla school, Sarat Chandra Bose, was shot dead in broad day light at Comilla while returning from the school. He was acting as a Government agent for the detection and suppression of revolutionaries, particularly students.

In the Deben Ghosh case our house was involved in an interesting way. During the Puja holidays several men were arrested including Shri Ramesh Banerjee, the agent of the Singer Sewing Machine Co. Our closest neighboursknew that Biren Chatterjee was very intimate with Banerjee. Biren borrowed a Singer Sewing Machine from Ramesh and his friends made Khakhi shirts and shorts. During the search these khakhi shirts and shorts were recovered. But the police did not bother to find how those things. came there. A few days after, during a marriage in the town, a lady who was our next door neighbour and whose sons were in the movement, told other ladies about the activities of Biren. One of the ladies, who came from Calcutta and who was the wife of a C. I. D. officer, heard everything attentively and in due course narrated everything to her husband in Calcutta.

The result was the arrival of an officer from Calcutta to enquire into the matter. Our servant Harendra, admitted the Singer Sewing Machine affair, but the police could not get Biren. When during the war time Biren was arrested in the Grier Park fight with the police in which Mr. Lowman's hand was dislocated by him, he was tried under section 110—a section under which people " leading a bad livelihood " were prosecuted —and our servant was the main witness. In many cases the police unjustly prosecuted revolutionaries under section 110, as in those days there was no other law, except the Regulation III of 1818, under which a person against whom there was no definite complaint and evidence could be detained for an indefinite period.

In 1912 this servant was taken to Calcutta by the officer in a second class compartment and was examined by higher C. I. D. officers, and during the case he was even interviewed by Rai Bahadur Basanta Kumar Chatterjee, a principal assistant of Sir Charles Tegart. I heard all these things from the servant on his return from Calcutta. Of course, Biren met him on many occasions before his arrest and told him to tell the truth in case he was called upon to give evidence. Biren did not want this poor man to suffer because of him. Such was the feeling of Biren for the poor.

Coming back to the main theme of my narration, we did not know much about the big scale attempts of the revolutionaries. But this much we knew that an effort was being made to make the country free during the war. We were making ourselves ready to play our part in our limited areas. In those days my trunk used to be full of cartridges and bottles of Picric acid were kept under my wooden bed. We decided that our task would be to capture the Chittagong Division, i. e., Chittagong, Noakhali and Tippera districts.

I was admitted into the Victoria school, attached to the Victoria College. The Head master, Sashi Kumar Bal, was a graduate of the B. M. College, Barisal, with which the name of late Aswini Kumar Datta was associated. The Head Master encouraged a social welfare organisation of the students styled " Little Brothers of the Poor " to help the poor and the needy. Discussions used to take place every Saturday after school hours. I regularly attended such programmes. Because of these activities the police had a suspicious eye on the Head Master.

Informally I was already in close touch with some of the Anushilan Samiti members. As a boy I had no knowledge of the national or international affairs. Only intense anti-Brttish feeling was roused in my mind by the environmental conditions. When the Governor of East Bengal, Sir Bamfylde Fuller, went to Agartala, the capital of Tripura State, two youths in saffron clothes were arrested as they were loitering in a suspicious way. They were brought by the police to Comilla for trial in November 1909. I went to see them in the court with an elderly neighbour, Dhiren Sen. They appeared to be handsome Sadhus. They were Shanti Mukerjee and Ashu Das Gupta, two important Anushilan leaders, as I came to know later. Though a boy, fresh from village life, I was much interested to see them because I was in search of such men.

Initiation to Secret Anushilan Samiti for me was only a formal matter. Fire extinction, nursing of patients, cremation of the dead, etc. were the work in which we were interested as students of the Victoria School. In fact my activities drew me unconsciously close to the Anushilan Samiti, whose members were also doing similar things. Even before my formal initiation I was thus working with them. In reality the organiser, Purna Chakravarty, told me that in my case no formality was necessary as I was the cousin of Biren Chatterjee.

The place at Comilla where my uncle's residence was situated was called 'Sonarang' Compound because one family from Sonarang in Bikrampur came to Comilla and settlde in this part. The Compound consisted of about a dozen houses and there was only one entrance. On one side of the entrance was the house of my uncle and on the other side was the house of a lawyer, whose cousin, Atindra Mohan Roy, was an important member of the Samiti. He was also my class mate. As in-Charge of the Violence Department of the Party in 1916 he led the group that murdered Rai Bahadur Basanta Kumar Chaterjee of the Calcutta C. I. D. who, as assistant to Sir Charles Tegart, had pledged to eradicate the revolutionary movement from Bengal during the First World War. Suren Roy, the younger brother of the lawyer, was also an important member of our party. Jiten Sen, the war time in-charge of the Jugantar Party at Comilla, was from this Compound. His younger brother, Dhiren Sen, was an important meber of Anushilan. Profulla Das Gupta who became an Engineer after being released from jail as a State Prisoner, came from this compound. My class-mate, Bipin Behari De, lived in the house of Das Gupta's uncle in this Compound. My cousin, Paresh Chatterje the eldest son of Bisweswar Chatterjee, was an Anushilanite from early boyhood. Another Jiten Sen, known as Kalababu, came from this compound too. He suffered jail and internment.

We started a literary club and Library at Sonarang compound, collected donations for it and in additoon we earned money by chopping firewood and used the money for running our Library.

During the war the Defence of India Act

was promulgated. The main purpose behind it was to check the activities of the revolutionaries. Lord Carmaical, the Governor of Bengal, advocated in 1916 strong measures for the complete eradication of the revolutionary movement in Bengal. This encouraged the C. I. D. Police to use a strong hand in suppressing the revolutionaries. Mr. Charles Tegart was the head of the Bengal C. I. D. at that time. He gave assurance to the Governor that with the help of the Government he would be able to dig out the revolutionary movement at the very root. Rai Bahadur Basanta Kumar Chatterjee volunteered himself to work as Tegart's assistant in this mission. Arrests and interrogations followed in large scale. Harrassment and house searches in mass scale were conducted by the police. 44000 houses were searched in a single year. When these oppressions reached an intolerable point, the revolutionaries also started retaliating. Rai Bahadur Basanta Kumar Chatterjee was battered to death in public in Calcutta, in July 1916. This culmination of several unsuccessful attempts on Chatterjee's life was one of the most daring exploits of Atindra Roy's leadership.

Our District organiser, Purna Chandra Chakravarty, left Comilla and took charge of Dacca, but he could not work there for long. One morning we read in the paper that he was arrested. Chakravarty left handing over the charge of the district to Prabodh Sen, a student. Sen drew the attention of leaders, because of his brilliant articles in our hand-written monthly Party Organ.

But soon Profulla, a new organiser, was sent from North Bengal to take charge from Sen. Meanwhile myself and Sen had gone to Chandpur and we received a wire indicating some trouble at Comilla. Sen stayed but I returned by a night train. Before day-break, as I entered Sen's drawing room, I found signs of house search even in the dark. Several places of the floor were dug up. I waited silently till his youngest brother came out. I met the afflicted mother, who wanted her son to be on the right path. This was rather a signal of the days ahead. Some absconded and some others kept themselves ready for any eventuality. We did not sleep in our houses during the night as we apprehended that a police party could suddenly swoop on us any time.

MY ESCAPE IN 1916

One day we received news that Prabodh Bhattacharya and another personfrom Mymenshing, both of whom later participated with Tarini Mazumdar in the attempt to murder Mr. Emerson, the District Magistrate of Comilla, were to come to our house by the midnight train. I waited and waited for them but they did not turn up. In the late hours of the night I did not go to my neighbouring shelter as that would have caused disturbance. So I slept in my place. At about 4.30 a. m. my cousin, Paresh Chatterjee, roused me from my sleep and told that the house was surrounded by the police. The police had an eye on our house since 1911.

Though there was nothing objectionable in the house, we closed the doors and windows and burnt the papers which contained some of our secrets. At day-break the D. S. P. and the S. I. entered the house with the neighbouring lawyer as the search witness. In the warrant of arrest my name was written " Jogesh Chandra Chakravarty or Chatterjee". The witness said, " He is not Chakravarty. He is not wanted." But the D. S. P. replied, " I have definite information that he is the person wanted. Though he appears to be very young, the charge is very serious against him." My room was searched but nothing incriminating was found. At this stage the Superintendent of Police arrived on the cycle to see the positions at different places, as a dozen houses were being searched that day simultaneously. Two officers went to the veranda to receive him and I took the opportunity to go out through the back-door, bare-bodied and bare-footed with a lota (brass tumbler) in my hand as if I was going to the latrine. The policeman, guarding the back door asked my name and I gave him a false name and passed by. Almost simultaneously they were after me, because the

S. P. wanted to see me. I ran and the policeman also ran after me. I entered a neighbour's latrine through the big soil cleaning hole and entered inside the house and again went out speedily by another door to the other side of the road in the opposite direction. I was thus beyond the reach of the police. I walked about 5 or 6 furlongs and took shelter in a students' mess. My host, our Party member, had a relative from his village. That gentleman suspected me, but I acted in such a manner as if I had a severe pain in my stomach and was going to the latrine again and again. So my host also could not go to the school.

In the afternoon the District Organiser came and informed me that my friend, Tarini Majumdar, had also escaped arrest. Tarini saw his house surrounded by the police when before day-break he was about to enter his house from his night shelter.

Even at the time of repressions, twleve simultaneous searches on a single day was an unusual matter. Myself and Tarini discussed this in our secret hide-out. We could not reach any conclusion. But later, some two months after my arrest in Calcutta, the matter was clear to me. Both Prabodh Sen and Jiten Sen, the two leaders of the two parties in Comilla had made a clean breast of everything to the police after they were arrested, and the searches followed.

I met Tarini Majumdar after night fall and we both proceeded to a house of a Dafadar

(village police petty officer) who was a relative of Tarini. To reach there we had to walk about 13 miles in heavy rains. The Dafadar told us that in the afternoon he noticed activities in the Thana (Police Station). So, though very tired, we left his house in the early hours of the morning. Shortly after we left, his house also was searched to find out a local absconder, a friend of Jiten Sen. Had we not left, we both would have also been arrested. However, we took shelter in a house of another relative of Tarini. This house had a big compound accommodating six families. So, to avoid detection by neighbours, we were lodged under a bamboo machang in front of which dhoties were hanged, as if these had been spread out for drying purposes.

A ROMANCE AT COMILLA

I had a romance at Comilla during the first World War days. So long only Anushilan branches were vigorously active in the district. But during the war, the other Calcutta group, popularly known as the Jugantar group, also became active. Our neighbour Jiten Sen, whose younger brother Dhiren Sen was an active associate of ours, deflected from us and took charge of the Jugantar group's organisation in our district. One afternoon I was standing outside his house with his younger brother. Suddenly I heard a bomb burst ; volumes of smoke came out of a room in his house. I stood guard on the road side and Dhiren ran round to see that no outsider came to know anything. Really nobody knew anything. Jiten Sen was safe but one of his friends, who was with him received several deep injuries on his face. I do not remember the name of the person.

Though by then I was a prominent Anushilanite, Sen recruited me to his party. Of course, I reported everything to my district organiser. He warned me to be very cautious but at the same time wanted to have me in the full confidence of Sen, so that I could get all information about his activities. Otherwise the safety of our party was at stake, because there might be police vigilance due to their activities and following that we might be taken unaware.

Sen gave me some fire arms etc. But I did not keep them in my house. At last I was ordered by Sen to participate in an armed dacoity. I was willing to go but my organiser would not allow me to do so. I was pressed to go by Sen but I gave the plea that a certain person of our household was suspecting me and that in case I joined the exploit he might divulge our secret to others. So it was decided that I would not participate in the dacoity but would accompany them to the railway station and help them to board the train with arms and ammunitions. Before we started for the station, I was introduced to the leader of the group whom I accompanied up to the train. The leader was Shri Naren Ghosh Choudhuri of Noakhali, subsequently transported to the Andamans to serve a life sentence for the Shivpur dacoity case.

Sen, however, asked me to meet him in the closing hours of the night. When I met him he handed over the booty to me in the dark. I kept everything outside my house along with the arms. The things were handed over to Sen next day. The booty included some gold mohars and a necklace.

Sen's organisation was so weak that he could not even maintain contact with revolutionaries who wanted to work with him or who belonged to the party of which he was a member. This was revealed to me much later when Shri Aswini Ganguli of Barisal, a co-prisoner in the jail, told me that he came to contact them all the way from Barisal but had to go back baffled as he failed to find them out.

A MURDER PLAN

Once we planned to kill the district magistrate of Comilla, Mr. Emerson. The scheme was that when the district magistrate was murdered, Sir Charles Tegart, the biggest target of revolutionaries at the time, would certainly come from Calcutta for the investigations. In that case he would be put to an end to at Chandpur where he would get down from the steamer and walk to board the standing train nearby. The persons, who were sharp shooters and were prepared to die, were deputed for this. It was decided that if they were arrested they would give a statement prepared by the party. Even this statement was made ready and handed to them.

But fortunately for Tegart, the plan of the murder of Emerson could not be executed. In the whole town only Emerson had a car and he used to go out every evening in that car. Our men were to stop the car just before the gate of his bungalow, where two stout trees stood on either side of the drive. They were to fasten a strong rope between the trees and thereby get the car stopped and shoot him dead. For 12 consecutive days our men were ready but he did not go out. We gave it up on the 13th day and that day he went out in the car. For the next few days he again did not come out. So out of sheer disgust we had to give up the idea.

HARASSMENT OF MY UNCLE AFTER MY ESCAPE

The District Magistrate, Mr. Emerson, came to my uncle's house in the Sonarang Compound after he received the news of my escape from there.

He threatened my uncle accusing him that he was himself a supporter of revolutionaries and, therefore, encouraged by him, I became bold and escaped. My uncle, though not a member of the revolutionary party, was a very bold man and told the Magistrate that he had no authority to threaten people in their own homes. Emerson left, but after this search parties came to my uncle's house on many occasions only to harrass him. Every time they came they invariably entered the kitchen, which in a Brahmin household meant that any cooked food exposed to their search was defiled and had to be thrown away, uneaten. They demolished ovens and broke open boxes and almirahs. And once about 300 policemen surrounded the whole Sonarang Compound and proceeded to destroy many things in my uncle's house. From our hide-out we were getting information of the police harassment of our house. But we were not then in a position to retaliate.

In our hide-out we had to spend the whole day lying on mats. But after nightfall we met our party members in the school building away from the village. One day we planned an excursion into the hills many miles away. After several hours' walk we arrived at a village where we took shelter in a hill-man's hut. Our guide introduced us as members of the local zamindar family. So we were treated as most esteemed guests. Women, who were almost naked like the males, avoided us and went inside their huts. But the men gave us utensils, rice, vegetables, etc. We took water from the nearby spring and cooked rice and vegetables offered by them. But they also presented a bird to us. On our refusal to accept the bird they felt offended and we begged to be excused. We did not like roasted meat as they did and meat cooked without spice and other ingredients we could never relish. Moreover, we were in a hurry to cross the hill section before dusk.

This adventure during the rains told upon my health so badly, that I ran a high temperature with shivering cold. I was down with malaria. Bagala Majumdar, a member of the Party, paid a visit to the house where I was sheltered. The house was his relatives' house, so none suspected anything.

Bagala delivered the message to us that on an urgent matter we were to go to a place 28 miles away. I felt so weak that it was not possible for me to walk such a great distance. But Tarini would not go leaving me in that condition. At my repeated request Tarini agreed to leave. He impressed upon his relatives that they should take special care of me. Then he embraced me and departed at midnight. How could I know then that this would be our last parting ? Next day a man came with a phial of quinine pills. This was the last gift of Tarini.

One night I came out of my hide-out and took the train from Laksam Junction for Chandpur. Bipin Bihari De came by this train from Comilla with my clothes. For years we were intimate friends and classmates in the Victoria School and College. When we were students of the 9th class I tried to recruit him into the Party by a frank and direct approach. He resented it so much that he vehemently insisted that as a genuine friend it was his duty to prevent me from going astray. The next morning he did not go with me to the tank for bathing nor did he accompany me to the school. This change of attitude of my friend pained me. But when I reached school he embraced me and expressed regret, stating that difference of opinion should not stand in the way of our personal relations.

Two years later when we were in the last year intermediate class, one day Bipin told me that he had watched us (the members of the Party) keenly all these years and thought over the matter from all points of view and that he was convinced that we have taken up the right path. Soon he became an important member of the Party.

Bipin came from a poor rural family. His father was a day labourer. But Bipin was so meritorious that he secured a scholarship from the village school and then came to the town for further studies with the help of generous persons. He was from a village near Kashipur from where came Basanta, Sashi, Kali Prasanna, Bagala, and the great martyr Tarini of the Mazumdar family. They were all revolutionaries. They were zamindars too. Bipin came to escort me and stayed with the family a few days. One day after we all took our meals together in the kitchen Bipin had to wash his plates himself, because the women members of the family knew his caste. This was very painful to us. Bipin came because I was there. The male members of the family were very much ashamed but were helpless before the prejudices of the women. The revolutionaries did not observe anything like that.

A word here about the social condition and the revolutionaries. Our brotherhood in the Anushilan Samiti not only made us staunch nationalists, but also advocates for the removal of social inequalities on the basis of caste. We had recruits from all classes and castes amongst the Hindus who were very orthodox. We were brothers at arms, a part and parcel of a semi-military organisation in which every one was ready to sacrifice himself before the alter of freedom. In such a brotherhood there was no question of differentiation and untouchability. We had no Muslims in our Samiti. As a matter of fact the Muslim community as a whole remained, by and large, unaffected by the revolutionary movement. There are several socio-historical reasons for this. To mention only one the religious orientation of the revolutionaries was more sympathetic towards the Hindu religion than to Islam. The revolutionaries were mostly inspired by a type of Hindu Nationalism. The rituals that we had to perform and most of the ideals that we held scarcely attracted the Muslims.

Our movement however did affect a small section of orthodox women. One night we dined together in a friend's house at Comilla. The cook served us the dinner. The lady of the house was requested not to bother about our dinner. This naturally aroused her curiosity. She came into the room where we were dining and next morning she told our friend that Satyayug had come. She knew we belonged to different castes. The very sight of our dining together without the distinction of caste thrilled her. And hence her remark. The Hindus believe that Satyayug is the beginning of the cycle of cosmic existence and that it is the purest and fullest of all the periods. In this yuga there is no distinction between caste and caste. But social prejudice dies hard. On another occasion when we were taking our food from the same pot in a Brahmin's house, a girl saw us and reported to her mother. She appeared in such a furious mood that we had to quit hurriedly, leaving everything.

On another occasion I stayed at Dacca with a Vaidya family. The first midday meal I had to prepare myself. But on my request I was later allowed to take food prepared by the ladies of the family. But the children of the family were not allowed to see me eating food cooked by the Vaidyas. They were afraid that the children might report it to outsiders that a Brahmin was taking food with them and cause a turmoil. Twenty-nine years later, one lady friend of our

Lucknow family used to come to us almost daily, help with the cooking and ate with us often. One day by chance I came to know this lady to be the daughter of the same Vaidya family with whom I stayed at Dacca. I narrated my story to all present and wondered at the great change that had taken place in our society within this 29 years.

After staying at Chandpur for some time, I accompanied Atin Roy who was also an absconder to Faridpur district crossing the great river Meghna in a small boat. Our object was to collect money through robbery. But the man on whom we were depending failed. He was a married man and hesitated. So we left for Calcutta.

I was to take charge of a district where I was to go from Calcutta. I was to live in the new place as a tutor. But it was already September and the Puja vacation was approaching. So it was decided that I should stay at 39 Pathuriaghata Street Calcutta till the vacation was over. From Mymensingh came a requisition for a boatman for a boat dacoity. I was bored with my idle life and was eager to go to Mymensingh district for this. But the leader, Jogendradas Bhattacharya, did not allow me to go.

I was forbidden to go out from the Pathuriaghata Street house because important C. I. D. watchers from East Bengal district had been brought to Calcutta and they were walking in the streets in batches for the arrest of absconders.

Some of our friends were already the victims of such watchers.

There was a large number of books in the house and I read them avidly. My other duty was to cook. Every noon and night a number of persons used to come to eat. I cooked rice and dal in a big pot and boiled potatoes. After every meal every body except myself used to go out. That was the daily routine. The time was very bad for the revolutionaries. The idea of war-time revolution could not be fulfilled. Frustration led to the shaking of faith and consequently discipline among the revolutionaries became slack. Government repression reached its height. Tegart's men created havoc. Thousands of houses were searched and thousands were jailed and interned under the Defence of India Act, 1915.

MY ARREST AT 39, PATHURIAGHATA, CALCUTTA

On the 9th October, 1916, only one person came at noon-time. Naren Bannerjee, a student of the Presidency College, who was the organiser of Calcutta at that time, had his meal with me and then left. In the night nobody came. I waited and waited and then at about 10 p.m. went to sleep. In the midnight I was awakened from deep sleep by violent knocks at the door. Somebody said "Open,

open, "—I thought that some of our men were at the door. But as soon as I opened the door several revolver barrels were pointed at me. Some were Bengal police officials and others were European police sergeants. Two Bengalees caught hold of me and pushed me into the room using me as a shield against any attack from inside.

It was the first floor. On the verandah on the other side facing the street, screens, rags and pieces of water-proof clothes were hanging to indicate that the house was occupied by some family. While passing through the verandah, I tried to pull down the clothes, but the officer said rather ironically, " Don't remove them. Let them remain as they are ". This showed that they possessed full information about this house. Long after this I came to know that Comilla information was given by Jiten Sen and Calcutta information by Prabodh Sen, the two one time head of two local units.

Before I proceed further with my story let me quote here the paragraphs in the Sedition Committee Report about this House at 39 Pathuriaghata Street (the head quarters of the All India Secret Anushilan Samiti at the time.)

" In October a confessing revolutionary in custody pointed out 39 Pathuriaghata Street as the resort of conspirators. The house was searched and among other documents found were cipher lists of names and addresses in seven districts of Bengal and also outside the province. There were also lists of depositories of arms and bombs.

" All the addresses in Bengal were searched and the results have been investigated by us. In all but one or two cases these results were of more or less importance, but we only take one as an illustration. One of the addresses at Faridpur was ' N. N. Chatterjee Hemanta Mukerjee, Pleader '. Hemanta was Chatterjee's uncle, with whom he lived. Another address was ' Prabodhendu Mohan Roy, 32 Sonarpura, Benaras '.

" A letter was intercepted written to this man from Bijnore in the Punjab. The writer was traced *as Prabhudayal Mehta, resident of Rohani, Punjab.* This man was arrested and in his possession was a book with nine addresses in the Punjab and also a suspicious letter of the 12th December, 1916, from Jabalpur giving the address of a student at Jabalpur to whom Prabhu should write. This led to enquiries at Jabalpur and the police was led to believe that there was a branch of the Dacca Samiti there, of which among others one Sailendranath Ghosh was a leading member. He was arrested and his letters intercepted. One came to him from Vinayak Rao Kapile from Calcutta. On the back in the cipher was the name of...Calcutta.......was arrested there and in his possession were cipher lists like those at No. 39 Pathuriaghata Street, containing, among others, the name of N. N. Chatterjee of Faridpur, with whose name the story started. Thus by following up a Benaras address given in the.....,

No. 39 Pathuriaghata Street, one is led from Benaras to the Punjab, from the Punjab to Jabalpur in the Central Provinces and from Jabalpur back to Calcutta and there a new list is found containing a name of Faridpur found independently in the list of No. 39 Pathuriaghata Street, from which we started." (p. 106)

To resume my narration, early next morning Sisir Kumar Datta Gupta, an absconder from Comilla, came to 39 Pathuriaghata Street from French Chandernagore. He had two revolvers wrapped in a small bundle. He was arrested by the C. I. D. men inside. At about 9 a. m. Jogendra Das Bhattacharya, was enterning the house and the C. I. D. officials tried to arrest him. He fired a shot and tried to run away. But he was followed and arrested.

Just at about night fall Atindra Mohan Roy, the then leader of the Violence Department, came to the house. He called me by my name, abused me for not lighting the house even after night fall and went up the staircase. But as soon as he was about to enter the room he received a heavy lathi blow. He turned and ran for safety. But a man caught hold of his shirt from behind. Fortunately for Roy, the shirt was very old and half of it remained with the man and Roy dropped through the staircase to the ground. He was hurt, but yet he stood up and ran away. Roy is now at Comilla in East Pakistan. Naren Banneriee who was also arrested from Pathuriaghata house is now in the Aurobindo Ashram at Pondichery.

On the Vijaya procession, a day previous to my arrest, I saw a man particularly looking at our house. I reported this to Naren Banerjee next morning when he came. He did not suspect anything. But next night I saw the same man with the search party and came to know that he was an officer in the C. I. D. Inspector Satish Mazumdar was in charge of the police party. The Bengali police officers were in plain dress and the Sergeants were in uniform. Mazumdar started abusive language and was frequently pulling my hair and even slapped me. We proceeded to Jorasanko Thana on foot. Even on the way to the Thana abuses and slaps continued as I remained silent to his questions.

The C. I. D. men left me in the Thana under the charge of a sergeant. He made me sit on a chair while he remained standing. We were talking. Suddenly a European Deputy Commissioner came and ordered me to stand up and asked the sergeant to take off my shoes. The sergeant, though no doubt reluctant to perform this mental act, was constrained to obey him. At his direction the sergeant caught hold of my handcuffed hands. The D. C. started his interrogations. My silence annoyed him so much that he gave me a blow. He then ordered the sergeant to send me to the office and went away. A Bengali clerk of the office told me in Bengali that I would receive brutal assaults. Soon a Police van came and I was taken to the C. I. D. Office at 4 Kyd Street.

On the first floor of the big police office at 4 Kyd Street lived Mr. Goldy, Dy. Commissioner of Police and on the ground floor was his office. The stable was divided into 3 cells. In the front was the barbed wire door and there were two rows of iron netting walls. Every important revolutionary arrested at that time had to live in these cells.

My shoes were taken off at the Jorasanko Thana and as soon as I entered the new office my coat and shirt were also removed and then I was odered to be put into the stable. When the sentry took me to the latrine he told me that I would not have any more chance to bathe or drink water. So I drank as much water from the tap as I could. Round midday I was given a dry chapati and a potato. I ate, but it only increased my hunger. I had only a dhoti on and slept in the stable cell spreading half of my dhoti as a mat. In the afternoon I was roused from my sleep by a harsh voice and as soon as I opened my eyes a man started abusing me. With blows and pushes I was brought to the office. A plump man of white complexion and bloodshot eyes was sitting in a chair. This was Manoj Pal, son of a Deputy Collector, who had inherited loyalty to the British. But how he could be so brutal, I do not know. The man who brought me was an office peon. Like peon, like officer. An armed police man was standing in the room with his rifle. The man seated started filthy abuses and put several questions to me. I remained silent. The officer's intention, of course, was to extort confession. Divulge the Party secrets, get the friends arrested and thereby accomplish the great mission of life, that of being loyal to the British crown—these were the instructions. My silence exasperated this officer. With filthy abuses he started striking me on bone joints so heavily that with every strike the joints swelled. Though I was silent the Bihari armed man could not tolerate the sight and turned his face towards the opposite wall. The officer was drunk and the peon appeared to be jubilant.

After about a dozen blows when he stopped to breathe the joints of my body were so swollen that it appeared as if I were suffering from some peculiar disease. But my silence made him more enraged and more abuses and more strikes followed. He struck my chest and back several times with the end of the stick. Blood came out from different parts of my body and there was suffocating pain in my heart and lungs. I sat on the floor with my hands on my chest. Questions and abuses continued. With nightfall the peon was ordered to bring a cane and brutal caning followed. I was made to lie on the table and my legs were raised and cane strikes went on underneath my feet. It was already late night and the officer had to leave me possibly for his drinks. I was sent to the stable cell with the strict order that I must not be allowed even to sit. I should be bayonetted on any such attempts. Yet the good sentries allowed me to sleep and instructed me to get up on their raising the alarm. I marked later that there was a sense of general respect for me even in this torture chamber, as on many occasions they showed sympathy for me. All were not brutes like Manoj Pal and his peon. One sentry on duty gave me also a lota of water, which I needed badly after all the inhuman tortures.

One day the drunk Manoj Pal became very angry with me and told the peon to bring pieces of beef from the Dy. Commissioner's cook and push those inside my mouth. Next the idea came to his mind to put urine etc. in my mouth. No sooner did he express an idea than a man in European costume jumped at it and helped in its execution. Owing to tortures, starvation and sleeplessness I was extremely weak. They caught hold of me and forced my mouth inside the commode. When I was on the point of being suffocated they released me Then they poured the urine mixed with excreta all over my body and locked me in the cell. For three days they did not allow me to have a wash. After three days I got the first chance of a wash in the Calcutta Presidency Jail.

Inspite of the arrests, tortures and slackening of discipline, work of the party went on vigorously. The war news also was encouraging and created hopes in the minds of the revolutionaries. Britain was terribly afraid and the next year in August 1917, Mr. Montague, the Secretary of State for India, came to India, peddled help and declared in Calcutta that after the war India would be given the right of self determination Because of such promises leaders like Mahatma Gandhi, Surendra Nath Banerjee and others lectured and worked in support of war efforts. But the turbulent youth did not like the idea. They were sure that nothing tangible could be had through compromise. This resentment of the revolutionaries came out in the open when a student threw a shoe at Surendranath Banerjee when he was lecturing in a meeting held at Lahore.

When the administration becomes weak, the police rule is established. Revolutionaries were direct actionists and therefore they were the most formidable enemies of the British raj. They had to be suppressed if the administration was to be carried on. The necessity become more pressing during the war, so brutal tortures were carried on. I was one of the worst victims because I escaped from Comilla and was arrested in Calcutta in the Headquarters of the Party Organisation. Inspite of all my efforts many of the secrets were known to the police as our district organiser had himself given much information in detail.

During the First World War the Government opened the Special Branch of the C. I. D. in

Calcutta to cope with the revolutionary activities and in 1916-17 the amount of Rs. 1, 400, 000 was sanctioned for it. We now read with creeping sensation about the torture chambers of the feudal days. Stories of Spanish Inquisition repulse us. But seldom did the outside world know that medieval tortures were being continued by the British Raj in India. From the point of view of brutality, British tortures on Indian revolutionaries can easily be compared with the brutalities of any other regime of terror in any part of the world.

To come back to my plight in police custody : From the torture house Sisir Kumar Datta Gupta and I were separately brought to the Dallanda House. The elderly officer in charge, a European, saw the marks all over my body. I could walk, but with difficulty. Sisir had high temperature as a result of the torture. Our names had already been entered into the Register. After that the European Officer in Charge saw our condition and refused to take us under his custody. By chance the army doctor of the Police Training School also came there. The doctor had seen Sisir that morning at the Kyd Street office and prescribed medicine. He also complained to the officer. So we both were sent back to the Kyd street office (the torture house) from where we were sent to the Presidency Jail, Alipore. But I had to wait for two years to ventilate my grievances even to the higher authorities of the Government. In 1918 I got the first chance to do so from the Rajshahi Central Jail in a petition to the then Viceroy of India, extracts from which were published by Ramananda Chatterjee in the August issue of the *Modern Review* of 1918 with the headline : " A State Prisoner's Petition". Let me quote :

" Early last month we received a copy of a petition submitted to His Excellency the Governor General in Council by one Jogesh chandra Chatterjee, a State Prisoner, now in Rajshahi Central Jail. It contains allegations of incredible cruelties and revolting ill treatment. One extract from it will suffice. The prisoner thus described what happend on the fifth day after his arrest : " That on the fifth day at about 5.00 P. M. I was again taken to the office of Kyd Street. There the officer of the first day, according to the proposal of an officer in European costume, called his men and they took me to the latrine. There one man took hold of my hands, another my head and the officer in European costume pressed my nostrils and the Sweeper Mehtar put a commodeful of urine mixed with stools and thrust and poured it all over my face. Then they kept me in my cell and did not allow me to have a wash. All these days I was not allowed to take my bath and got only 2 or 3 luchies for food and that, too, not every day."

EDITOR'S COMMENT : " We do not know whether this petition has reached the Viceroy's hands. If it has, the public should be informed what has been done with it. If it has not, it is to be hoped His Excellency will order it to be placed before him, and cause an open enquiry to be made."

Various were the methods of torture at Kyd Street. My legs were forcibly taken apart, one leg standing about two feet away from the other and an iron bar was put between my two legs to prevent me from drawing them together. In this position I was made to stand for hours. When this failed to accomplish their purpose, they kept the lower part of my body on the table while the other portion remained suspended in the air. This was also done for hours together. When even this was not enough, the police took recourse to a peculiar method of torturing me. They stripped me naked while my hands and feet were chained. Then one man masturbated with me for hours. This they did to make me a nervous wreck. Such and many other inhuman tortures were perpetrated on me and other revolutionaries who were arrested in that period.

A leader of Anushilan Party, Nalini Kanta Ghose, was being transferred from the Kyd Street office after torture to Dacca Jail for trial. On the way he succeeded in sending word outside. By this way the news of brutal tortures on revolutionaries found a place in the newspapers. Mrs. Annie Besant challenged the Governmement on this ;

and long after this a whitewashing committee was appointed to enquire into the matter. This committee did nothing. Had there been any real enquiry many things would have been revealed. For example, the records in my and Sisir Datta Gupta's names in the Register of Dallanda House would have been a convincing proof of the tortures prepetrated on us and the record in the Register of Presidency Jail of the marks all over my body, which did not exist after a month, could have convinced anybody about the tortures perpetrated on us.

Akhil Chandra Datta of Comilla as the President of the Provincial Congress Conference held in Hooghly, expressed his feelings against the ill treatment of revolutionary detenus and said that this was the "massacre of the innocent". But the Anglo-Indian papers as the mouth piece of the alien rulers, raised a hue and cry against Datta's words. He was hardpressed to withdraw the words. Local papers supported him firmly and B. G. Tilak wrote to him to stick to his stand. Of course Datta was firm.

Tortures have been perpetrated on many important revolutionaries. In some cases the police was successful in extorting confessions. But all this failed to suppress the movement. Even when some people were acting as police informers, the movement went on quite vigorously. Various devices were adopted by the revolutionaries to save themselves from being detected by the police. Umbrellas played a big part in avoiding detection by the watchmen in prominent places like the railway station, bazar and streets. There were various methods of cipher writings. The police had experts for deciphering ; but they often failed to know the code word. The man through whose information the Pathuriaghata Street search took place also helped in deciphering the ciphers found in the house by the C. I. D. This was a big help to the police.

To resume my story, " 44 Cells ", of the Presidency Jail, where I was lodged, created a history. The under trial prisoners of the first Alipore Bomb Case were detained there. Shri Aurobindo occupied one of these cells. Revolutionaries under capital sentence in Calcutta were kept in these cells before their execution. The scaffold was situated just behind these cells. In fact one of the cells had a door opening to the scaffold. Kanai Lal Dutta and Satyendra Nath Bose were hanged there in 1908, and so was Gopinath Saha in 1923 and many others. Revolutionaries under transportation for life were kept in these cells prior to their transfer to the Cellular Jail in the Andamans.

I was lodged in Cell No. 6, the very cell in which the famous Bengal revolutionary of Anushilan Samiti, Trailokyanath Chakravarty, was kept. I saw on the wall clearly written a stanza from an inspiring poem by Rabindranath Tagore and under the stanza was the name 'Maharaj', —

legendary Trailokyanath's secret name. On another side wall he wrote a few lines and signed " Kalicharan", his other secret name and yet on another wall was his own composition in verse bidding adieu to Mother India before his departure for the Andamans and hoping to come back again and devote the rest of his life in her service. I still remember the few lines written in Bengali. Underneath was the signature, Biraja, another secret Party name. As I know all these Party names, I was sure that Trailokyanath was kept in this cell before his transfer to the Andamans, only a few months before my arrival. This gave me encouragement and accentuated my sense of responsibility and determination.

I stayed in " 44 Cells " that time only for a month. The cells had no windows. The only inlet for air was a hole in the roof.

Parallel to the main high boundary walls were two rows of cells, 22 in each row. In between were two big open yards. The European Warder-in Charge had a seat in the middle from where he could watch both the sides. Gurkha military personnel were kept on duty with their open Kukries. No Indian jail warder was allowed to enter this yard. Even the jail doctor had to take permission of the European Warder-in-Charge when he had to come in and the doctor was to talk with us in English in the presence of the European Warder.

I was brought to the cell in the evening. I was

in semi starvation condition in the torture house and hence I enjoyed that evening's ordinary jail diet because I got a bellyfull for the first time after my arrest. I also enjoyed a very sound sleep in the night. The next morning the Warder awakened me. The Superintendent and the Jailor were to come on their morning round and preparations were completed. There was the shout " Sarkar Salam " ("Salute to Government ! ") and then passed the Superintendent under a big umbrella, the Jailor following him.

At noon the European Warder came before my cell with a very big Register in which my name etc. were entered. Special marks of the body were also noted. The young Warder seemed to be a new man. There were marks of beating all over my body. He asked who beat me and in reply I said that C. I. D. people had done so. Yet he noted down in the Register all the marks of beatings I had on my body.

One noon I was taken to the jail office. A European officer was seated there. After my entry the door was closed and I was told to sit on the opposite side of the table. He then started interrogations. I was silent, as was the case in the torture chamber. He started writing, " I came to Calcutta from Comilla by aeroplane, etc." and asked me to sign it. He had a big sized revolver on one side and a batton on the other. On my refusal to sign, he freed his shirt sleeves from his wrists, stood up with the batton in his hand as if to start beating me. I also made myself ready to counter-attack as there was no other person in the room. I thought that this was perhaps another torture chamber. But after this menacing attitude the officer sat down on his chair, rang the bell and asked the man who brought me there to take me back to my cell. I came to know later that this was Mr. Colson of the C. I. D. the prosecutor of the Barisal Conspiracy Case.

After a month's stay in the jail myself and Naren Banerjee were taken out one evening and lodged in the cells of the Police Training School in the Dallanda House. I came to know afterwards that this was necessary because under the Defence of India Act a man could not be kept in jail for more than a month. So we were brought to Dallanda House again. Similar was the case with many others. We were to be kept in jail under Regulation III of 1818 as State Prisoners. This required sanction from the Government of India, Pending this sanction important revolutionaries were kept here. On two occasions two leaders of Anushilan Samiti had escaped from Dallanda House detention. One was Nalini Kanta Ghose and the other was Prabodh Chandra Das Gupta. Meanwhile a lot of correspondence went on between the different authorities of the Government. I come to know about these much later. So let me quote the relevant portions from these correspondences.

National Archives, New Delhi, Home-Poll-1917-January 364-372 and K W Part—A.

Extracts from the above file of Archives :—

Page 34

Statement of Jogesh Chandra Chatterjee of Gaodia, PS Lohajang, Dacca.

" My name is Jogesh Chandra Chatterji. My father's name is Bepin Chandra Chatterji. He keeps a timber and corrugated iron sheeting shop at Daulatkhan, Barisal.

I am aged 20 and am unmarried. We are 3 brothers......and 3 sisters.......

I was educated in the Comilla Victoria School, from where I matriculated in 1915. At Comilla I have been living all alone in the house of my maternal uncle, Bisweshwar Chatterji, pleader in Sonarang Compound. I joined the Comilla College in 1915 and then read upto 2nd year IA class.

I left my place of resort about a week ago. The police arrived to search my house about a month ago. They said they wanted me. I gave them the slip by the back door on the pretext of going for a wash. This search took place about a month ago. After escaping from the house I went and took shelter in the house of a poor man in a village—some distance from Comilla (says again not Comilla) by giving bribe of Rs. 7. I will not give out the name of the village or the name of the man with whom I took shelter.

I then met some Sinha in Comilla, who

brought me down to Calcutta. I will not give out the name of the man as I took a vow not to give it out. He comes from East Bengal. He brought me to Calcutta and took me to the house at 39, Pathuriaghata Street. He left me there saying that he would meet me later on.

I have saved Rs. 60 from the money which used to be remitted to me from time to time by my father while I was residing at Comilla. I have still Rs. 40 left with me in 4 GC notes of Rs. 10 each. The rest I spent in travelling and my fooding expenses here. I refuse to make any further statement.

8th October, 1916. Recorded by B. Mukherji "

Note of C. Tegart on Jogesh Chandra Chatterji :—

"It will be seen from the statement of Jogesh Chatterji, a copy of which is attached, that he has declined to account for his conduct, his associates or his movements. He is undoubtedly a dangerous criminal, and should be dealt with under Regulation III of 1818 without delay.

Calcutta,

The 3rd November, 1916. C. Tegart

for Deputy Inspector General of Police,

Intelligence Branch".

National Archives, Home-Poll-Jan. 1917-No. 364-372 K W—Dept. A

Page 4 Appendix.

From Hon'ble Mr. J. H. Duboulay KCIE, CSI, Secretary to the Government of India,

Home Department

To J G Cumming CSI, CIE, ICS Additional Secretary to the Government of Bengal, Political Department

No. 3232 (Political) dated Delhi, 25th November, 1916.

" Would you kindly refer to your letter No. 5418 of the 9th November in which you send up the names of four persons (Narendra Nath Banerji, Jogesh Chandra Chatterji, Sishir Kumar Dutta Gupta, Jogendra Das Bhattachaya) recommended for treatment under the provisions of Regulation III of 1818. The necessary warrants have doubtless reached you by now, but I am to draw attention to the examination of Jogesh Chatterji by Mr. L. H. Colson. You will see that in one place Mr. Colson warned him that his answers would entirely ruin any chance of mercy, and further on threatened that on the evidence against him he would be punished, and that if he chose to make a full disclosure of his knowledge he might hope that some mercy would be shown him. There are further remarks in the record showing an intimidatory attitude on the part of Mr. Colson against Jogesh. This is not in the opinion of the Government of India a proper method of interrogating an accused person, and if it were believed to be the common practice, it would go far to endanger the credibility of the various statements that have been made by persons dealt with under the. the Defence of India

Act and Regulation III of 1818. I am, therefore, to suggest that with the approval of His Excellency the Governor some admonition should be addressed to Mr. Colson so that any examination he may conduct in future should be free from these objectives."

Note of L. H. Colson on Jogesh Chatterji on 23rd October, 1916.

Note, —

" This appears to be a very hardened and dangerous youngster. He has been consistantly defiant throughout the proceedings. I forgot to mention I also told him that many leaders of his party had made full statements and he could save neither himself nor the Samiti. To which I received no reply.

The 23rd. October, 1916. L. H. Colson."

National Archives, Home-Poll-1917-Jan. 364-372 and K. W Part A.

Page 54

"His Excellency the Governor General in Council being satisfied that the interests of the state demand the close restraint of the above conspirators (four), has been pleased to direct the issue of warrants under Regulations III of 1818 for their confinement in the Presidency Jail, Calcutta.

Delhi J. H. Duboulay.
5th January, 1917. Secretary to the Government of India."

Note to Secretary of State for India :—
No. 1 of 1917
Government of India, Home Department,
Political.

To

The Hon'ble Austin Chamberlain,
His Majesty's Secretary of State for India,
Dated Delhi, the 5th January, 1917.

Sir,

In continuation of our secret despatch No. 15 (Political) dated the 3rd November, 1916, we have the honour to report that we have found it necessary to issue warrants under Regulation III of 1818 for placing under personal restraint the four persons named below, in circumstances detailed in the annexed proceedings :—

1. Narendra Nath Banerji alias "Scientist" alias Pratul S/o Uma Charan Banerji.
2. Jogesh Chandra Chatterji S/o Bepin Chandra Chatterji
3. Sishir Kumar Datta Gupta S/o Nagendra Kumar Datta Gupta
4. Jogendra Das Bhattacharya alias Jogendra Nath alias Master Babu alias Jyoti alias Justidhar alias Dada, alias Maharaj S/o Haridas Bhattacharya.

We have the honour to be,
Sir,
Your most obedient humble servants

R. S. Craddack
W. S. Meyer
C. H. A. Hill
C. Shankaran Nair
G. R. Lowndes

DALLANDA HOUSE AND KYD STREET C. I. D. OFFICE

To come back to the Dallanda House, I saw there the two leaders of Comilla, Prabodh Sen of Anushilan and Jitendra Sen of the Jugantar Party. We were behind the bars but these two were on the opposite side of the big compound. Their cells were not locked any time of the day or night. Yet I did not suspect them. Many days after this I came to know that my Comilla arrest was made on the information of Jiten Sen and the Calcutta house at 39 Pathuriaghata Street, was pointed out to the police by Prabodh Sen. Jiten Sen has died but Prabodh Sen is now a professor in a big institution.

Prabodh Sen had a favourite student at Comilla named Ramesh Bhattacharya, whom he made his assistant. This student as an agent of Mr. Tegart did a good deal of mischief to the revolutionaries, first in North Bengal and then in West Bengal. When he was a student of Bankura College, his College Hostel associates among whom were some revolutionaries including Charu Ghosh, suspected him and even opened his trunk in his absence. They found a letter of Tegart introducing him as an agent. He, too, on his return to his room suspected that his trunk was searched and left the College immediately. Charu Ghosh told me this in Rajshahi Central Jail. In 1923, Ramesh met me at a Ghat of Benaras. He was then a professor in Bengal. As soon as he accosted me, I gave him such a reply that all people present were astonished.

Rai Bahadur Bhupen Chatterjee of the Calcutta C. I. D. used to pay daily visits to the Dallanda House. He visited us casually, but spent much time with the two Sens. Prabodh Sen told me that people, who were detained in Dallanda House were sent to different Jails as State Prisoners and that it was always better to be interned in a camp from where one could escape. He also told me that we should try to escape as new developments could take place in favour of revolutionaries. It was a part of a conspiracy between Sen and Chatterjee. One evening I was again sent to the torture house ; but this time they did not ill treat me much but the food supplied was not edible. Mr. Colson came one day and narrated to me some details of my stay in Faridpur district. I was sure that there was something seriously wrong with our organisation or else how could he know the things which he told me ? This dampened my spirit and I wanted to leave that hell somehow, so that I could be spared the agony of listening to the acts of betrayals of my own associates.

One day I saw one finely dressed person under police guard. I asked the Havildar about him and he told me that he was from Singapore and was helping the police. He was a Bangkok lawyer who betrayed the Indo-German conspiracy to the police and got a big amount of money in return. He was Kumud Nath Mukherjee. He had a serious difference with " Father Martin " (Naren Bhattacharya, later M. N. Roy) and for this he went to Singapore and gave out all information to the authorities there. In this way the whole Indo-German affair came to the direct knowledge of the British Government and they took all possible precautions. Thus the Indian revolutionaries could not get the German help in their greatest hour of need.

I was restless to leave the hell. I could not understand why they were detaining me. I found that the armed police and the officers doing clerical work were all sympathetic to me. Perhaps it was because they all knew how I had stood firm against all brutal tortures. In fact one day a South Indian clerk told me that Europeans were afraid of dysentery and advised me to approach the Deputy Commissioner and tell him that I was suffering from dysentery. I did so. Promptly after this I was sent to the Presidency Jail. At the Jail gate I met Naren Banerjee, who was also brought from the Dallanda House. We both were sent to the European Ward, where the good cells on the ground floor were under occupation and so we were kept in cells upstairs.

CALCUTTA PRESIDENCY JAIL

So I was back in the Calcutta Presidency Jail.

The European Ward was a small enclosure in which there were ten cells. It was two storied, five cells on the ground floor and five on the first floor. Naren Sen, the well known leader of Dacca Anushilan was there in a cell. Jogendra Das Bhattacharya and Sisir Kumar Dutta Gupta also came there.

Our cells were locked the whole day. Only one person was unlocked at a time for going to the latrine. We were not supposed to have any talk between us. Here also there was one European Warder who sat on the Verandah and one Gurkha military man was on duty on the first floor. We had no means of communication, no book or newspaper and no association. A portion of Alipore was visible from my cell, as also the back side of the jute mills inside the Jail where prisoners worked. Despite all these precautions we, however, had one means of communication. We were given a slate and a pencil for whiling away our time. So we wrote on the slate and sent it through the Gurkha to others. We wrote on it in Bengali and exchanged our views when a good warder was on duty. Otherwise we got tired of sitting or walking inside the cell.

After a few months Naren Banerjee and I were suddenly transferred to the 44 Cells. The European ward was much better. The cells were very good and well ventilated. But cells in " 44 " were very bad.

This time we were detained in the jail under Regulation III of 1818. This Regulation was enacted at a time when the British rule was not well consolidated and was used as a measure to keep the revolting princes under restraint. This they were applying in the present century against their political opponents. Lala Rajpat Rai and Sardar Ajit Singh were its first victims in 1907 followed by nine leaders of Bengal in 1909. During the war the Regulation was applied freely to the revolutionaries. Out of the thousands arrested and detained in Bengal, nearly 140 persons were kept in the jails under this Regulation.

The rules of the Regulation stated in the Preamble ; " A State Prisoner is called a prisoner, because there is no other term to express the idea. The person under whose custody such a prisoner is kept will see whether the allowance fixed for him is sufficient both for himself and his family." This was the spirit of the rule framed by the Government. And what was the treatment meted out to us ?

We were kept inside the cells which had no window. There was nothing in the cell except a small mug of water, an enamel mug and a plate, one blanket and two earthen pots for easing. No reading and writing material was supplied to us even when all of us were young and came from educated middle class families. To remain confined day and night inside cells without anything to do was a terrible strain on our minds and hardly within a year and half three of us turned lunatic. Two were sent to the Lunatic Asylum. The third a Vice-Principal, was interned outside, but within a short time he died in the Medical College hospital. One person was kept in one cell and two cells on either side were kept vacant with the purpose of ensuring of absence of communication between prisoners. Vice-Principal Manindranath Sethi of Daulatpur College was on the third cell on my right. One evening he suddenly started singing a stanza from a song common in Bengal. He sang the same thing again and again and used the mug and the plate to produce the musical accompaniment. He paid no heed to the warder and the same was the case when the jailor came. The Jailor questioned me about him. But I had no personal acquaintance with him.

My father came to see me. A C.I.D. officer was with him to hear the talk and we were separated by two rows of wire partitions. This was disgusting and I finished the interview within a minute though the allotted time was five minutes. I requested him not to come again. My father left some new clothes for me. But later when I asked for the clothes I was told to write home for that, and I refused to do so. The jail authorities gave me two small pieces of Dosuti cloth, usually given to C class prisoners on release. They were like thick loin cloth which I wrapped round my waist like a lungi.

After three persons had turned lunatic, the authorities became a bit lenient towards us. We were allowed to walk a little in the yard in the morning and evening and books from the jail library were supplied to us. This was a great relief.

The next year my uncle came to interview me. He was pleading with the C I D officer to help him in securing my release. This I resented, and I told my uncle that those were the very people who tortured me brutally to get promotion in their service.

Besides Naren Banerjee, my friend Atindra Mohan Roy, Jiban Thakurta of Faridpur, Jiban Chatterjee of Vikrampur and a relation of mine, Suresh Chakravarty and Sisir Ghose and many others were there. Atin, Suresh and Sisir participated in the murder of Rai Bahadur Basanta Chatterjee. But the police had no concrete evidence against them. Another prisoner who joined us was Krishna Lal Saha of Faridpur. He had many exploits to his credit. But for reasons best known to him he faltered from the path of the revolutionaries and gave information to the police which led to the police raid of Gauhati in which there was a regular fight between the police and some other important revolutionary leaders.

A number of political prisoners used to be brought to the jail and taken out. We used to see them walking in and out of the cells. But we could not contact them. Once two Muslims came and stayed for some time in our cells. They were not revolutionaries. They were Khilafatists and were against the Britishers because Turkey was England's enemy.

The Superintendent of the Jail, Lieut-Colonel Thomson, was a dry sort of man, devoid of any human sentiment. From the beginning to the end I was never on good terms with him. He derived sadistic pleasure in oppressing not only us, the political prisoners, but also the ordinary criminals. He did not think that the prisoners were human beings.

When we were in the European ward there was one habitual convict, a non-Bengali hardened criminal. He came there as a cleaner of the Ward. When the Warder on duty was a lenient man. this cleaner would come in front of my cell and talk to me for hours on the conditions of prisoners in the jail. He also spoke of officials, warders and doctors. He was very bitter against the Superintendent, who never cared to hear any complaint of the prisoners. From his talks I got a good deal of information on the general conditions prevailing in the jail. He was an illiterate man. On his request I used to write letters for him. These letters he smuggled out. And from what I wrote for him I knew he had intimate relations with a big gang of criminals, many of whom were in Alipore jail. He was ready to be my messenger in return. But I felt I could not trust him that much.

The Jailor, Mr. Hill, an Irishman, amassed much wealth extorting bribes from prisoners and also by stealing from the jail supplies. We were not much concerned with him and he met us very rarely. On the eve of his going home on long leave, one night he had a serious attack of high blood pressure and expired within a few hours.

The District Magistrate, Mr. Prentice, I. C. S. used to visit the jail once every month. But he was never in a mood to hear anything. He had a patent reply " Tell my friend, Colonel Thomson, the Superintendent." So we were also indifferent to his coming and going. Prentice developed a sentimental attachment to Bengal and its coast line. Many years later I learnt that after his death his body was cremated and the ashes were thrown into the Bay of Bengal according to his wishes.

My father had met the then Home Secretary Mr. J. G. Cummings. The latter told him that he had seen me in jail and that I was in good health. He told my father that although he was a very good man, I was very turbulent and misled. Mr.

Cummings came to see us only once. As soon as he heard my name he looked at me sharply and went away saying, " You were arrested in the Pathuriaghata house."

Sir Walter Buchanan was the Inspector General of Bengal Jails. He also paid us a visit. The jail was cleaned and whitewashed and everything was made neat and clean. He simply passed by our ward accompanied by the officials ceremonially but did not exchange a word with me or any one of us. I spent in total nearly a quarter of a century in the Bengal, Bihar, U. P. and Punjab jails, and I never again saw such an imperial I. G. of Prisons anywhere, neither did I meet another I. G. P. with a title of Sir.

Mr. Tegart also came once to our ward ; but did not talk with any one.

Mr. Hugh Stephenson, Additional Secretary, Government of Bengal, used to pay monthly visits to the jail. He used to stay for long and had talks with individual prisoners. We all knew that he was making a keen study of the subject. He was later knighted and became the Chief Secretary and then Home Member and officiated as Governor. After retirement from the I. C. S. he became the Governor of Bihar and after that the Governor of Burma. All these visits made it clear to us that the Government was much concerned and purturbed over the actions of their direct enemies—the revolutionaries.

After Lord Ronaldshay's visit a slight change in our plight was effected. But even then our condition continued to be miserable. In all fairness it must be said here that the conditions in the New Alipore Central Jail were much better, thanks to the efforts of the Jail Superintendent, Colonel Malvini, an Irishman.

Colonel Malvini was strict in the observance of rules. He did not illtreat a political prisoner even if pressure was brought on him. Unjust directives even from the Central Government failed to change his attitude. He managed the jail affairs in England perfectly and for that reason he was given the charge of constructing the New Alipore Central Jail on the English model. After the construction of the jail he was appointed Superintendent of the jail and also acted as the Deputy I. G. of Prisons. But he had to lose his job because of his strict adherence to jail rules even in the case of revolutionary prisoners. The Government brought pressure upon him to act differently ; but he did not budge. After some years the newspaper *Forward* founded by Deshbandhu C. R. Das, published some letters sent to Colonel Malvini by Government of India. These letters gave an inkling of the plight of the political prisoners and also showed Colonel Malvini's integrity.

At the approach of the summer of 1918, almost all of us were sick and some lost their mental balance. The Superintendent wouldn't even allow me to send an application for transfer. But eventually when it was allowed by the District Magistrate the reply came from the Government within two weeks that " Government are not prepared to transfer you." My health was so bad that a minor operation on my foot took more then a month to heal up and I was getting only one motion in a week, and that too, after taking a double dose of saline purgatives. This reply was intolerable to me. Without a sound body what would be the value of my life ? The Government was determined to kill us slowly and I could not think out what was to be done.

HUNGER STRIKE

One noon no sooner was the plate of food served than I kicked the plate away. The Warder asked the reason but I was silent. The Jailor came and I told him that I would not touch food unless either I was transferred to some other jail or conditions were improved. I learnt soon that all the ten political prisioners also did the same. So it took the form of a hunger strike, though I had no such idea when I kicked away the plate. I could not even dream then that on a later occasion I was destined to break the world record in hunger strike behind the bars. From the next day the Superintendent stopped visiting our ward. The District Magistrate came and I gave him in writing that either I must be transferred or given better treatment ; or I shall fast unto death. All others, I learned later, did the same.

For five days nobody came near me, neither the Superintendent nor the Jailor nor the Warder. On the sixth day, after noon, three of us were taken out, weighed and then locked again in the cells. In the evening we all three were marched to the jail gate with our kits. Three European sergeants took charge of us, I was sent to Rajshahi, Atin Roy to Dacca and Jiban Thakurta to Midnaore jails. Myself and Atin Roy met again at the Sealdah Station. Though we were fasting for six days, we two friends enjoyed the evening at the station after nearly two years in hell. We also took some fruits and sweets because the main grievance was redressed as we were being transferred. The victory in the fight also gave us much pleasure. What happend in the new jails we would see. The train journey I enjoyed so much that I could not sleep the whole night. In the morning we boarded a steamer on the great river Padma—a river with which I grew since my childhood. I enjoyed the steamer journey to my hearts content. My dishevelled hair, grown beard and pale face attracted the attention of other passengers, particularly because of the police guards. But I was absorbed in enjoying the steamer breaking the waves and passing from place to place. And the sweet, humid breeze from the river Padma was playing with my long hair. I felt like jumping into the water and playing a thing which we enjoyed so much in our childhood. My mind ruminated on the sweet memories of the mighty rivers. Suddenly my dream was broken at the harsh horn of the steamer and when I looked at the other passengers they were all busy preparing to get down with their baggage.

I now saw that the time was near to enter another jail. Who knows what would be the situation there? At any rate shortly I would again be locked behind the high walls, only heaven knew for how long!

Chapter IV

IN RAJSHAHI CENTRAL JAIL

The massive gates of the Rajshahi Central Jail opened and took me inside its walls. There was no European there. I was taken to the jail office. After I sat down the officer-in-charge of the state prisoners came near me. He was very gentle and courteous. He sent for the barber, gave me a clean towel for washing, and then with great hesitation raised the question of my food. He said, " You are not taking food for seven days and so the Superintendent instructed us to give you a cold drink." I said, " Yes, I would relish a cold drink." I then told him that I had already broken my fast at Sealdah Station as our main demand had already been conceded. At this he seemed to be much relieved.

I entered the jail with the officer and on reaching the corner of the hospital I found other state prisoners waiting there to receive me. I had known none of them before. But as revolutionaries we were friends, known or unknown. So far as I remember at this distant date after 47 years, they were five, Satish Pakrashi, Rasik Sarkar, Purna Das, Girin Banerjee and Naresh Chaudhury. They had heard that I was on hunger strike and therefore thought that I would continue the strike. They said that because of this they were allowed to receive me outside the cells.

Purna Das and Girin Banerjee were transferred to the Rajshahi jail after their hunger strike in the Midnapore jail. Shortly after my arrival the hunger strikers of the Alipore New Central Jail who had been transferred to the different jails of U. P. and Madhya Pradesh started arriving at the Rajshahi jail one after another. Thus Suresh Das came from the Agra Jail and Bhupen Dutta came from the Bilaspur Jail.

Like the 44 cells of Presidency Jail, here also the state prisoners were kept in the condemned cells. Professor Jyotish Ghosh turned lunatic because of the inhuman conditions in which he had to live in this jail and had to be sent to the Lunatic Asylum. Naresh Chaudhury was also almost on the brink of losing his mental balance due to the hard confinement in the cells of this jail. But by the time I arrived at the Rajshahi Jail hunger strikes in other jails had led to a slackening of the tortures of confinement and this saved Naresh Babu.

Prabodh Das Gupta, who escaped from the Dallanda House and while absconding participated in the Gauhati encounters with the police, was arrested and sent to this jail. It may be mentioned here that this Das Gupta, a few years after his release was sentenced to 5 years' R.I. in a currency note forgery case in 1925. He attempted this forgery to help the revolutionary party. Pratul Ganguli came from Raipur Jail. Another person who joined us was Mani Choudhury. So this jail earned the reputation of being the prison for "all dangerous." Therefore the jail authorities were more cautious in their behaviour. The Governor of Bengal had called a conference at Darjeeling of all those jailors where state prisoners were detained and there it was decided that they should be given better treatment. The Government realised that the revolutionaries would retaliate against any ill-treatment and that might cause a county-wide ferment. So the plight of the political prisoners changed everywhere for the better; but in Rajshahi jail it became really good. We were allowed to play badminton outside our enclosures and were permitted to walk on the lawns.

No Indian newspaper was allowed in the jail. But we managed to smuggle in a copy of Amrita Bazar Patrika everyday. The smuggled newspaper was delivered to Purna Das who used to give the same to Pratul Ganguli. Pratul Ganguli and I sat in his cell with a slate. Ganguli used to read and I used to take notes. Then the paper was returned. After lunch we used to sit in one cell where Pratul Babu with the slate in hand used to tell the daily news to all. This was done everyday, regularly. For our smuggling work we had to distribute various articles to the petty officials. We had to part with cheese, oil, sugar, flour, clothes, shoes, shirts, soaps, tooth powder, tooth paste, etc. But we were getting good service in return.

For our demands, we first used to think over the matter thoroughly. Then we placed our demand before the authorities and we did not stop till it was conceded. We were cautious and because of this grievances were invariably redressed in the Rajshahi jail.

In the summer cellular confinement at night was a painful thing. We had disturbed sleep because of the extreme heat. Government had made it a rule that we would be kept confined in cells at night. The cell in the European Ward in the Calcutta Presidency Jail was quite good and even in hot weather it was not trying. But the cells of Rajshahi Jail were worse than even those of the 44 Cells of the Presidency Jail. 44 Cells had a broad yard in front but here the yard was very narrow and hence there was no proper ventilation. For this reason cellular confinement in this Jail was a genuine grievance and we placed this before the authorities again and again but nothing happened.

A TRAGEDY IN THE JAIL

Rasik Sarkar of Mymensingh district. a member of the Dacca Anushilan. was in this jail. His family was not very well off financially. Though not much educated he was a good worker in violent activities. He participated in the murder of Sarat Bose, the Headmaster of the Zilla School, Comilla, in broad day light. He also murdered a C.I.D. officer in Mymensingh along with a child who was in the officer's lap. In the jail he remembered, these things.

After serving one year R.I. in Dacca Jail, he was transferred to Hooghly Jail, where he was confined in a cell. The front side of the cell was kept covered with a gunny cloth. Nothing outside was visible to him. He could only look at the empty walls of his cell. On top of all this frequent questioning by the C.I.D. officials were continued. All this caused terrible mental disturbance to him, so much so that he lost his mental balance.

At this stage he was transferred to Rajshahi Central Jail. As members of Anushilan, Pakrashi and Sarkar were naturally more close to me. Rasik Sarkar became more intimate with me because he had a great craving for knowledge. He did not know English. Books in English I had to read and explain to him in Bengali. Even today I distinctly remember that I read out Rousseau's Social Contract and explained to him word by word in Bengali. He did not talk much and often remained in a pensive mood. In the afternoon during our permitted walks he very rarely walked together with others. He used to sit in the lawns alone. Though young and robust his hair had grown grey in jail.

An interned detenue, Das Gupta, had committed suicide in an internment camp in North Bengal and he left a statement which was published in the papers months ago. Sarkar one day asked me whether I remembered what Das Gupta had written. I told him that he should not think of these things in jail. I tried to distract his mind from morbid thoughts. From his behaviour I knew he was always brooding and most of it was centred round his family. He could not get out of the jail by betraying his revolutionary friends. But from inside the jail he could not do anything for his family.

So he applied for the grant of a family allowannce. That was rejected. He received a post card from home that his family was suffering from financial difficulties.

One afternoon Sarker played badminton as my partner very enthusiastically. After the games he walked a little in the lawns and then went inside his cell. Long after, when I reached my cell I saw his cloth and towel spread for drying in my antecell. This was a bit unusual but I did not think it was serious. When we were being locked up, he came in front of my cell and addressed me with folded hands and I came to know later that he did so that day in front of every cell. We could not even imagine that he was bidding good-bye to us for ever.

At midnight the duty of guards changed. Rasik shouted to Girinda and Pratulda that it was a late hour of the night and that they should go to sleep. Girinda told him that he was going to bed at about 1 A.M. About half an hour after this flames were visible in Sarkar's cell. I clearly saw the reflection of the flame on the wall in front of Rasik's cell. One guard tried to shout: "Chabi" (Key) but out of fear his voice was choked. We shouted: "Chabi", "chabi". The Gurkha guard was not talking. Later we came to know that he was trying to throw mugfuls of water on the fire. But the fire was behind a cot fitted with a mosquito curtain. The guard of the hospital told our guard to whistle and as soon as he whistled other whistles rang from all sides and the jail gong also went in action. The Jailor, Upen Mukherjee, came and was so nervous that he sat down on the ground outside our ward and the doctor and the Chief Head Warder took the keys from him and opened the door of the cell. So long Rasik was standing but he dropped on the cot when the doctor caught hold of him. When the cot reached the hospital Sarkar was dead. The District Magistrate came for enquiry and all that we could do was to give him which Rasik had received from his home in which his brother wrote about his family's economic hardship.

We said to the Magistrate and every other officer that we would like to have a last look at the body of our departed friend. That was not granted, though the officials told us that they would allow us to see the dead body. It was stated later that the body was so much disfigured that we would have been pained to see it. I came to the Rajshahi Jail in May, 1918, and this happened on the 16th of June.

The next day Mr. Stephenson with Rai Bahadur Bhupendranath Chatterjee came from Calcutta. No body had the least inclination to have any talk with Chatterjee. Our spokesman, Girin Banerjee, told Stephenson that had we been put together in a barrack such a tragedy could have never happened. Our suggestion was that a portion of the first floor of the hospital building could be set apart for our night accommodation. The jail authorities' opinion was that would be unsafe. The war was over by that time and we assured Mr. Stephenson that the Government could depend on our words. Stephenson turned to Prabodh Das Gupta and said, "What has Pradodh got to say ?" Prompt was the reply of Prabodh, who, after his escape from the Dallanda House, had remained underground for nearly two years, "Did you believe me ?" But on his going back to Calcutta Stephenson telegraphed to the Superintendent : "Keep state prisoners in hospital building upstairs and tell them that I depend on their honour."

Another serious thing happened in the Rajshahi Jail. Girin Banerjee was the oldest person among us. After we were locked up, Banerjee was talking to the officer who came with the Jamadar for locking us in. The Gurkha Guard roughly said, "Don't talk." In the same way Girindra said, "Keep quiet ; you have nothing to do with this." Next morning this guard entered Girindra's cell and roused him from sleep with his kukri drawn. It was a terrible sight for him. He jumped up from the bed with a shout and ran to the lawns where we were. The guard was after him with the open kukri in his hand. We surrounded the guard and asked the hospital Warder to whistle. With great reluctance he complied. The Chief Head Warder came and ordered him to sheath the kukri and he did so. We lodged a complaint. But the guards and warders said that our complaint was a piece of fabrication. In protest we started a hunger strike. We gave in writing that unless this practice of giving duty with kukri was not stopped, we would take no food.

One evening, before lock up time, when we were shouting slogans on the lawns, the Jail Superintendent came there. But we did not even look at him. He came near me and putting his hand on my shoulder said, "You are too young to go on hunger strike." Bhupen Datta reminded him that I was transferred to Rajshahi Jail because of hunger strike. Then he laughed and said, "You all take your food. I have already sent this batch of Gurkhas to Dacca and have written to the Commander of guards that the next batch should give duty here without kukris." So we went to our cells satisfied and welcomed food after lock up.

Through Rasik Sarkar's death we gained another thing. The Magistrate, Mr. Cassels thought highly of us. When in his presence the witnesses to the enquiry whom he had brought with him from the city expressed doubt that Rasik's death could not be a case of suicide as the dying man did not even stir while being burnt, we ourselves told him that there was no foul play. Cassels knew that we could easily put the jail authorities into difficulty by making the allegation that Sarkar had been killed and then burnt. That could create a great agitation in the whole country. We did nothing of the kind as falsehood and deceit were never our forte. So he was very pleased and at our request he asked the Principal of the Government College. Rai Bahadur Kumudini Banerjee, a great educationist, to supply us books from the College. This was a great privilege to us. We wrote to Banerjee and he himself selected the books and sent them to us. In this way we were borrowing about 25 books per month from the College Library.

I was immensely benefitted by my transfer to

Rajshahi Jail. Almost all the prominent revolutionaries of Bengal had been to this jail during the two and a half years of my stay there. Their constant association was a boon to me in many respects. I mixed with all irrespective of party affiliations. Because I had no prejudice in my mind I respected all the revolutionary leaders deeply and they also in their turn had good feelings towards me. My main objective was to acquire as much knowledge as was possible and the opportunity was limitless. When we could not get good books from outside I learned history from Girin Banerjee. His knowledge of history was so good that even without any text book he taught me the history of India and of modern Europe. Besides Girin Banerjee, Pratul Ganguli, Bhupen Datta and Basanta Banerjee of French Chandernagore, took a good deal of personal interest in my studies. Sometimes I studied economics with Monoranjan Gupta. Then French Language Class started and I joined it.

We were not only reading for hours and hours but also we had lively discussions on interesting subjects. Very often we carried our discussions into the night. And the discussions were so lively that we lost all sense of time till someone told us that the sun was rising. We were so absorbed in our studies and discussions that very often we thought that we were the members of a residential university.

We got the news through the magazine "Twentieth Century and After" that there had been a successful revolution in Russia and Czarism had been replaced by Socialism. Before this we read only a little about Socialism in books on economy. We wrote to Principal Banerjee to supply us some books on Socialism. But unfortunately there was only one book on Socialism in the College Library—Sombart's Socialism. In the introduction it was stated that this book had been translated into 26 languages of the world. So it became more attractive to us. We read it again and again and took extensive notes.

We also read classical books of famous authors in the original as well as in translation. Once it struck us that we should study the cooperative movement of Europe and we read some books on this as well. Previously, while we were not in jail, we read the Economic History of British India and Victorian Age by R. C. Dutt, the Prosperous British India by William Digby and Poverty and un-British Rule in British India by Dadabhai Naoraji.

I remember one day a Muslim Deputy Magistrate came to visit us. He saw a book on economics by Gide with Pratul Ganguli. He asked what was his academic qualification and when he learnt that he was not even a graduate he remarked that Ganguli would not understand a book like that.

Girin Banerjee retorted that Ganguli possessed so much knowledge that he could teach an ordinary graduate for many years and it was really so.

I utilised my time in the jail to the best of my ability. All were helpful to me in my efforts. The jail at this period was a place of learning. Our confinement was not very rigorous as before and we were reading and writing. So we prepare for the next stage. We were more busy in acquiring knowledge than were the post ra duate students who carry on research work for the preparation of their thesis. The advantage here was that we had no other preoccupation.

My elders helped me in the choice of books that I should read. Books in connection with revolutionary movements in other countries we read very attentively because this was the subject nearest to our hearts. History of India, ancient and modern History of Europe and of Asia, particularly of China and Japan I also read. In economics Marshall and Gide we read and took exhaustive notes. We also read general literature in English and Bengali and the classics of different European nations in translation.

I was the youngest among the State Prisoners in this jail but later a younger friend came, Jiten Chaudhury of Lamchar, Noakhali district. I did not come from Calcutta or Dacca, the two big centres of culture, and my experience of revolutionary activities were mostly confined to the district of Tripura with its headquarter at Comilla, although I had connections with some neighbouring districts of East Bengal. Therefore, the association in Rajshahi jail with the veterans had a very beneficial effect on me.

Pratul Ganguli, Purna Das, Girin Banerjee, Rabi Sen, Manoranjan Gupta, Hemendra Prashad Acharya Chaudhury of Muktagachha, Mymensingh, Bhupen Datta, Bhupati Mazumdar, Satish Pakrashi Prabodh Das Gupta, Mani Chaudhury, Suresh Das, Basanta Banerjee and many others were there Pratul Ganguli was the most important leader of of the Dacca Anushilan Samiti. He was sentenced to 10 yeaɹs' transportation by the lower couɹts in the Barisal Supplementary Conspiracy Case but was let off by the Calcutta High Court along with Ramesh Chaudhury, elder brother of Naresh Chaudhury, who was in the Rajshahi Jail. The credit for the release of these two leaders of Anushilan goes to C. R. Das, who defended them. Both were made state prisoners on their acquittal by the High Court. They were both taken out of Presidency Jail gate and told, " You are released and rearrested" and taken to the Alipur New Central Jail as state prisoners.

Purna Das was the leader of the Faridpur Conspiracy case. He was described in a Government Commission Report as the " notorious student of the Bangabasi College." He had his own

Faridpur group and worked with the Jugantar party since the outbreak of World War I. Chittapriya, Monoranjan and Niren were his men. Chittapriya died in the fight with the police on the bank of the Muribalam in the Mourbhanj district, and Monoranjan and Niren were hanged. Purna Das had a grievance that three of his best men died with Jatin Mukherjee.

I had very good relations with Girin Banerjee and Bhupen Dutta even after our release. Rabi Sen was a leader of the Anushilan. He showed us the Ghany, where he was pressing oil as a convict in 1911. That was the way political prisoners were treated when the revolutionaries started their Movement. No distinction was made between the ordinary criminal and the political prisoners. He is still alive and holds an annual gathering of Anushilanites in Calcutta. Bhupati Mazumdar was arrested in a ship on his way to America and was kept in Singapore fort from where he was sent to Rajshahi Jail. He was a Minister of Bengal Government in Independent India. Satish Pakrashi suffered imprisonment in 1911 when he was a minor. He was an absconder for seven years before he was arrested and sent to the Rajshahi Jail as a state prisoner. Hemendra Prasad was a big zamindar and a group leader. He sent his brother to England as a revolutionary to learn the techniques of revolution and contact the India revolutionaries abroad but he returned with an English wife. Our Jail Superintendent, Dr. Ashe, was a a family doctor of the Muktagachha family when he was the Civil Surgeon of Mymensingh. So once when Sir Walter Buchanan, the I.G. of Prisons, came to visit the jail the Superintendent introduced Hemendra Prasad to him as a big zamindar of Muktagachha. Sir Walter said, "Yes, being a big zamindar he had ample opportunity of doing mischief." Another co-prisoner in the Rajshahi Jail was Basanta Banerjee of Chandernagore. He was devoted to literature from his student life when he wrote the life of Guru Govind Singh in Bengali. He helped and encouraged our reading and writing habits.

REVOLUTIONARY CONVICTS IN RAJSHAHI JAIL

On thing used to worry us, we were getting such good treatment while there were others in the same jail, our convicted friends, who were suffering as ordinary C class prisoners. A half shirt and a short were their dress. They had to carry an iron ring round their necks which passed through a wooden plate hanging on their chest in which were inscribed their numbers and the dates of sentence and the dates of release. An iron saucer was the only utensil supplied to them for all purposes, for taking food, storing drinking water, for washing, for taking bath, etc. Some coarse rice, dal (lentils) and vegetables were their daily food.

What a tragedy. We were living in such good conditions while in the same jail so many intimate associates of our were passing their lives in misery. It was very very painful to all of us. But there was no remedy. We were detained without trial and they were kept in separate wards at a distance and we could not even see them. They themselves were kept in separate wards in such a way that thye could not come in contact with one another.

My friend and an important member of Anushilan, Prafulla Roy of Sylhet, was sentenced to 12 years R.I. At Dacca when C.I.D. officials followed him to the Railway Station, he fired at the police men, ran away and while doing so his legs were caught in some iron wirings, he fell down and was arrested. He was sent to the Rajshahi Jail. Naren Banerjee of Banaras, an absconder of the Banares Conspiracy Case, who fought with the police when they surrounded the Gauhati house where he was living,was another importaנu person who was undergoing his conviction in the Rajshahi Jail. He was sentenced to 10 years' rigorous imprisonment.

Prafulla did not like the idle life in the jail. He was eager to escape from it. I managed to give him my woollen wrapper so that he could use it for scaling the wall and for covering himself up. But the Warder, who promised to help him, betrayed him at the eleventh hour and he was locked in the Cubical Ward.

There was some other political convicts. They were being ill treated. They resented this and went on a hunger strike. In the face of deliberate oppressions they had no other alternative but to resorting to hunger strike. The news reached us and we also went on hunger strike.

Prafulla Roy was transferred to another jail and others were given opportunities to mix with their fellow convicts and better treatment followed. But we did not give up our hunger strike till we got the formal news. Next morning when the jailor entered our ward he had to face a very awkward situation. All were in a fighting mood and abused the jailor bitterly. But the ever gentle Girin Banerjee came to his rescue. Soon we got the news of the improvement of the lot of the political convicts formally and our hunger strike ended.

At this time there were new arrivals of state prisoners. Khetra Sen, Charu Ghosh, Sarat Guha, Kuntal Chakravarty, and others joined us. The District Magistrate, Mr. Cassels was transferred and the new D. M. Mr. Stork was a different sort of man. Letters were our only source of information about our friends and relations. The C. I. D. censor of our letters was very irritating. They cut and disfigured the letters to such an extent that some letters were so thoroughly spoiled that no meaning could be made out of them. Most of us had grievances against this. So we complained to the authorites. The D. M. came with a file of our complaints. He came to our ward and asked about a certain application. I said it was mine. He said that if I wrote such applications against the police, they would not only be not considered, but would be thrown into the waste paper basket. When he was asked under what rule this could be done, he did not reply but made an about-turn and went away in the midst of various questions. An application complaining against the behaviour of the D. M. was sent to the Government of India. In the afternoon the jailor requested us to withdraw it. Our protest had its effect. For contrary to the rules, Mr. Stork did not come to our ward for many months. He was transferred and Mr. Reed came as the D. M.

After Dr. Ashe, Major Goel came as the jail Superintendent. He was a weak person and so he was very submissive to his superiors and very troublesome to his subordinates. Once he ordered that the state prisoners must return their old clothes before new ones were given. An application to the Government of India stating all the wrong things that were being done in the jail was submitted. The Jailor tried to mediate so that the application was withdrawn. This was done when the Superintendent agreed that he would not disallow any article indented for through the Indent book. We made it a point that we would not make unreasonable demands but that we would not tolerate any cut in our indents.

Our jail experiences demonstrated that to suffer silently any wrong was improper. If the Government were allowed to do what they pleased, the valuable lives of revolutionaries would have been ruined in the jail. To suffer tyranny lying down without any protest or resistance is cowardice. The revolutionaries were not cowards. They adopted the only possible means of resistance by resorting to hunger strike resolutely. This means of resistance brought about a change in the general situation. The authorities bowed down to our demands creating better circumstances for us which helped us to enhance our cultural and educational knowledge.

We started a hand written monthly paper in the jail. The name was "Bhanga Kula" (Broken Cleaner). Most of us contributed articles. The most notable feature used to be the short stories by Kuntal Chakravarty who was a brilliant young man and a good short story writer. He had a rare capacity of grasping the ideas of the books he read. He had also a very loveable character. Charu Ghosh also had a very tender heart full of nice human qualities. After release Charu Ghosh developed tuberculosis and Kuntal looked after him. He also somehow caught the contagion and met the sad end shortly. The revolutionaries lost a brilliant man with an inexhaustible store of human sympathy. Charu Ghosh survived a few more years.

Bhupen Dutta left him at Comilla sometime in 1922 for a month or so and I looked after him there. But soon he left Comilla. The last time I met him was at Banaras in 1923. His mother was with him. They stayed there for a few days on their way to Chunar. His condition was very critical. I sat beside his bed to relieve his mother. Charu objected to my sitting very near him as he was apprehensive of my getting the fatal disease, so deep was his concern for others. One day they left for Chunar and I accompanied them up to Moghal Serai station. This was our last parting. Charu died shortly after this.

CLASH OF IDEAS IN RAJSHAHI JAIL

I have already stated that Girin Banerjee was the oldest among us and he was well read as well. Surendra Nath Banerjee was his grand father through his mother's side. Yet he was extremely conservative in his ideas. He was a great supporter of the caste system. Even in the jail he was not ready to take food prepared by a non-Brahmin, It was a peculiar mentality for a man who knew practically all that was to be known international politics. There were also some others who were conservative in their attitude. Purna Das, Suresh Das, Mani Chaudhury could be counted among them. Pratul Ganguli, Bhupen Datta, myself, were the liberals. We did not find any justification for the caste system, untouchability or unequal status of women. Satish Pakrashi took much interest in the changing ideas in Russia and other countries but rarely expressed any opinion in discussions.

Owing to the constant difference in outlook and in thinking there arose among us a difference of a lasting nature. We were called free lovers by the conservatives and we in our turn, christened them as Achalayatan, 'the immobile' taken from the name of Tagore's satire.

Girin Banerjee told me that his grand father Surendra Nath Banerjee's daily diet consisted of two chickens. But he himself was such a staunch vegetarian that he could not think of taking any meat. He had no objection if others took it. But if a Hindu ate chicken, he felt disturbed. We could never propose that chicken be cooked in our kitchen. So we prepared chicken outside our ward and ate it there. When the news reached him he was very much displeased with us. He asked me if I ever ate chicken before coming to the jail. When my reply was in the negative, he cross-questioned me as to why I ate chicken at all. I said that I had no objection to eating chicken even before coming to the jail, but I had no occasion to do so. The attitude and views of men like Girin Banerjee were exceptions rather than the rule among the revolutionaries. However by some curious socio-cultural logic the Hindus of Bengal thought that chickens could only be eaten by non-Hindus.

DURGA PUJA IN RAJSHAHI JAIL

We did not ask for any grant for religious purposes. Now it struck us that we should ask for a grant to celebrate Durga Puja, the biggest religious festival of the Bengalees. We applied for a grant. The Jailor persuaded the Superintendent to write to the headquarters recommending the proposal. pointing out that as the jail officials observed the Puja ceremony every year, the state prisoners also could be allowed to join the same, provided an amount of money was sanctioned for the purpose. The Chief Secretary of the Bengal Government, Sir Hugh Stephenson, sanctioned some money with the remark that proper security arrangements had to be made.

Though many of us had no faith in the Puja, yet we wanted it to be celebrated as it would mean a little change in our jail life, and the jail rigors also would be slackened.

The mandop (pandal) was erected on the right side of the compound in front of the jail gate. The gate was opened in the morning for us. In the afternoon we all sat in the compound where chairs were arranged. We thus freely mixed with the outsiders. One significant point may be mentioned in this connection that the goat offered to the Goddess was a white goat, symbolic of the white man with whom the Indians identified the British.

In the night a cinema show was arranged. The Elphinstone Company was called from Calcutta for this purpose. The screen was fitted up just in front of the jail gate. Chairs were arranged inside the jail gate on the space between the inner and outer gates. In the midnight we were taken out from our barracks and seated in the chairs between the gates, with our faces towards the screen. The Jail Superintendent also occupied a chair.

Mainly the war documentaries were shown. The war was over and everybody knew that our release was not far off. The authorities, therefore, were not very strict. But a deep sorrow soon befall us.

Along with the rest of India, the revolutionaries had a great respect for Lokmanya Bal Gangadhar Tilak. The entire nation mourned his sudden passing away in a Bombay hotel on 1st August, 1920. We were all in mourning for 10 days in the jail as is done when a near relative dies.

The daily "Statesman" of Calcutta wrote editorially: "By his death India is purged of a much maligned and degraded character." This editorial note on the demise of the most respected son of India was so much resented by the people of Bengal that an agitation started for the boycott of the Anglo-Indian paper. The campaign was so strong that its circulation among Indians in Calcutta dwindled into insignificance and the paper was compelled to come out with an apology.

When after the World War Indians were to select three representatives to the Peace Conference at Marseilles, the first choice was Tilak, second

Gandhi and third Hussan Imam. Mrs. Anne Basant wrote in her paper that Tilak should not be the representative of India, because he did not know English. But Bipin Chandra Pal replied that Mrs. Besant wanted to say that the author of the 'Orion' and the 'Arctic Home of the Vedas' did not know English. This was one of the reasons why during the special session of the Congress in Calcutta in 1920 Mrs. Besant was not allowed to speak even after the request of Pandit Malavya, although 3 years earlier in 1917 she was the President of its Plenary Session held in Calcutta.

One day a C.I.D. Inspector came to see me from Calcutta. He showed me a list of certain properties, mainly a box full of books and other articles stated to have been recovered from 39 Pathuriaghata Street, Calcutta. He said that he had come to deliver these articles to me. After hearing all this I told him that I was not arrested at 39 Pathuriaghata Street and so I could not take delivery of the articles. Had I accepted the articles it would have been a clear proof of my being arrested in that dangerous house. My denial had a good effect. Four persons were arrested in connection with this house. But no name of the persons was mentioned although the Sedition Committee report devoted nearly two pages on this house.

King's Proclamation for the release of political prisoners was made not long after. Many leaders were released. Even many of the leaders of the Alipore Bomb Conspiracy Case, Barin Ghosh, Upen Banerjee, and others were released from the Andamans.

Two C.I.D. officials, one European and one Indian, had seen me once and told me that they could slacken the rigors of my confinement if I gave them a verbal undertaking that I had changed my views. I left them stating that I had not changed at all.

A few months after that we were called to the jail office. The Jailor informed us that Mr. Nelson, Additional Secretary and Mr. Dixen, D.I.G., C.I.D. had come to interview us. We had earlier learnt from Kuntal Chakravarty that these two officials invited him once the Dacca Jail office, but did not offer him a chair to sit. So he had refused to talk to them. We, therefore, told the Jailor that we must be assured of civil behaviour. Reluctantly the Jailor conveyed our message to them. They went away and we came back to our ward.

This news came out in the *Amrita Bazar Patrika* with strong editorial comments in which the questions of how and for what reasons the officials were sent to Rajshahi jail and drew their travelling allowances for their journey were raised.

The Governor was at that time at Dacca for a Council meeting. The Chief Secretary, Sir Hugh Stephenson came in the Commissioner's motor launch to Rajshahi and met us individually in our respective cells. He came to my cell and discussed with me my course of action after my release.

DAYS OF THE FIRST WORLD WAR

I have stated how the revolutionaries tried their utmost to avail of the opportunity offered by the War. After Bengal Partition agitation the political life of the country took a new turn and the energy of the secret revolutionaries burst out through large scale violent attempts and court-cases. Ultimately they were subjected to detention without trial under the Defence of India Act of 1915 and the Regulation III of 1818. This was done to avoid the propaganda that open trials might have created. The other object was to detain those persons who were suspects but could not be brought under the grip of law. Detenues were kept in camps in remote places under strict vigilance of the police. The important leaders were lodged in the jails under Regulation III of 1818.

As I have stated elsewhere the revolutionaries inside the country and abroad were deeply engaged in the single task of ousting the Britishers from India. For this purpose, immediately after the war started, the revolutionaries abroad established contact with the German Government and succeeded in getting some substantial help. Inside India they established wide contact with the army. Though they were not successful in India, they achieved success in capturing Singapore temporarily.

THE ROLE OF THE CONGRESS

After the war started Gandhiji and other top Congress leaders helped the Britishers in their war effort. Among the top leaders only Tilak was of the opinion that Congress should not help in the war effort till Britiain's promises were fulfilled.

S.P. Sinha, as the President of the Congress at its Bombay Session in 1915, stated in his written address that India was not fit for self determination. That clearly showed the pro-British stand of the Congress during the war period. The role of the Congress till that time was ultra-moderate. They were not ready even to bargain with the Government. The demand put forward by Tilak was opposed by Gandhiji himself who was of the view that Great Britain should be supported unconditionally in its war efforts as he was confident that if the British won they would not forget the services rendered by India.

But revolutionaries kept the flame of the spirit of freedom burning, Even in schools and colleges their propaganda literature found their way. The principal of our college used to warn us that students who had anything to do with the revolutionaries degrade themselves by such activities and that they should have the courage to come forward and confess. He used to look at the faces of students. Those who were trained to observe secrecy, how could they be affected by such lectures ? I rather helped the revolutionaries in their recruitment,

The principal did so, because being a very loyal person, he used to go to the District Magistrate with the pamphlets which we distributed to the students. Naturally the D.M. must have asked him to detect such students. This was beyond his power, because the revolutionaries were no fools, neither had he the courage to do any harm to them. He knew too well the result of such an action.

The revolutionaries carried on their propaganda mainly through their secret pamphlets. But their actions were more successful as propaganda. Though not very big in number, yet many of the best students joined them, attracted by their pamphlets and actions. A political money action was always a different matter than an ordinary dacoity committed by the criminals. Even the persons in whose house a political dacoity was committed were often a bit happy as they thought that the money would be utilised for the country's cause. In fact, I know of a young man who made efforts to come in touch with us after a decoity was committed by our party in his village home in the district of Mymensingh in East Bengal. Thus political dacoity served two purposes—it gave us the much needed fund and it acted as a propaganda. It also served as a training ground for making us dare-devils, a thing which we thought would be much needed in the ultimate fiight.

The other methods of propaganda were the big actions, like the throwing of the bomb by Khudiram Bose and Prafulla Chaki at Muzaffarpur and the throwing of the bomb on the Viceroy, Lord Hardinge in Delhi, the open fight with the police as at Baripada in Orissa by Jatin Mukherjee and others, the fight with the police at Gauhati, at Atgharia, Pabna, and Kalta Bazar, the murder of Saunders by Bhagat Singh, Chandrasekhar Azad and Rajguru, or the killings of high English officials in Bengal beginning with the Chittagong armoury raid, etc. Events like these shook the country from one corner to the other and roused the patriotic feelings in the hearts of innumerable Indians. Most of them were not active but they had sympathy and a good number of them also helped directly or indirectly in revolutionary or other patriotic activities.

GENERAL FEELINGS DURING AND AFTER THE WAR

The Partition Agitation in Bengal was a mass movement, but since its annulment there was no mass movement in the country. Anti-British feeling, however, continued. Then the war broke out and the patriotic feeling was manifest through the happiness of Indians in getting the news of British setbacks during the war.

People used to read papers with interest for war news and they appeared to be jubilant to read about the reverses of Britain and the British gains in war made them unhappy. The disgust of the people for British rule was the source of sympathy for the revolutionaries in India, because the revolutionary movement was the only active movement in the country which was carrying on an all out fight for India's freedom. In Bengal and the Punjab it was fought more fiercely. The feeling of a revolution was most intensified in Bengal from the Partition days and in the Punjab it was inspired by the Ghadar Party. Prosecutions and persecutions were also more severe in these two provinces. Thousands of houses were searched and thousands were thrown into prison or sent to detention camps.

The suppressed feelings of the people burst out to oppose the Rowlatt Act of 1919 when it was brought forward after the war to curb the activities of the revolutionaries. It took its most acute form in the Punjab and the result was martial law and the Jalianwala Bagh Massacre.

Britain promised substantial reforms after the war. But before the reforms were introduced the British Government brought forward the Rowlatt Act to curb the activities of revolutionaries. The Rowlatt Act was followed by the Government of India Act, 1919, based on the Montague-Chelmsford report of 1918. These reforms came into operation in 1921.

It is an undeniable fact that the countrywide

agitation against the Rowlatt Bill was the expression of the people's love for the revolutionaries because of their sustained sufferings and sacrifices for the country's independence. For this very reason the Britishers suppressed the agitation so ruthlessly. But the harvest was reaped not by the revolutionaries, but by the Congress. In fact Gandhiji took up the leadership of the country along with C.R. Das and Moti Lal Nehru just after the Jalianwala Bagh Massacre.

Chapter V

ABOUT FIVE DEAD FRIENDS

1. Tarini Prasanna Mazumdar

The zamindars of Kashipur of Tippera district were a family of revolutionaries. Basanta Mazumdar and his wife Hemaprabha Mazumdar were Congress leaders of Tripura and had sympathy for the revolutionaries. His younger brother Sashi Mazumdar, his cousins, Kali Prasanna Mazumdar and Bagala Mazumdar were all very important and active members of Anushilan. Their nephew Tarini Prasanna Mazumdar laid down his life in the Kalta Bazar fight of Dacca along with Nalini Bagchi, another brilliant Anushilanite.

Tarini was not only an intimate friend of mine, but also shared equal status with me in the Tripura district organisation. We both started shooting practice together, both became circle leaders and sub-division supervisors at the same time. I was looking after the Chandpur Organisation and Tarini looked after Brahman Baria sub-division. We both absconded together in 1916. On many occasions we travelled to distant villages in the night. In our day to day life also we were very often together. We used to go out for morning walks in batches of 3 or 4. The first to rise used to sing from the street and on hearing the song others knew that the time for morning walk had come. We walked 2 or 3 miles away from our home. Our walk terminated at the newspaper agency shop. We used to collect the papers, read them sitting at a ghat and then go back home.

That was our routine work. In the evening we used to walk in batches as a part of our training as secret revolutionaries. This sharing of the common things of life made our group cohesive.

Tarini was 6 feet tall and well-built. His arms were stout and long. He was always cheerful and even in a difficult situation his mood remained unchanged. As an absconder for two years he had many exploits to his credit. Once when the house where he took shelter was surrounded by the police, he went up on the roof and jumped for the next roof, but missed it. One of his ankles was dislocated, yet he managed to escape. His health improved even as an absconder.

When I was transferred to Rajshahi jail, Satish Pakrashi told me that the present leader of our party was a person the like of whom he had never seen before. He said that the leader was of gigantic stature and had a long beard. He did not know his antecedents or real name. But he knew his secret party name. When I wanted to know the name Pakrashi said it was "Star". I told him that he was from Comilla and was an intimate friend of mine. His real name was Tarini Prasanna Mazumdar. Pakrashi told me that Mazumdar was a very daring and heroic person. That he performed many daring and arduous tasks in those bad days of the party. Shortly after this we came to know in the jail about his martyrdom in Kalta Bazar fight on the 15th June, 1918.

After our release I heard the details about the fight at Kalta Bazar house from an eye witness named Aswini Kumar De. He also had a history behind his simple life. He had no relative on earth except a maternal uncle. He was working at Comilla as a domestic servant for some time and served in our house also. He was not only a reliable man but also was intimate with us even in our secret activities. Tarini knew him and took his help when he was absconding. That was how Aswini was living in the Kalta Bazar house as domestic servant under the assumed name of Hari Chaitanya.

After the fight he was arrested from this house, tortured and then given a heavy sentence. He put up with all these things as a revolutionary does. After the King's proclamation he was released and met us at Comilla. He was hard pressed even after his release, because we were not in a position to help him. He told us how, after the Kalta Bazar house was surrounded by the police, Tarini rushed from the latrine, took out the Mauser pistol from a box underneath the wooden bedstead and started fiighting bravely along with Nalini Bagchi and others. They seriously injured two C.I.D. inspectors and one Havildar was killed. At last Tarini fell dead having received seven bullets. Nalini Bagchi also received several bullets and died in the hospital.

2. Prabodh Bhattacharya.

As I have already stated, Tarini and I was to go to an action some 28 miles away from our hide-out. Owing to my high fever Tarini had to go alone. A decoity at Laliteswar was the purpose. Tarini joined it, with the rest. Krishna Saha led the group. It was a rainy night and when one of them, Prabodh Bhattacharya, was taking out money burried in the ground, he was bitten by a poisonous snake.

It was a critical situation. The group consisted of a small number and Bhattacharya was losing consciousness and so he had to be carried away without any delay. When the villagers saw them in this plight, they challenged and tried to attack them with lathies and other weapons. In self defence they had to open fire. Several died and many were wounded. Bhattacharya breathed his last. The group left him under a big tree in a bush and escaped.

Next day the dead body was exhibited in Comilla but nobody could identify it. Later police came to know that it was Prabodh Bhattacharya of Rajshahi district. He was the only son of a widow. While a B.A. student, he was arrested and interned. He absconded from internment and shortly after came to Comilla.

3. Bipin Bihari De.

My boyhood friend and classmate, Bipin Behari De, also sacrificed his life at the alter of revolution. As a school boy he tried to persuade me not to be a revolutionary and after two years' close watch he was convinced and then formally joined the party. He was not only a meritorious student but also a staunch moralist. There was a warrant to arrest him and hence he had to abscond. When circumstances became hard for him in Bengal due to police vigilance, he shifted to Bihar. He lived there as a Bihari. One day he fell down from the roof of a building accidentally and died in hospital after three days. Khetra Sinha was in charge of the Bihar Branch of the party and he arrived at Monghyr after he expired. The Bengali Civil Surgeon told Khetra Sinha that from the utterance of the deceased in delirium he came to know that he was a Bengali, though dressed as a Bihari.

4. Rebati Nag.

He was a brilliant student and a zealous worker of the party. As an absconder when the situation in Bengal became very critical for him, he, too, had to go to Bihar as a student. He showed his capacity as an organiser. This is how even the Sedition Committee Report mentioned him as the most prominent organiser of the Anushilan Samiti in Bihar. Party discipline at the time had reached such a rigid point that for a minor lapse the party decided to murder him and it was executed. This news shocked us in jail. His elder brother also was a leading Anushilan worker, who worked in Bengal and Burma but died of T.B. His only surviving younger brother was drowned in a pond.

5. Pulin Mukherjee of Comilla.

He was Dr. Abinash Banerjee and Ramesh Banerjee's sister's son. He was also an important member of the Comilla Anushilan. Though Pulin did not play any important role in organisational work and in violent activities, he had to abscond when the first World War started. As an absconder he came in touch with the Jugantar Party, and took leading part in their violent activities. He even led many of their taxi decoities in Calcutta. Unable to get hold of the son, the police terminated his father's Government services. After his arrest, Pulin faultered and confessed to the police and his father was reinstated in his services. The demoralising effect of this incident was visible in him after his release from detention. He could not survive long after release.

CHAPTER VI

RELEASE FROM JAIL

One evening my release order was received. Next morning on the 1st September, 1920, I was released and went straight to Calcutra to join the Special Session of the Congress which was held from the 4th of September under the Presidentship of Lala Lajpat Rai.

In Calcutta I stayed in the Y. M. C. A. Hostel in Beniapukur Road. Some released political prisoners were sheltered here temporarily under the charge of Nalini Kishore Guha. I joined the Congress as a Pandal volunteer.

This was a very important session of the Congress. Due to the Rowlatt Act and the disappointment because of the Montague-Chelmsford Report and the Government of India Act of 1919, there was a great discontent in the country. The Special Session was called to decide what stand the country was to take. There was the proposal of responsive co-operation by Tilak and non-violent non-cooperation by Gandhi. These two proposals were to be placed before the special session. But unfortunately about a month before the session Tilak died. And so Gandhiji's proposal was the one to be discussed in this session. When Gandhiji stood up, there was a pin-drop silence in the big assembly. There was no microphone in those days and Gandhiji's voice was not very loud. Yet, due to the eagerness of the audience all were listening to him so attentivly and silently that in a gathering of about twenty thousand people. Standing at the farthest corner I could hear every word he spoke.

Gandhiji promised that if the people followed his advice, he would get them Swaraj within one year. I could see that the audience was captivated by his promise of Swaraj in one year. After the Congress Session I went home. I was about to enter the room when my mother prevented me from doing so. I thought my grandmother might not be alive. So I was to observe something defore entering the house. My mother led me to a Tulsi plant for worship. How could she know that I had no faith in such things ? However, I obeyed her and then saw my grandmother hale and hearty. Village elders came and requested me to wear a sacred thread. I told them clearly that I had lost my faith in that.

Village ladies were happy that my mother was now relieved of the pangs of separation from her son. My mother did not participate in any village festival during my imprisonment. Only once she went to lunch with other ladies of the village at the request of the head of a family. But while eating she suddenly started shedding tears as she remembered me. Other ladies also were touched by this and it was a sad scene.

After a few days I went to Dacca to meet Pratul Ganguli. We had met in Calcutta during the Congress Session and he requested me to come to Dacca. There we discussed the organisation of the party, particularly at Comilla. He had already visited Comilla and gave me some general idea about state of affairs there. I was going to Comilla and he advised me to stay there till his arrival and then accompany him to Chittagong. Reaching Comilla from Dacca I found that Pratulda had given me the correct information about the position inside the party at Comilla. He came to Comilla within a week or so. He met the Party members at Comilla, gave them necessary instructions and then left for Chittagong. Pratul Ganguli activised the Chittagong workers and gave Girija Chaudhury the charge of Chittagong. Here he had long talks with Surjya Sen, the martyred leader of the legendary Chittagong Armoury Raid Case, in 1930.

Pratulda then left for Dacca and I went to Daulatkhan to meet my father, uncle and others. Here I was depressed to see that my father's business was in a miserable plight. My elder brother had gone away with some money. My father was passing his days with one assistant who was realising arrears from persons, but was not depositing properly the amount collected. He could not suggest anything for my future. My uncle said that I might go ahead with the business but he was not willing to place some money at my disposal, although he had at least a few thousand. My uncle was in Government service.

ATTEND NAGPUR SESSION OF CONGRESS

So I came to Calcutta. The plenary session of the Congress was going to be held at Nagpur. I attended it as a Bengal delegate. Bengal's stand was to oppose Gandhiji in his scheme of non-violent non-cooperation as this was once tried in Bengal after the Bengal Partition of 1905. Charkha, Khaddar, National education, boycott of British goods and use of Swadeshi goods were already tried in Bengal and had failed. Gandhiji wanted to do the same on an all-India scale.

Bengal Congress passed a resolution to oppose it. Then the leaders left for Nagpur. Next day about 200 delegates, started for Nagpur by the Nagpur-Bombay mail. I carried 10,000 copies of the printed resolution. But as soon as we arrived at Nagpur, we came to know that C. R. Das had accepted the major part of Gandhiji's programme. So the copies of the resolution were only used by us as fuel for making tea, etc.

We, a batch of three, Rabi Sen, Prabodh Das Gupta and myself, visited Allahabad, Banaras and Patna on our way back to Calcutta. At Patna we stayed at the Sadaquat Ashram started by Barristar Majrul Haq. The old leader embraced us very cordially saying, "You are madmen of the first rank and we are of the second." We stayed there for three days and were much pleased to meet the inmates. Baba Khaleel recited his own poems to us, which were very popular throughout northern India.

Our difficulty in the Ashram was that we did not know Hindi. There were two Bengali youths in the Ashram. They very gladly worked as our interpreters. All were very enthusiastic, because all were inspired to create a new India. Majrul Haq helped the absconding Bengal revolutionaries who were in Bihar. It may be mentioned here that Acharya J. B. Kripalani, as a Professor in Bihar, rendered monetary help to the absconding revolutionaries. I heard this from Kshetra Sinha, who was in charge of our Bihar Party.

We saw the Anand Bhavan and other things at Allahabad. But at Allahabad we did not know any revolutionary. At Banaras we had two such persons and they received us very cordially. We visited many important places at Banaras and we also went to the residence of Naren Banerjee, who was convicted in the Gauhati Case and was serving his sentence of 10 years R. I. in Rajshahi Jail when we were there. We met his mother and gave her consolation after having paid our respects.

We heard at Nagpur what Gandhiji wanted to be done in order to obtain Swaraj in a year. C. R. Das had already given out to his personal friends even at Nagpur that he would give up his lucrative legal practice and devote himself entirely to the country's cause. He did so, as everybody knows.

COMILLA AGAIN

From Calcutta I went to Comilla. Before me there was a problem. On the one side there was the gigantic movement to be launched for the country's freedom and on the other was the miserable economic condition of my family. Every member of the big family was looking to me for relief. What would happen to my father, mother, grand-mother and others, who were so dear to me? If I took up the responsibility of the house-hold affairs, the task was so big that I would be merged into it, no time and opportunity would be left for me to serve the country to which I had pledged myself and for which I had suffered so much. This mental conflict gave me a great deal of pain. A relative also was trying for a job for me. At Comilla I received the news from him that he was not quite sure, but yet I should go to his place. This gave me a little relief from the mental anxieties and I made up my mind to devote myself to the great national freedom movement of the country.

Political awakening of the Muslims was very remarkable at this time. Near our house was the Munsif's house, a well-to-do middle class Muslim family lived in it. Three brothers of the family were in high government service. The fourth brother, although he was also a brilliant student, became crippled and gave up studies before he became a graduate. We used to go for bathing purposes to their pond. This gentleman, the Maijha Mia, as we called him, used to sit in front of the house in a deck chair. He supervised the studies of boys in that house and also looked after the household affairs.

Since the Comilla Hindu-Muslim riot, he was a

bit communal in outlook. He suspected some of our secret party members and even talked about them disparagingly. He did not suspect me, at least that was what I understood from his talk. But one afternoon when I was riding a horse on the road beside his house he called me waving his hand. As my horse neared him he admonished me not to be intimate with the Mazumdar family, as he saw that the horse was owned by Basanta Mazumdar of the Kashipur zamindar family, who were known, for their anti-British feelings. All this happened before I went to the jail. But after my release from jail when I arrived at Comilla, this gentleman welcomed me open heartedly. He called us national heroes, all of us who had returned from jail. He regretted that the Hindus were so much advanced and the Muslims lagged behind in the movement of national freedom. His enthusiasm for the appreciation of revolutionaries went so far that one day a police officer came and warned him not to do so.

I was intimate with a Vaidya family of the Sonarang compound. Two sons of theirs were also revolutionaries and Bipin Behari De, mentioned elsewhere was also living in that family. But I did not visit them on my first arrival after my release. When I came to Comilla the second time my revolutionary friend of the family was also there. So I went with him to his house. The family members complained that I did not see them when I came to Comilla on the first occasion. I told them that I did not come as some of the members of the family were Government servants and as my visit might have jeopardised their positions. Their reply was that they took me as a member of their family.

At that time there was no Congress office at Comilla but there was something like a Peoples' Assciation. Under the leadership of Ashrafuddin Chaudhury the Khilafat Committee with its office at Charta, very near our residence was functioning at Comilla. Ashrafuddin was two years' senior to me in the Victoria School.

On behalf of this committee Ashrafuddin Sahib arranged a reception to the three released State Prisoners, Atindra Mohan Roy, Sisir Kumar Dutta Gupta and myself. A big meeting was held at 'Maheshprangan' under the chairmanship of Akhil Chandra Dutta. The principal speakers were Basanta Mazumdar, Prakash Das and Ashrafuddin.

Soon there was a by-election to a Council seat. The Constituency was a Muslim one. Nawab Faruqi who was a loyal zamindar, was a candidate. Ashrafuddin did not like him to go unchallenged. So he decided to put up a Muslim against him on behalf of the Khilafat Committee. It was in the Zamindary of the Nawab which was under Court of Wards and on behalf of the Court of Wards, he himself was the manager. I was given the charge of two polling booths, Barkanta and Daudkandi. With the local revolutionary friend, Ananga Sarkar, and others I reached round sun-set the

Barkanta Bazar. We heard that long before our arrival the Superintendent of Police came to the bazar with policemen and threatened the people that if anybody said anything against Farqui's candidature, he would be prosecuted. We gathered some men and declared in a challenging way that we had gone there to put up a tailor against the Nawab on behalf of the Khilafat Committee and we challenged the police to arrest us if they had power to do so. We then invited some of the influential persons of different villages to meet at a certain place in the night. They appeared to be mostly in favour of us but they regretted that there was very little time left. Next morning was the polling. So they had no time to take an organised stand.

During the polling the Nawab told me that as this was his zamindari of which he was also the manager, we could not expect any vote. But in spite of all that twenty eight votes were recorded in our favour.

Next day was the polling at Daudkandi it was under my uncles' zamindari and he had given me a letter for the Naib. Therefore we secured more votes. So the Nawab's candidature did not go unchallenged.

After the Nagpur Congress, Gandhiji gave a call to the students to take part in the 'Movement.' He stated : "Education may wait but Swaraj cannot." There was a storm among the students of the country. The Victoria College was not far off from our compound. One Saturday after the college hours, a group of students assembled in our Sonarang compound, to decide how to respond to Gandhiji's call. They called a meeting and requested me to preside. As it was a serious matter, I told them to go ahead themselves. So they decided to join the movement leaving the college. My cousin, Paresh Chatterjee, took a leading part in it. The exact date of leaving the college was decided in another meeting. And a big number of students plunged themselves into the freedom movement.

BARISAL CONFERENCE

The Bengal Provincial Political Conference was to be held at Barisal, A large number of persons from Comilla and other parts of Bengal assembled there. All were full of enthusiasm and the conference was a grand success. The country adopted Gandhiji's programme and the Conference also did the same. All realised that a non-violent fight was ahead of us. The programme was the subject of discussion inside the Conference as well as outside. Our revolutionary friends from different districts had also assembled; we had also discussions amongst ourselves and decided that we would also join the movement. We returned to Comilla with this decision.

DESHBANDHU C. R. DAS AT COMILLA

Deshbandhu C. R. Das had already given up legal practice after his return from Nagpur

Congress and plunged himself whole-heartedly in the movement. He was touring in Bengal and his tour programme included East Bengal and Assam as well. All preparations were made to give him a grand reception at Comilla. Myself and a friend of mine were given charge of it by the local Congress Committee. The office bearers of the local Congress Committee were the following: President, Akhil Dutta; Secretary, Ashrafuddin Chowdhury; Assistant Secretary, Atin Roy; and office Secretary, Surendra Chakravarty. Before the arrival of Das, a large number of students gave up their studies. C.R. Das came and stayed with Akhil Datta. A meeting of lawyers was held at Mathur Deva's residence. Das appealed to them to suspend their practice for three months. My uncle Bishweshwar Chatterjee, was the first person to stand up and offer to suspend his practice for three months. Many more lawyers followed him. But all eyes were on Akhil Dutta, leader of the Bar and Congress President. He was hesitant; next day was the public meeting at 'Maheshprangan'. Eventually shortly before the meeting Akhil Datta agreed to suspend his practice for three months.

After the departure of C.R. Das, there was another big meeting to chalk out the programme of action to be followed. My uncle, Bishweshwar Chatterjee, was unanimously elected to preside over the meeting despite his reluctance to do so. After the meeting, the lawyers, students and other workers sat together and decided a detailed programme. One non-cooperative lawyer was given the charge of an area controlled by one thana (police station). One important worker was deputed to assist him and a batch of about a dozen non-cooperative students and others were also asked to work with him. I was placed as an assistant of a lawyer in charge of Sarail thana in Brahamanbaria Sub-division, with ten non-cooperating students mostly of B. A. class. There were some others connected with the revolutionary movement with us. My uncle took charge of Daudkandi thana which was in his own zamindari. He along with a batch of non-cooperating students and others and a singer of patriotic and inspiring songs went there and started the work of political upliftment. He tried his best to create an environment in the masses so that they could grasp clearly the non-violent non-cooperation movement of Gandhiji.

We made village Kalikachha our headquarter. This was a very famous village in the district of Tippera. The well-known revolutionary pioneer, Ullashkar Dutta, came from this village. His father, Dwijadas Dutta, was also a well-known person because of his erudition and strong moral character. Dr. Mahendra Nandi of this village was not only a famous doctor but also carried on with chemical research work on various things, maintaining an expensive laboratory and workers for several decades. This was a prosperous and big village. A maternal uncle of our revolutionary associate, Pulin Gupta, had a brick-built house in that village and our friend offered it for our accommodation. His uncle as the head of the police of Tripura State, was living in Agartala. His son who was living in the village helped us a good deal.

The incharge of our group was Haladhar Babu, a lawyer of Comilla. There was also one Maulvi, educated in Deoband, with us. We had divided ourselves into batches and then started work simultaneously in different areas. I took two party workers and the Maulvi with me and started activities in our area.

We established ourselves in a house of a village. There was enough accommodation in the house as a number of inmates had died due to cholera. Our object was to gear up public opinion for non-cooperation. Every morning we used to go to a village. There we collected important men of the village and told them the real situation in the country and our duties regarding it and then persuaded them to become four-anna members of the Congress. After it we formed a village panchayat in that village and explained to them that they should try to settle all disputes in the panchayat and refrain from going to law courts of the British. In the afternoon we held a meeting in the same village and in the evening went back to our centre. This was our daily routine.

A very important member of our secret revolutionary party, who was incharge of Brahmanbaria

Sub-division died due to a fatal accident. While he was heating old cartridges to make them dry, one exploded and killed him. He was Lal Mohan Saha, son of Lari Saha of village Uroail. His father had a shop in the market of the village. We made a sub-centre in that shop. The local youths were much influenced by him. That is why the young men extended their helping hands towards us as they knew that we were doing some sacred work there. Some time we held public meetings in which all the members of the group used to participate. On a few occasions these meetings were held at Kalikachha also.

Though I came from a village, I never studied the life of villagers so thoroughly before. I noticed in the villages signs of extreme poverty. There were families who did not have even proper utensils. They used only earthen utensils. They were not properly fed, dressed and sheltered. Even four-annas for the membership of the Congress was a strain on their meagre incomes. These scenes always pained me. I always thought whether our movement would be able to bring about any real change in the condition of the suffering people. I had the previous experience of the Swadeshi movement after the Bengal Partition. This new movement also might be ended abruptly one day without producing any fruitful results. This idea always pressed me even in the midst of all my activities, though it never affected any work.

As everybody knows, neither Swaraj could

be attained in a year, nor the movement continue for long. The high hopes entertained by the villagers as well as by the workers were also not fulfilled. The economic plight of villagers remained where they were. The only thing we gained was the spread of political consciousness among the people. But even that, I wonder, was not very deep and strong.

Among the non-cooperative students of our group, one was Gopal Chakravarty, a scholarship holder from Noakhali. He used to deliver very fiery speeches. This was in 1921 and next I saw him in 1938 when I went to Comilla after a lapse of fifteen years. I was presiding over a meeting in the Town Hall and Jai Prakash Narain was delivering a lecture on Socialism. I marked in the meeting that Gopal Chakravarty was taking notes of the speech. After enquiry I came to know that he was a C. I. D. Inspector at that time. Two days after this, I was served with an order of externment from Bengal and in this connection went to the Police Superintendent's office. As soon as I got down from the carriage, Chakravarty came forward and asked, " What do you want ?" Certainly he must have thought that I would not recognise him after a lapse of fifteen years but when I asked him. " How are you Gopal Babu ?", he was astonished and ashamed. He then took me to the waiting room and arranged the interview with the S. P.

Another person in the non-cooperating students'

group was B. K. Mukherjee. He joined the Railways Service at Jamalpore but was dismissed. He started work in the Railway labour unions. Ultimately he became the General Secretary of E. I. R. Union and later became an M.L.A. at Lucknow and thereafter became a Member of the Rajya Sabha.

Two non-cooperative students, Prabhat Chakravarti and Dinesh Chakravarty, were sheltered in my uncle's house. Prabhat gradually became a revolutionary. He carried on Congress work vigorously but Dinesh continued his studies in the National School and later in the General School and College and attained much success in life as a highly placed employee in an Insurance Company. Prabhat became very prominent as a revolutionary. Prabhat and I had something to do even after the non-cooperation movement was over. Let me narrate it here.

After I started my political work in U. P., once I went to Bengal. The year was 1924. When I went to Comilla the police there were too much vigilant to trace me out as I had disappeared from Banaras in the same year. I somehow managed to reach my place in the night but early in the morning I was informed by our partymen that the clerk of my uncle who was formerly helping in our secret work had turned to be a Police informer. So I had to pass the whole day in another house. Late in the night I came to my uncle's place, took my meals there and after midnight left for the Railway station with Prabhat Chakravarti. It was raining heavily. I waited outside the station while Prabhat bought two tickets and boarded a compartment. I stood all alone on the other side of the compartment and boarded it when the train was just about to move. So I escaped from Comilla untraced. From Chandpur also, I did not take the regular steamer route. I went to Rajabari by one steamer and from there to Goalundo by another steamer. From Rajabari I sent back Prabhat to my village with a letter. This letter was the only source of information that my family got about me. Prabhat was thus introduced to my family members as a very trusted member of our secret party. I was arrested and jailed not long after this and Prabhat thus secured a very safe shelter for more than two years in my village home with an assumed name as my cousin. While in jail I was always getting the news of Prabhat's welfare through my sister's letters. Sometimes the letters were in Prabhat's handwriting.

Prabhat escaped from internment camp and when rearrested was involved in the Inter-Provincial Conspiracy Case and was transported to the Andaman Jail along with Sita Nath De and Purnananda Das-Gupta, after having been sentenced for life. He is now in the Communist Party.

A WORD ABOUT THE NATIONAL SCHOOL

The Congress leaders wanted to open one National School at Comilla. They fervently requested my uncle to persuade the proprietor of Ishwar Pathshala, Mahesh Bhattacharya, to convert it as a National School. Bhattacharya did not agree with the proposal but promised to donate a big sum of money if a new school was opened. And it was done. A prominent teacher who left Ishwar Pathshala, was made the Headmaster of the National School. But this School did not last long. The Hedmaster had also to rejoin the former school as a newly appointed teacher.

My cousin Paresh Chatterjee joined the National College in Calcutta. He was a very favourite student of Subhas Chandra Bose who was the Principal of the College. Years after this when Bose came to Comilla as the President of the Indian National Congress, he lunched with my uncle.

The degree awarded by the National College was not recognised by the Government and thus the students of the National College were often in great difficulties. I know at least of three brilliant students who faced great difficulty in starting their careers after their graduation from the College. One of my co-villagers had to pass B. A. and B. L. from the University of Calcutta after his graduation from National College before he could start practice as a lawyer. Another brilliant graduate had to become a shop assistant and the third one who was also a brilliant graduate, had to start a stationery shop.

The National School started one weaving class with a science graduate weaver as its teacher. He is now a 'Kaviraj' at Banaras. Our Anushilan leader Pulin Gupta started a factory for the manufacture of Charkha and looms. I purchased two charkhas from here and brought them to my village but the thread produced had no market. So like the former 'Swadeshi' movement this time as well the movement was of temporary duration. The Charkha and Khaddar even today are not profitable concerns although they give employment to a huge number of workers because they are subsidized by the Government.

COOLIE EXODUS FROM TEA GARDENS OF ASSAM

As the result of C. R. Das tour a new life was instilled into the people of Assam. Youths and other workers became very active. The biggest and most profitable industry of Assam was tea. European planters were making huge profit from tea gardening at the expense of the labourers who were treated almost as slaves. These indentured labourers were recruited from the backward places of Madhya Pradesh. Eastern U.P. and Bihar. These poor people were given high hopes by the recruiting agents who brought them as prisoners to the tea gardens of Assam. Here in the tea estates their lives were completely cut off from the rest of the world. A coolie could never leave the estate and he could not handle any cash. Their essential needs were supplied by the shops on the basis of contract on the production of slips issued by estate officers.

And these need were always fixed at the subhuman level.

As a result of the non-cooperation movement the political workers penetrated into the tea estates of Assam. The proprietors, managers and the high executives of the tea estates were Europeans. The political workers had to go there at great risk because the European staff there used to be very much alert ; but yet the political propaganda reached the coolies in wide scale. They became a bit self-conscious and the result was that a large number of coolies was suddenly dismissed from service. They left the garden and took trains to go back to their respective places. They could easily board the train and come up to Chandpur, the railway terminus, because the railway staff was very sympathetic to the movement. They allowed the coolies to travel without tickets. Everybody was aware of the miserable conditions of the Indian coolies under the European owners and managers of the tea gardens. So coolies in thousands arrived at Chandpur but from there they were not allowed to proceed further by the police. Chandpur was too small a place for accommodating such a huge number of men and on the wake of their arrival Cholera broke out there in an epidemic form. J. M. Sen Gupta came from Chittagong and Akhil Dutta from Comilla. The Assam-Bengal railway employees were on strike. It was a very big problem both for the people and the Government. C. R. Das also came from Calcutta and so did Sir Henry

Wheeler, executive member of the Bengal Government. The heroic part in this affair was played by J. M. Sen Gupta. Large amount of money was required for the expenses and Sen Gupta mortgaged his own house at Chittagong and brought a huge amount to meet the expenses required in helping the coolies.

At last a compromise was reached ; the strike was given up and the coolies returned to their gardens with a distinct change in their life.

During the coolie exodus, the Gurkha military units were brought to Chandpur from Dacca. All the coolies were kept behind a cordon of the Gurkhas. Outsiders were not allowed to mix with them, because all along the Government effort was to send back the coolies to the tea estates. But for one man there was no barrier. This was Atindra Mohan Roy, the famous revolutionary of Comilla. These Gurkhas were on duty in Dacca Jail where Roy was detained. So they knew him and they allowed him to go inside the cordon freely.

I have already stated that the Assam-Bengal Railway staff was very sympathetic to the movement and they were always ready to help the coolies in all possible ways and in fact the railway strike was interlinked with the coolie exodus. Of course, the officers of higher ranks were hesitant. That was not the case with the general staff. Once we wanted the Assam Mail to stop at Comilla at 1-30 A. M. and not to proceed further. Before the arrival of the Mail, we approached the Station

Master to stop the train there. The general strike was going to take place and we knew that some of our men would stop the train after it left Comilla. But on further thought we decided to stop the train at Comilla so that passengers in the train were not put into unnecessary inconvenience. If the train was stopped at a way-side station, the passengers would not have found any place to stay in after getting down from the train. Comilla was a big place and it could conveniently accommodate the passengers who would be forced to alight there. That is why we approached the Station Master of Comilla. The Station Master did not agree with us. But when the train came, we approached the driver and the guard. They agreed and refused to drive the train any further. We arranged alternative accommodation for all the passengers and tried to provide them with all possible facilities.

The strike was so effective and complete that all the courts of Comilla remained closed for twenty-one days. We maintained the communication links between different places with the help of bicycles squads, organised by Congress organisation. During the days of strike supply of kerosene oil from the local stockists who had a big stock, was difficult task, but Amulya Mukherjee and Manindra Chakravarti managed the whole affair in such a manner that the people did not face any difficulty at all.

But the condition at Chandpur became worst. The coolies in thousands were kept there under the custody of Gurkhas. The authorities were not taking any effective steps to solve the problems. Those who came from outside to extend their helping hands towards the coolies were also kept aloof and put in trouble. After seeing tyranny the staff of the steamer companies could not remain unmoved. Thus a steamer strike also took place. Steamers stopped plying from Chandpur to Goalando, Chandpur to Narainganj, Chandpur to Barisal and to Assam.

So Sir Henry Wheeler was compelled to discuss the problems with C. R. Das. It was decided that the coolies would be allowed to go to their homes or gardens at Government's expenses. The Government did take the proper course but the situation had already turned seriously against them. People saw the inhuman treatment meted out to the coolies and the natural reaction to it was that there was nothing but hatred towards the Government. So in the struggle the Government was the loser.

People also learnt through these actions that alien Government do things only when they are compelled to do so due to great public pressure. This encouraged the people for a righteous fight against the Government.

It will not be out of place to mention here that it is a pity that the whole incident received a very unfair treatment in the hands of Dr. Pattabhi Sitaramayya in his book 'The History of the Indian National Congress.' Dr. Sitaramayya has only two sentences to write on the whole affair. He writes on page 370 in his book : "Another mighty undertaking was the strike in Chittagong. Chittagong is a port in East Bengal and the labour strike, organised by Sen Gupta, cost the Congress over a lack of rupees." He gives the same treatment to even C. R. Das's efforts. For on page 475 of his book he writes on Das : C. R. Das : "Here was Das who had organised in Bengal the Chittagong strike of 1921."

It is an undeniable fact that the coolie exodus and the railway steamer strike occupied a major place in the political movement of the country that year. But I completely fail to understand the motive of the Congress historian in neglecting these and distorting and under-estimating their effects. He devotes thirty-four pages in his book to narrate the general movement in the country in 1921. Out of it two complete pages are given to narrate the Mopla rising in Malabar. I agree that arrests in big numbers were not made and the police did not open fire at Chittagong or Chandpur. But arrests in large number and firing are not the only criterion to judge the merits and importance of a movement. The authorities as a matter of policy after their experience of partition of Bengal and the consequent national revolutionary movement did not take these aggressive steps, in Bengal as they knew that suppression would beget more trouble for them.

After the strike was over and the coolies had returned to the tea estates or to their respective homes, there seems to be a general slackening everywhere. The lawyers started their practice in courts and most of the students returned to their schools, and colleges. And we resolved to continue our activities through the Congress organisation. The Congress activities were carried on vigorously. Our friend Atindra Roy did not allow it to be slackened. The main work of the Congress was carried on by him. Ashrafuddin Sahib, the General Secretary, spent most of his time in his village and sometimes came down to issue some general instructions. Atin Roy spent all the time in the Congress Office at Maheshprangan. President of the Organisation, Akhil Dutta, was living nearby and it was very easy to contact him. Among other leaders, Basanta Majumdar, Kamini Dutta, Ananga Ghosh, Prakash Das and Dhirendra Dutta took active interest. Amongst our revolutionary friends besides Atin Roy, myself, Pulin Gupta, Suren Chakravarti, Prafulla Chakravarti, Jiten Bhattacharya, Amulya Mukherjee, Manindra Chakravarti, and others took active part.

BHARAT SEVAK SANGHA IN 1921

During the railway and steamer strikes I had an urgent call from Calcutta from our party leaders. Travelling was a problem during the strikes as no means of conveyance was easily available. Only one train, the Assam Mail, was running regularly to carry the mails. Mainly the loyal Anglo-Indians were working in it. I managed to travel by that train upto Chandpur from where I went to Goalando by boat in two days. In Calcutta there was a meeting to discuss the proposal to start a social service organisation named Bharat Sevak Sangha. This organisation proved to be very helpful for the Anushilan Samiti to get itself re-established in every district. Pulin Das headed tbe organisation and Naren Sen and others were his responsible colleagues. I was given the charge of Tripura district with headquarters at Comilla and I established branches at Chandpur and Brahamanbaria. From our headquarters at Calcutta we started a weekly paper 'Shankha' and also a printing press named 'The Calcutta Printing Works.' We received some donations from different individuals for this purpose. And the Anushilan Samiti got a new life and again became very active in every district. Pulin Das took up his work with all sincerity but others took it up as a means of reorganising the Anushilan Samiti and actually within this period the Samiti was really re-established in all districts.

MAHALLA COMMITTEES IN 1922

When the movement got slackened, we resolved to continue some sort of activities. Though we were working in the Congress which had an open programme, as members of the secret party we had to take special precautions against the police. We thought that if we were to work among the youth, the suspicion of police on us should be avoided through every possible means. The movement had kindled a political consciousness among people. We wanted that to be retained in the youth. It is association with great things that begets a mental state conducive to logical thinking and analysis. It compels one to think and to act upon what is thought out. In this way inertia and inactivity vanishes and action, unity and consequently invincible strength generates in the individual as well as in the society. We tried to do away with the stagnation in our life. Some creative programmes were chalked out. The Mohalla (area) Committees were formed in which discussion on character building, educational problems and other subjects of social moral and intellectual upliftment took place. Except in one Mohalla Committee, no political discussions took place. Myself and Atin Roy were behind this move ; we did not openly participate although we took much interest and attended all the meetings.

But it was due to the untiring efforts of Amulya Mukherjee, Manindra Chakravarti and Jogesh Chakravarti that these committees achieved wonderful success. We aimed at the harmonious development of the personality of the youth. For mental development the study of good literature and discussion of intellectual topics of high standard were encouraged in youths. Emphasis on health was laid as health was the stepping stone of all success in life. If a model personality, mental and physical, is built it makes out its successful way in the world. When the parents saw it, they appreciated the aims of the committees and very soon the committees became very popular in the city.

On certain Sundays the committees held a joint meeting. On such occasions debates, essay reading and recitation of poems took place. I also regularly attended the general Sunday get-togethers as well as the big meetings. I always took a keen interest in these activities. At this time the work of the Congress was also going on very satisfactorily.

We all knew that non-cooperation movement was not going to produce any desired result. But as it was launched on a mass scale, the revolutionaries and real patriots could not resist themselves and joined it whole-heartedly. They played a major part in the movement in Bengal. But the movement, as did the movement of 1905 after the Partition of Bengal, abruptly ended. We foresaw it very clearly that freedom was not going to be granted through charity. The movement could ensure for the country some concessions and privileges only. But for complete freedom armed rising was necessary which would completely tear off the alien Government machinery and force them to quit. Compromise on it was not possible as any compromise on fundamentals always begets degeneration.

The interests of the oppressor and the oppressed are always diagonally opposite. That is why the revolutionaries never preferred a middleway. They thought it worth its while to live in glory or die with honour. The gradual way to constitutional independence sounded to them stupid and a self-conceited fallacy. Nothing lies in between complete freedom and total slavery. One who cannot die for life, does not live in reality. The revolutionaries loved the freedom of the mother-land and they happily offered their lives on its alter. Even during the First World War ' Liberty ', the leaflet of Anushilan Samiti declared : " Our object is not to gain a few privileges but to create a nation of men fit for independence. " Any departure from this stand was impossible for the revolutionaries. They adamantly adhered to it till the last. They could use the Congress movement for their ultimate purpose. As their lives were completely devoted to the service of the community and country, they served them through the Congress programmes during the non-cooperation movement but they were never detracted from their firm convictions.

MOHALLA COMMITTEE, CONGRESS AND BHARAT SEVAK SANGHA

In the district three different but inter-connected activities were going on. The Mohalla Committees were functioning in a very satisfactory way under the charge of Amulya Mukherjee and Manindra Chakravarty. The Congress organisation work was looked after by Atindra Mohan Roy and Surendra Kumar Chakravarti. As I have already stated, myself was in-charge of Bharat Sevak Sangh in the district. The spirit behind all these activities was one and the same, i.e. the spirit of dedication and service, so there was no strict clear-cut divisions between the functions of these three organisations. We were doing work in the Congress organisation, in the Mohalla committee and in the Bharat Sevak Sangha as well. In Bharat Sevak Sangha we took up the work of helping patients by supplying medicines and doing nursing. My revolutionary friends engaged themselves in social service. Though we got a very meagre amount as a grant for the Sangh and we were already passing through hardpressed days, our spirit was high and our determination was firm.

We tried our best to utilize all our activities to enhance the cause of revolution. Naren Sen, who was the second man in command next to Pulin Behari Das in our secret revolutionary party, was also the Secretary of Dacca Congress Committee. And the Assistant Secretary was also our man. In this way the Dacca Congress was also in our hands. The Bharat Sevak Sangha published a leaflet 'Hak Katha' in Calcutta. That paper, in thousands, was sent to me as I was the organiser of the Sangha at Comilla. In this paper the Non-cooperation movement was criticised. As we were running the Congress in East Bengal, we never wanted to encourage the criticism of the Movement and thus the leaflets were not distributed but destroyed. To cite an example would not be besides the point. A missionary came to Dacca to inspect the work of the Bharat Sevak Sangha. Naren Sen showed him the work undertaken by the Sangh there and also four night schools which were not run by the Sangha, though the Sangha used to give them some help. An impression on the missonary was created that these schools were also run by the Sangha. He was very much pleased and submitted a very good report, appreciating our work in Dacca. As a result of this report, the amount of grant was increased. We never took these matters seriously as our main object was to strengthen our secret revolutionary party. The official Congress party leaders seldom suspected our motives. Many of them thought that we had eschwed the path of violence and were sincere believers in the Congress creed of non-violent non-cooperation. But we took the Congress work only as a camouflage for the achievement of our end.

HOUSE OF LABOURERS

It has already been stated that Dr. Mahendra Nandi maintained a laboratory at Kalikachha. He invented a handlever match machine. His nephew Kamaniya Sinha (his sister's son) opened the Pioneer Match Factory at Comilla and Prafulla Chakravarti, our revolutionary friend and an inhabitant of the village Kalikachha, became its manager. The main purpose behind the opening of this factory was to help our movement. Swadeshi Movement created a market for the indigenous products. The factory which was completely Swadeshi by nature earned profit and also became a subject of peoples, respect. The manager of the factory Prafulla Chakravarti was a secret Anushilanite and had suffered imprisonment also. He worked throughout the day in the factory and in the night when all the work was over, I and few other friends used to meet together. Prafulla Chakravarti wanted me to start some industry. We all thought that industry is the key to a nations' progress. The prosperity of the poor masses could be brought about only through industriasization—that was what we thought. Industrialization would increase production and stop the financial exploitation of poor Indians by the Europeans. All these were undoubted facts but I was hesitant to draw up a path for starting a production centre. Money was the primary requisite to start that. Apart from money, experience and mechanical know-how, were also basically necessary. But Prafulla Chakravarti's pressure was increasing day by day and he and others had immense confidence in my abilities. They thought that if I became involved in their plan, it would be carried out successfully, irrespective of all these difficulties. I would take up the matter very seriously and with all sincerity. At last the idea struck me one night and I agreed and resolved to draw up such a plan.

Nothing is impossible in the world is the dictum in which the revolutionaries always believe. I took up this work with the same spirit. To me it appeared as a part of our party work. To start with money was our immediate need. I left Comilla for Calcutta to arrange few things for the prospective industry taking only Rs. 30/- with me. Some money was spent in the journey and the remainder I put into the box of a revolutionary in Calcutta. In my absence the box was broken and the money was stolen. When I came to know this, I was very much perplexed as no money was left with me even for going back to Comilla. I thought it advisable to take the help of our secret party leader. I went to Ramesh Acharya, the leader of Barisal Conspiracy Case, and a very important leader of our secret party. I narrated the story to him. He gave me two hundred and fifty rupees. Taking the money from him I did some necessary purchases for the industrial project and came back to Comilla. Before leaving Comilla, I had written a few letters to my relatives and friends for some financial help to start the project. When I arrived at Comila, I found that Rs. 900/- sent by my relatives and friends had already reached. My revolutionary friends also took keen interest in it. Naren Sen contributed Rs. 300/-.

We were busy to tap the various resources and had very big plans for the future. A Match factory was to be started first and then textile factory and iron works. After these three industries were well established, we planned to start an automobile industry, and even ship building and aeroplane production. Comilla was not a suitable place for such big industries and we thought we should prospect in Chittagong for the purpose. Prafulla Chakravarty and Jitendra Bhattacharjee went to Chittagong to find out some suitable location for the industry but I did not agree due to practical difficulties. At Comilla everybody knew us and any kind of help could easily be summoned ; but Chittagong was a new place and to start a new industry there even on a small scale was a very difficult task. So it was decided that the venue of the industry would be Comilla.

With high hopes and huge schemes in mind, we started the House of Labourers in Fabruary 1922 in an humble way. By the side of the National School Building, we ourselves constructed the factory. I took timber on credit from my uncle's timber company. The structure was erected by us and tin sheds were put. We made a bamboo curtain and fixed it on all sides. In this way a factory was constructed. The opening ceremony was performed with the staff of two carpenters, two iron smiths, myself, two brothers of Prafulla Chakrvarti, Prabodh and Pramode Chakravarti.

The first work we undertook was the production of a rotary match machine. Dr. Abinash Bhattacharjee, who was in Germany during the First World War, opened a Chemical laboratory at Konnagar in Hooghli District. He also had taken part in revolutionary activities during his stay in Europe. His elder brother was the district engineer at Comilla. Abinash Bhattacharjee told us that an old

German rotary match machine, which was brought by some Marwari firm during the Swadeshi movement but could not be used, was lying at Konnagar. Myself, Prabodh and Pramode went to Konnagar and studied thoroughly the making of the machine. Prabodh, a very good student of mathematics, was trying his level best to get well versed in engineering. But Pramode had real mechinical aptitude. We came back and copied the rotary machine in the House of Labourers. It was a successful effort and the new rotary machine started functioning wonderfully.

As a result, the Pioneer Match Factory of Comilla went into liquidation as its hand-lever machines could not compete with our rotary match machines. The Proprietor of the Pioneer Match Factory got very annoyed with me, but I was helpless. Our machine produced twenty gross of matches per day. We fitted the first machine in our factory and advertised the sale of other machines. Prospective buyers came and saw our machine at work and placed orders. Our daily production of matches was purchased by a firm. We received our first order from the district jail Comilla to supply twelve Salvation Army Pattern of Handlooms, within twelve days. We supplied the order in time and to the best satisfaction of the jail authorities. This created a goodwill for us in the city. People were surprised how a factory in its initial stage could supply things in such a short time. We employed extra carpenters for the work and I personally went to Dacca to bring the teak. From dawn to dusk work continued and the necessary arrangements for meals, etc. were made in the factory itself.

With the closure of the Pioneer Match Factory, Prafulla Chakravarti along with a few technicians also joined us in our work. Jitendra Bhattacharjee joined us after his examinations. Atindra Roy showed a very keen interest in our work and Amulya Mukherjee and Manindra Chakravarti and others also came very often to the factory and took interest in what was going on there. So from the very beginning it took the form of an institution. It was not only a centre of production but also a place with inspired patriotic youngmen to collect and take up the work in a missionary spirit with national perspective. Some Muslims also joined us enthusiastically.

With the expansion of work and increase in the number of men working, more finances were our imperative need. This was a very difficult problem. We always thought of the possible financial resources. One day one of my friends, who was running a Vivekananda Ashram, asked me to accompany him to Mukunda Das, the great dramatist and actor who stopped at Comilla on his way to Sylhet and Chittagong. My friend wanted to request him to donate some money for his Ashram. I, though reluctantly, accompanied him. During our talk Mukunda Das enquired about me. When he was told about the House of Labourers, he showed keen interest in it and put so many questions to me.

I told him that our work was expanding but we were short of finances. He enquired how much money was immediately needed for the work. I told him that we needed Rs. 2,000/- immediately. He proposed that on his way back from Chittagong, he would give a performance at Comilla and the money, thus collected, which he expected to be two thousand rupees, would be placed at our disposal as an interest free loan. He asked me to reserve Maheshprangan for his performance.

To get the consent of Mahesh Bhattacharjee for the proposed performance in Maheshprangan I called on him. I told him about the programme and asked for his permission for the performance to be staged in the Maheshpragan. He enquired hom much money we needed and up to what extent the performance would be able to meet our needs. I replied that two thousand rupees were immediately needed and we expected the same amount to be collected through the performance. He did not like the idea that only for two thousand rupees we were seeking an obligation from Mukunda Das. He said that he would extend an interest free loan of two thousand rupees to us. I naturally became very happy to see his sympathetic attitude as our attachment with Bhattacharjee, a very big businessman and a renowned philanthropist of Comilla, would increase our goodwill, financial security and provide incentive to our newly established work. Meanwhile my uncle, after seeing our dedication in the work and being fully convinced that our work was on the right, direction, spoke a word to Mahesh Bhattacharjee in our favour. Janaki Nath Sarkar was the headmaster of Ishwar Pathshala. He was also an ex-member of secret Anushilan Samiti. He was enjoying full confidence of Mahesh Babu and was looking after his household affairs. He always had a very soft corner for us. He also spoke to Mahesh Babu. Mahesh Bhattacharjee advised me that to carry Rs. 2,000/- with me in Calcutta was risky and that I could open an account with the cashier of his firm and do the necessary purchases by issuing a slip to the concerns to get the amount cashed from Bhattacharya & Co. So I travelled to Calcutta with a letter from Mahesh Babu addressed to the Manager of his Calcutta head office. I was surprised to see the goodwill of his firm in the market as every one readily gave us articles agreeing that the costs would be collected from Bhattacharjee & Co. I did the necessary purchases and came back to Comilla.

After seeing the pace of progress of the factory, Bhattacharjee advised us that it could no longer be accommodated in the small shed, we had erected ourselves beside the National School Building, and offered us a plot of land, free of any charges, near his residence where we ourselves constructed a big factory building using iron bars and tin sheds. Bhattacharjee also offered one big room in his residence for housing our office. In those initial stages, such a rapid and methodical expansion of our work was an extremely difficult task, but it was only due to his helping hands that everything could become possible. After shifting to the new factory building, the pace of our work speeded up. An All India Industrial Exhibition was to be held in Calcutta at that time. We decided to exhibit our rotary match machine there. We exhibited it there but got orders only for four machines, though it attracted the attention of owners of big factories. They started productoin of the same kind of match machines through casting in which much less cost was involved and sold them at much cheaper rates. This competition with the comparatively better and cheaper machines affected our business and ultimately we gave up the production of match machines.

Meanwhile we got an order for setting and fitting machines from a tea estate. Our technicians did this job very efficiently and we charged considerably less amount of money from the owners of the estate. For the same work they used to seek services of European firms in Calcutta, and very heavy charges were always demanded for that. The tea estate people were very pleased with us and issued a very fine recommendatory letter in our favour. Consequently, a new avenue was opened for us and the number of orders increased day by day.

From the very beginning the House of Labourers earned the reputation of a nationalist institution in which the revolutionaries and non-cooperating students of the town were working. The house had red uniforms for its workers. In every public meeting, processions and national functions the workers in their uniforms used to participate. In social service activities. nursing of patients and helping the cremation of dead bodies. the workers of the house always rendered their full help. In this way the team of red uniformed young men became a symbol of self-service and efficiency in the city. They enjoyed respect and affection from all the patriotic people of the city. Our procedure of recruiting the workers was that one had to learn the technical work for six months, on one's own expense. After six months, we managed to give board and lodging to the trainee and watched carefully his capacity to work and his mechanical aptitude. According to the ability of individual trained worker, the salary was decided, and he was considered to be an employee of the House. It will not be out of place to mention here that Mahesh Bhattacharjee was kind enough to grant a few apprentices free board and lodging in his Ramtara Chhatravasa. a free students, home for 80 students.

Owing to our faith in socialism, we ran the factory on socialistic lines. All those who belived in socialistic thinking there, were considered as members of the Brother-hood which was the main executive body. They were not entitled to any salary and were getting only an allowance. The amount of allowance was only fifteen rupees per month. Those who were not in this brother-hood, were considered as regular employees of the House and they were getting salaries according to their qualifications. The surplus money went into the Reserve Fund for further development of the Industry.

One day a C.I.D. Inspector called on the office of the factory and wanted to see the muster roll to note down the names of the workers. I refused and challenged his authority. He threatened me and said that someday he might come with the warrants of District Magistrate and collect all the papers there. I said that he was free to take any legal step ; but I was not prepared to show him anything. When I reported this matter to my uncle and Mahesh Bhattacharjee, they said that there could be nothing wrong if I showed the muster roll to the inspector. But I thought that C. I. D. interference would increase in the House due to my presence there. I also resolved that freedom of the country was the first and important necessity. I met Naren Sen and Pratul Ganguli, two important leaders of Anushilan Samiti and asked them to allot some full time revolutionary work for me.

It would be interesting to cite one instance here. One day I and Jitendra Nath Bhattacharjee happened to go to the Technical School. There, accidentally, we met the police superintendent, Mr. Hodson, who also had come there. He knew Jitendra Bhattacharjee by his face but did not know me personally though he had heard so much about me. During the course of conversation with Bhattacharjee he wanted to know who I was as I was standing just beside. When he heard my name he looked surprised but resumed his conversation. I assured Mr. Hodson that though we were revolutionaries and political suspects in the eyes of the police, there was absolutely no political motive behind the House. I told him that we were patriots and whatever work we would take up in life, there would definitely be patriotic ferver in it but I could very well assure that behind the House of Labourers, there was no revolutionary conspiracy brewing or any political motive involved. Few days after, the S. P. came personally to the factory and wished to see it. I was not present at that time, others who were present obliged him and took him round the factory.

One evening the 'Peshkar' of the District Magistrate told me in private that one show-cause notice, as to why the Indian Factory Act should not be enforced on the House of Labourers, would be served on us. He told me how to reply to that notice. The notice was served and I gave the reply.

As a result of my request to the leaders of the Anushilan Samiti, Pratul Ganguli, wanted me to go to Assam where, as he told me, the party work was not running satisfactorily. It was in the later part of 1921. He gave me a few addresses also. I visited Silchar, Sylhet, Karimganj and Sunamganj. During my tour I met Nihar Ranjan Ray, now a Prafessor in Calcutta University and an M. P., in Sylhet who was closely connected with the Janashakti weekly paper. He introduced me to the Editor of the Janashakti. In Silchar the most important worker of our party was a shop assistant. He also introduced a few persons to me. In Sunam ganj Sub-division, I met an important worker of our party, Dharani Goswami, who was doing farming and working among peasants. He was later arrested in Meerut Conspiracy Case and joined the Communist Party.

After this tour, I was instructed to go to Bombay. Pratul Ganguli apprised me of the situation and the method of work there. He gave me copies of the 'Socialist', a paper run by Dange and told me that the main field of my activities should be among the labourers. But this programme did not ultimately materialise and I had to wait for some new assignment.

One representative of the party was urgently needed to be sent to U. P. Pratul Ganguli was in search of some suitable man who could be entrusted with this responsibility. His assistant Ashit Bhattacharjee suggested my name. Ganguli very happily agreed to the suggestion. Incidentally, I also went to Dacca for purchasing teak wood for the House of Labourers. When I saw Pratul Ganguli there, he happily remarked that it was very good that I was there at that time. He asked me whether I would like to go to U. P. I gave an affirmative reply. So our discussion on the detailed programme started. He told me about the situation in U.P. I personally liked to go to U.P. more than to Bombay.

Bengal and the Punjab were the two hot beds of revolutionary activities. Between these two provinces lay U. P. and Bihar. I knew about the activities of Rash Behari Bose in U. P. and the Banaras Conspiracy Case, the Mainpuri Conspiracy Case, etc. There as I thought a methodical revolutionary work with accentuated speed was required to be started. I thought if we could activise our party units in U. P. it would be a great help to the revolutionary activities in Northern India. Our units in U. P. would be able to serve as links between Bengal and the turbulent Punjab.

I left the House of Labourers leaving the House in the hands of three Chakravarti brothers, and Jitendra Bhattacharjee. It was a pity that Atin Roy was already arrested by the police and sent to jail. Had he been free, the House of Labourers could be left in very efficient hands. Owing to the absence of proper leadership Jitendra Bhattacharjee found himself alone on one side and the three brothers on the other. Meanwhile they developed differences with Mahesh Bhattacharjee also. When we were there, we always honoured the advices of Mahesh Babu and tried our best to learn something from his experience and foresight in business. Our successors took his advice in a different light and protested against the interference of Mahesh Babu. Mahesh Bhattacharjee had given the House 22 thousand and 6 hundred rupees in all. After some differences with him they wanted to return the amount taking loan from a Bank on twelve per cent interest. About the House of Labourers late Mr. Mahesh Chandra Bhattacharjee wrote in his autobiography that he wanted to invest up to one lakh of rupees in it. But due to differences he could save himself.

Really the change in the attitude of the Chakravarti brothers caused the ruination of the Institution. Bhattacharjee advised them that if they repaid such a high amount all at once, it would affect the business of the House badly. He suggested that the amount could easily be paid in many small instalments. The House was made a limited company. By this time the House of Labourers had gained so much popularity that men like Sir P. C. Roy, and Ramananda Chatterjee, Editor of "The Modern Review" came to see the House, were very much impressed and in Calcutta they wrote articles in the monthlies praising the House of Labourers and its working on idealistic principles. When it was declared as a Limited Company, offers for buying shares came from far and near. Money was sent by money orders by a number of persons to purchase shares and branches were opened. The House of Labourers soon became the Managing Agents of three important big concerns— the Comilla Electric Supply Co. Ltd. which was supplying electricity to the Railway Station and the city, the Steel Construction Co. Ltd. and the Peerless Tea Estate Ltd. The business flourished but due to heavy loans taken from the bank, the

House was going under the grip of the bank day by day. As long as there was flourishing business, the House was paying the interest to the bank. But during the 1929-30 economic depression, the House's business was affected. The Bank had its own designs for it since very long. The business decreased and a fall in the income was noticeable. In those bad days, one day in the general meeting in which Prabodh Chakravarti explained the situation before the members, Naren Dutta, the banker pleaded that the House was passing through a critical financial duress and the bank which had extended loans got possession of the House. The Chakravartis started their own contract business and entered in litigation with the Bank. Jitendra Bhattacharjee took over as the Manager on behalf of the Bank.

We had started the House of Labourers as an ideal nationalist institution. We had created a feeling of brother-hood and comradeship. Dignity of labour was our motto and all of us did all sort of work from brooming the floors to carrying heavy loads personally. No one felt shy in doing any work. When we left the place, the successors decided to run it, with all bureaucratic pomp and modern business house paraphernalia. They forgot that this house was a symbol of patriotism, selfless and dedicated service for the community and the country. Overambitious schemes and the rise of over-night bureaucrats played havoc here also with all its disastrous consequences, resulting in dissolution of the temple of labour, self-sacrifice and national dignity we erected.

ABHOY ASHRAM AT COMILLA

When the Non-Cooperation Movement was started on a large scale, the British Government got very much perplexed as it was fearful of a general upsurge of the ever suppressed Indian masses. All the leaders, C. R. Das, Motilal Nehru and others were arrested but the authorities did not dare to arrest Gandhiji when the movement was at its climax. He was arrested after he called off the movement because of the Chourichoura incident. The movement was no longer there; but problem of exploring new avenues for social and nationalist activities faced all those who joined the movement, resigning from high positions in Government and other services. Two prominent non-cooperators of Bengal came to Comilla in the later part of 1922. They were Dr. Prafulla Chandra Ghosh, who was a former member of the Anushilan Samiti, and Dr. Suresh Chandra Banerjee who had connection with one Jugantar group in his student life. Dr. Prafulla Chandra Ghosh, a D. Sc. in Chemistry was appointed as Deputy Alloy-Master in the Calcutta mint, a post which he relinquished because of the movement. Dr. Suresh Chandra Banerjee was a Civil Surgeon and he resigned and joined the movement. After the movement slackened, they came to Comilla to start an Ashram for the propagation and encouragement of 'Charrkha' and 'Khadi'. For some time they discussed the matter with the important local leaders. Akhil Chandra Dutta and Kamini Kumar Dutta, the two leading lewyers of Comilla started taking interest in the plan. Forty thousand rupees were collected for the opening of an Ashram. A big tank, which was situated on the outskirts of the city was chosen as the venue for it. They took it on lease and started Abhoy Ashram there. ' Charkha ' and 'Khaddar' promotion were kept in view; the Ashram also took up social service. A medical clinic and a school were started by the Ashram.

In this way almost simultaneously two ideal nationalist institutions grew up at Comilla—the House of Labourers and the Abhoy Ashram. Though ours was an industrial production centre and the Abhoy Ashram was a socio-economic-political centre on Gandhian lines, the political motive behind the both was one and the same,—service to the community and the country, all round progress and freedom for all.

Allow me to digress a little. Once it so happened that I and Ashrafuddin Chaudhury Sahib boarded a steamer from Chandpur for Goalando on our way to Calcutta. Ashraffuddin Sahib was then the General Secretary of the Comilla District Congress Committee. Later when Subhas Chandra Bose had strong differences with the Congress High Command, he became the General Secretary of the B. P. C.C. The Bengal Congress was staunchly behind Bose. In that condition Ashrafuddin Sahib as Secretary of B. P. C. C. steadfastly supported him. When the Congress formed an ad hoc committee in Bengal, Ashrafuddin Sahib became the Bengal Secretary of the Forward Block.

To resume my narrative, we sat together in the steamer. We also talked about the House of Labourers and the Abhoy Ashram among other things. Ashrafuddin Sahib said that the lawyers of Comilla collected so much money for the Abhoy Ashram which was comparatively of lesser importance. The House of Labourers which had a creative programme and which was doing more important work should have been helped.

CHAPTER VII

DEPARTURE FROM COMILLA FOR U.P.

It was July 1923. After my talks with Pratul Ganguli in Dacca, I came back to Comilla. It was sad that the time had come again to leave the town where I had spent ten years—the best part of my youth. The place where I was going would be an unknown one for me. Those feelings were natural. When I told Atin Roy about my programme, he was very much annoyed. He even stopped talking to me. He did not like the idea of my leaving the House of Labourers after starting it. I did not tell anything to Jitendra Bhattacharjee because he had come to the House of Labourers only due to my pressure. Prafulla Chakravarti and Prabodh Chakravarti also disapproved the idea but when I told them that I was going for a nobler cause, they agreed with me. I was very much disturbed at that time. The night when I was to leave, Atin Roy talked to me. We talked about everything in detail. In the Register of the House, my name was the first. For a very long time I was simply marked absent.

Concerning my relatives, with whom I was residing, my uncle went to Dacca to appear in some law case and my aunt had gone to her village. My cousin, Paresh Chandra Chatterjee, was the only responsible family member present. He was a member of the Anushilan Samiti. I told him everything and left with him a letter for my uncle. It was just a matter of chance that my uncle went to Dacca at that time, otherwise it would have been a very difficult task to talk to him about my departure. He was full of affection for me and his personality always impressed me. I know that he would not object to my leaving the house. He was always too reticent to express his feelings and was a great devotee of individual freedom ; so much so, that even if his heart broke, he would not have stopped me from following my own chosen path. But to part with such a man would not have been easy for me.

I can never forget that cloudy day when I had to start for Banaras. I went home to see my family. Practically that was my last adieu to my family. I had crossed the Rubicon and there was no going back. I asked my sister to pack all my woollen clothes and shoes in a box. My sister did so. I took my meals and when the time of my departnre came, she asked me why was I taking all the woollen clothes with me in the month of July. She guessed that I was going to some distant place. She reported the matter to my mother. My mother was by nature a silent and patient lady. But as she heard my sister, tears rolled down her cheeks. My sister, also started weeping. I knew that I was going to leave them without any one on whom they could depend. My father was very old. My elder brother was not in a position to support the family. The entire family was looking toward me. I also knew that I was going for an unknown journey. What assurance could I give to the rolling tears ? My conscience felt a sense of guilt and injustice which was being done to those who had brought me to this earth. I was caught in this emotional vortex. The 'Mallah', boatman, was calling from outside that if I had to catch the steamer, I should not delay any more. I could not miss the steamer and the train to Banaras, as a man would come to receive me at Banaras station at the appointed time. So I hardened my voice and told my sister that weeping at the time of departure was a sign of evil portents and that this they should not do. I left the house and went to the boat. From the boat I could see both my mother and sister standing in drizzling rain and looking at me as long as the boat was visible. It was a gloomy day and inside my heart was also a gloom. The gloom of weather cleared away but the gloom inside continues to haunt me even now.

SITUATION IN U. P. BEFORE MY ARRIVAL IN THE MIDDLE OF 1923

The 'Swarajya' a weekly Urdu paper, started at Allahabad in 1907 by Mr. Shanti Swarup Bhatnagar, was in one sense a pioneer organ in preaching revolutionism in U. P. This extremist paper openly supported the revolutionary activities in the Punjab, Maharashtra and Bengal. Four editors of this paper were sent to the Andamans under heavy sentences for writing articles espousing the cause of the revolutionaries.

Though not connected with Bengal, Mr. Sachindra Nath Sanyal had started an Anushilan Samiti at Banaras in 1909. The name was subsequently changed, as the Anushilan Samiti was banned by the Government. In 1913 Sanyal went to Calcutta and came in touch with Mr. Pratul Chandra Ganguli of Dacca Anushilan and was also introduced to Mr. Rashbehari Bose of Chandernagore. Bose was carrying on revolutionary work in north India and Sanyal became his lieutenant in U. P. with his headquarters at Banaras. Rashbehari Bose was an employee in the Forest Research Institute at Dehra Dun. Sanyal, Girija Babu and other were clapped into jail and given heavy sentences in Benaras Conspiracy case. Sanyal was sent to the Andamans and Girija Babu died in Agra Central Prison.

An exceptionally enthusiastic youth from the Chambal Valley area in the border of Etawah and Agra districts, named Pandit Gendalal Dixit, was inspired with the ideas of revolutionism and he started secret revolutionary activities very earnestly. He travelled to distant Bombay, also got inspiration from Calcutta in pursuit of his objective and eventually succeeded in gathering a band of youths around him and gave them revolutionary training. As a teacher at Auraiya in Etawah district he got the opportunity of recruiting youths.

When the organisation took some shape, the

need arose for money and he had to adopt the same old method of forcible collection of money. The inevitable consequence was arrest and a conspiracy case,—the Mainpuri Conspirary Case of 1918. Gendalalji was the leader of the conspiracy. But he managed to escape from the jail with the approver. Many were sentenced, but were let off after compromise with the authorities. Gendalalji had a very hard life as an absconder. He collected a gang of criminals with the hope that they would turn patriots. But in this he was not very successful. He was betrayed, fought bravely with the police and was captured with severe wounds and thrown into Gwalior Fort. He, however, managed to come out, but died in Delhi on 21st December 1920 of T.B. in great distress.

Wide scale revolutionary activity again started in U.P. in 1923 and it took a sharp turn after I joined Sanyal early in 1924. I took the charge of U.P. and Sachin Sanyal went over to Calcutta.

AT BANARAS (U.P.) AND KANPUR.

Bengal had a close relation with Banaras. The Bengali population constitutes a considerable part of the city's population and the locality 'Bangalitola' is just a miniature Bengal inside the city of Banaras. Before the First World War, Shashi Mazumdar who belonged to a zamindar family of Comilla, and younger brother of Basanta Kumar Mazumdar, worked in Banaras. He was a member of our secret party. Kedareshwar Sen and Tarani Shom, two important Anushilan members, were sent to Banaras by the Samiti and they joined the Banaras Hindu University as students. At the time of the Non-Cooperation movement of 1921, Upendra Dhar, who was also an Anushilanite, joined the movement. Upendra Dhar and Vichitra Narayan Sharma (later a Cabinet Minister in U.P. and now holding a very high position in Gandhi Ashram affairs) were fourth year students in Banaras Hindu University when the movement started. They left the University and joined the Gandhi Ashram there. Vichitra Narayan Sharma used to live in the Ashram and Upendra Dhar spent the whole day in the Khaddar Bhandar of the Ashram.

I knew that U. P. required a methodical plan for revolutionary activities. The facts about the Banaras Conspiracy Case of 1915 and Mainpuri Conspiracy Case of 1918 were known to me. While coming back from the Nagpur Congress in 1920, I stopped at Banaras and met Prabodhendu Roy, whose name and address also came in the Rowlatt Report. I was happy that such an opportunity was offered to me.

When Anushilan Samiti decided to work with the Rash Behari Bose group, Nagendra Nath Datta of Sylhet, who was known as Giraja Babu in the party, was sent to Northern India by the Anushilan Samiti to work with him. He worked with Rash Behari Bose and Sachindra Nath Sanyal. In the Banaras Consparacy Case along with Sachindra Nath, Girija Babu was also arrested and sentenced in 1915. He died in Agra Jail early in 1918 during the tenure of his imprisonment. I had contacts with him at Comilla as he was a leader of our Samiti.

When I arrived at Banaras, I was received at the station by Satish Sinha, the incharge of our party there. He made arrangements for my stay in a room of Ganesh Mahal where he himself was staying. I was very intimate with him and his elder brother Khetra Sinha. They belonged to Chandpur and were very important members of our Samiti. I took charge from Satish Sinha and he went back to Bengal. He gave me some addresses and other things.

I think it would not be out of place here to mention another important fact. In Godholia, a place in Banaras, Swami Satyananda Puri, a 'Sanyasi' who was a revolutionary and who played a big part afterwards with Rash Behari Bose in the formation of the Indian National Army, had opened an 'asharm' named Kalyan Ashram. Though he had left Banaras by the time, I arrived there, there was another 'brahmachari' staying in that Ashram. This 'Ashram' was the centre of revolutionary activities before my arrival.

The Brāhmachari's real name was Sachin Chakravarti. In 1925 he was sentenced to 5 years R. I. along with Prabodh Das Gupta in a currency note forgery case, which they were doing for the Samiti in a place in the district of Dacca.

He introduced me to all the persons he came in

contact with during his stay at Banaras.

Another young man, Sachin Bakshi, became a full-time worker for the Samiti. His family had a big house in Pataleshwar mohalla and his father was the proprietor of Sikrol Ice Factory, not far off from the Banaras Cantonment station. So he had no family worries and devoted all his time for the secret revolutionary work. Another member of the Samiti, Manmatha Gupta was a student of Gandhi Vidyapith and even at that time he evinced literary talents. He was recruited to the Party through his younger brother Manmohan Gupta. Still another member of our Samiti, Pranabesh Chatterjee was a student of Vidyapith. He recruited Chandra Shekhar Azad to the Party.

Sudarshan Ganguli and Jitendra Bhattacharjee, two school students and Prabodhendu Roy were also very active in revolutionary work. So the beginning was quite encouraging. In the Hindu University two students were sent by the Samiti, one was Maitra of Rajshahi, student of Engineering, and the other was Modak of Mymensing District, a student of the Intermediate class. Maitra later gave up engineering and passed M.A. and L.L.B. Modak joined the engineering college after doing his Intermediate,

Early in 1922, Shyam Chakravarti of Chandpur came to Banaras for a change. He was an active Anushilanite at Chandpur. Then came Kshetra Sinha and Satish Sinha stayed. I relieved him in July, 1923.

My arrival at Banaras was with a firm determination and solid purpose. The others came only for a short time, they did some work and went back to their places. My case was different as I came to stay there and merge myself completely in revolutionary activities. I found a favourable atmosphere. A number of enthusiasts, whose names I have mentioned above, were also keen to gear up revolutionary activities. So I along with them accentuated the pace of our work. I was young and energetic at that time. My companions were also very young. We never grudged footing down long distances and roaming about the city, meeting different people, persuading them and tapping all the possible resources for the encouragement and enhancement of revolutionary activities.

Before my coming to Benaras I requested Pratul Ganguli to give me an introductory letter for Sachin Sanyal, even though I was well acquainted with him in Calcutta. Pratul Ganguli told me that a letter was not needed as Sachin Sanyal, after coming back from the Andamans, told him that he would not participate in revolutionary activities any more. But when I arrived at Banaras, I came to know from Satish Sinha that Sachin Sanyal had started taking interest in revolutionary work again. I decided that I would meet him at Allahabad. But let me narrate certain things that happened in Banaras.

The Gandhi Ashram shop at Dasaswamedh was centre where different types of people used to gather

Upendra Dhar, a member of the secret anushilan Samiti, was the incharge of this shop. Daily in the morning, he and Vichitra Narayan Sharma used to carry the Khadi clothing etc. in a ‘ Thela ’ (hand cart) from the Gandhi Ashram. Besides this small shop was the Star Company. It was run by the Lahiri family. I also made that shop my centre for getting acquainted with the people and the way of life in U.P. Upendra Dhar was always ready to help me. He introduced me to Vichitra Narayan Sharma who offered me accommodation in the Gandhi Ashram as it was a central place where I could meet so many people without any risk of being suspected by the C.I.D. men. As I had to carry on secret work, I did not think it advisable to stay in the Ashram. It was through the Gandhi Ashram shop that I came in contact with Rajendra Nath Lahiri, a young and very sincere energetic student. He was recruited to the secret party by one of my predecessors, Shyam Chakravarti, but I did not know why he dropped him from the party. When he left Banaras, he asked Satish Sinha not to include Rajendra Lahiri in the Party. Satish Sinha did not ask the reason for it. When Satish Sinha was leaving he told me something regarding the inclusion of Rajendra Nath Lahiri. Rajendra Nath Lahiri, as I found, was very keen to know about the revolutionary activities. He came in touch with Sachin Sanyal also. He also went to Dr. Surendra Mukerjee, who was a known revolutionary, and was detained during the wear period and was doing homoepathic practice in Banaras at that time and told him that he was interested in revolutionary activities. He promised Rajendra Lahiri to introduce him to Sachin Sanyal when he came to Banaras, and he did so. When I met and Rajendra Nath Lahiri came to know me, I found him very eager and inquisitive to know more and more about the revolutionary movement. We used to talk for hours together about the subject. Rajendra Lahiri very keenly wanted to know more about various aspects of Revolutionary Movements in India and abroad.

These conversation and the overwhelming patriotic trait of his personality, made us very intimate. I was surprised that he was excluded from the party by my predecessors. I was watching the development of the young man but I never wanted to attract him towards ourselves as he had already come in contact with Sanyal Babu.

After a considerable consolidation of the organisational work in Banaras, I decided and went to Allahabad to meet Sanyal. I went to Allahabad and called on him. We already knew each other. During our talks I told him that I had been sent to Banaras by the Anushilan Samiti as its representative. I thought and the party men also advised me that I should definitely meet and take his advice when I was so near. We had long discussions about the affairs in U.P. Sanyal Babu suggested that I should sever my connections with the Anushilan and work with him in U.P. I expressed my regrets as it was not even imaginable for me to drift from

Anushilan Samiti which deputed me there as its representative. On my polite refusal to his suggestion, he wanted me to ask some other responsible member of the party in Calcutta to come and have talks with him. When I told him that I did not know any one's address in Calcutta and that if he liked I could write to Pratul Ganguli in Dacca, he did not seem to be pleased with the proposal. He said that he had addresses of Ramesh Chaudhuri, the incharge of our party in Calcutta and asked me to write to him. I wrote a letter to Ramesh Chaudhuri in Calcutta. Sanyal Babu discussed so many other subjects also. Soon after I came back to Banaras.

After sometime in the same year 1923, Pandit Madan Mohan Malviya called an open session of the first Hindu Mahasabha at Banaras. It was organised on a very large scale and representatives from all over India came to Banaras to participate. It was during this session that Ramesh Chaudhuri and Nalini Kishore Guha came to Banaras from Calcutta. Nalini Kishore Guha, who was an editor of a daily paper, participated as a press representative in the confernece. Ramesh Chaudhuri came along with him. He had given information about his arrival to Sachin Sanyal. Sanyal Babu also visited Banaras at the same time. Ramesh Chaudhuri and Sachin Sanyal met but no fruitful decision came out of the talks.

Ramesh Chaudhuri brought a letter from Abani Mukherjee, a well known revolutionary, for Shiva

Prasad Gupta, a well known philanthropist-patriot of Banaras. Both had very intimate relations when abroad. In the letter Abani had requested him to render some financial help to the secret party ; but Babu Shiva Prasad Gupta declined to give any help and said that he was now only interested in non-violent activities. Ramesh Chaudhuri and I had gone to see Babu Shiva Prasad at his residence with that letter.

A young party worker who was living in the Ashram of the Swamiji in Godholia wanted to go back to Bengal. I had no money at that time to meet his journey expenses. When Nalini Kishore Guha came to Banaras, I requested him to take the young party worker back to Calcutta bearing his journey expenses. Nalini Kishore Guha readily agreed and the young man accompanied him.

I hope it will not be out of place to pay tribute to Swami Satyananda Puri, the founder of the Ashram in Godholia, who lived and died for the service of the country. He was Prafulla Sen of Faridpur, from East Bengal and was a brilliant student. He was an important member of the Anushilan Samiti and later he turned a 'Sanyasi' but even then he was a staunch patriot. Even as a 'Sanyasi' he was helping the secret party work and so his Banaras Ashram was under the vigilance of the C.I.D. From Banaras he went to Ranchi and later left India and established himself at Bangkok, the capital of Siam. He lived in there for several decades. His eminence in that country grew very high and he was adorned and worshipped there as a great spiritual saint. His humanitarian outlook impressed the people there and even the King of Siam became his great admirer and devotee. During the Second World War, Rash Behari Bose the veteran Indian revolutionary came from Japan to Saigon for a few days and stayed with Swamiji, who helped him a good deal in the formation of Indian National Army. However, when Swamiji and Sardar Pritam Singh were flying to Japan for meetings, the plane fell down into the sea resulting in the death of a great patriot, spiritualist and saint.

My revered uncle, Bishweswar Chatterjee, who had alwas been a source of inspiration to me was shocked very much after my departure from Comilla. He loved me like his own son. During the Puja vacation, my uncle along with his son, Paresh Chatterjee, come to Banaras with the intention of taking me back home. Letters had already been exchanged between us. At Banaras they stayed with a relative. Having come to know about his arrival, I went to the place where he was staying and very respectfully touched his feet. He was much enraged due to my leaving a comfortable life at Comilla. He asked me whether I had ever thought of my family, old father, mother, younger brother and sister. On whom would they depend if I lived in such a way ? I kept silent. His objections were really very genuine. I had no answer to offer. He asked me to be wise enough to go back to Calcutta. There I and my cousin, Paresh Chatterjee, would study the trend of the markets and then set up a business. He said that he would give twenty-five thousand rupees for that. If it was not possible for me in any case to go back to Calcutta, I was advised to start some business in Banaras itself and for the same he offered five thousand rupees but on one condition that I would give a word of honour to him to leave all connections with the secret revolutionary party. It is obvious that it was not possible for me to do so.

All through his stay at Banaras, I was with them. But when the time of departure came, he gave me money for buying three inter-class tickets. I purchased only two tickets and returned the rest of the money. He again was enraged. I accompanied them from Banaras Cantonment station to Kashi station and got down there, bidding them good-bye, silently touching his feet.

Coming back to Sanyal and his activities, it would be interesting to reveal a fact here. Long after my meeting with Sachindra Nath Sanyal, I came to know the thoughts Sanyal Babu entertained about me and our party members. It happened like this.

Amulya Lahiri, a seasoned Anushilanite, who came from Pabna district of North Bengal, was well known to me. He was a cousin of Rajendra Lahiri who also belonged to the same district. Amulya Lahiri due to some reasons of health wanted a change in climate and decided to go to Chunar for some days. While on his way to Chunar, he stopped at Banaras and stayed with Rajendra Lahiri for some time till all the arrangements for his stay at Chunar were made. As we knew each other, our frequesnt meetings were natural. Once I went to Rajendra Lahiri's house along with Amulya but at that time Rajendra was not there. Rajendra Lahiri who was in contact with Sachindra Nath Sanyal started to persuade Amulya for the revolutionary activities without any knowledge of Amulya's background as an old member of the Anushilan Samiti. Amulya, very much amused, told me not to meet him publicly as that would take away the fun. To hide our friendship from Rajendra Lahiri, Amulya called on my place at night and told me the contents of the talks that took place about me and our party between him and Rajendra. Rajendra told him that Sachin Sanyal said that Anushilan Party had sent to Banaras a very important member. Sanyal Babu told him that Anushilan is an organisation of the revolutionaries of East Bengal only. They were stern and stubborn and wanted to dominate everywhere they went. It was very hard to follow the strict party discipline and very strong organisational fellowship of the Anushilan Samiti. He gave Rajendra Lahiri the impression that it would be very difficult for him to adapt himself to the matrix of Anushilan ; but he could very easily apply his own initiative and work freely on the advices given by Sanyal Babu. He said so many other things.

He created this impression on Rajendra Lahiri only to keep him on his side.

In Banaras our recruiting work was going on satisfactorily. The main objects of our work was to instill a strong sense of patriotism among the recruits. Literature that could help in that kind of mental build-up was given to them. Discussions were arranged and debates frequently took place on the formation of a clear cut conception about the situation in the country and on the duty of young Indians. To establish contact with as many persons as possible and to inspire them to the service of the community and the country was part of our routine work, I remember one bright young recruit specially. He was Rabindra Nath Kar. He was an important recruit at Banaras. He had taken training in auxiliary force. He was a very good shot. His end was very unfortunate as he died of tuberculosis.

Financial insecurity always surrounded the secret revolutionaries, They could not tap any financial resource on a big scale due to strict police vigilance. I also worked under extreme financial duress in Banaras. I had no other alternative but to earn some money by taking private tuitions. I managed one tuition for teaching English to Pranabesh Chatterjee. I was getting Rs. 13/- per month.

My next teaching experience was as an honorary teacher in a school of Banaras. The headmaster of this school was a Law student in the Calcutta

University. He joined the non-cooperation movement from there in 1921. He came to Banaras in a vacation. There was a small school with one teacher and a very meagre number of students. He foresaw a very good opportunity. He met the teacher of the school and after some time managed to become its headmaster. One day, one of our common friends, introduced me to him. When we came a bit more close to each other, he insisted that I should also take a keen interest in teaching as well as in the affairs of the school. My other friends also said the same to me. I started going daily to the school and teaching the students ; but I refused to accept any remuneration. My interest grew in the school and I devoted more of my time in teaching the best students there. Throughout my stay in jail, I had been studying various subjects. I got the opportunity of utilising what I had learned. Apart from taking regular classes, I encouraged the poor students to keep their head high despite poverty. Consequently, the number of students grew very speedily and the parents showed a very keen interest in the school affairs. It was a well established school by the time I left it. Long after this one of my friends told me that the same school had grown into a big educational institution in a new site of its own. The Ramakrishna Mission and other organisations helped it to grow.

During my stay in Banaras, I maintained my relations with the District Congress Committee also. I was not living in Banaras with an assumed name. I thought it advisable to join the Congress and establish my contacts with the Congress Committee there. I became a four-anna member. Sampurnanandji was the General Secretary of the District Congress Committee at that time. I attended the Provincial Conference of the Congress held in that year. The election for central legislature also took place while I was at Banaras. The late Motilal Nehru was the candidate for it. I did canvassing for him in the Bengalitola. C. R. Das sent Basanta Kumar Majumar, a leader of Comilla, for canvassing among the Bengali population in favour of Motilal Nehru. We met and mutual exchange of views and elaborate talks took place.

After the arrest of Gandhiji in 1922, the country faced a political chaos as no programme was clearly visible to those who joined non-cooperation. To decide the further step to be taken, a special session of the All India Congress was called in Delhi in 1923. Most of the important members of our party also came to Delhi to attend the session. I also went to participate in it as a delegate from Dacca and Banaras. When I reached Delhi, we decided that my delegation from Banaras be cancelled. Three groups of persons participated in it. One group was composed of staunch Gandhiites and was trying to keep itself engaged in tho propagation of 'Khadi' and Charkha', etc. only. Another group was the group of secret revolutionaries who extended their work throughout the length and breadth of the country after the Non-Cooperation Movement. The third group was constituted by prominent lawyers who placed the resolution for Council entry before the Session and got it passed. After this they formed Swaraj Party inside the Congress and contested elections for entering into the Provincial and Central legislatures. The members of our party who came from Bengal also attended it. After this session some of us toured U. P. We went to Hardwar and after visiting Mathura, Brindaban and Agra we arrived at Banaras and all of my associates stayed at my place. From Banaras Pratul Ganguli and Naren Sen boarded a train for Calcutta while Purnananda Das Gupta, Atindra Mohan Roy, and Dhirendra Ganguli, the late Curator, Victoria Memorial Museum, Calcutta, who died in 1963 remained in Banaras for some days. Dr. Dhiren Ganguli was the younger brother of Pratul Ganguli. On the next morning we read in the newspapers that arrests had commenced in Bengal. We sent one person by the next train to stop Naren Sen and Pratul Ganguli at Patna. From Calcutta also somebody was sent for this purpose. They were contacted at Burdwan station and thus they escaped arrest and went underground.

I must narrate another incident. While we visited Agra, we saw the Taj in the day time. In the evening we decided to go to Taj again and see it in the moonlight. On our way to the Taj, Naren Sen sat down on a bench in the park adjoining the Taj premises and told others to go and see while he would remain sitting there. I also did not go and sat beside him. We talked on so many subjects but the most remarkable thing that he foretold that time, I still remember very well. He said that our association of so many persons together would not last long. He had a wonderful capacity of foresight and he clearly saw the impending arrests and repressions. Not only on this occasion but also on so many other occasions he studied the course of happenings and formed conclusions about the future which later came to be true. His mind had that capacity to anticipate things after due consideration of the past and the present. Within a very few days after our talk in the park, arrests of revolutionaries started in Bengal, and Sen and Ganguli also would have been arrested in Calcutta had not their journey been shortened at Burdwan. Atin Roy was arrested on his arrival at Comilla and thrown behind the bars.

The other conference I attended in Banaras was the conference of the Khilafat Movement. Though I did not follow much of Urdu language at that time, I gathered the impression that the Khilafat Movement lacked the touch of genuine patriotism which the same movement I saw at Comilla in 1920 possessed. Those who understood the contents of the speeches fully were even less happy towards the attitude which the conference adopted.

It would be interesting here to reveal a few sensational facts. After my meeting with Sanyal Babu at Allahabad, we happened to meet often and talk about our work. It was at this time that a cruel episode happened at Kanpur. The police of Kanpur tyrannised the labourers there and as far as I remember firing and death also took place, and consequently a great agitation was afoot in the city against the place. Sanyal Babu one day talked to me in this connection when he came to Banaras. He proposed that the S. P. should be murdered. The next proposal he placed was for the murder of Rai Bahadur Jitendra Nath Mukherjee, the then Dy. S. P., C. I. D. in Banaras. I agreed on the proposals and told him that he should arrange for the murder of the S. P. at Kanpur and that after it was executed, I would deal with Jitendra Nath Mukherjee at Banaras. We had built up a strong organisation in Banaras and it was not very difficult for us to execute this plan. I had revolvers and men who would shoot him. But the murder of the S. P. at Kanpur, Sanyal had to arrange and naturally he was depending on his recruits for it.

Due to the failure of the plan at Kanpur, our plan at Banaras was not executed, though we were fully prepared. Even earlier than this plan, Sanyal Babu authored a more adventurous plan. He was interested in the murder of the then Viceroy of India, the Earl of Reading. For the same purpose he sent Chheda Lal Mishra, who came from Hardoi district and was working at Farrukkabad district, to Simla to watch the movements of the Governor General there. But Chedda Lal Mishra did not succeed in this plan as an iron organisation with men of staunch faith and unshakable conviction were needed, to execute it. An amateur like Chedda Lal Mishra could only watch the movement of the Viceroy but could not give any precise information. For the execution of this plan, Sanyal Babu went to Calcutta and met C.R. Das there. He placed his plan before him and asked for some financial help for its completion. C.R. Das gave him some money for his purpose. But the matter did not proceed any further. He was not a fit man to execute such a plan in which only seasoned and expert men could succeed.

After a satisfactory consolidation of our organisational set up in Banaras, I could afford to divert my attention to some other districts of U.P. I received instructions from Pratul Ganguli in Dacca who gave me a few addresses in U.P. While I was taking charge from Satish Sinha at Banaras, he also handed over to me a few addresses of persons in the different towns of U.P. So I chalked out a tour programme. I toured a few towns and cities of U.P. During my tour I realised that there was an imperative need for a unit of our party at Lucknow as it was the headquarter of the Provincial Government. I arrived at Lucknow and met Chaudhuri Khaliquzaman, the then Chairman of the Municipal Board Lucknow, for whom I had an introductory letter from Pratul Ganguli. I appraised him of my aims. He agreed with me that I should set up one unit at Lucknow and promised that he would extend his helping hand by trying to look after some financial needs of the recruits at Lucknow. In Lucknow I met a few other persons also. All of them showed a sympathetic attitude. From there I came back to Banaras and thought that Sachindra Nath Bakshi, who was the best man in our Banaras organisation, would be the fittest person to be deputed to Lucknow. I introduced him to Chudhuri Sahib and a few other persons. He stayed at Lucknow to start the work there.

As I have stated earlier that I was not known as a revolutionary in Banaras and so without any intereference from the C.I.D. my work was going on smoothly. But this secrecy could not be maintained for a long time due to the betrayal of Kartik Brahmachari, who was neither our Party recruit nor living in Godholia Ashram but used to visit the Ashram very frequently. Swami Satyananda was a very great man and this Kartik Brahmachari without any affiliation with the secret party work, used to go to Swamiji. It was natural that the purpose of my stay at Banaras was not hidden from him. The C.I.D. officials suspected this Brahmachari and interrogated him. He in a state of nervousness exposed to the C.I.D. that though he was not involved in any such type of activities, he knew one person who had specially come to Banaras for such a purpose. The C.I.D. people must have forced him to reveal the name of the person. He might have told them my name and promised to identify me some day before the police. One day it happened that I and Modak, who was a student of Intermediate class in the University, were going to the Godholia side from my place at Ganesh Mahal. The Brahmachari met us on the way and proceeded with us towards Godholia. All of us walked to the centre where many streets met. There was the house in which the C.I.D. Inspector, Jatin Sen was living. When we reached the front of the Inspector's house, the Brahmachari asked me to come into the house. Now I was placed in a very awkward position. To run away from there was more dangerous. It might have affirmed their suspicion more. I signalled to Modak to go away and I with the Brahmachari entered the house. He introduced me to the C.I.D. Inspector, Jitendra Sen. He came from Mymemsingh district in East Bengal. I told him that I had come to Banaras only for a change of climate as I was not keeping good health. But everything was known to him. I was known to him as I was not staying in Banaras with any assumed name. Since that time the C.I.D. people were always after me like a shadow. I had already changed the room where I stayed after my arrival. Now I was putting up in an old house of a relative of mine at Pataleshwar. One day when I was coming back from shopping, I saw Rai Bahadur Mukherjce, the C. I. D. Dy. S. P., standing on one side of the house and gazing very intently toward it as if he was doing some minute study of the architecture of the house. I decided that it was high time for me to leave Banaras. Otherwise my my contact with other recruits would expose them before the police.

As the C. I. D. vigilance grew daily and I was thinking of getting an opportunity to leave Banaras, a very important development took place in our party. I have already stated that I met Sanyal at Allahabad and he expressed his views that it would be more convenient for him if I worked with him without any affiliation with Anushilan. When we could not compromise on it, Ramesh Chaudhuri was requested to visit Banaras for elaborate talks with Sanyal Babu. The talks took place but no decision came out. In the second round of talks, Sanyal while in Calcutta, talked to Pratul Ganguli but he did not agree with Sanyal's views and the talks again failed. Then the third time Sanyal Babu contacted Trailokya Chakravarti, a veteran Anushilan leader, known for his liberal views, and equally respected by other parties also. Trailokya Chakravarti was teaching in the National School in Calcutta at that time. Trailokya Babu agreed with Sanyal and an amalgamation was the result. Sanyal Babu virtually joined the Anushilan ; but, as Anushilan was very popular in Bengal only, for working outside of Bengal, even as a unit of Anushilan, some other party name was required. So the formation of another party as an offshoot of the Anushilan took place in the village Bholachang of Brahmanbaria Sub-division in Tippera district, East

Bengal. In the presence of Pratul Ganguli, Narendra Mohan Sen, Sachindra Nath Sanyal, whom Amulya Mukherjee escorted from Mymensing, the Hindustan Republican Association was formed. After this amalgamation Sachindra Nath Sanyal came back to Banaras and gave me the news of these developments. He brought one letter from Trailokya Babu for me wherein he suggested that I should go to Calcutta, where he (Trailokya Babu) would give me two revolvers.

Meanwhile, Prabodh Das-Gupta, who was with me in Rajshahi Jail and who was an intimate friend of mine and an important member of the Anushilan, came to Banaras as his mother was living there. He brought one letter from Trailokya Babu for me. It was a detailed letter. Afterwards I went to Calcutta for detailed talks with Trailokya Babu. In our conversation he took up every point with its various aspects. He gave me the two revolvers also. Sanyal had asked for two revolvers and Maharaj (Trailokya Chakravarti) promised to give two more revolvers for U. P. I came back to Banaras with the revolvers. I gave these revolvers to Sanyal Babu. At that time he had only one revolver with him. How he got that revolver had also a story behind it. Actually what happened was that one foreigner came to Banaras and stayed in a Hotel. He had a revolver with him. One of the waiters stole the revolver and sold it to Dr. Surendra Mukherjee at fifty rupees. Mukherjee gave that revolver to Sachindra Nath Sanyal. That was the only revolver Sanyal had. This revolver was later seized by the police and was exhibited in the Kakori Conspiracy Case. It was a six chambered Webley 55 bore revolver.

It may be mentioned here that when Ramesh Chaudhuri approached Babu Shiva Prasad Gupta for financial help with a letter from Abani Mukherjee, he replied that he was not interested in encouraging violence but shortly after this Dr. Jadu Gopal Mukherjee of Calcutta, who belonged to the Calcutta Jugantar Party, accompanied by Sachindra Sanyal, approached Babu Shiva Prasad Gupta. Guptaji gave him twelve hundred rupees out of which six hundred rupees were taken by Sanyal Babu himself. Babu Shiva Prasad Gupta's refusal to give money to Ramesh Chaudhuri was only due to the fact that he did not approach Guptaji with proper and convincing credentials. How could he judge the authenticity of the letter of Abani Mukherje, which Chaudhuri brought for him, especially when he had no earlier acquaintance with Guptaji. Dr. Jadu Gopal Mukherjee went with Sanyal Babu, who was well-known to Guptaji.

Sanyal Babu was a man with family liabilities. He had to look after the financial demands of his family. There was of course no source of regular income. He therefore thought it advisable to shift to Calcutta with his family. There he hired a house in South Calcutta and started living incognito. There also, as he gave us to understand, he was not financially well off and he had to work hard to make both ends meet. But in spite of these practical difficulties, he had to continue his activities and maintain his leadership as well. It was during this time that some very promising young members of the Anushilan Samiti came to know him. And he, of course, tried earnestly to lead them in his own way. Jatin Das was the most remarkable among them. He became a martyr afterwards.

After the formation of H. R. A. when Sanyal Babu came back, it was decided between us that I would shift to Kanpur and set myself up there.

Mr. Sanyal kept it a close secret that he was regularly getting rupees 150/- per month from Babu Shiva Prasad Gupta of Banaras. This was continued even in jail though there he told me that he was getting only Rs. 10/- per month from Guptaji for books. He once casually mentioned to me that Deshbandhu C. R. Das offered him Rs. 10, 000/- for killing the Viceroy. This he told me shortly after the amalgamation.

" Fame ", as Milton said " is the last infirmity of a noble mind ". Possibly one can appropriately substitute the word " fame " by " leadership ". Absolute perfection in human character is only a hypothesis. And one is judged by the maximum number of virtues one possesses. Sanyal Babu's infirmities may be neglected and even forgiven. He fought throughout his life against the British and had many virtues and if sometimes he was impatient or spoke a few words against other party leaders, who were actually the pillars of the secret party, it should not be taken seriously.

In Banaras my identity was already exposed to the police. At Kanpur I could devote my time to my mission without attracting the notice of the police. So before leaving for Kanpur I gave the charge of the city unit to Rajendra Nath Lahiri and Modak was deputed as incharge of the University unit. At the time of my departure I had to take every precaution against the C. I. D. So I adopted the same method when I left Banaras as I did at the time of my departure from Comilla. Probodh Das-Gupta went to the station with my luggage. He purchased my ticket and occupied a seat in a compartment. I was waiting on the other side of the train where there was no light. When the train started Das Gupta got down and I entered the compartment and took the seat. It was already decided that I would stay in the mess of Suresh Bhattacharjee. After my arrival at Kanpur, I straightaway went there.

The Patkapur mess of Suresh Bhattacharya where I stayed needs a word here. The Anglo-Bengali School was being run at Kanpur under the patronage of Dr. S. N. Sen a well known medical practitioner. Suresh Bhattacharya was its Hindi teacher. There were five teachers, including the headmaster, in the school.

All of them were taking their meals in the mess; but only Suresh Bhattacharya and another teacher who came from Banaras were living in the mess.

All the teachers knew that Suresh Babu was an ex-revolutionary and they were sympathetic to him as well as towards the revolutionary activities. So when I stayed there, there was no need to hide the purpose. Of course I lived there with an assumed name P. C. Roy. But popularly I was known as Roy Sahib. The police also had no ground to suspect me as my stay in that mess where two Bengali teachers were living and three other Bengali teachers came daily to take their meals, did not appear to be strange. The headmaster and the other four teachers of the School knew who I was and why I had come there. Suresh Bhattacharjee was also looking after the 'Vartaman', a daily local paper, as its paid editor. Ganesh Shankar Vidyarthi secured him this job. Bhattacharjee also enjoyed the confidence of Dr. Sen, the patron of the institution. This confidence was amply demonstrated when Dr. Sen came forward as a defence witness of Suresh Bhattacharjee in the Kakori Conspiracy Case and gave a fine statement in the court in Bhattacharjee's favour.

Soon I hired a double storeyed house situated near the mess but in the interior of the street. I stayed there only for a month. The difficulty in keeping this house was that except myself there was nobody to occupy the house. The financial difficulty in meeting the rent was the second obstacle. Moreover, I thought that my staying alone in a double storeyed house without any ostensible source of income might have created some suspicions. So

I left that house and came back to the mess.

It was during the time of the Non-Cooperation movement that National Schools were established at many places of India. I have given reference earlier to the National School at Comilla, and to the National College in Calcutta. These institutions were the centres of national and patriotic activities where revolutionaries as well as non-violent Gandhiites got due place. There was also a National School at Kanpur. Manilal Avasthi was the headmaster of the School and Vir Bhadra Tewari was the first man whom Suresh Bhattacharjee introduced to me. He was a recruit of Suresh Bhattacharjee. He was an active man. The headmaster, Mr. Avasthi, who living with his family in a quarter inside the School, had also a sympathetic attitude towards us but was not active. So I found the first active man for our organisational work at Kanpur in Vir Bhadra Tewari and Kailash Narain though the former was more active. The National School also became a centre of our activities due to them.

My next acquaintance at Kanpur was a group of Arya Samajists. I came to know them casually but this gradually developed into friendship. One of the members of the Arya Samaj, Desh Bandhu Vidyalankar, was a sportsman and was very enthusiastic in our work. Another became a Vaidyaraj. He was also a Snatak of the Gurukul and studied Ayurved. He had a Ayurvedic dispensary at Nai Sarak. That dispensary also became a centre of our activities. Desh Bandhu asked me to read

'Satyartha Prakash' and supplied me with a copy of it. I read 'Satyartha Prakash' very thoroughly and was very much impressed. Though the basis of the book is the Vedas, the feeling of overwhelming patriotism is its outstanding feature. I realised the intense national feeling that Swami Dayananda Saraswati had. Just like Swami Vivekananda, who advocated more liberal views for the material and spiritual upliftment of the Indians as well as of the entire suffering humanity; Swami Dayanand Saraswati too was a great soul who gave a nationalist and patriotic lead to the Hindu society, suffering from horrible superstitions, ritualism and fantastic misconceptions. I was further thrilled to know that Shyamji Krishna Varma, who was a great supporter of the Indian revolutionaries in London, and who afterwards shifted to Paris, was a devotee of Swamiji and staunch believer in Arya Samaj. My reverence for Swami Dayanand Saraswati, and my understanding of the Satyartha Prakash also helped me in coming in closer contact with the group of the Arya Samajists at Kanpur.

Like the National School and the Ayurvedic dispensary at Nai Sarak, the Anglo-Bengali School was also a centre of our activity. All the teaching staff of the school were sympathetic towards me and in addition to them some students were also taking keen interest in our activities. The most remarkable students who were the students of Class IX and were recruited to our party were Bijoy Kumar Sinha, who was afterwards arrested in the

Lahore Conspiracy Case and transported to the Andamans to undergo life imprisonment; Batukeswar Dutt afterwards arrested in the Assembly Bomb Case with Bhagat Singh, also transported to the Andamans and Ajoy Kumar Ghose, who was also arrested in Lahore Conspiracy Case, acquitted and later joined the Communist Party of India and died as its General Secretary. Batukeswar Dutt was a very frequent visitor to our Patkapur mess as he was very close to Suresh Bhattacharjee. Bijoy Kumar also used to come to the mess.

One day Bijoy Kumar told me that his elder brother Raj Kumar Sinha, who was a B.Sc. student in Banaras Hindu University was interested in revolutionary activites and, if approached properly, could become an active member of the Party. I talked over this matter to Suresh Bhattacharjee but he told that Raj Kumar had applied for some job in the C. I. D., so it was not proper to take him in the party. But my impression was that from this solitary instance his entire character could not be estimated. So I told Rajen Lahiri and Modak to watch the movements and psychology of Raj Kumar in the University. Both of them observed his activities and later recruited him to our Party.

A word for an honest, genuine and competent teacher of A. B. High School is also required here. He was Nepal Banerjee, who was our sympathiser and not a member of our Party He always spoke highly of us and praised our ideas and way of life before the students. He had the character of a resolute man and he came to witness the Kakori Case trial in Sessions Court and remained there the whole day which an ordinary man would never dare to do for fear of catching the eyes of the police. He later opened a branch of the Ramakrishna Mission at Kanpur and become a monk.

From Kanpur we tried to expand our organisation to other district of U. P. also. Our first contact was with a respectable person of Hamirpur in Bundelkhand. Bundelkhand is well known through folk songs as a birth place of heroes and guerilla fighters like Alha and Udhal. The story of Alha and udhal in verses are sung in most parts of U. P. These songs are speciality of this area. The memories of Bundela heroes are kept ever fresh there by bards and singers. So it was not surprising to find that our heroic activities received a ready response from Bundelkhand.

Pandit Parmanand, who was a great fighter, arrested in the Lahore Conspiracy Case and transported to the Andamans, belonged to Hamirpur. He made Hamirpur a good field for our activities. Diwan Satrughna Singh also, through contact with him, became interested in the fight for freedom. Diwan Sahib was known to Suresh Bhattacharjee since he was interned and Suresh Babu made him our party member. He introduced me to Diwan Sahib. He came to my house at Kanpur and we had long discussions on our future activities. We tried to visualise a picture of free India.

I also came in contact with those who were

connected with the Mainpuri Conspiracy Case through Rana Pratap Singh and one Mr. Saxena. I went to Mainpuri and stayed with Rana Pratap Singh. Our next step was to contact Ram Prasad Bismil because Rana Pratap Singh was his associate in the Mainpuri Conspiracy Case. He accompanied me to Shahjahanpur to meet Ram Prasad Bismil. It was just a chance that he was out of station at that time. But we had talks with other persons who were friends of Ram Prasad Bismil. We met there Pandit Ram Dev Shukla, who was a student of M. A. class at that time and Prag Dutt. They seemed to be sympathisers. I came back from Shahjahanpur without meeting Bismil. But soon I went back to Shahjahanpur and met him. We had long talks and I wanted him to join our party. As he was already a seasoned fighter which he demonstrated in the Mainpuri Conspiracy, he understood our point of view very thoroughly and then agreed to work with us. He joined our party very earnestly and remained sincere to it up to the last moment of his life.

Suresh Bhattacharjee introduced me to Krishan Gopal Sharma, who was his fellow-journalist at Jhansi, and a local Congress Leader. I enquired from him about the general political conditions and the prospects of revolutionary activities in Jhansi. I accompanied him to Jhansi and stayed with him. It is through him that I met Rudra Narain, who was a teacher and well known sculptor there and generally known as 'Master Sahib'. There I met

Mr. Kanchan, who was a businessman and worked with us with full interest and enthusiasm. Mr. Kanchan introduced me to Mr. Sanyal, a good Bengali lawyer there. He had a good legal practice and showed keen sympathy for us.

After these contacts with the different districts in U.P. the arrival of a youth, who become a very remarkable man, took place in the Patkapur mess. First, however, I must narrate the background. I have earlier mentioned the name of the historian Jay Chandra Vidyalankar. He was a Professor of History in the National College of Lahore. He was also incharge of our secret party in the Punjab. He *noticed an intense patriotic urge and revolutionary* fire in the heart of a young Sikh student, Bhagat Singh. He was a very promising young man with a patriotic family background. His uncle was the famous revolutionary Sardar Ajit Singh, and Sardar Kishan Singh was his father. Bhagat Singh came in more close contact with Jay Chandra Vidyalankar. Vidyalankar recruited him to the party. But a disturbing state was created. Bhagat Singh's family and especially his grandfather insisted on his marriage in his life time. Bhagat Singh was now greatly perplexed. On the one side he had an intense urge to engage himself in the revolutionary activities and fight out British Imperialism in India and on the other side there was the proposal for marriage. Family pressure was trying to detract him and he went to Jay Chandra Vidyalankar for a solution of this problem. But what remedy could

Vidyalankar suggest? It was during this time that Sachindra Nath Sanyal happened to arrive at Lahore. Vidyalankar told Sanyal about the case of the zealous young Sikh student. Sanyal expressed his willingness to see Bhagat Singh and eventually when they met Sanyal Babu asked Bhagat Singh whether he was fully ready to devote his life for winning the freedom of his motherland? Whether he was ready to leave his family and relations for the cause? The replies to these questions were of course in the affirmative. So at that very time the turning point in Bhagat Singh's life came. Sanyal Babu gave him a letter for me and sent him to Kanpur. It was in the day time that he arrived at our place and gave me that letter. We talked but I did not know where to put him up for the night. I was staying in Bengali mess where all the members were Bengalees. The sudden presence of a Sikh youth might create suspicions with the police. However, he had to be accommodated in the same mess. While coming from the station he put his luggage in some Dharamshala. He did not know the name of that Dharamshala. He and myself both went out to find out that Dharamshala and bring his luggage. We searched most of the Dharamshalas near the station but did not find the particular one in which he put his luggage. At last when we decided to come back to our mess disappointed, postponing the search for the next day, at about 10 P.M. he could find out the Dharamshala and we brought his luggage to the Patkapur mess. That was the beginning of a new life at Kanpur. Although he had a full grown beard he was only a youth of seventeen at the time.

Since he was staying in the mess, his first acquaintances in Kanpur were its members. But he used to pass most of his time with me. He was an intelligent and very inquisitive youth, and he expressed his interest in many things. We used to talk and discuss for hours the general political life in the country, the form of revolution most suitable to the Indian conditions, different aspects of the revolutions in other countries and particularly in Russia which was looked on by the entire world as a laboratory experiment and pilot project, so to say, for the new systems to be introduced after the great coming of world revolution. Bhagat Singh wanted to know what the Communists stood for. His inquisitiveness was insatiable ; and he was no blind-follower. His youthful mind was ever alert to assess and grasp any new idea.

It was the time when the Kanpur Bolshevik Conspiracy Case trial was going on in the sessions court and it was a topic of discussion everywhere in the city. Four persons who were accused in it, Nalini DasGupta, Dange, Muzaffar Ahmad and Shaukat Usmani were charged with having established contact with M.N. Roy who was incharge of the Eastern Section of the Third International with its headquarter at Moscow.

I also witnessed the trial in the court with the help of one of my intimate friends, Satya Bhakta.

He was a Hindi writer and read widely books on socialism. He used to come to our mess and we had very long discussions and he helped in our work though he was not a member of our party. One day he asked me to accompany him to witness the trial. I did not want to go to the court as at that time I was living incognito. He gave me repeated assurances that nothing would happen and I accompanied him to witness the proceedings of the trial. During the recess when the C.I.D. people left the court, he introduced me to all the accused. Not long after this each of them were sentenced to four years' rigorous imprisonment.

In the district of Rai Bareily our party agent was Banwari Lal. He had some connections with the Pratapgarh district also. He was living a comfortable life and the party had also to send some money monthly. It will not be beside the point to mention here that once a Kisan rally took place at Rai Bareily district under Baba Ram Chandra, the well known Kisan leader in Eastern U.P. I also went there and saw it although I could not take any major part in it as I had gone there incognito. Banwari Lal was also with me. Sometimes I used to go to Rai Bareily to see how our work was going on there. Banwari Lal used to come to Kanpur occasionally.

We tried more and more for the expansion of our organisation in different districts of U.P. At Farrukkabad we were much helped by a man popularly known as Panditji as he was a school teacher though he was not a member of our Party. He is now working as incharge of the Gandhi Ashram in the same district.

We also established a unit of our party in Etawah district. Pandit Jyoti Shanker Dixit was a secret agent of ours there. He was keenly interested in our work. I used to go to Etawah quite often to review the position of our party there. Pandit Jyoti Shankar became an important man in the Congress and eventually became the Secretary of U.P. P.C.C. But later he left the Congress and joined the Hindu Mahasabha as its U.P. General Secretary. He was arrested in the Kakori Conspiracy Case, but let off in the lower courts as no proper evidence was found against him.

After the inclusion of Ram Prasad Bismil, Shahjahanpur became a strong base of our party and I had to visit the place frequently. At Shahjahanpur I was introduced to Ashfaqullah and Thakur Roshan Singh, two important members of our party. Both of them were given capital sentences in the Kakori Conspiracy Case. Like Ram Prasad Bismil, they took up the membership of the secret party with all earnestness and worked passionately towards the final goal. I was also introduced to some other members who were with Ram Prasad Bismil.

It was through Ram Prasad Bismil, that I came in contact with two other important persons who were connected with the Mainpuri conspiracy. They were Deva Narain Bharti of Shahjahanpur and

Bhagwan Singh of Pilibhit district. Both of them were prominent in the political fields of their respective districts and later became members of the U.P. legislature.

In Allahabad Jitendra Nath Sanyal, younger brother of Sachindra Nath Sanyal, was the incharge of the organisation. He was working as the incharge of the Book Depot of the Indian Press, Allahabad, at that time. He had a good house and was living with his mother and younger brother Bhupendra Nath Sanyal, who was then a student. When Sachindra Nath Sanyal was in Allahabad, he with his family was living with him.

Bishnu Saran Dublish of Meerut, who non-cooperated as a B.A. student, and suffered imprisonment during the Movement of 1921, joined our party through Sanyal Babu. He was the incharge of our organisation in Meerut area and was looking after the work very earnestly and passionately. It would be interesting here to mention an incident. Once Sanyal Babu was going to Lahore and on his way he dropped at Meerut and stayed with Dublishji. Next day when he went to the Meerut Railway station to board a train for Lahore, he took the ticket but he found that his pocket was picked and all the money, six hundred rupees in all, was taken away. He was put in a very awkward position and had to go back to Dublishji. Dublishji managed to give two hundred rupees to Sanyal with which he went to Lahore.

It would be interesting to mention a few more

incidents here. The Ayurvedic dispensary of Vaidyaji at Nai Sarak, Kanpur, was a centre where we used to gather in the summer noons. From there we used to go to the Ganges to swim. This was almost a regular programme in the summer. All of us, Bhagat Singh, Deshbandhu, Vaidyaji and I, once went to Unnao and had mangoes from the orchard there. After that we started for Kanpur. At the railway station I wanted to purchase tickets but my friends stopped me and asked me to enjoy ticketless travelling as an adventure. We entered a compartment when the train had already started and incidentally a ticket checker also followed us into the same compartment. When he asked for tickets, we pleaded that as we were in a hurry to catch the train we could not purchase the tickets. But the ticket checker demanded payment with penalty. We did not have enough money so we promised to pay at Kanpur station. A cousin of Vaidyaji was working as a Goods Clerk at the Kanpur station and we thought that we would borrow the requisite money from him and pay for the tickets. When the train reached Kanpur, Bhagat Singh, calling me on one side, told me that he had kept a ten rupee note as safety money. If I needed that for the payment he could give it. I took that money from him and paid for our tickets.

Since the arrival of Bhagat Singh at Patkapur mess, we were cautious because the presence of a Sikh youth in a Bengali mess might have attracted

15

the notice of the police and made them suspicious. We had no source of income and consequently the financial duress was very hard. The addition of Bhagat Singh to our mess worsened our financial plight. We thought about the matter but there was no suitable place where Bhagat Singh could be shifted safely. It was at this time that a remedy to these problems was worked out by the circumstances. Jai Chandra Vidyalankar happened to come to Kanpur for some work. He also saw the practical difficulties involved in Bhagat Singh's stay at Patkapur mess. He met Vidyarthiji and referred this to him. Vidyarthiji gladly said that he would give a room to Bhagat Singh in Pratap office. Bhagat Singh would learn journalism there and it was a place where so many persons came, his stay there would not attract any suspicion. He gave Rs. 10/- per month to Bhagat Singh as scholarship to learn journalism. Bhagat Singh's room where he shifted from our mess was in the inner side of the building. So in this way the problem of his stay as well as of financial assistance were solved and we also felt relieved.

The National School of Kanpur was a centre of our activities. The headmaster Manial Avasthi and Vir Bhadra Tewari who was a teacher in the school, had contacts with professional outlaws and undesirable elements. One of the persons of that nature was introduced to us. His name was Chatarpal Singh. He was introduced to us as a revolutionary but later it was revealed that crime was his profession and he had no political affiliation. We chalked out a programme to commit an action in Fatehpur district on Chatarpal's information. The place where the action was decided to be done was roughly ten miles south of Khaga railway station. We went there but at the time of action Chatarpal Singh failed to locate the place and we had to come back disappointed. This incident is enough to show the lack of seriousness of purpose of this man.

Another centre in Kanpur where we used to get together was a fuel wood stall. Thakur Jang Bahadur Singh, after leaving the educational institution where he was a student, opened this stall near Patkapur. He was a genuine party member. Pandit Shiva Saran a friend of Jang Bahadur Singh who used to come there also became our sympathiser. He was a handsome man. He had a licensed gun, a pistol and a rifle. Thakur Jang Bahadur Singh's brother also had a licensed gun.

With the expansion of our contacts our expenses also increased. The meagre income that we got from some sources was not enough to meet our expenses. It was a state of increasing financial stringency and no probable solution seemed to be visible in the near future. I received a demand for money from Banaras and many other places. In this financial duress, I thought of arranging some action. One day at the wood stall I talked to Thakur Jang Bahadur Singh in this connection. He suggested one place in Allahabad district. I accompanied him, for an on-the-spot study of the situation, to the village where the action was to be committed. We went and stayed at the house of one of his very intimate friends who was also living in the same village. I studied the location and other important facts of the house where the action was to be committed and came back to Kanpur. Here a plan of action was chalked out. Then the members, who were to take part, were requisitioned from our Banaras, Allahabad, Kanpur and Shahjahanpur units. So far as I remember now three persons came from Banaras,—Manmatha Nath Gupta, Rabindra Nath Kar and Pranabesh Chatterjee. Banwari Lal came from Rai Bareilley and from Kanpur Bhagat Singh, Jung Bahadur Singh, Vir Bhadra and I joined. Ram Prasad Bismil came from Shahjahanpur and for someone from Allahabad I asked Jitendra Nath Sanyal that if some local member accompanied us, it would be better. Jitendra Sanyal brought Pandit Keshav Dev Malviya who was then a student of the B. Sc. class in the University of Allahabad. After my talks with him I decided that it would not be advisable to take him with us. From Allahabad we went to that village and the action was committed out in the night. But we did not find any money there because they hid it under the earth. We thought it very wrong to inflict physical torture on the inmates of the house and we had to come back disappointed. The other disgraceful thing that took place there, which we came to know the next day, was that one person of the adjoining village received a bullet shot and died. It added to our disappointment and I decided that it was not worthwhile to arrange such actions in U. P. villages. In U. P. inhuman torture was needed to get the confession of the hidden money and jewellery which was very often so little that it was of no consequence to us. No one except us had any information about this unsuccessful action even later.

But one day our defence lawyer in the Kakori case, Barrister Chaudhuri of Calcutta, told me when we were being tried in that case, that Mr. Horton, the Chief Prosecutor of the Kakori Case said that there was a case in which I could be given even capital punishment. I immediately thought that the reference was to the Allahabad village action. Ram Prasad Bismil and Sachindra Sanyal and I had discussions on it and all of us came to the conclusion that Banwari Lal who was a participant in it, had made a clean breast of everything to the police. In this connection it may also be mentioned here that Pranabesh Chatterjee sent from jail after his conviction a statement to the Chief Court, in which he mentioned this action among other things.

We failed to collect any money from Allahabad action. The pressure for money from all sides was getting heavier. Sanyal Babu asked for money from Calcutta as he said that he had to take delivery of arms from European sailors. Rajen Lahiri was also very hard pressed in Banaras and he had taken a loan from some other sources. So he was also very much in need of financial help. Apart from these demands we had to pay some person. monthly. At Kanpur itself money was needed to pull on.

Meanwhile an opportunity was provided to us. Thakur Todar Singh of Aligarh started a National School in his village. For that institution he was in need of a suitable man to be the headmaster. He talked to Vidyarthiji in this connection. Suresh Bhattacherjee was also contacted regarding this. Thakur Todar Singh saw Bhagat Singh and was very much impressed and wanted him to be the headmaster of his National School. Bhattacharjee told me about it and I had a talk with Thakur Sahib. I asked Bhagat Singh and he agreed to go to Aligarh. So I sent him to Aligarh to become the headmaster of the School. Though I thought that since he belonged to a good family and was brought up in the city, he might feel some difficulty in a village, yet Bhagat Singh happily affirmed that he would pull on there without any difficulty. So at the time of departure I embraced him and told him that whenever he felt like leaving Aligarh, he could come to Kanpur, without any hesitation.

I told him that he had enjoyed a reputation in in the circle of acquaintance for his intelligence and and strength of character and that he should keep his head high wherever he went. It was virtually our last parting as I saw him only once more, when he came into the court where we were being tried in the Kakori case. And that was the last time I saw the magnificent young lion of Punjab, nay of the whole of India.

There were two motives behind my sending Bhagat Singh to Aligarh. The financial trouble was of course acute but we were pulling on somehow. We needed to expand the organisation and Bhagat Singh's going out as a headmaster of a school opened a great opportunity to us. His going to Aligarh meant an addition of another centre for our activities.

The pressing need of money became so acute thatit seemed now impossible to pull on without financial help. This need for help led me again to go to East Bengal from where I had slipped out previously. The police in Bengal was still trying to trace my where-abouts. But there was no other alternative left and I took the risk. I decided to go to Comilla and obtain some money from Mahesh Bhattacharjee. So from Kanpur I went to Calcutta and stayed with Sachindra Nath Sanyal. I knew the address of the house where he was living incognito with his family. There I met Jatin Das for the first time.

SECRET TRIP TO COMILLA

From Calcutta I started alone for Comilla. I boarded the Assam Mail which reached Comilla at midnight. Though there was risk of being seen by the C. I. D. officials, I had eluded them so many times previously and I knew the method of getting out of the platform safely. I opened my umbrella and hid my face behind it, gave the ticket to the ticket collector and crossed the gate amidst the hustle bustle of other passengers without being noticed. After reaching Comilla I went to my uncle's house and stayed there for the night. The next day, before dawn, I met Manindra Chakravarti. He advised me not to stay at my uncle's residence, as it involved a real risk. One of the clerks of my uncle who was previously our helper had become a police informer. So I decided to shift and the whole of the following day I stayed at another place and met my friends and partymen. It was in the night that I along with Prabhat Chakravarti went to see Mahesh Bhattacharjee at his place.

I told Mahesh Babu the situation the pressure of which had brought me to him. I told him that on a previous occasion I had agreed that I would not indulge in revolutionary activities as long as I was working in the House of Labourers. But as I had decided that the fight for freedom was the first and foremost duty of my life, I had left the House of Labourers and devoted my life for the freedom fight againt British Imperialism in India. Now I had gone underground and was working as a wholetimer, with all my capacity and strength, for revolutionary party very far from Comilla, out of Bengal, but as the revolutionaries always face financial duress, I was also its victim. Our moribund condition compelled me to come to Comilla, taking great risk of being identified and noticed by the C. I. D. people who all knew me, and to see him in this connection.

Bhattacharjee appreciated my plight and gave me a patient hearing. He asked me to come the next day and take one thousand rupees from him. But he also said that in case he failed to collect the whole of the promised amount he would give me whatever he could collect. During our talks he revealed an important and interesting fact. He told me that before the Alipore Conspiracy Case Aurobindo Ghosh along wlth Ullaskar Dutta came to him for obtaining some financial help and that he gave them money. He had a lion's heart and he never hesitated to help the needy, the poor, the patriot and the revolutionary. When I went to seek financial help from him, his greatness was again demonstrated. He even made a kind offer for rendering me regular help. He said that I should not come personally as it involved a great risk. I should, whenever help was needed, send one man in whom I had full confidence, to him for money. That man should go to him and tell him the pass word 'Haran'. That was the name by which he was known in his childhood and nobody except himself knew it then. Next night at the appointed time I went to his place and took one thousand rupees from him. The train by which I wanted to travel to Calcutta used to leave Comilla after midnight. So I had enough time at my disposal.

I went to my uncle's home with Prabhat Chakravarti. I went to the first floor of the house and stayed in the room of our sister. She herself brought my meals to avoid the notice of the servants and the cook. While I was taking my meals Sailesh Chatterjee, my cousin, youngest brother of Paresh, who became afterwards a martyr in Deoli camp, came there after attending some function. He was tired and slept there while we continued our conversation. My uncle also came twice into the room but seeing me taking meals, he went back to his bedroom. My aunt came upstairs and we talked for a long time. It was about twelve when I left that room to start for the station. I went to my uncle's bed room where he was lying on bed. I hesitated to wake him up. But he said that he had not slept so far. He must have been very much worried about me, so he could not sleep. He said that what could he tell me : I must go carefully avoiding all chances of being noticed and caught by the C.I.D. From his voice the heaviness of his heart and the grimness of his mood was clear. I respectfully touched his feet and left, never to meet him again on this side of the valley of death.

He was a fountain of inspiration for me. I always respected and adored him. When I was taking leave, he asked that I must have been in need of money but I told him that I had enough. I reached the railway station and applied the same old trick of boarding the train. Prabhat Chakravarti took my ticket and entered a compartment to ascertain that no one in it knew me while I was waiting on the other side of the train. When the train started I entered the compartment. He also accompanied me. After coming to Chandpur I did not take the Chittagong Mail steamer to Goalando but went to Rajabari by another steamer. From there I boarded the Dacca Mail instead of the Chittagong Mail. On the way came Lahajung, which was the only steamer station near my village. I wished, I could get down there aad go to my home to see my family but there was much risk involved. The entire area was flooded with water and my home was under the strict watch of the police. If my arrival was noticed, I could have no way to escape. So I did not think it proper to take the risk. I gave one latter for my sister to Prabhat Chakravarti. He got down at Lohajang to go to my home with my letter.

As a result of his visit to my home with my letter, he became familiar with my family. After a month when I was arrested he had also to go under-ground. In that state, my home was the best shelter for him and he stayed there for about two years with an assumed name of one of my cousins. My younger sister, Induprabha, was keenly interested in our activities and she worked for the secret party as its member. Once Prabhat Chakravarti caught small pox in Dacca and our partymen brought my sister there. She nursed him in Mitford Hospital of Dacca. He was admitted to the hospital with an assumed name and my sister nursed him and nobody could know that he was an absconder.

I came to Goalando and took the train for Sealdah. On reaching Sealdah, I went to Sanyal Babu's house. He was very much pleased. He was also in need of money and took three hundred rupees from me. He told me that he was hard pressed for money and that he was getting money from different sources and yet he kept Rs. 300/- from me. That was not proper, yet he did it. He was always writing to me for money although I had no source in U. P. for getting money. He utilised the U. P. sources for his personal expenses in Calcutta.

During my stay in Calcutta I had discussions with Sanyal Babu, Trailokya Nath Chakravarti and others. The other important fact to be mentioned here is that at that time the party was trying to forge hundred rupee currency notes. Trailokya Nath Chakravarti brought one forged note to Sanyal Babu's place. I also saw it and compared it with a genuine note and found that there was not much resemblance between the genuine and the forged one. The ten rupee note which the party forged previously had a more genuine look and I myself cashed four of those notes in the market.

They accepted my view and those hundred rupee notes were never circulated. The other important thing that is worth mentioning is that the party needed one man to be sent to foreign countries for establishing foreign contacts. For this purpose I suggested the name of Keshav Chakravarty, who had a shop of old books in Cornwallis Street at that time. He was a recruit of our party at Banaras but not much known among the party men in Calcutta. I personally met him and he agreed to go abroad as a Muslim sailor. I brought him to Biren Chatterjee, my cousin, who was working in a business house of our maternal uncles. We dressed Keshav Chakravarti as a Muslim sailor, putting on a Lungi and a cap etc. Then he accompanied me to South Calcutta where I introduced him to Sushil Banerjee who had connections in the circle of sailors. In the way Keshav Chakravarti was successful in going abroad disguised as a Muslim sailor and there he established some contacts.

From Calcutta I started for U.P. I stopped at Banaras and cleared the debts of Rajen Lahiri. After that I made an extensive tour of the different places in U.P. where our centres of activities were functioning. Money was paid wherever it was badly needed. And then I came back to Kanpur.

Rajen Lahiri and Ram Prasad Bismil used to visit Kanpur very frequently. For their stay I made arrangements in the 'Pili Kothi' Dharamshala which was situated in Pilkhana. It was near the Pratap office and they could stay there safely. Ram Prasad Bismil developed friendship with the Brahmin cook of the hotel which was in one part of the Dharamshala. Bismil used to take only one meal in twenty four hours. In the evening he took only milk. He maintained a very good physique. Physical exercise was a part of his daily routine and whenever at Kanpur, we used to go to an

Akhara on the bank of the Ganges. The Brahmin cook used to serve him very hospitably at the dinner time. So Bismil got something in return for his friendship.

I was also a frequent visitor to Shahjahanpur. There the routiue of Ram Prasad Bismil was the same. In the day time he worked in his silk factory and every evening he used to go for a stroll on the bank of the river. I accompanied him in his strolls. There after crossing the railway bridge, he used to do physical exercises. He passed two or three hours daily there. Ashfaqullah also used to go with us to railway bridge. We used to sit some time on the railings of the bridge. Bismil knew good Bengali and sometimes insisted that I should sing a Bengali song. I used to sing for him and he very much enjoyed it.

During the period of my stay in Kanpur, our contacts expanded and units of our secret party started functioning at different places in U.P. So now it was thought proper to consolidate that expansion and then to proceed on more planned and methodical lines. A review of the work done previously and cool thinking on the prospective programmes was needed. After returning from Calcutta, when I made an extensive tour of all our centres in U.P., I had that idea in my mind and so I talked to my associates in all these places about the indispensable need of a provincial conference. And thus the Provincial Council of the Hindustan Republican Association was called at Kanpur, the headquarters of the Party. The members of the Council came to attend the Council meeting. Those who attended it included Rajen Lahiri, Suresh Bhattacharjee, Vir Bhadra, Ram Prasad Bismil and myself. Bishnu Saran Dublish could not come from Meerut as the railway train stopped running that area due to a breach in the the railway bridge owing to heavy floods. All of them stayed at the Pilikothi Dharamshalla and the Conference was also held there. It reviewed the previous work that the party had done. Resolutions were placed before the Council for the prospective programme. The detailed discussions on the constitution of the H. R. A. will come in connection with the Kakori Conspiracy Case, but its fundamental principles may be mentioned here.

The Party aimed at setting up a republican form of Government in India. The Conference decided that the free Government of India should be against every form of exploitation of man by man. The party should hold progressive views, and preach and propagate the communistic principles and ideology. As regards the tapping of financial resources for the running of the party, the Conference resolved that the party would try to meet the requirements by contributions. Though it was not mentioned explicitly, it was in our minds that for meeting expenditures, the Party would not resort to money actions and dacoities.

In the meeting of the executive Suresh Chandra Bhattacharjee represented the Jhansi Division but it was decided. before the meeting, that next time Sachindra Nath Bakshi, whom I was going to set up at Jhansi from Lucknow, would represent Jhansi Division. Bakshi was set up at Lucknow but unfortunately no remarkable success in work could be achieved there. So we wanted to utilise his talents in Jhansi. It would not be beside the point to mention here that when I came back to U. P. as an undertrial in the Kakori Conspiracy Case, I came to know to my surprise that Sachin Bakshi was not given the chance to attend the next Provincial executive council's meeting, held at Meerut, as the representative of Jhansi. It was, as I took it, a big lapse of the organisation because of which this injustice was done to Bakshi. He was a very sincere and an efficient worker and was one of the senior most members of the Party in U. P. Even the idea of his being neglected by other members during my long absence pinched me.

To come to the point again Bakshi accompanied me to Jhansi. There I introduced him to all the important persons with whom we had contact. They all accepted him sympathetically and in an appreciative mood and promised to render every help to Bakshi in his work. Bakshi very earnestly set himself up at Jhansi and engaged himself wholeheartedly in the party work. He achieved a remarkable success in creating a very favourable ground there for revolutionary ideas and activities. The reference to a few important facts is enough to show his success there. It was in Jhansi that

Chandra Sekhar Azad found safe shelter and stayed for a long time. A revolutionary cannot shelter himself safely unless he is baeked, helped and loved by the people.

M. N. ROY ESTABLISHES CONTACT

Pandit Ram Charan Lal Sharma of Etah, U. P., was under warrant of arrest in the Kanpur Bolshevik Conspiracy Case of 1924. He evaded arrest and went to French Pondicherry and declared himself a political refugee, and the Pondicherry Government put him under restraint. He was confined in a high walled house in a small township not far off from Pondicherry. Just in front of his house, opposite the gate, was a house from which both British and French C.I.D. people kept a day and night vigil on him.

His confinement was undoubtedly very strict, yet from this place he maintained contact with M. N. Roy through Paris. Evidently, Roy was not really satisfied, though he must have thought that at the initial stage this was of much importance. Pandit Krishna Gopal Sharma of Jhansi had connections with Ram Charan Lal Sharma through the Madras representative of Ram Charan Lal.

From Krishna Gopal I received four undated letters from Comrade M. N. Roy, in two of which he particularly mentioned the names of Pratul Ganguli and Dr. Jadugopal Mukherjee, the two important revolutionary leaders of Bengal. Roy expressed great eagerness to establish contact with them. This was a great attraction for me, because foreign contact was very essential to carry on secret revolutionary activities against a powerful colonial rule.

Ever since I received the letters, I had a mind to make an attempt to exploit this source, although Krishna Gopal stated to me that the source was under the watch of the police. He also said that he was getting some money from time to time through this source, but the latest sum remitted was seized by the Government. Still I was ready to tap it even at a risk because if successful, this could be of immense help to us.

How I wished that I could consult Pratul Ganguli on this, but he was not available. We had lived together in Rajshahi Central Jail and I knew his ideas quite well. We read about socialism there and I knew how keen he was for socialism. He could certainly guide me in this. I had no inclination to have any talk on this with Sanyal Babu, because I knew thoroughly well that he was not for socialism. As a matter of fact, between myself and Sanyal Babu, my faith in socialism stood as a stumbling block and I found it almost impossible to work with him.

This was the trend of my thought at that time, but later when I came to know all the facts, I realised how mistaken I was. M. N. Roy had sent his own representative, Nalini Das-Gupta, for establishing contact. Das Gupta came to Bengal and he was sheltered by the Anushilan leaders, because

M.N. Roy's former associates, the so-called Jugantar or Calcutta Party leaders, were not very active in secret work, and could not give shelter to Das Gupta. Their ideas did not have the least similarity with those of Roy's. But as I had no direct contact with Bengal Anushilan leaders at that time, I did not know the real anticident of Das Gupta. He knew how to make bombs, because during the First World War he worked at the explosive factory at Glasgow in U. K. The Anushilan Leader Pratul Ganguli gave him shelter at Dacca and naturally Das Gupta came in contact with many workers of the Party and they were very much attracted to Das Gupra when the latter started teaching them bomb-making. Taking advantage of this position, Das Gupta even succeeded in making many of them anti-Ganguli thereby partly disrupting the party organisation.

About the same time the old Anushilanite revolutionary, Abani Mukherjee, also came from Moscow. When M. N. Roy sent Nalini Das Gupta to establish contaet with the Bengal revolutionaries in the hope that they would give their recognition to him and work in India in collaboration with him, Abani Mukherjee also took a great risk and came to Bengal with the same objective that he might be given the recognition. At this Das Gupta was much annoyed and, as I learnt, went so far as to shoot at him. After this the Anushilan leaders could not entertain high hopes about Das Gupta. They, however, sent Gopen Chakravarty to M. N.

Roy. Roy was satisfied with him and wanted more such young men to be sent. Abani Mukherjee also was not successful in his mission. He remained underground and left the country in that condition, but was very generous to advise the Anushilan leaders to develop contacts with M. N. Roy. When Gopen Chakravarti came back he was not hailed by the Anushilan leaders and gradually he went over to the Communist Party.

From what I have stated above it would appear to be clear that the Bengal revolutionaries, particularly the Anushilanites, who were all along carrying on an active secret organisation, could *very well establish contact with Mr. M. N. Roy* and thus create a powerful liaison with international Communism. But they did not.

Long after I was released from jail, I asked Pratul Ganguli why he could not utilise this source for our cause, as I knew he had the proper outlook for it. He stated in reply that he had the idea but he was surrounded by such a leadership in the Party that it was not at all possible.

I was quite ignorant of all these developments in Bengal. But from outside Bengal I was feeling a great need for the expansion of the organisation.

M. N. ROY, THE FAMOUS INDIAN REVOLUTIONARY

M. N. Roy, a Bengal revolutionary, became a world revolutionary figure, especially after he took up the charge of the Eastern Section of the Third

International at Moscow under Lenin's guidance.

Roy later entered India in disguise but was soon betrayed and arrested and was given a heavy sentence. He had been sentenced in U. P. in connection with the Kanpur Bolshevik Conspiracy Case.

After release he resumed his work and succeeded in getting a good number of brilliant youths to work with him. When we were released from the Kakori case he sent us a wire of congratulations from South India and after meeting him, I with some others decided to work with him. But we could not pull on together long and we subsequently joined the Congress Socialist Party.

AT FRENCH PONDICHERRY :

After the Council meeting at Kanpur I posted Sachindranath Bakshi at Jhansi and from there started for Pondicherry to exploit the chances, if any, of contacting M. N. Roy. That great risk was involved and that I knew ; but I was quite optimistic that the main persons, though suspects, would at least be reliable. I went to Madras and lodged myself in a hotel in the Triplicane area. My addressee, Krishna Swami, was an inhabitant of Triplicane. He was a Brahmin and Triplicane was a Brahmin area in 1924 and even now it is mainly so. From the hotel I searched for Krishna Swami and found him.

He received me with endearing terms and requested me to leave the hotel and come to his home. I did so, because that was safer. He introduced me to his family members and I became one of them. Swami sent a message through his source to Ram Charan Lal.

He introduced a Muslim young man to me, who did not know English but knew Urdu quite well. I thus stayed for three days in Madras and the Muslim youth was my constant companion. Madras eity was not much developed in 1924. We visited almost every place in Madr as in three days' time. I was thus thoroughly acquainted with the city. I introduced myself as a silk merchants's agent from northern India, because my associate, Ram Prasad Bismil, a Kakori martyr, was a silk manufacturer at Shahjahanpur. In fact I was wearing a silk chaddar over my coat, It was decided that one messenger would be sent first to Pondicherry and then Krishna Swami would go personally. I decided to go to Pondicherry after his return. The plan was executed and after his return, I boarded a train for Pondicherry. Swami told me how to reach the house where Ram Charan Lal was detained. The house was situated about six miles away from Pondicherry city. I had no difficulty in reaching the place and locating the house. Ram Charan Lal received me enthusiastically. He said that much risk was involved but the gain, if our plan could materialise, was great. We had elaborare talks on the general political movement in India, more particularly on the revolutionary side and some other plans and programmes. And then I unfolded my plan to him for which I took the risk of going there. I told him that Kanpur was central and industrial place in India. Fortunately it was also the centre of our revolutionary activities in U. P. In Kanpur, we had connections with the people, engaged in the press, papers and publications. We also knew many other working people in the city. Our plan was that if we could get some financial assistance from Moscow through M. N. Roy, we would start a press and bring out our own publications. This would help us to a very great extent to speed up our activities as well as to solve our financial problems ; for a press, run properly, wouid definitely yield a good income. Ram Charan Lal was very pleased to know about this plan and he spoke with full confidence that M. N. Roy would definitely extend his helping hand.

Ramcharanlal put a particular proposal before me. He took me aside in his residence and showed me a very fine tiny five chambered revolver. He said, he kept it for killing Mahatma Gandhi, because the latter was the highest obstacle in the path of an armed revolution. I vehemently objected to this idea, because thereby the revolutionaries would alienate themselves from the people and Gandhiji would become a martyr. I also told him that the small revolver that he had would never be able to kill a man unless its shot entered some very vital part of the man's body. After discussion he agreed with me that he would give up the idea.

He said that he had kept some clothes for his

brother Shivcharan, who was to be released soon. I told him that I would be able to arrange for the clothes to be sent to him through a friend,—I meant Ram Prasad Bismil of Shahjahanpur, who being a former Mainpuri Case absconder must be knowing Shivcharanlal.

I sent a percel of these clothes to Ram Prasad from Madras with a letter in it. Ram Prasad recruited him to the party and even made hi n a member of the Provincial Council.

I found another young man from Jhansi named Ayodhya Prasad, living with Ram Charan Lal. When I was at Jhansi, I was told about him. Ram Charan Lal told the C. I. D. people, who used to visit his place, that I was the uncle of Ayodhya Prasad and that Ayodhya Prasad's father had sent his younger brother to take the nephew back to Jhansi. It was a very natural explanation. The C. I. D. people also did not suspect anything. Ram Charan Lal further advised me to go to the Police Station and disclose the same identity and the purpose of my visit. He said this would eliminate all possible doubts from the mind of the police. I did so.

Now I had to leave the place to come back to Madras. The C. I. D. was very vigilant. Ram Charan Lal devised a plan to elude the C. I. D. In the house, adjoining the back part of his house, one Mr. Chettiyar, a merchant was living. He was Ram Charan Lal's very good friend and used to visit his place frequently. I was also introduced to him but my political identity was not revealed. Now his help was required and so the real motive of my visit was disclosed to him. Ram Charan Lal asked him to hand a rope ladder from his house in the night by which I would reach his house, and from there I would take the road leading to the railway station at a distance of 28 miles. He agreed to help. In the night we waited in vain for the ladder. That plan failed. We had to think of some other way to leave the place safely. So I and Ayodhya Prasad both decided to go to Pondicherry. One C. I.-D. man also followed us. After reaching Pondicherry, we roamed about the city to give the impression that our main object was sightseeing. Then we went to the residence of a barrister, who was the most prominent barrister of Pondicherry. It was a huge building. In one part of the same building his son-in-law, Mr. David, an advocate, was also living. He was the man who had connections with Paris. Ayodhya Prasad went in and talked to David and then he came out. It was decided between us that Ayodhya Prasad would go out and roam around the city to delude the C. I. D. man as he would naturally follow him everywhere and in the evening he would again come back to the barrister's residence on his way to the railway station. When the C. I. D. man would follow him, I would leave Pondicherry. He did so. The C. I. D. man also followed him and then I went inside and talked to David. He assured me that our message would definitely be conveyed to

Paris. He called his younger brother and told him something in his own language. I followed his younger brother who led me by the back door of his house to a bus driver's place. The driver was his trusted man. He told me to wait beside a pucca ghat of a tank on the roadside about three miles away from the house. I left the house and waited there. After the bus came there,. the driver signalled by footing his horn. I knew the meaning of the signal. So I quietly approached the bus and sat beside the driver. On the border of French Pondicherry, the usual searches were made by the authorities. I reached Cuddallore from where I boarded a train and reached at night time Egmore station of Madras. As I was acquainted with the roads, I straightaway walked to the residence of Mr. Swami in Triplicane.

CHAPTER VIII

FOLLOWED FROM MADRAS & ARRESTED IN CALCUTTA.

Next day in the morning I purchased a third class ticket for Calcutta and decided to board the train silently without being noticed and detected by the C. I. D. people. But it sounded to me very surprising when my host Mr. Krishna Swami insisted on accompanying me to the station to see me off. I told him that he was a suspect and his presence with me in the railway station would definitely catch the eyes of the police which would not be good for me in any case. But inspite of my persistent requests he insisted to see me off. I suspected some bad designs behind this insistence but as he was my host, I could not afford to be discourteous. He came to the station to leave me, but he did not insist on going inside. His designs were definitely to help the C. I. D. people by identifying me. I boarded the train. The compartment was full of passengers. I did not know that I was being followed by three C. I. D. officials. The Inspector was travelling in a Second class compartment. All of them were in plain dress. Early in the morning the train reached Vijayawada. There all the passengers of the compartment got down. Then my suspicion that some evil intention was involved in Swamy's activities eased for the time being and as the people get down, new passengers filled the compartment. I thought that the risk of being shadowed was over. But it was not the actual position. Among the people who boarded the train from Madras, I alone was left in the compartment. Then the new passengers filled the compartment on the same station. There two C.I.D. people also entered the compartment, one was a Hindu and the other was Muslim who belonged to Hyderabad seemed to be quite talkative and intelligent. He sat beside me and talked with me. The Madras Police must have informed the Calcutta Police about my jonrney. The Calcutta special branch of C. I. D. sent two officials in advance to Kharagpur junction. When the train reached Kharagpur the C.I.D. officials from the Calcutta Special Branch entered the compartment. An Assistant Sub-Inspector of the Calcutta Special C. I. D occupied a seat just in front of me and opened a book and started reading. It was not a book but an album bound as a book. In that album photographs of revolutionary absconders were pasted and he was studying my face to compare it with my photographs in the album. They followed me upto Calcutta. After reaching the Howrah station I got out on the platform. I saw a very poor man standing outside the station. He begged to be employed as a coolie by me and I gave my attache case to him. While crossing the Howrah bridge for boarding a tram to go to south Calcutta, I found that I was surrounded by a number of C. I. D. people. I had a very important document in my pocket. I first thought of throwing it into the river but there was every possibility of being caught and the papers being snatched away by the people who were following me just like my shadow. I came to know later that fourteen C.I.D. men were following me on the bridge. I crossed bridge and just on the junction of Strand Road and Harrison Road I asked the coolie to hand over the attache case as I could get a tram from there. As I was saying this to the coolie, two C.I.D. officers caught me simulataneously from my front and started fumbling into my pockets. I just laughed and told them that there was nothing in my pockets. The Assistant Sub-Inspector of C. I. D. who was following me from Kharagpur, with a view to giving the impression to his superior officers that he had earlier succeeded in identifying me, held my photograph in the album before me and said, "Jogesh Babu, here is your photograph." They did not make a thorough search there. I was led to an Ayurvedic Dispensary of a Ceylonese 'Kaviraj'. The compounder of the dispensing shop was a police informer. When I was taken there by C. I. D. people, the Kaviraj was not present in the dispensary. I sat there on bench and on my right sat the C. I. D. Inspector. Now a thorough search was to be made and the articles found with me were to be recorded. Some eye witnesses were also needed to sign the inventory of things found with me. The C. I. D. men caught hold of an Imperial Bank employee for this purpose. Some members of his family was ill and he came to buy some fruits. He just by chance passed through that way and was asked by the C. I. D. people to be an eye-witness of the search. Meanwhile when they were busy, I found a good opportunity. I loosened a button of my coat and took out that important document from my pocket and silently put it under the 'shitalpati' (a country made mat), spread over the wooden bedstead. Nobody noticed it except the compounder of the shop. To my surprise, he signalled the C. I. D. officer. It was beyond my expectation as generally people used to extend their sympathy and helping hands to those involved in political cases. The C. I. D. officer came to him and the compounder again pointed towards the edge of the shitalpati. The officer pulled out the document from underneath the shitalpati. I raised my objection very loudly that it was only a mischievous manoeuver of the C. I. D. to produce a paper from there about which I did not know anything. I said that the C. I. D. men always wanted to implicate others like that and that I had a thorough experience of such activities. Its effect was good. The search was made. The articles found with me were listed. But when the eye-witness, signed over it he put a footnote that all the articles except, item No. 1 (that document), were found with me in his presence. The C. I. D. men did not like this note and demanded that he should clarify his remarks, which meant a threat to an Imperial Bank officer.

So to further elucidate the matter, he added one more line that since he was standing on the other side, he did not see whether the document was recovered from me or not.

The Ceylonese Kaviraj came after the search affair was over and appeared to be very sympathetic to me. He offered me tea and a cold drink but I declined the offer with thanks, although I was very hungry and thirsty. The conduct of his compounder had annoyed me. Later I came to know in jail that the Ceylonese Kaviraj was a sympathiser of the revolutionaries and so his offer was quite genuine. This must be the reason why his compounder, a poorly paid man, was made an informer by the C. I. D. This man, as a well dressed Kaviraj, gave evidence against me, in Kakori trial court.

The police officers took me in a taxi to the Head Office of the Special Branch at Elysium Row. On the way they stopped the car before a sweetmeat shop and purchased quite a good amount of the best quality sweets. They offered and insisted that I should take some , but I had not the least inclination even to touch the sweets. They were jubilant because they could arrest me and hence enjoying sweets at my cost.

After arriving at Elysium Row, I was brought before the Assistant Commissioner of Calcutta, C.I.D. Police, Mr. Nalini Majumdar, who was then the head of the special C.I.D. police, under Deputy Commissioner Mr. Mills. In 1916, I had met him for the first time in the torture house at 4 Kyd Street, when he was a Sub-Inspector of the Special C.I.D. Branch. After I had been tortured under orders of Manoj Pal from 6 p. m. till midnight, Majumdar had come on duty at midnight. I was put up before him in a very much exhausted condition and he gave me a little food and water with some sweet words. Then I was locked up in the stable-cell. All these I remembered when I saw Majumdar.

Majumdar offered me a chair. He was leafing through the files and also was talking to me. I saw that he had come to know that I was very hungry and yet I disliked taking sweets from his colleagues. So he offered me sweets and tea. I declined with thanks. But I took a cold drink. He said that there was no hotel near about that place. One Muslim Havildar said that he had meat and chapati ready and I might take that if I liked. But I declined this too with thanks.

They were all anxious for my meals, because they had come to know from their agents, who were following me very closely all the way from Madras to Howrah for nearly two days and nights that during this period, I did not take anything but fried gram and water. The watchers were under the impression that I was short of money. The Muslim watcher had even told me at Kharagpur that the train would stop at Kharagpur for long time and I might take my meals there. But I had replied that I would take my meals after reaching

Calcutta. Naturally they thought that I had no money. But they were astonished when they saw during the search that I had with me four ten rupees G. C. notes, two one rupee coins and another eight anna bit and a pice.

The thing is that when I came to U. P. to work for the revolution I was a very determined man. I had left my family in a bad plight, left the House of Labourers which I had helped to create and then at Banaras rejected the good and generous offer of my uncle when he suggested that I should start a business with my cousin in Calcutta and for which he promised to give a sum of rupees twenty five thousand. I thought and acted on it firmly that when I had dedicated my life for the cause of the country and the party even at the cost of sufferings which my departure brought to my family, then I personally had no right to spend much money on myself. I made it a matter of principle that I would not spend more than four annas on my meals at a time. That was the only reason why I did not take any meals except gram etc. on my way from Madras to Calcutta, as with four annas no other food could be had at the railway stations.

As I was arrested in the Bara Bazar Police Station area, my case had to be registered there. Nalini Majumdar asked his Assistant to telephone to the Incharge of Bara Bazar Police Station to manage for my meal from some local hotel. When I was taken to the Bara Bazar the Incharge asked me whether I had any objection to taking food cooked at his own place. I told him that I hat no objection. So a very nice meal was served to me in his family quarter situated in the police station itself. I was very hungry as I had not taken any meal for two days ; so I enjoyed it. After taking my meals I thanked my host for entertaining me so cordially, and then the official formalities were conducted.

Then I was taken to Lal Bazar lock-up by my escort. There a room was vacated for me. Three Chinese were kept in this cell. They were shifted to some other cell and I was put into it. The Chinese left their blankets in this room and when I entered it, I found a filthy and suffocating odour. But as I was very tired after the long journey and because of the strain of C. I. D. detention, I had a sound sleep. It was the plan of the police to detain me for some days without producing me in a Court. They knew that very shortly an ordinance was going to be promulgated by the Viceroy under which a large number of arrests and detentions of political leaders and workers would take place. That was the only reason why though the police followed me in my journey yet I was not arrested till I stepped into Calcutta. When I arrived at the Howrah Railway Station, the C. I. D. followed me just like a shadow but arrested me only when I crossed the Howrah Bridge and entered Calcutta. The reason behind arresting me in Calcutta was that the Police Commissioner, Calcutta, was bestowed with powers of a first class Magistrate. I was produced before him. And after I was locked in Lal Bazar, I was daily escorted to the Police Commissioner's office just to fulfil the formality of receiving a remand to detain me for the next twenty-four hours. It was an illegal detention. The Calcutta High Court gave this ruling after some time in a Case, that the first class Magistrate's powers of the Police Commissioner should not be misused in this way and consequently this practice of receiving remand from the Police Commissioner was stopped.

I have stated that in the Lal Bazar lock-up cell I had the dirty blankets left by the Chinese. To use dirty blankets was revolting to me. But in an October night blankets were necessary, so I wrapped myself in them and slept very soundly. Cells in the jails are not so dirty. They are kept clean on sanitary grounds. But there was not the least sanitation in these cells of police stations. Netaji Subhas Chandra Bose had to pass a night in one of these cells and let me quote his words. He wrote in his book 'The Indian Struggle' on page 182: "The room in the Police station was a dirty hole and thanks to mosquitoes and bugs, it was impossible to have a wink of sleep. The sanitary arrangements were horribly bad and there was no privacy at all. I then realised the truth of what others had said before, namely, that if there is a hell on earth, it is the Lal Bazar Police Station."

I was lodged in this hell on the 18th October, 1924 and was kept in it till the 25th when an

Ordinance was promulgated and a large number of revolutionaries were arrested and thrown into the prisons. Some of them were brought by batches to Lal Bazar lock up. Others we saw from the windows sitting in Police vans. One day I was taken into one of these vans along with many others and was brought to the Presidency Jail.

AGAIN IN CALCUTTA PRESIDENCY JAIL

Thus I was again in my old 44 cells in the Calcutta Presidency Jail. This time we were kept unlocked in the day time. There were old associates as well as many new ones.

The most remarkable thing that I saw on entering the yard this time was a very bold writing in Bengali on the wall which means : Non-violence has no place in world politics,—with the signature below : Gopinath Saha. Saha wanted to kill Sir Charles Tegart, but by mistake he murdered Ernest Day and was hanged in the Calcutta Presidency jail, not long before our arrival. This writing indicated how much pressure was brought on him on this question of violence and non-violence. Gandhiji brought the new technique of non-violence and it caught the imagination of the unarmed country and they stood solidly behind him in the 1921 movement. But the movement was called off in 1922 without any material gain. The Government thought that revolutionaries had changed their line of action and that the movement for national emancipation would not again take this course of violence.

Therefore, they must have disturbed Saha too much with the question of violence and non-violence. The police must have insisted that by resorting to violence Gopinath had gone against the country's adopted principle under the leadership of Mahatma Gandhi. He must have left a reply to that by writing on the jail walls.

In fact it was a matter of big controversy throughout the country. Bengal Provincial Political Conference at Serajganj passed a resolution eulogising the bravery of Saha. Deshbandhu C. R. Das also participated in it. About this Netaji Subhas writes in his book 'The Indian Struggle' on page 145 : " Another resolution was discussed and passed which was to stir up a hornet's nest in the days to come. This was the Gopinath Saha resolution. Some months earlier, a young student named Gopinath Saha, had attempted to assassinate the Commissioner of Police of Calcutta, Sir Charles Tegart. Through mistaken identity, he shot at and killed another Englishman, Mr. Day. At the trial before the High Court of Calcutta, Saha made a statement which created a sensation at the time. He stated in effect that he really intended to murder the Police Commissioner and expressed his sincere sorrow for having killed the wrong person. He was glad to pay with his life and hoped that every drop of his blood would sow the seeds of freedom in every Indian home. Saha was sentenced to death by the High Court and duly hanged."

Colonel Simpson was the Superintendent of the Jail at that time. I complained to him one day that the cell life was telling upon my health and that really I was feeling giddy and also that I had a slight temperature. The Superintendent told the doctor to send me to the hospital for a check-up. I had been in this jail in 1916, 1917 and 1918, but those were very hard war days and our confinement was very strict. So to go to the hospital was unthinkable then. But I hankered after seeing the hospital, as this was the place where during the first Alipore Bomb Conspiracy Case Satyendranath Bose and Kanailal Datta had shot and killed Naren Gosain who had turned approver in the case.

The hospital became a very comfortable place for me. A sub-deputy collector sentenced for the misappropriation of a big amount of Government money, was there as a convict assistant of the doctor. In the absence of the officials he was all in all there. He was spending money for giving tips and every comfort was there for him. After the Superintendent's visit when the doctor also left after prescribing some medicines for me, the doctor's assistant asked me what food I would like to have. I could not understand the question properly and for clarification asked him what food would be available. He said in reply that he would get whatever I liked. He said I could have eggs, meat or fish ; as I was a bit indisposed I should have rice, vegetables and fresh fish. He showed me that everything was available. For bath he supplied hot water, towel, soap etc. and showed me the closed bathroom on the ground floor.

In the afternoon, I was shown the places where Satyen and Kanailal were and how after the first shot Naren Gosain ran towards the office and Kanailal also followed him firing the revolver and Gosain dropped dead near the Jute Factory.

Next day I told the Superintendent that I was alright and that I would like to go back to my yard. He allowed me to go back. This Colonel Simpson later became the Inspector General of Prisons and he was shot dead by the revolutionaries in his office in the Bengal Government Secretariat.

From the Presidency Jail a few of us were often taken in batches to the C. I. D. office for interrogation. That was a new type of mental torture. They had some small chambers. We were taken individually to separate chambers and were forced to sit there for hours. Each chamber had two small chairs and a small table. To sit for hours in this condition was a terrible strain on the mind. Some officers would come and sit on the other chair for some time and would talk on some irrelevant things and then go away. One day a muslim Inspector sat before me. He said, he was Office-Incharge of Lohaganj Police Station. He had once gone to search my village residence where my sister gave them a lot of trouble. When I enquired from him the whereabouts of that brute of a man named Manoj

Pal who had brutally tortured me in 1916, he became very angry and threatened me saying that I was under arrest and such things might be harmful to me. I said in reply that once I was under their clutches they would do whatever they could. But inspite of his threats I would not change my opinion about Manoj Pal. Then he calmed down and told me that Manoj Pal was the son of a Deputy Magistrate and also that Manoj Pal was dead.

I have mentioned that Mr. Mills was at that time the Deputy Commissioner of Police in charge of the Special Branch, C.I.D. On one occasion I was taken to his room. He ordered everybody, even his orderly, to quit. Then he got up and bolted the door from inside. I have stated that Mr. Colson did so once in an office room in the Calcutta Presidency Jail in 1916. I could not understand his motive and was very curious. . He sat before me and made a very earnest appeal to tell him one thing, whether I had been abroad. At first I tried to be evasive and told him that I would be the last person to confess anything to the police. He said again appealingly that he would not put a single cross question. At this I said that he might take it that I had not been abroad. He was thankful and I left his chamber. It was absolutely clear from his query that the police had no information about me after I left Banaras and shifted the Party Provincial Headquarters to Kanpur. Here my underground life was quite successful till I was betrayed by Krishnaswami at Madras.

BEHRAMPORE JAIL

Shortly after this some of us were transferred to Berhampore Jail. Netaji Subhas Chandra Bose had already been transferred there from Alipore New Central Jail. The entire jail population was accommodated in a very big double storeyed building. After winning the battle of Plassey the Britishers erected a number of magnificent buildings on the bank of the river and one such building which was once an army hospital was the Berhampore Jail. The Hospital, the workshops and the convicts were accommodated on the ground floor and we, more than twenty ordinance detenus and five state prisoners under Regulation III of 1818, including Bose, were accommodated on the first floor. On one side of the building on top of the hospital, was the Female Ward. During my imprisonment it was mostly vacant.

The Superintendent of the Jail, who was also the Civil Surgeon, was an Ulster Irishman. He was a good doctor, but on one point he was a bit eccentric. He would discuss politics and would pass objectionable remarks about the leftist Indian Leaders, for whom we had great regard. This gradually took an unpleasant turn. We, therefore, requested him not to have any political discussions with us. But he could not help it. One day I took a strong objection to one of his remark and I said that we would not talk to him till he withdrew his remark and tendered his apologies. All our associates stopped talking to him from that day. A struggle started and we elected one of us, Kshitish Banerjee, as our representative to talk to the officials in this connection. Everybody had full confidence in him. People of different groups were there, but the majority belonged to Anushilan and Kshitish Babu was one of them

The Superintendent used to come on his daily visit and we were indifferent to his coming and going. We did not even stand up when he came. The five state prisoners were separated from us by a partitioned wall ; but there was no restriction to our meeting them. Shri Bose did not like this silent protest, but there was no way out. We wrote to the authorities about our difficulties regarding medical needs. The I. G. came and talked to us for nearly half an hour, but Kshitish Babu did not raise the delicate point of our relation with the Superintendent although we all knew that the I. G. was in the know of everything. When I raised the matter the I. G. became resentful and said that Government would not care for our health. "We won't care for the Government then", was my retort. The I. G. sullenly got up and walked out. But within a week or so the Superintendent was transferred and Dr. Hazra, a reputed surgeon, came as the Civil Surgeon and Jail Superintendent. We were relieved of a constant unpleasantness.

As a pastime in jail, many of our friends wished to celebrate Saraswati Puja. A Government grant was necessary for this. But the question was what could we do if the Government did not grant our request. We could never take a refusal lying down. So, it was decided that we should consult Netaji Subhas on this. Myself and Pratul Bhattacharjee met Bose. He supported the idea readily. With hesitancy I asked what had to be done in case the request was not granted. Prompt come the reply, "We shall resort to hunger strike". We did not expect this from him ; we were pleasantly surprised. When the news was broken to other friends all were jubilant. An application was forwarded to the authorities for this. Suddenly on the 25th January, a telegraphic transfer order for Netaji came. We knew only that he would be taken to Lalbazar Police Station in Calcutta.

We suspected that the news that Bose was ready to resort to hunger strike, must have reached the authorities and that might be the cause of his transfer. Naturally we apprehended the presence of some police agents among us. When Bose sent for me and asked me my opinion I told him that regarding his arrest there was difference of opinion amongst the C. I. D. officials and that his transfer from the jail might be a prelude to his release. But none of us apprehended that he would be sent to distant Mandalay Jail in Upper Burma. It is a well known fact that he resorted to hunger strike even in that jail and that it was terminated through the mediation of Maulana Shaukat Ali. His hunger strike in Alipore New Central Jail and subsequent release and escape to Kabul in 1941 are now parts of thrilling history.

We held a meeting that day to give him a hearty send off and the words of Shri Anil Baran Roy still ring in my ear : "Subhas Chandra is the rising sun of India." He was undoubtedly the rising sun in the political firmament of India, but unfourtunately for the country the sun set at a time when the need of it was the greatest.

After the transfer of Bose from Behrampore Jail, one day in the couse of our talk Professor Anil Baran Roy, who was then a trusted lieutenant of Deshbandhu Das and was a Swarajist M.L.A. told me how intimate Bose was with Das, He told many anecdotes on the relation between the two. To mention one such incident : Deshbandhu had invited Bose and Roy to take meals with him and Basanti Devi, the wife of Deshbandhu, was herself serving and while doing so she made a certain request to Das. But as no response was forthcoming she remarked, "You won't even listen to me, if Subhas says you would respond promptly." So intense was the feeling of Deshbandhu Das for the future Netaji Subhas. The jeweller of men knew the mettle of his disciple.

We had established secret contact with our Party men in the town and through our source secretly received on a particular day a copy of the leaflet printed outside. In this connection later Sachindranath Sanyal was tried at Bankura and was sentenced to 2 years' rigorous imprisonment.

This leaflet came up very prominently in the Kakori Conspiracy Case at Lucknow, but that is something which I shall narrate later.

We used to prepare a hand-written monthly in which Netaji wrote one article on the Independence of Poland. Professor Anilbaran Roy used to edit the articles. The last article I wrote for the monthly was on the Easter Rising of Ireland. I was transferred to Hazaribagh Jail the very day I finished it. I have forgotten the name of the monthly.

Shortly after our arrival in Berhampore jaii we proposed to have a competitive game of badminton between the State Prisoners and the detenus. From the detenns, myself and another young friend from Mymensingh were selected and from the State Prisoners Netaji Bose and Professor Anilbaran Roy played. We won both the games very easily. I easily became the Champion later, as even two could not beat me. As I had no rival I had to give up playing badminton. Many years after this when I was a Kakori convict in U. P. Jail, Netaji Bose visited Comilla as the President of the Indian National Congress. He took his lunch in my uncle's house. When he was taking his lunch, my name came up in the discussion and Bose stated that I was such a fine badminton player that I could be a champion. Such was his impression about my game.

We were arrested under the Emergency Ordinance (called Bengal Ordinance) promulgated by the Viceroy at midnight on October 24th, 1924.

It had to be passed by the Legislative Council within six months. A Bill was, therefore, duly introduced and the Government strained every nerve to have it passed into Law. The Government was worried whether they would be able to carry the Bill through because of the strong opposition of the Swarajists. Deshbandhu Das was then resting at Patna as he had been suffering from a nervous breakdown. But in spite of his ill health, he resolved to inflict a crushing defeat on the Government. On the appointed day he arrived at the Council Hall in time and had literally to be carried in an invalid chair. Once again the laurels of the day were his. "The bill was thrown out, but by virtue of the extraordinary power given to the Governor under the Constitution, the Governor was able to certify the Bill as law," writes Bose in his book.

THE BENGAL CRIMINAL LAW AMENDMENT BILL, 1925

Sir Hugh Stephenson, the Home Member, Government of Bengal, in moving the Bill before the Legislative Council made a comprehensive statement in strong support of the Bill. He fully utilized the two documents, the "Revolutionary" leaflet and the document recovered from me after my arrest. Prior to this the Home Member mentioned the Rowlatt Committee, whose report brought havoc in its wake in India in 1919. The Home Member stated, "In the view of Government there are weighty reasons for enacting the Bill in a permanent form." Then he said, "This was the view of the Rowlatt Committee who says : 'The powers which we shall suggest for dealing with future emergencies must be ready for use at short notice. They must, therefore, be on the statute book in advance." The Governments' plea was that the Bengal Criminal Law Amendment Bill was the first step in pursuance of the Rowlatt Committee's recommendations for the suppression of revolutionary activities.

Sir Hugh mentioned Sachindranath Sanyal and quoted the following passage from the "Revolutionary" leaflet. "Those who say that there is no revolutionary party in India and so the promulgation of the repressive laws is an oppression, are not telling the truth ; for such an organisation of a very big size really exists in India. This party is endeavouring to bring about independence of India through armed revolution." After this he quoted a synopsis of a document alleged to have been recovered from a state prisoner.

Without mentioning my name (because of the adverse remark of the search witness) he stated that as regards the extent of the conspiracy he would refer to papers found recently with another member who was under restraint under the Ordinance and who had been commissioned to organise revolutionary activities outside Bengal by a secret Committee. These papers mentioned 23 districts in one area outside Bengal where there were district organisers at work. A copy of the resolutions of that Committee was also found on him. I will quote five of these resolutions :—

(1) That only two departments be set up at present :
   (a) Department for Propaganda and
   (b) Department for the collection of funds and arms,

(2) That the following immediate steps be taken to do propaganda through newspapers and magazines :
   (a) To start a campaign against the C. I. D. authorities ;
   (b) To start a campaign against repressive laws and measures ;
   (c) To criticise Congress activities that hinder revolutionary work.
   (d) To collect stories, episodes and other materials in connection with revolutionary activities for publication.

(3) That every possible care be taken as regards the secrecy of the activities of the Association ;

(4) That every district organiser should try his best to help the local clubs and associations which follow the principles that may directly or indirectly promote the cause of revolution and try to become member of the Congress and take part in its activities whenever advisable keeping in view the rules of the Association.

(5) To provide workers with work it is necessary

to divide the district activities into three categories :

(a) Village upliftment

(b) Secret revolutionary activities

(c) Local social functions and activities connected with the clubs and associations.

The motion was lost by 66 votes to 57. After being defeated, the Government took to the device of legalising the illegal law. The Governor certified the Act.

To come back to our life in Berhampore Jail : In the Baleswar fight at Baripada, Bagha Jatin and Chittapriya Roy laid down their lives in a trench fight with the police and Niren and Manoranjan were hanged. The only survivor in this fight was Jatish Pal, who was sent to the Andamans under transportation for life. In the Andaman Jail he had lost his mental balance due to inhuman treatment and as a consequence thereof he was sent back to Bengal and was kept in the Lunatic Asylum at Berhampore. The news reached us one day that Pal had expired there. We were all mortified to hear this. Of the five Baripada heroes he was the only person alive. Who knows what had happened there in that memorable fight between the underground revolutionaries and the police force, headed by Sir Charles Tegart ? I wrote an article in our handwritten monthly under the caption "Homage to Jatish" and in the same issue another article on him was written by Santosh Datta, a colleague of theirs.

Once Gandhiji paid a visit to Berhampore town. He was once passing by the river side and many of us stood on the roof of the building from where everything was visible. The slogans of the procession attracted us to the roof. Seeing us on the roof Gandhiji left his car, stood up on a big wooden box provided by a Pan shop owner and waved his chaddar to us. We also shouted slogans.

We planned to escape from the jail and we sent the message to our friends outside. That was a serious matter and the local friends could not give any answer without consulting the leaders. So it took a long time to receive the reply. Four of us were permitted to make the attempt at escape. On receipt of this information we started our preparations and planning.

At this stage suddenly we received news that we need not now make any attempt at escape, as the question of our general release was in the air. In fact, our top leader, late Narendra Mohan Sen, who was then underground, personally came to Berhampore and conveyed the news to us. He was sheltered in a house visible from the jail.

Deputy jailor, Jamini Mukherjee, who had come from the Calcutta Presidency Jail on special duty as incharge of the affairs of the detenus, took me aside one day and told me that we might be released. I told him in reply that he had chosen an elderly man to cut jokes with. He was taken aback at this and stated that he had never been in light mood with me and that he respected me. Mukherji's uncle was an Inspector of the C. I. D. and I thought that he must have come to know this from his uncle. We had already received such news from our friends outside and after Sen's arrival at Berhampore we knew definitely that we would all be released. One day the Superintendent, Dr. Hazra, also told the same thing to Professor Anilbaran Roy.

There was indeed a prolonged negotiation between Deshbandhu C. R. Das and the Government which the public came to know long after. About this let me quote what Netaji Subhas wrote in his book ' The Indian Struggle '. No one in India felt these persecutions more than Deshbandhu Das did. In a magnificent speech delivered from the Mayoral Chair of the Calcutta Corporation, he gave vent to the deep indignation which stirred the public at the time. He accepted full responsibility for what the Chief Executive Officer had done and challenged the Government to arrest him. The Government did not accept the challenge but replied in a different way. They opened negotiations with him for a settlement of the entire Indian question. At that time, Mahatma Gandhi was politically a back number. He had confined himself to the Khadi campaign, having retired from the political movement which was under the control of the Swarajist leaders. The memory of the negotiations in December, 1921, had left an impression on the official mind that it was possible to come to an understanding with Deshbandhu C. R. Das if the major issues were tackled in an earnest and sincere manner. Lord Lytton personally had a very high appreciation of him as a man. And at the time no official felt the pressure of the popular movement more than the Governor of Bengal did. In those days, to settle with the Congress meant to settle with Deshbandhu C. R. Das. Therefore, unknown to the outside world, negotiations between the Deshbandhu and the Governor of Bengal, Lord Lytton, went on for some months. With his shrewd political instinct, the Deshbandhu thought of making use of the public feeling roused by the arrests of October, 1924. He appealed for a fund to be used for national reconstruction. The economic situation in the country was not favourable and many people thought that the response to the appeal would be disappointing. But the leader knew better. In spite of unfavourable forecast, he had a very good response and that was a further proof of public confidence in him. At the end of the year, the annual session of the Congress was held at Belgaum in Bombay Presidency. This Congress was presided over by Mahatma Gandhi and it was the last Congress attended by Deshbandhu. The proceedings were marked by extreme cordiality between the Mahatma and the Swarajists. The principal programme of work adopted for the coming year was extension of home spinning and home weaving and it was enjoined on every member of the Congress to produce a certain quantity of yarn as his membership subscription. The only other significant fact about the Belgaum Congress was the attempt of Mrs. Besant to get her Commonwealth of India Bill ratified by the Congress. The Bill which was to confer Home Rule of India, had been drafted by her and her intention was to have it introduced in the British Parliament as a private Bill. She felt that her hands would be considerably strengthened if the Congress gave the stamp of approval to her pet constitution, but none of the Congress leaders could be drawn into her. net. She therefore, had to leave the Belgaum Congress disappointed. Page 155 : of the 'Indian Struggle' by Bose " The political situation remained unchanged when the year 1925 was ushered in. Deshbandhu Das continued in power. In the early part of 1925, there was further trial of strength between the Government and the Swarajists in Bengal. The Ordinance which the Governor-General promulgated in October, 1924, conferring on the Bengal Government powers of summary arrest and imprisonment without trial, was to expire in April, 1925. Thereafter, if the Bengal Government desired to have those powers, they would have to introduce legislation to that effect in the Bengal Legislative Council.

"It has already been shown how the Bill was rejected and the Governor had to certify it." (p. 153) On page 157 Bose continues that soon after the Faridpur Conference, "Lord Reading left India for London, as the Conservative Cabinet and the Secretary of State for India, Lord Birkenhead, wanted to consult him. But that time it was in the air that negotiations had been going on between Deshbandhu Das and the Government though hardly any one knew the details. It was announced that after consulting Lord Reading, Lord Birkenhead would make an important pronouncement about India. Every one in India awaited his speech with the greatest interest and eagerness.

"Then came a sudden bolt from the blue. In June 1925, when Deshbandhu was having a rest in the hill station of Darjeeling, the summer capital of the Bengal Government, he fell seriously ill. After a brief attack he suddenly died."

Before I come to the reaction of Das's passing away, I would like to quote more paragraphs from Indian Struggle. "The death of Deshbandhu on June 16, 1925, was for India a national calamity of the first magnitude. Though his active political career consisted of barely five years, his rise had been phenomenal. With the reckless abandon of a Vaishnava devotee, he had plunged into the political movement with heart and soul and he had given not only himself but his all in the fight for Swaraj. When he died, whatever worldly possessions he still had, were left to the nation. By the Government he was both feared and admired. They feared his strength, but admired his character. They knew that though he was a hard fighter, he was also the man with whom they could bargain for a settlement. He was clear-headed, his political instinct was sound and unerring and unlike Mahatma, he was fully conscious of the role he was to play in Indian politics. He knew more than any one else, that situations favourable for wresting political power from the enemy do not come often, when they do come, they do not last long. While the crisis lasts, bargain was to be struck. He knew also that to sponsor a settlement, when public enthusiasm is at its height, needs much courage and may involve a certain amount of unpopularity. But he was nothing if not fearless. He was conscious of his exact role, namely, that of a practical politician, and he was therefore never afraid of courting unpopularity.

"In contrast with the Deshbandhu, the role of the Mahatma has not been a clear one. In many ways he is altogether an idealist and a visionary. In other respects, he is an astute politician. At times he is as obstinate as a fanatic ; on other occasion he is liable to surrender like a child. The instinct, or the judgement, so necessary for political bargaining is lacking in him. When there is a real opportunity for a bargain, as in 1921, he is liable to stick out for small things and thereby upset all chances of a settlement. Whenever he does go in for a bargain, as we shall see in 1931, he gives more than the takes. On the whole, he is no match in diplomacy for an astute British politician." (p. 158) Bose further writes "After the death of Deshbandhu Das the Mahatma spent several months in Bengal trying to raise a memorial fund in honour of the departed great and helping to reorganise the Congress machinery in the absence of the leader. His public activities, nevertheless, continued on the whole to be non-political in character and the political mantle of the Deshbandhu therefore fell on Pandit Motilal Nehru, the Swarajist leader in the Assembly. While Lord Reading was still in England and Lord Lytton, the Governor of Bengal, was acting as the Governor General of India, the Pandit attempted to resume the threads of the negotiations which the Deshbandhu had been carrying on with the Government. But the Government in London had already decided to drop the negotiations for the time being and watch developments. Nothing therefore came out of this attempt of Pandit Motilal Nehru." (p. 159)

The sad and heart-rending news of the death of Deshbandhu was given to us by a professor of Berhampore College in the night by shouting from outside the jail walls. We were all stunned. It was really a bolt from the blue for all of us.

The next day, the citizens of Berhampore went round the town in a huge mourning procession and they stopped for long outside the jail as we all stood on the roof. A mourning song was sung by one man and it was repeated by others in a chorus. Bengal was in deep mourning. On the Sradh day a song was composed by Jitesh Lahiri and we sang it in chorus and processions of the town again stopped outside the jail walls silently till our song was finished. The question of release vanished in the thin air as England changed its mind.

I had already read in the newspapers that a large number of persons had been arrested from different places and transferred to Lucknow Jail after the Kakori train dacoity. One was arrested from Berhampore, brought to our jail and then sent to Lucknow under fetters. Sachindra Nath Sanyal was arrested and was being tried at Bankura. Rajendranath Lahiri was also arrested at the Dakshineswar Bomb Factory. These were all very bad news for me. I also read that Banarsi Lal of Shahjahanpur had given an incriminating statement to the police. I told my most intimate friends that I might also be involved in the matter.

Soon the C. I. D. officials from Calcutta came to take our photos and specimens of handwriting. We were a big number and they took about three days to complete their work. This was advantageous to me. I could guess that if there be a conspiracy at Lucknow then there was every likelihood of my being involved in it and in that case the paper recovered during my arrest would certainly be utilised againts us.

Ramesh Acharya, the principal accused in the Barisal Conspiracy Case of 1913-14, was with us in the Behrampore Jail. Generally handwriting experts are put up for giving evidence in proof of hand-writing. In Barisal Case a hand-writing expert was produced and examined. So Ramesh Acharya had knowledge of it. I received detailed instructions from him about the method and gave the specimen in bold letters writing very slowly. Rameshda told me not to write in the characteristic way. I attained grand success in this, as will be told in connection with the Kakori Conspiracy Case.

My days were numbered in Berhampore Jail. We were not in any way interfering in the affairs of the jail so far as the convicts were concerned. But once when we were downstairs we heard a pathetic shriek from the Oil Mill Factory. Myself, Santosh Dutta and Syamananda Sen stepped in and found a young good looking convict who was working in mills bleeding profusely. We all saw that about 5″x 2″ of his back was badly bruised. We rebuked the convict in charge for this and slapped him. The Head warder became very angry and he complained against us to the jailor and the Superintendent.

Next morning the Superintendent asked us what had happened and he understood the real position.

TO HAZARIBAGH CENTRAL JAIL IN BIHAR

Winter was approaching and we asked for winter clothes. But nothing was supplied. One afternoon when we were taking exercise in the field we were told that we were under orders of transfer to Hazaribagh Central Jail, Bihar. We said that we could not be transferred to a Hill station without adequate winter clothes. Because of this dispute the authorities did not allow us to go in, as they sensed that in that case we might resist with the help of other friends. So we were taken to the jail office and our friends shouted from the roof and many outsiders gathered outside the jail walls.

The Police Superintendent came and brought a dozen of constables. They decided to lift us forcibly. As we were taking exercise we had nothing on us except a dhoti and a vest. In lifting us forcibly our scanty clothes gave them maximum trouble. I was taken up with my head down and there was a fresh shout from my friends. They dumped us into horse driven carriages and took us to the Berhampore Railway Station. Police officials physically carried us from the carriage to the waiting room and when the train arrived they carried us to the compartment.

At Sealdah station in Calcutta we were carried to the prison van from the train. From the railway platform to the police van was a long distance. We were taken to the Howrah Station which was over-crowded. People crowded to see us. One European Inspector and a sub-inspector with a dozen constables were escorting us from Berhampore to Hazaribagh. In the month of November three almost unclothed persons were being physically lifted from place to place. This was a very unusual sight. But people understood we were political prisoners. We were dumped into a compartment of a train bound for Hazaribagh.

When the train arrived at Hazaribagh Road Station, we posed a greater problem for the police, because we had to be lifted through the railway over-bridge. It was really a very hard job for the police, particularly because Santosh Datta had a huge physique, 6 feet tall and equally bulky.

I was running high temperature and was shivering but the European Superintendent of Police of Hazaribagh who came to the station to escort us to Hazaribagh Jail at a distance of nearly 44 miles, was very rough in his behaviour. He made me sit in a van which was over-crowded.

When we reached the Hazaribagh Jail gate in the night, I told the Jail Officer that I was ill and also that I needed medical help. He sent for the doctor. My temperature was 102 degrees. I was given four blankets and was locked in a cell.

In the night my temperature rose to 105 degrees and then I became almost unconscious. The next morning the Superintendent saw me and sent me to the hospital. So I was separated from my friends for some days.

The news of our transfer in such inhuman way was published in the newspapers and Deshapriya J. M. Sen Gupta gathered all the information and shortly after he moved the historic motion in the Bengal Legislative Council. Only a day earlier, SenGupta had been at Hazaribagh on a professional call. This was also advantageous to him.

Let me quote from the official proceedings of the Bengal Legislative Council. Mr. J. M. Sen-Gupta moved a motion for the adjournment of the business of the Council at its sitting on Tuesday, the 18th December, 1925 at 5 P. M.

" Mr. SenGupta : Sir, I beg to move for an

adjournment of the Council to discuss a matter of urgent public importance, viz., the recent treatment of political prisoners as evinced by the transfer on the 22nd November. 1925, of political prisoner Jogesh Chandra Chatterjee (Ghosh by mistake) Syamanda Sen (Somesh Chandra by mistake) and Santosh Kumar Datta from Berhampore Jail to Hazaribagh Jail without any sort of clothing or without giving them any notice to make provision for their journey. Sir, it is prefectly clear from the wording of the motion that the attention of the House is drawn to the question of the treatment of political prisoners as a whole and as an example... Sir, I will not refer today to the feeling in the country against the Ordinance or Regulation III. The opinion of the Council has been expressed against them unequivocally more than once. We have condemned both the measures. We have asked the Government to repeal Regulation III and we have refused to pass the Bengal Ordinance under which most of the prisoners are being confined at present. Today I shall now refer, and I am sorry, I shall have to refer only to the three prisoners but I hope I shall be able to satisfy the House—and even though I am confined with regard to this resolution only to the case of three political prisoners, I hope I shall be able to satisfy the members of the House that such treatment should never be meted out to political prisoners by any Government which desires to call itself civilised.

"What are the facts of the case ? The facts

are perfectly clear. On the night of 22nd November these three prisoners received a chit from the Superintendent or jailor that they were wanted at the office. At that time they had no clothes on the upper part of the body as they were taking some exercise. They were immediately marched before the jailor and then were told that they would have to take a journey immediately—a long journey from Berhampore to Hazaribagh. They had to go via Calcutta. They protested. They said they had asked for warm clothes from a month before. No winter clothes had been supplied. They said that they ought to be allowed to go back to their cells to get whatever clothes they could get hold of, warm or otherwise...That prayer was also refused. They were compelled to take their journey that very evening without any clothes and we know that these facts were published in the Press and the Government knew it on the morning of 23rd. Sir, happily or unhappily, I was at Hazaribagh on the night of the 21st as also on the 22nd when I travelled down to Calcutta. I know that at that time of the year it was very cold at Hazaribagh—much colder then we have had here in Calcutta, or in this side of Bengal this season. Not only were they not given any warm clothes but they were actually taken without any covering on the upper part of the body from Berhampore to Calcutta, at any rate. After that what happened I do not know. But I do charge the Government with mal-administration and illtreatment of political prisoners after detention without trial. It may be that they have been under detentien without trial, that they were confined under an Ordinance which we wanted to throw out—it may be that some members of the House opposed us at that time as they were convinced that there were some reasons of State for such detention without trial—and I ask today the members of the House opposite, particularly my English friends that they should not complain if the Indians think that they follow the Government into the lobby on every question without caring whether the Government is right or wrong. The question today is not whether the Ordinance is being administered in the spirit and according to the letter of the law. What do we find ? Some of the prisoners are confined under the provisions of Regulation III of 1818. Section 6 of that Regulation says :

'Every officer in whose custody any State Prisoner may be placed shall, as soon as after taking such prisoner into his custody as may be practicable, report to the Governor-General in Council whether the degree of confinement to which he may be subjected appears liable to injure his health, and whether all' allowance fixed for his support be adequate to the supply of his own wants and those of his family, according to their rank in life."

Section 6 is almost verbatim reproduced in Section 21 of the Bengal Criminal Law Amendment Act of 1925 which replaced the Ordinance. That Section runs thus :

'The Local Government shall make to every person, who is placed under restraint by reason of an order made under sub-section (1) of Section II, a monthly allowance for his support of such amount as is, in the opinion of the Local Government, adequate for the supply of his wants, and shall also to his family, if any, and to such of his near relations, if any, as are in the opinion of the Local Government dependent on him for support 'an allowance for the supply of their wants suitable in the opinion of the Local Goverment to their rank in life.'

"It is the Government's case that we look after them well, we house them well, we give them proper clothes, but for reasons of State we keep them confined. Once that is admitted, I ask you, is there any justification for not allowing these prisoners to go and get their clothes from their cells ? Is there any justification for dragging them away on a wintry night without any clothes to cover them ? There can be justification only if the Government's case is this, namely, that we are treating them in that way so that their lives may be jeopardised, so that when they come out they will not be able to follow the ordinary advocations of life, they may not be useful to society, that their health may be undermined to such an extent that they may not carry on the work which they started —the work for the freedom of the country. Therefore, I ask the members of the House opposite who have all along supported the Government in passing the Ordinance into Law—I ask them today to think and ponder whether they will by thire action tonight allow the Indian public to be more firmly convinced in their belief that the English members of the House do not care anything for the merits of any question and that they only want to follow the Government into the lobby simply because they think that the Government must be supported at all costs. I am sorry that I cannot give other instances by reason of the ruling of the President under which I am suffering tonight as we have suffered on many occasions on this side of the House. I am sorry I cannot give other instances of recent ill reatment of political prisoners, which horrify the members of the House. But if they will come to me—if the President will allow me another motion, I will cite other instances which will show that the treatment of political prisoners is a disgrace to the Government. We talk of the dignity of the House': We cannot protect our own citizens. We cannot protect the members of this very House. We ought to hang down our heads in shame for the humiliation and insult that have been offered to the members of this House."

Sir Hugh Stephenson, the Home Member, gave a reply to this. But the Government case was very weak. With very scanty clothes on we were forced to spend two winter nights in the latter part of November. Mr. Sen Gupta or the public did not know that I was attacked with fever and my condition became even critical as a result of the inhuman way I was treated.

There were two non-official visitors of Jail at

Berhampore as members of Legislative Council. One was Kumar Srish Chandra Nandi, the landlord of Cossimbazar and the other was Khan Bahadur. Srish Nandi came to our Ward only once and was accompanied by the Divisional Commissioner, Mr. J. N. Gupta, son-in-law of the great scholar R. C. Dutta. Though a jail visitor Nandi was usually debarred from visiting us, the political prisoners. Only Khan Bahadur was allowed to visit us.

During the debate on Sen Gupta's adjournment motion, the Khan Bahadur supported the Government case very strongly stating that the state prisoners and the detenus in Berhampore jail were having a very comfortable life. They were well-fed, well-clothed and every care was taken by the Goverment for their health and general well-being. According to him they were living in veritable paradise. If I remember correctly after such a long time, some members perhaps asked the Khan Bahadur if he would be ready to exchange position with the prisoners.

After the Khan Bahadur, Kumar Srish Nandi of Cossimbazar stood up and said that although he was also a non-official visitor of Berhampore jail he was not allowed to visit the political detenus there. After Sen Gupta's stirring speech, the speech of Kumar Srish Nandi added fuel to the fire. The Kumar was not a revolutionary nor had he anything to do with politics. Not to allow such a person to meet the detenus, clearly indicated that there was something wrong. Sen Gupta gave a spirited reply to the speech of Sir Hugh Stephenson and it was a crushing one. When the Adjournment Motion was put to the vote it was carried by the House by 58 to 50.

The Superintendent of Hazaribagh Central Jail was an Indian Christian from Madras and his wife was an English lady. He took much care for my speedy recovery in the Hospital. I was then removed to our cell yard where my two associates were lodged. Hazaribagh Central Jail was a celluler jail. One cell wing was meant for us. Besides ourselves a sweeper was locked up in one cell. A convict cook came in the day time to prepare our meals. We were getting a daily allowance and food articles were supplied according to our choice.

The Head Jailor was a Bengalee. Everyday he and the Superintendent used to visit our yard. His attitude was also good towards us. I shall narrate one instance to give an inkling of this. Being Bengalees we were all very fond of fish. The Jailor had only one daughter and no son. The daughter was also very fond of fish. So the Jailor always tried to get fish for his daughter and we were also getting some occasionally, though it was difficult to procure fish at Hazaribagh. This Jailor was in Mandalay Jail when Lokmanya Bal Gangadhar Tilak was there. He described to us how this great man of India passed his days deep in piles of books. Tilak wrote his Geeta Rahasya while in Mandalay Jail.

The news of the adjournment motion in the Bengal Council and the Government's subsequent defeat and the public knowledge of the manner in which we were transferred to the Hazaribagh jail made the local jail authorities a bit nervous. We were complaining to the Superintendent about our loneliness. He told us they would feel relieved if we were transferred back to Bengal.

We were supplied necessary clothings, both cotton and woollen, because we came only with one dhoti. Later we also received all our articles left in the Berhampore jail. So we had double sets of clothes.

Gardening was our only pastime. The Brahmin convicted cook was a vegetarian, yet he cooked our meat and fish. But he would not touch an egg. So we had to give up eating eggs. The Santal sweeper was an interesting companion. He was a tall and stout man and very simple. The greatest trouble for him in jail was that he could not get any liquor. Often he would entreat us to allow him to make liquor from rice. But how could we allow him to do that in Jail? He was given 5 years, rigorous imprisonment for murdering a woman who was supposed to be a witch. He told us that he was not the culprit and that the police falsely implicated him.

A simple man as he was, he was taking our jokes to be real. Once we told him that Santosh Datta after release would go to his place and start family life there by marrying a Santal girl. He stated that he would bear the expenses. He had left Rs. 50/- buried under earth and he would spend that amount for the marriage ceremony. He was also teaching us Santal dance and songs.

One day we read in the 'Statesman' a long report on Kakori Case. A Special Magistrate had been appointed and three persons who were already in police custody would be transferred to Lucknow; they were Sachindra Nath Sanyal, Jogesh Chandra Chatterji and Rajendra Nath Lahiri. The jail officials did not read this elaborate and detailed report.

My two friends were unhappy to read this news. From that day they made it a rule that our lunch would consist of Polao and meat, because as a Kakori prisoner I was likely to be sentenced to long term imprisonment and in the U. P. jail I would be given food not to the taste of an average Bengalee.

Within a fortnight or so, the Superintendent on his daily round asked me if I would like to go to some other jail. He refused to discuss the matter further. We discussed amongst ourselves and we were sure that the order for my transfer had arrived but the jail authorities could not know the real thing because they did not know that I was under warrant in the Kakori Case which was to begin shortly at Lucknow. The Superintendent, however told me one morning that I would be transferred to a place that very day, but that it would be a temporary transfer. The transfer order was like that. I was to go as a Bengal detenu, not as an undertrial in the Kakori Conspiracy Case.

Before the lockup time I was brought with all my belongings to the jail office.

CHAPTER IX

TO LUCKNOW JAIL AS A KAKORI UNDERTRIAL

The parting with my friends was very painful. They were overwhelmed with grief that I was going to face a big trial at a place far off from Bengal. We embraced one another very feelingly and warmly. But worse was the condition of the simple Santal sweeper. Ever since he kenw that I would be going away he wept like a child. Before my departure he was locked up in his cell. When I approached him he was weeping bitterly even in the presence of the jail officials. It was very painful to me as well. What loveable fellows they were: They were, as it were, nature's own children. Work, eat, drink and be merry, were their motto of life.

On my arrival in the jail office I saw that I was to be escorted by one European Inspector of Police, one havildar and four constables of the armed police. Leaving the jail gate our vehicle reached the European club where the police Superintendent had a look at me and then when we went to Hazaribagh Road Station, we sat in the crowded Waiting Room, where all eyes were on me, but nobody dared to come near me. A well dressed person under such an escort was really an object of curiosity. I was talking to the Inspector on various subjects and was astonished to know that he was a Theosophist of Annie Besant School. He believed in the birth of a superman under whom there would come the millenium. I utilised this weak point of the man throughout our long journey from Hazaribagh to Lucknow. He was enthusiastic when I supported his views and we became friends.

We travelled by an Inter Class compartment in Bombay Mail upto Moghul Sarai from where we boarded a train which brought us to Lucknow in the afternoon. At Mughul Sarai I purchased a big quantity of guavas and apples, because I knew that my passage money had to be spent.

At Banaras Cantonment Station I saw Jitendra Nâth Sanyal, the younger brother of Sachindra Nath Sanyal. He did not look at me but I saw that he boarded the third class compartment next to mine. He occupied a seat which was visible from my seat, but he was not at all looking at me. Some children were near me. So in order to attract the notice of Sanyal, I gave some fruits to the children with the permission of the Inspector. When they were taking the fruits from me, Sanyal saw me, came near my compartment and took a seat adjacent to mine. We talked in Bengalee—a language which others could not follow. He got down at Jaunpur station and stood in front of our compartment. I told the Inspector that he was a lawyer and I was going to Lucknow as an undertrial and hence I was taking his advice. Sanyal informed me that he and others would be ready to help us to escape if circumstances forced us to try that.

Our train arrived at Lucknow where an armed police party under the S. P. was ready to receive us. As soon as I got down the policemen cordoned me. But my escorting Inspector objected to this. So I walked fanked by the S. P. and the Inspector while the policemen followed us. They took us through a side door to the police van and we reached the District Jail within a few minutes and soon we were sitting in the Superintendent's room. The jailor was on his round making sure that all the locks of the jail were put. On receipt of the news of our arrival he hurried to the office and stood near me. When I asked his name he said Champalal and when I asked his title, I meant surname, he said that he was Rai Sahib. At the first sight I took him to be a good man, but on hearing that he was a Rai Sahib I thought that I was mistaken. He must be an exceptionally shrewd man, outwardly he had the appearance of a good man, but inside he must be quite different, that was what I thought. But I had to live long in this jail and soon I learnt that a more tender hearted jailor I never saw.

The Inspector handed over his charge to the jailor and offered to pay the money that was saved out of my food allowance on the way. The jailor politely declined saying that he might return the money to those who gave him, if he so liked.

The Inspector took leave of us telling the jailor that he had a pleasant journey with me.

Then the jailor led me to the Civil Ward. On the way he showed me the Circle, the cook house and the condemned cells. By the side of the Civil Ward was a factory, where Pandit Motilal Nehru and Pandit Jawaharlal Nehru were kept when they were imprisoned in the Civil Disobedience Movement of 1921.

It was dusk when we reached my ward. My boxes and bundles were heaped up in the small barrack. A lantern was supplied. The jailor wanted to supply my meals for the night from his place, telling that he was also a Brahmin. But I declined the offer with thanks and asked for some milk. My bed was spread out on a cot. When the jailor and the deputy jailor went out, I dropped down on the bed to spend my first night in a jail in U. P. where I was destined to spend another nineteen years.

THE KAKORI CONSPIRACY CASE

While leading me to my ward the Jailor told me that I would be put up for identification and if not identified then I would be sent back to Hazaribagh jail. That must have been the directive, because, as I started earlier, the Superentendent of the Hazaribagh Central Jail had also told me so. But I knew that the main approver, Banarsilal would easily identify me, because I had stayed in his house for six days. So in my mind I knew that a prima facie cause would be established against me and that I would certainly be roped in.

One afternoon, Syed Ainuddin, the special magistrate for this case, made his appearance with a smiling face and started talking to me, of course in English, as if he was a personal friend of mine. He wore a big Turkish cap and Achkan. I thought he spoke in a friendly way because I was a privileged detenu under the Bengal Criminal Law Amendment Act certified that very year by the Governor.

The next time the Magistrate came for my identification with a few more persons including Mr. N. N. Mitra, representative of A. P. I. (Associated Press of India). Mitra was a student at Dacca and was an enthusiastic member of the secret Anushilan Samiti there. Because the Magistrate was on very intimate terms with him our friend Ram Prasad Bismil took him to be a friend of the C. I. D. and even made some remarks against him in the Court. Yet Mitra did never in any way act against our interest.

I was mixed up with some persons in the identification parade. Banarsilal, the main approver identified me. On another day the confessing accused, Banwarilal, also came and identified me. Before the Magistrate came to see me in Jail, our defence lawyers were also informed about my arrival in Lucknow District Jail. One day Pandit Harkaran Nath Mishra, Bar-at-Law, came to see me. He was accompanied by another young lawyer. After introducing himself, Mr. Mishra also introduced his friend as Mr. C. B. Gupta. I had no talk that day with Mr. Gupta, but the smart looking short-statured young man's dress attracted me much. The way he wore his dhoti twisted round his legs and his big white turban looked unusual. I looked at him again and again with curiosity. Who knows Harkaran Nath Mishra now ? Gupta is now one of the top political leaders of U. P.

The jail population took me to be a Raja, because privileges in the jail were reserved for that class only. The jail authorities were very much perplexed with the problem of my expenses. I told the jailor that it was a simple matter. As I was still a Bengal detenu my expenses would be incurred by the Bengal Government and actually they were doing so when we were in Bihar jail. But authorities seemed that they failed to understand the position. They, therefore, referred tne matter to the U. P. Government.

When after the identification I was made an undertrial in the Kakori Case I insisted that I should not be kept separate from other accused. They did not accept my plea. But I established private contacts with my friends. One day, shortly after my arrival, Ram Prashad Bismil and Roshan Singh came in front of my ward gate and we exchanged greetings. They were being taken out under fetters.

One day I was shifted to the circle and allowed

to live with the other accused but my privileges as a detenu were withdrawn. I protested against this but who was there to hear my protests? I thought of resorting to hunger strike. But in the circumstance in which we were placed at that time, hunger strike was inadvisable. So I protested in writing to the Bengal Government who took up the stand that as I was under a different Government they were unable to interfere. It was a wrong stand on the part of both the Governments, because in case of my acquittal in the Kakori Case, they would not have released me and would have detained me again as a Bengal Detenu. Later Gopinath Srivastava of Lucknow wrote a forceful article on this problem which was published in the Forward, a daily from Calcutta, under the headline: "A Detenu's Privileges go".

THE ORIGIN OF THE KAKORI CASE

The provincial Council Meeting held at Kanpur on the 3rd October, 1924, was the last time when I had direct connection with the party. After the meeting I went to Pondicherry and was arrested in Calcutta on the 18th October 1924. One resolution of this meeting states: " That at least Rs. 100/- (considered to be the least expenditure in case of dire necessity at present) be raised by subscription from members and sympathisers." This shows how the Association resolved to carry on the organisational work depending on its own resources.

But with the expansion of the organisation the expenditure also increased. So the problem of money became more acute. When the necessity was great, means were also to be found out to meet the increased demand. Forcible collection of funds followed. Though the revolutionaries never wanted to take recourse to this method of collecting funds they were helpless in the face of dire necessity. This compulsion is evident from what Ram Prasad Bismil wrote in his autobiographical sketch only two days before his execution. He wrote how he was compelled to take away the railway collections. Ashfaqullah vehemently protested against the proposal. His argument was that the organisation was not strong enough to save itself against a strong onslaught from the Government. But Ram Prasad was in charge of the organisation and he had a great responsibility. He had written how the organisers of different districts were already burdened with loans and he himself was indebted. So he himself took the responsibility of the action.

It was the 9th of August, 1925. The 8 down Passenger train was, as usual, running from Saharanpur for Lucknow. At about dusk it left Kakori station for Alamnagar, near Lucknow. The alarm chain was pulled from a second class compartment, the train slowed down and stopped. Shots were fired and the passengers were warned to keep themselves inside the compartments and close the windows. The guard was told to lie down with his face down. He obeyed. The Anglo-Indian driver thought that "discretion was the better part of valour" and lay flat with his face down. The iron chest carrying the day's collections from all stations was thrown out from the brake-van, broken open and its contents taken away. The Doon Express from the opposite side passed by in the meantime and the chest-breaking operation was temporarily stopped. Then the whole party of only ten armed men made away with the booty.

Long after a relief train with officers came to the spot and discovered that a passenger was lying dead on the side of the track. But no trace of the people responsible for the action could be found. This sensational incident is known as the Kakori Train Dacoity. The daring train loot and the dramatic escape of the looters wtthout leaving any trace of any kind was an object of astonishment both to the Government and to the public.

When I read the news from Berhampore Jail, Bengal, I thought that this might be the work of my associates. Such a daring action in such a manner could not be done by ordinary dacoits. The men were determined and well disciplined. They shouted to the passengers to get inside telling them at the same time that they were taking away Government money, but not of the public. Only one passenger, a Muslim Mukhtiar, came out to see his wife in the female compartment and was unfortunately shot dead by a stray bullet. The three persons who pulled the chains from the second class were in Khaki short and shirt and felt hat. They reached Lucknow safely and most of them passed the night in the Banarsibagh.

The action was a challenge to the Government, in other words to the police, who were guardians of law and order. Therefore, the C.I.D. were alerted and deployed into action under the leadership of its Special Superintendent Mr. Horton. Their eyes were on the political suspects. Mr. Horton succeeded in getting a clue at Shahjahanpur, where the vigilance was specially concentrated as three currency notes looted from the train were found there. Ram Prasad Bismil, a suspect since the Mainpuri Conspiracy Case of 1918, was living at Shahjahanpur. Police also came to know that Bismil was absent from Shahjahanpur, on the 8th, 9th and 10th August, 1925. During further investigations they came to know that a student of the Government High School received letters for Bismil and handed them over to him. For the police to discover the address for correspondence with the leader of the secret party was a very important matter. Mr. Horton arranged with the Head Master of the Government School, Khan Saheb Idris Ahmed, that he would open and copy out the letters addressed to Indubhushan Mitra and send the copies to Mr. Horton. The original letters would then be sent to Indubhushan. Thus Horton was getting the information contained in all the letters addressed to Bismil. Bismil had written a letter to his associate at Aligarh. This letter was intercepted but the addressee was not arrested. This letter referred to a meeting of the Council to be held at Meerut Vaishya Orphanage. More things were known to Horton through this man and also through other letters. Bismil was convinced of this when, after he was arrested, he came to know certain things from a C.I.D. officer, which were not known to anybody else. Horton came to know of more things.

When Horton came to know of the Meerut meeting from different sources, he sent Sub-Inspector of the C.I.D. Burma Singh to watch the meeting. He had a local assistant, Pheru Singh. Meerut meeting took place on the 13th and 14th September, 1925.

On the 26th September, there were province-wide arrests and searches. Nearly forty persons were arrested from different parts of the province and more were arrested outside the province also. A letter to Indubhushan gave the clue that articles were kept in a student's room at Banaras. This room was of a Hindu University student. The police broke open the lock and they found in a box two rifles. The student, Rajkumar Sinha, was arrested at Kanpur. A letter addressed to Ramnath Pande of Banaras was recovered from Bismil and Pande was arrested. In the mantime Indubhushan wrote to Pande giving the information that Bismil had been arrested. On this Indubhushan was also arrested at Shahjahanpur. Banarsilal gave the news that he received the "Revolutionary" leaflets through a registered parcel from Banaras. On the basis of this information Rai Bahadur Jitendranath Mukherjee found out that four more registered parcels of consecutive numbers were sent from the Kamaksha post office to four different addresses. Kanpur addressee was Gopinath. On arrest he confessed and became crown witness. The student addressee of Raibareli was Kanwar Bahadur. He too confessed on arrest and became a prosecution witness. He gave the address of a relative of Banawarilal. While searching that place police found a trunk in which were a pistol, a 55 bore Webley revolver and some cartridges. The other addressee was Pranabesh Chatterjee of Jabbalpore. He was also arrested. After Indubhusan's arrest the Head Master, Khan Sahib Indris Ahmed, received another letter written from Chanda in Central Provinces. The name of the writer of the letter was Mohanlal Khatri. Police traced out Ramkrishna Khatri and arrested him at Poona.

Sachindranath Sanyal and Rajendranath Lahiri were brought from Calcutta after the latter was given 10 years, transportation in the Dakshineswar Bomb Case. Sachindra Nath Bakshi, Ashfaqulla and Chandrashekhar Azad went underground. Bakshi and Ashfaqulla were tried in the supplementary case after arrest. Bakshi was given transportation for life and Ashfaqullah was given capital sentence. Azad kept his promise and remained Azad (free) till he breathed his last.

As I have already stated, in the early hours of the 26th September, 1925, there was general round up of political suspects in various places of U. P.

People were also arrested in Bengal, Central Provinces, Maharashtra and the Punjab. All of them handcuffed and with barfetters, were brought to Lucknow District Jail under heavy police escorts. These wholesale arrests and ill-treatment of arrested persons, many of whom were men of public position, created a public resentment against the foreign rulers. In fact, Mr. Horton, the Special Superintendent of the C.I.D., had very little material in his possession for such large scale indiscriminate arrests and infliction of insults and humiliation on arrested persons. But he was very fortunate that after the arrests, damaging confessions were made by some of the accused persons. The interception of many letters also gave new clues for strengthening the case. Rai Bahadur Mukherjee played a big part by finding out the rifles from Raj Kumar Sinha's box. It was Mukherjee who traced the Post Office from where the parcels of "Revolutionary" leaflets were sent to different addresses. These proved to be very damaging for those who were accused. Really these things ultimately established the case. The main approver, Banarsilal, could not give any material evidence to prove the Kakori money action. But it was Banwarilal's confession that helped to prove the Kakori action, because Banwari had participated in it..

As the police eyes were fixed at Shahjahanpur, they succeeded in arresting Ram Prasad Bismil, Roshan Singh, Hargovind, Banarasilal and Prem Kishen Khanna. Prem Kishen Khanna was taking great interest in what police was doing when they were searching Bismil's house. Khan Bahadur Tasadduq Hussain of the Imperial C. I. D., therefore, made private enquiries about him and sent for him to be present in the Police Station with his licenced Mauser pistol. When he came he was arrested and sent to Jail. At Banaras Manmatha Nath Gupta was arrested. Suresh Chandra Bhattacharjee, Ram Dulare Trivedi and Virbhadra Tewari were arrested at Kanpur. Govind Charan Kar was arrested at Lucknow, Vishnu Saran Dublish at Meerut. A big case was about to be opened at Lucknow.

Pandit Motilal Nehru, the Swarajist leader in the Central Legislative Assembly, came to Lucknow and stayed with Pandit Jagat Narayan Mullah, the most prominent criminal lawyer of the Lucknow bar. Motilalji requested Pandit Mullah to take up the Kakori Conspiracy Case on behalf of the defence. Pandit Mullah was agreeable to the proposal, but stated that he would work for this case for 20 days every month and 10 days he would devote to earn for his family. This was evidently absurd and Nehruji went away disappointed at the attitude of Mullah. Before leaving Lucknow Pandit Motilal formed a Defence Committee for the case under the leadership of Pandit Govind Ballabh Pant. Saheed Ganesh Shankar Vidyarthi was an important member of this Committee and raised the major portion of the much needed fund.

The very next day after Motilalji left, Rai Sahab Durga Prasad, the Deputy S. P., C. I. D.

Assistant to Mr. Horton, gave Pandit Jagat Narain the offer to take charge of the prosecution and the Pandit readily accepted it and thus became the prosecution advocate in the Kakori Conspiracy Case. His nationalism vanished in thin air before his lust for money. Pandit Motilal resented this so much that he ceased to have anything to do with his family any more.

Half of the arrested persons were let off one by one even before the case came up in the Court. This was because Banarsilal and Indubhusan Mitra of Shahjahanpur turned approvers and Banwarilal of Raibareli became a confessing accused. From them the police came to know who were the persons really connected with revolutionary work.

Many lawyers joined the defence committee. Two Congress leaders, Pandit Pant and Mohanlal Saxena stood by the accused. Pandit Harkaran Nath Mishra came forward and also Shri C. B. Gupta, who had joined the bar that very year. Shri Manilal Kothari also joined the defence counsels' team along with eminent lawyers like R. F. Bahadurji, Ajit Prasad Agarwal and Daya Shankar Hazela.

WHAT THE KAKORI CASE WAS

Though the case started with the incident of a train money action, the Government realised that the real cause behind the train action was a very serious one. It was an armed challenge to the foreign domination of India by the dare-devil revolutionary youths, who did not believe in reformism but wanted to free India by an armed revolution.

The prosecution case was that there was a conspiracy to deprive the King Emperor of his sovereignty over British India by an armed revolution. The Kakori train action was only one of the incidents for the furtherance of the conspiracy to overthrow the foreign Government and thereby to make India free.

THE REAL BACKGROUND OF THE CONSPIRACY

Let us have a bird's eye view of the whole situation and try to realise how all these things came about.

During the First World War (1914-18) any Indian revolutionary actively tried to make India free from British yoke by an armed revolution with the help of England's deadly enemy, the German Government. The Indian revolutionaries inside India and abroad had combined in this great effort. They made immense sacrifice and stood intolerable suffering during the course of their activities. A glimpse of it can be had if one cares to read carefully the Sedition Committee Report, prepared and published by the Government of India not long after First World War was over.

The revolutionaries who had a hold on the youths had no faith in constitutionalism either. They continued with their task of making India free through an armed revolution though they had plunged themselves into the non-cooperation movement as well. But they knew that India could not be made free through open mass movements. So they briskly formed a net work of secret revolutionary organisations throughout the length and breadth of the country. They were never for compromise or reforms. Their goal had always been complete independence.

The U. P. Branch of the organisation was not an isolated body but a part and parcel of the All India organisation. Documentary evidence proved this fact conclusively in the Kakori Conspiracy Case, as we would see when we discuss the case.

A few sentences will show how the Kakori Case was closely linked up with the entire secret revolutionary activities in the whole of northern India in the period between 1923 to 1930. A member of this organisation, Dr. Sailendra Nath Chakravarty of Allahabad, received the maximum sentence in the Deoghar Conspiracy Case in east Bihar as one of its leaders. Jogendra Sukul, a recruit of this organisation at Banaras, became prominent in more than one case in Bihar and was ultimately transported to the Andamans. Though not declared absconders, the police were in search of Sardar Bhagat Singh in the name of Balwant Singh, the name that I gave him at Kanpur, and also of Jatin Das, whose name came in connection with the Kakori Case as Kali Babu and Kamini Kaka for whose identification, Banwarilal had gone to Calcutta, but failed to identify him. They were both in the Lahore Conspiracy Case in which Bhagat

Singh was hanged and Jatin Das laid down his life by hunger strike. Those who escaped from Lahore Conspiracy case were later roped in the Delhi Conspiracy Case. Chandrasekhar Azad, the Supreme Commander of the Hindustan Socialist Republican Army, was declared absconder in Kakori, Lahore and Delhi Conspiracy cases.

To take up here Dakshineshwar Bomb Case, we see that Rajendra Nath Lahiri who was a leader of Kakori Conspiracy Case, was also a leader of Dakshineshwar Bomb Case and was awarded the maximum punishment among those involved in it. It happened like this : Ram Prasad Bismil of Shahjahanpur wanted to learn the art of bomb making. Rajendra Lahiri, who had connections with Jatindra Nath Das, managed through Das that Ram Prasad Bismil would be taught bomb making and Das wrote Lahiri to send Ram Prasad to Calcutta. Lahiri wrote to Ram Prasad but due to some reason, he could not go. Rajendra Nath Lahiri himself went to Calcutta instead. Bismil had a grievance against Lahiri for this, as he expressed to me in jail.

In Calcutta Jatindra Nath Das introduced Rajendra Lahiri to persons who were experts in bomb making and thus he got himself associated in the experiment for bomb making in a hired house at Dakshineswar, a suburb of Calcutta. They hired two houses for this purpose, one in Dakshineswar and the other in Sobha Bazar. There was great enthusiasm among them for this kind of experiment.

One glaring example of the enthusiasm can be cited here. One of the accused in Dakshineswar Bomb Case, Dhrubesh Chatterji, sold war bonds worth ten thousand rupees, which was all that he had, for meeting the expenses of the experiment. When the police raided the houses many persons were arrested and revolvers, pistols, live-bombs, cartridges, chemicals, explosives and acids along with some literature and books on the art and science of bomb making were found.

After they were sentenced in the Sobha Bazar-Dakshineswar Case, Rajendra Lahiri was brought to Lucknow as an accused in the Kakori Case, and the rest of the accused were sent to Alipore New Central Jail. There Rai Bahadur Bhupendra Nath Chatterjee, of the Special Branch of C. I. D. used to pay frequent visits to have a chat with political detenus to find out some more clues about revolutionaries outside the jails.

This act of a C.I.D. Officer in jail was very much disliked by the accused in Sobha Bazar-Dakshineswar Bomb Case. They protested that C.I.D. men had no jurisdiction inside the jail. But their protest went in vain. So they planned to put an end to Chatterji's life. They were kept in cells and the outlet of the enclosure was through a narrow lane. One day when Bhupendra Nath Chatterji was passing through that lane, they caught hold of him and gave him a sound thrashing. He died on the spot and for this murder two were given capital sentences and the rest were awarded heavy punishments.

It was a militant group of revolutionaries who were accused in the Bomb Case and then in the murder of Chatterji. The more explosive expression of the militant spirit of the group was Chittagong Armoury Raid Case led by Surjya Sen, which took place in 1930 after four years of Dakshineswar Case. Surjya Sen himself was connected with the Kakori prisoners. After the Chittagong Armoury Raid, he absconded and was arrested after three years and hanged.

Thus it will be seen that the Kakori Conspiracy Case had a very great significance in the revolutionary activities of northern India. Normally a man is an ordinary being but under abnormal circumstances at times he can work wonders. This happens when he gets inspired. The potential energy in him becomes kinetic. He is aroused and awakened from slumber. He kicks and jumps and works with great energy. That was the U. P. organisation at that time and whoever came in close touch with it was inspired.

What has been written above would show that our organisation was fairly big and within the course of a few years it spread widely. In all parts of northern India and even beyond, the work was progressing with much energy and drive. In fact, the work was not new. The tradition and history of the past was there and the field was more or less prepared. Large number of old revolutionaries also came forward and added stimulation to the movement which redoubled one urge, energy and vigour.

New recruits were found everywhere.

During the 1921 Movement, Mahatma Gandhi had given the slogan : "Education may wait, but Swaraj cannot," And youths came forward into the movement and pushed it forward. But when the Movement was suddenly withdrawn these youths were taken aback. Some rejoined colleges, some went to service, some took to other avocations ; but the dare-devils amongst them were disgusted. They searched for new avenues and easily became recruits to the revolutionary movement as soon as they came in touch with the secret organisations. The revolutionaries were thus getting the better elements from the youth. Only they could make the utmost sacrifices for a worthy ideal. The purpose was such that it inspired confidence in them. They could go to any length for the attainment of the greatest objective fixed before them.

Sets of such persons had collected in northern India in nineteen twenties with the object of removing the country's bondages. The Kakori Train Dacoity was the work of a batch of ten such persons. They did not hesitate the least to stop the train, overpower the men, break open the iron safe and decamp with the money quietly while in the train itself there were fourteen armed men and two more armed European army men (vide Ram Prasad Bismil's autobiography). These armed men dared not face those dare-devils, who were firing shots every five minutes to keep the men in the train inside the closed compartments.

CHAPTER X

KAKORI UNDERTRIALS BEFORE THE SPECIAL MAGISTRATE SYED AINUDDIN

I have given a brief review of the general position of the revolutionaries at the time when they were arrested from different places in connection with the Kakori Train Dacoity.

The undertrials were at first kept separate from one another and later in a separate barrack in the jail outside the Circle. The ration supplied was unedible and therefore they had to spend their own money to supplement the ration. The jailor, Rai Saheb Champalal, was a good man by nature. This was the only good thing in a foul atmosphere.

The law court gives much importance to identification of the accused persons. But the police are clever enough to befool the court, of course in collaboration with the jail officials. The police have the closest relationship with the jail staff. They can, therefore, have any man identified by anybody. Undertrials to be identified were to stand in a line, called parade, mixed up with some other people. They were to be picked up from the parade by the person, who came for the purpose of identification. The jail warder, who escorted the man would tell him the positlon of the man on the identification parade or the police man or the jail officer accompanying the Magistrate would point towards the position of the man to be identified and accordingly the man charged was picked up easily on the parade. In a political case in the British days even Magistrates aided the prosecution for personal gain. The case of Syed Ainuddin, the Special Magistrate of this case, was a typical one in this respect. He had no scruples in damning the enemies of his masters. He earned Government titles, promotion, etc. married an Anglo-Indian girl and after retirement from Government service became more notorious as a manager of a native state by perpetrating various sorts of oppressions on the people. Britishers also selected Muslims to deal with the revolutionaries because the latter thought that the revolutionary movement was mainly a Hindu movement and Muslims would not, therefore, make common cause with the accused.

The Magistrate chosen to try us was a Mohammadan, Syed Ainuddin. Before the Kakori arrests Mr. Horton, we have seen, had concentrated his attention on Ram Prasad Bismil of Shahjahanpur and that was the reason why Khan Bahadur Tasadduk Hussain, Dy. S. P. of the Imperial C. I. D., a Muslim, was deputed to Shahjahanpur. Mr. Khairat Nabi was the Prosecuting Inspector and was assisted by the Khan Bahadur during the proceedings of the case. And the man sent to Howrah station with a party of a dozen men to arrest me in Calcutta in 1924 was Inspector Mohammad Ismail of the Special Branch C. I. D. All these show how the British relied more on the Muslim officials than on the Hindu officials.

Though some Muslims benefited much in this way by acting against the revolutionary movement, the revolutionaries did not take my notice of this. Although they were quite conscious of this, they did not take it very seriously because they were patriotic enough to disregard the nefarious policy of the Britishers. Divide and rule was the general policy of Britain in India and they followed this even in their dealings with the revolutionaries. The revolutionaries were far above these things. Revolutionary brotherhood had reached a stage where there was no caste or even religion, no untouchability or even separate identity. Success they knew was remote, and sufferings and sacrifices were their constant companions.

The Special Magistrate, Syed Ainuddin, was a very clever person, and was a master in the art of stabbing a man from the back. He would keep one fascinated by his manner of talking sweetly and laughing all the time. But if one reads his report of the identification parade or the Commital Order one would at once realise that he was a more bitter enemy of the revolutionaries than the Britishers themselves. He did not hesitate to give false evidence against us on oath before the Special Sessions Judge that myself and Govinda Charan Kar knew Urdu, although he wrote in a note while taking my statement in his court : " He does not know Urdu.

Therefore, his statement is taken in English." On this our Counsel, Mr. B. K. Chaudhury, Bar-at Law, wanted to cross examine him to prove that he was biased against us. But the Special Sessions Judge, Mr. Hamilton, threatened him that if he failed to prove that the Magistrate was biased, he would write remarks against him in his judgement. Ram Prasad Bismil, who was undefended, also was not allowed by the Judge to question him. Such was the impartiality of the British Judge.

IN THE COURT OF SPECIAL MAGISTRATE

The case started in the court of the Special Magistrate on the 4th January, 1926. Before the case started in the court police had withdrawn cases against many, who were evidently harassed and humiliated for no fault of theirs. The following were the persons let off: Mr. Shitala Sahai, Mr. Chandradhar Jauhari and Mr. Chandrabhal Jauhari, Mr. Ramdutt Shukla, Mr. Mohanlal Gautam, Mr. Baburam Gupta, Mr. Harnam Sundarlal, Mr. Devendra Bhattacharjee, Mr. Sarat Chandra Guha, Mr. Kalidas Bose, Mr. Bhairon Singh and Mr. Indravikram Sinha.

Twenty-five accuseds were put up before the dock that day. Cases against two-Virbhadra Tewari and Pandit Jyoti Shankar Dixit were withdrawn. Two became approvers,—Banarsilal and Indubhusan Mitra,—both from Shahjahanpur, and they were granted pardon.

So the number of accused in the Magistrate's court finally was 21. From the very beginning the case was not called the Kakori Dacoity case but the Kakori Conspiracy Case.

Banarsilal, the main approver, was the first witness examined by the prosecution lawyer, Pandit Jagat Narain Mullah. Let me quote an extract from his statement before the court, as recorded by the Magistrate: "In 1924, at the end of the hot weather or at the beginning of rains a man came to Shahjahanpur. He passed himself off under names which were clearly fictitious, "Roy Mahashay" or "Roy Dada". This man (identified Jogesh Chandra Chatterji) is the resident of a village in the Dacca district of Bengal. According to the approver this meeting was to discuss the formation of a branch of a revolutionary society at Shahjahanpur. Ram Prasad was appointed Provincial Organiser. Ashfaqullah was appointed his assistant. According to Banarsilal, Roy Mahashay had said that the English were to be slain and turned out of India by force and an independent Indian Republic was to be established. He said that all the public of India was to be armed and to be made acquainted with the aims and objects of this revolutionary society. He also said that the money required was to be obtained by dacoities. It was to be collected for getting arms and for propaganda. This was to be by pamphlets, books, leaflets and other printed matters. Roy Mahashay said names should not be given or asked and any harm caused by any member of the society would be punished by death."

Our defence had decided that witnesses would not be cross examined in the lower court. So the Magistrate was recording the prosecution evidence only and our counsels were also watching the proceedings. In all there were 56 hearings and 247 witnesses appeared. At the end statements of 21 accused were recorded, but they all reserved their real statements for the Sessions Court.

There was nothing very remarkable in these proceedings, except a few things which deserve to be mentioned. The accused were brought every day to the Court under heavy armed escorts. The undertrials used to be in one big bus in between two buses full of armed escorts. We were all under bar fetters. We used to shout slogans and sing inspiring nationalist songs when we were brought to the Court. Sometimes the songs were accompanied by the sounds produced by striking our fetters against one another. Every day when we were driven through the different routes from the jail to the court and back, crowds of men lined up on the road side out of curiosity. This went on for a year and a half in the city of Lucknow and it was itself a big propaganda for the death-defying revolutionaries of India.

From the very beginning Pandit Harkarannath Mishra took much interest in our defence, but we were becoming suspicious about him. Gradualy it was well established that he was a friend of the prosecution and not of the accused. So we became a bit careful, but it was too late.

One day the Magistrate subtly suggested that Mr. Mishra being a senior man may act as the leader of the defence. At this remark of the Magistrate every one was astonished. Pandit Gobind Ballabh Pant stood up and objected to this in a mild but dignified manner. Immediately after he resumed his seat the Magistrate apologised. This proved to us that Mr. Mishra was too much friendly with the Magistrate and our conclusion was that he was a friend of the prosecution too.

When the case was to be started in the Sessions, Babu Mohanlal Saksena guggested to us that we should apply to the Government for a lawyer for our defence at Government cost. We wanted to mention Mohanlalji's name as our lawyer in the application. But though agreeable to our suggestion, he was definitely against mentioning any name. He stated that if our petition was granted we might suggest his name. This was a mistake and he realised it later. In reply to our application, the Government announced the appointment of Mr. Harakaran Nath Mishra. We replied that we had no confidence in him and boycotted him. So throughout the eight months trial Mr. Mishra was defending the confessing accused Banwarilal, who required defence and he (Mishra) was drawing from the Government rupees sixty five per day for a work which he never did.

Mr. Mishra was after Pranabesh Chatterjee, too, in collaboration with Pranabesh's elder brother, Sukumar Chatterjee, who was himself an approver in the Sanfransisco Conspiracy case in America. Sukumar Chatterjee wanted Pranabesh to make a clean breast of everything and thereby get out of the jail. Mishra too was trying the same thing. Pranabesh was even separated from us and kept in the Central Jail for some months. He was meeting us in the court and did not like to betray his friends for personal safety.

But after the Sessions Court judgment when Pranabesh was kept alone in a district jail, his brother succeeded in getting a statement from him and placed it before the Chief Court appellate judges. A new charge against me was brought in this statement. But the judges could not accept it as evidence according to law. They said that they prosecution might start a separate case if they wanted. What did Pranabesh gain by making the statement ? His sentence was reduced only by a year from five to four. The statement was embodied in the judgement of the Chief Court. So Pranabesh was badly exposed by the Chief Court. This must have been a terrible shock to Pranabesh and the poor fellow committed suicide in Delhi after his release. What a tragedy.

In his statement dated 24th July, 1927, addressed to the Chief Court, Pranabesh stated how he was recruited when a student of the Kashi Vidyapith by Manmatha Nath Guha, how Jogesh Chatterjee became his teacher, how Rajen Lahiri sent him to Allahabad along with M. N. Gupta, how he met Jogesh Chatterjee there and then participated in a village money action. He did not, however, mention one very important fact that it was he, Pranabesh Chatterjee, who recruited Saheed Chandrashekhar Azad, the future commander of the Party whose statue stands at the Azad Park, where he laid down his life in 1931.

Another notable happening was the arrival of Sardar Bhagat Singh at Lucknow when the case was proceeding in the lower court. One morning when our buses were turning from the Abbott Road to the Cantonment Road towards the Roshanuddaula Court at Kaiserbagh, Bhagat Singh was standing near the corner of the turning and after we had taken our seats in the dock inside the court room, he too, entered the court room along with other visitors and occupied a seat very near us. Till then he was a Sikh, wearing an embroidered turban and Jodhpur Khaki breaches. He kept seated the whole day and was all along quiet with his usual smiling face. The policemen, the formidable C. I. D. brains were there as also their pet Magistrate. But nobody took any notice of this fine looking and well-attired Sikh youth. He stood in the garden in front of the Court when our buses were turning. This was the last time that I saw Sardar Bhagat Singh.

In the Magistrate's Court another note-worthy occurrence was the sudden release of Virbhadra Tewari of Kanpur on the 29th January, 1926. This was unexpected as there was sufficient evidence to give him a long sentence. Sanyal, Ram Prasad and myself had a long discussion about it and reached the unanimous conclusion that he had managed to become a favourite of the police.

The lower court hearings gradually came to an end. The Government prosecutor, Pandit Jagat Narain, made his concluding speech in a packed court in the presence of all our defence lawyers. Why I do not know, he spoke highly of me. His word I still remember. "Now I have come to know the whole life history of Jogesh Chandra Chatterji and I can say without any hesitation that he is a great patriot. Had I been a revolutionary I would have made him my leader, but not the great Pandit or the showy Sanyal." These were his words. As soon as he sat down I asked Jagat Narainji whether he would help me with money when I was free again. He said, "Yes, provided you do not shoot me." He was alive for some years after our release. But I had not the least intention of meeting him.

The Magistrate took an unusually long time in preparing the Commital Order. However, when it was out the reason of the delay was crystal clear to us. He left no stone unturned in drawing the worst picture of each and every accused person. Of course, it is a fact that I took a leading part in the conspiracy. But the prosecution evidence was very weak. Our defence Counsel, Mr. B. K. Chaudhury was absolutely sure that I would have been released even if the lower court gave me any sentence if our case went to the Calcutta High Court. In the Sessions Court my case was to be argued by Mr. Mohanlal Saksena, because two of the Assessors did not know English and therefore, Chaudhury did not like to argue. When Saksenaji studied the case throughly he told me that the case against me was very weak.

There was no evidence from Banaras or Kanpur. The approver had told in his original statement to the police that I came to Shahjahanpur and stayed with him in his house for six days. But he changed it in the court and stated that I was putting up with Ram Prasad. This change was essential for the prosecution, because Banarsilal's servant and neighbour identified M. N. Gupta and others, who stayed there only for a day, whereas they could not identify me, though I really stayed with him for six days.

The next evidence against me was the recovery of the documents from me at the time of my arrest in Calcutta. On this the search witness wrote, " All except the item No. 1 in the first page found in my presence." At this the police officer threatened him and compelled him to write again, "N.B. Item No. 1 in page 1 was found out by a police officer which is alleged to have been picked up by a gentleman present on the spot." This was an important document in the Kakori Conspiracy Case as Exhibit 198.

Syed Ainuddin tried his best to prove me as the leader of the Conspiracy by various inferences, real and imaginary. In his committal order on page 17 the Magistrate writes, "In the words of Banwarilal he met Jogesh in hot weather of 1923 at the Purshottam Das park at Allahabad who had asked Banwari's name and address. When Banwari met Jogesh the first question which the latter said him was about Bandijiban. When Banwari said that he liked the book very much, Jogesh promised to give him more books free of cost provided he gave them to other persons also to read. Here it is described in a manner as if Jogesh was living at Allahabad. But the Diary of Rai Bahadur J. K. Mukherjee Dy. S. P., C.I.D., says that Jogesh Chatterjee arrived at Banaras and lived at 164 Ganesh Mahal for 3 months and shifted to 20 Pataleswar."

The Committal Order continues "At first Banwari thought that this man, that is Jogesh, was Sachindra Sanyal, but Rajendranath Lahiri told him afterwards that he was Jogesh Chandra Chatterjee. Rajendra also told him that the mission of Jogesh was to set up revolutionary societies in these provinces and that he had come from Bengal only for this purpose." Then Banwari stated that Jogesh sent him to Pratapgarh where he formed a society. He further stated that Jogesh received him at Kanpur and introduced Rajendranath Lahiri to him and said that in future he should deal wit Lahiri under whose command the district of Pratapgarh had been placed for spreading the revolutionary movement.

To hide the weakness of the prosecution argument because of my long presence at Allahabad and my frequent conversation with Banwari the

Magistrate stated. "It would appear from the story given by Banwari that when at Banaras Jogesh used to visit Allahabad with the object of spreading revolutionary propaganda there. There is no reason to disbelieve it specially when evidence has been tendered to show that the Sanyal family was residing at Allahabad and a Hindi translation of the of the book Bandijiban was published from there. Naturally Jogesh would turn to Allahabad and hold consultations with Sachindra Nath Sanyal, who must have been known to him as a prominent revolutionary." Here the Magistrate without any evidence connects me with Sanyal as co-conspirators, evidently to show his overloyalty to the foreign rulers and thereby meet personal ends at the cost of the revolutionary fighters for the country's freedom.

The Magistrate further stated "Banwari's statements further shows that Jogesh had entrusted the work of Banaras to Lahiri and thus explains the transfer of his activities from Banaras to Kanpur and other places."

He continued : "Banwari has fixed the presence of Jogesh at Kanpur in the hot weather of 1924 and he is supported by the evidence of Rai Saheb Durga Prasad, who says that according to his secret sources he had come to know in the month of July 1924 that Suresh Bhattacharya was associated at Kanpur with a suspect Bengali, known by the name of Roy. Here again is the further corroboration to the evidence of Banarsilal, the main approver, that Jogesh was called Roy Mahashay by Ram Prasad when he came to Shahjahanpur to establish a revolutionary society there. From Kanpur Jogesh directed his attention to different places and amongst such places he visited Jhansi and placed Bakshi at that place in order to spread the revolutionary propaganda. It should not be forgotten that this is the same S. N. Bakshi, who had rented a room for Jogesh in house No. 164, Ganesh Mahal, Banaras."

"After Jhansi we find Jogesh at Shahjahanpur in the beginning of the rainy season of 1924 vide Banarasilal. Banarsi was taken to meet Jogesh by Ashfaqullah to the house of Ram Prasad. He was introduced to Jogesh and was taken in confidence. Ram Prasad was appointed the organiser and Ashfaqulla his assistant, while Banarsi being a married man, was made a sympathiser."

"We find Jogesh again at Kanpur in the first week of October 1924 when a meeting of the Provincial Council of the revolutionary society was held at that place. There could not be a better corroboration of this statement than paper recovered from the person of Jogesh. This paper is really a record of the proceedings of the meeting of the Provincial Council at Kanpur on the 3rd October 1924. Its writer has not been discovered but Jogesh is certainly responsible for its contents as long as he is unable to explain how he got it and what it is about. This paper says that more or less efficient representative acting as district organisers had been posted at Banaras, Allahabad, Pratapgarh, Kanpur, Lacknow, Fatehpur, Mainpuri, Jaunpur,

Jhansi, Hamirpur, Farrukkabad, Etawah, Agra, Aligarh, Mathura, Bulandshahar, Meerut, Delhi, Etah, Bareilly, Pilibhit, Shahjahanpur, Muzaffarnagar, etc."

Then we read : "We are now at a stage at which revolutionary centres were established throughout these provinces. We also know by now the names of Jogesh, Suresh, Pandit, Banarsilal, Indu, Lahiri, Banwari, Bakshi, Ashfaq, Roshan Singh, Ram Dulare, G. C. Kar, Ramnath Pandey, M. N. Gupta, S. N. Sanyal, and Pranabesh, as those who were connected with the revolutionary movement. Jogesh has had his full share in the movement. His arrest in Calcutta in October 1924 and subsequent detention under Bengal Ordinance, prematuraly put a stop to his activities. I have dealt with the activities of Jogesh in great detail. He being one of the founders of the revolutionary societies in these provinces, naturally his movement form an important part of the evidence of conspiracy in the case."

After we were committed to the sessions there was a distinct change in the general attitude. The fear of betrayal by weaker friends was no longer there. All had the stern reality before them. Ashfaqullah and S. N. Bakshi, too, had been arrested and a separate case was started against them. They wanted to go undefended, because by our example they had come to know that in a case like this the defence was meaningless. Still we requested Mr. C. B. Gupta to defend them.

But they did not agree to the proposal of Mr. Gupta. Then I wrote a personal letter to Bàkshi through Mr. Gupta that when in the original case we put defence, the supplementary one going undefended would have no effect on the public. They agreed to put up defence and Ashfaquallah was defended by Gupta.

HUNGER STRIKE

All the Kakori undertrials were now in a fighting mood. We had already paid thousands of rupees in supplementing the jail ration and we were determined not to do so any more. We decided to start a hunger strike demanding special treatment as political prisoners. Prior to this I had a severe attack of fever and was in hospital for many days. I was an old hunger striker and also the prime mover in this. But my friends would not allow me to join the strike because of the extreme weak condition of my health.

Hunger strikers were kept in separate groups and non-hunger strikers, myself and Lala Hargovind of Shahjahanpur were sent to the hospital. The Superintendent of the jails, Captain Salamatullah, knew well that I was the prime mover and as I was not on strike he had a great suspicion on me and transferred me to the Central Jail where Rajendranath Lahiri was confined alone. He too, was not on hunger strike as we requested him not to do so. I was to be sent under bar-fetters but I protested strongly and the jailor, Rai Saheb Champalal, agreed to send me unfettered after I had argued with him.

In the Central Jail again the Anglo-Indian Head Jailor came for the same purpose of putting me under fetters. I vehemently protested stating that I could not be fettered in the normal course unless and until I committed some very serious jail offence and were punished for that by the Jail Superintendent. Moreover, I was only an undertrial and therefore, the question of putting me under fetters could not arise at all. The jailor said that he was acting under the orders of the Superintendent. I said in reply that the Superintendent could not give any arbitrary orders and even if he did so, I would refuse to obey it The jailor went away disappointed.

Next morning the Superintendent was very angry with me and said that so many were on hunger strike and that the addition of one more would make no difference. After the Superintendent left the ward I took the decision to join the hunger strike even against the friendly entreaties of Lahiri. I gave the formal notice in writing that I was on hunger strike. My stand was that I did not start it earlier due to poor state of health and also because of the request of friends. I further stated that I had to go on hunger strike and that as a true revolutionary I had no other course open but to accept the implicit challenge contained in the jail Superintendent's words. I made it clear that the Rubicon has been crossed and that there was no going back.

Fortunately for us, Lahiri had two convict overseers to alternately watch on him. Both of them were old men, sentenced to transportation for life in a Hindu-Muslim riot case and they were very sympathetic to the political prisoners. I was to be removed to the hospital cell, where a new man-height wall was being erected. I got this information through the two watchmen. Next day I was actually taken to the cell, which now had two doors, the second one was fixed on the next wall which was erected only the previous day. The key to the outer door was kept with the Head Jailor and the one of the inner door was with the senior Doctor, so that my cell could not be opened unless both the jailor and the doctor were there. But an old convict was also locked up with me. This caused a good deal of trouble. The man was addicted to chew tobacco and he was in great distress first due to confinement and more so because he could not get tobacco which though a prohibited article was available in jail.

When I was leaving the European Ward, where Lahiri was kept, I left instructions and some money with him to send the news of my hunger strike out. This was done and the news alarmed the Superintendent. He came prepared to feed me forcibly. I objected and stated that I was not weak and hence required no food so soon. But he came determined. Unable to pass the tube properly through my nostril he spread milk deliberately over my pillow, nose and clothes ; much milk entered both my ears. My pillow, which was my own, was taken away on the plea that it was wet. But when I received it back after the hunger strike was over, I found it cut in several places with razor blade. Evidently the cotton was taken out in search of contraband articles, money, paper, pencils, etc. From the noon time I felt severe pain inside my right ear and the pain became unbearable. I shouted for the doctor for nearly two or three hours but there was no response from any quarter. Late in the afternoon the doctor came after both the gates were opened. The compounder gave me fomentation for a long time and only then I was relieved of the terrible pain.

Owing to our hunger strike the Court could not be held. The authorities wanted to hold the court inside the jail. The question was whether the accused under hunger strike could attend the court. The Jail Superintendent expressed doubt. The Civil Surgeon Col. Hunter, was sent to examine us and report. My condition was bad. The Col. was brought to my cell by the Superintendent. The latter asked me to get up from the bed and walk a little. I did so. The Civil Surgeon felt my pulse and asked me to lie down in bed. Then he examined me. He asked me : 'How do you feel ?' I described my condition stating at the same time that I had been on hunger strike several times before. After hearing me he said that my description of the state of my body was quite correct. He also gave me the information that once as a doctor he abstained from taking food for three days with the object of feeling the symptoms which fasting develops in the body. He reported, even if the Court was held in jail, I would be unfit to attend it.

Now the Government had no other alternative than to come to a compromise. The Magistrate along with the Jail Superintendent made their attempts to revoke our decisions. Both were Muslims. When they failed the Judge came forward. Sanyal Babu was negotiating and we gave him full authority to do so. But ultimately Ram Prasad Bismil intervened and settled that we would get articles worth ten annas per head per day for our food and also extra vegetables from the jail garden. Our demand was that as political prisoners we deserved special treatment. This was of course for the undertrial stage. The Judge promised that he would write in his judgement that we were political prisoners and in fact he did so.

PLAN TO ESCAPE

Ram Prasad was hoping against hope that he would not be hanged. While the case was in lower court he was not agreeable to escape from the jail though it could be arranged without much difficulty. It is said that he refused to escape because that would have jeopardised the position of a constable in the jail who came from Shahjahanpur and that of jailor Champalal who was very nice to us.

But I did not think that this had anything to do with his refusal. I had much private talks with him on these points. He did not care for a life transportation and he said to me that he would come out with his health in tact even after serving fourteen years in jail as an ordinary prisoner. I believe that he could do so, so fine was his health. At the beginning myself and Sanyal were not in favour of putting up defence but Bismil was keen on it. Due to this we decided to put up defence. In the Sessions Court he fully realised that he would be given capital punishment. Now he himself pressed me to plan for jumping the jail. But the jail authorities, too, had by now taken special precautionary measures.

I made a plan, read it out to Bismil, ciphered it and sent it to Mr. Jitendranath Sanyal, whom I had met while I was being transferred from Hazaribagh to Lucknow. I took Mr. Chaudhury into confidence about this and he gave full approval as the court was determined to give us the maximum sentence.

Hacksaw blades were smuggled inside and gratings of the windows of Bismil were cut unnoticed. Bismil, myself, G. G. Kar and M. N. Gupta—these four were to escape. We were to scale the inside row of walls and go near the drain of the main wall and push through a stick, the other end of which would be fastened with a string which again would be held by our friends outside. As soon as we pushed the stick the friends would know of our arrival and would throw a rope ladder over the wall for us and catch hold of the other end and thus we would scale the wall one by one.

We administered sleeping drugs to one of the two warders on duty outside and also to the two convict watchmen inside our barrack. The warder outside was fast asleep under the influence of the drug, but the second warder was very alert. The drug did not have much effect on one of the convict watchmen also. He was feeling sleepy but was struggling to keep himself awake, particularly because the warder outside was again and again shouting to keep him alert. Because of this we could not get out.

Outside the main wall our friends, including one very important person, who made history in the revolutionary movement of India, the great martyr Surjya Sen, or the immortal " Masterda " of the Chittagong Armoury Raid of 1930, were waiting with the rope ladder, arms and even bombs. When they came to the spot they found an armed warder was patrolling covering that part of the wall only which was over-looking our barrack. When they saw this they themselves formed into two groups, one for over-powering the armed warder and the other to help us to get out by throwing the rope ladder for us and then to see that we could jump down smoothly. They remained there the whole night and went away diasppointed owing to our failure to get out of our barracks.

There were three important documents in possession of the prosecution in the Kakori Conspiracy case which are enclosed, (1) The Constitution of the Hindustan Republican Association, (2) The 'Revolutionary' a pamphlet distributed on behalf of the association and (3) the Proceedings of the Council Meeting.

DOCUMENT NO. 1

"THE HINDUSTAN REPUBLICAN ASSOCIATION"

NAME :

The name of the Association shall be the Hindustan Republican Association.

OBJECT :

"The object of the Association shall be to establish a Federated Republic of the United States of India by an organised and armed revolution.

"The final form of the constitution of the Republic shall be framed and declared by the representatives of the people at the time when they will be in a position to enforce their decisions.

"The basic principle of the Republic shall be universal suffrage and the abolition of all systems which make any kind of exploitation of man by man possible."

CONSTITUTION : GOVERNING BODY

"The Governing body of the Association shall be the Central Council composed of the representatives of every province of India. All decisions of the Central Council shall be arrived at by unanimous consent. The Central Council shall be vested with absolute powers.

"The principal function of the Central Council shall be to supervise, adjust and coordinate the activities in the different provinces of which it shall have full knowledge.

"The Central Council shall be in direct charge of the work to be carried on in countries outside India."

PROVINCIAL ORGANISATIONS

"There shall be a Committee ordinarily of five (5) men representing the five (5) different departments of the Association in every province which shall regulate all the activities of the Association in the province.

"All decisions of the Committee shall be arrived at by unanimous consent."

DEPARTMENTS

"Every Provincial Organisation shall have the following departments :

1. Propaganda.
2. Collection of man.

3. Collection and storage of arms and ammunitions.

4. Collection of funds and terrorism.

5. Foreign connection.

6. Propaganda shall be carried on :

a) by an open and a secret press

b) through private conversations

c) through public platforms.

d) through a system of organised Kathas and

e) through magic lantern slides.

2. Collection of men shall be done by organisers in charge of different districts.

3. Funds shall be collected generally by means *of voluntary subscriptions and occasionally contributions* exacted by force. In extreme cases of repressions by agent or agents of a foreign government it shall be the duty of the association to retaliate in whatever form it shall consider suitable.

4. Every effort shall be made to arm every member of the Association, but all such arms shall be stored at different centres and be used according to the directions of the Provincial Committee only.

No arms shall be removed from any place in the district or used without the knowledge and the permission of the district organisers or the officer incharge of this department,

5. Foreign Connections : This department shall carry on its work under the direct order from the C. C.

DISTRICT ORGANISER : HIS DUTIES :

'The district organiser shall be in sole charge of the members of the district.

'He shall try to start branches of this association in every part of his district. In order to have efficient recruitment he should keep himself in touch with the different public bodies and institutions in his district.

'The district organisers shall be subordinate in every way to the provincial committee who shall supervise the district into separate groups and see that the different groups do not know each other.

'So far as possible the district organiser of any province must not know the activities of each other and if possible they must also not know each other by person or by name.

'No district organiser shall leave his station without previously informing his superior.'

QUALIFICATIONS OF A DISTRICT ORGANISER :

1. He must have the tact and the ability to guide and handle men of different temperaments.
2. He must have the capacity to grasp political, social and economic problems of the present day with special reference to his motherland,
3. He must be able to grasp the spirit of the history of India, with special reference to the particular civilisation which India has evolved.

4. He must have faith in the mission and the destiny of a free India, which is to bring harmony in the different spheres of human activities both spiritual and material.

5. He must be courageous and self-sacrificing without which all his brilliant qualities will have no real value.

PROVINCIAL COUNCIL AND CENTRAL COUNCILS :

P. C. and C. C. members must see that every member of this association gets full scope and ample opportunity to develop and use his individual abilities, without which the association will tend to disintegrate.

PROGRAMME

All the activities of the association shall be divided into two parts : Public and Private.

PUBLIC

1. To start associations in the forms of clubs, libraries, seva samitis and the like.

2. To start labour and peasant organisations suitable men must be engaged on behalf of the association to organise and control labourers in the different factories, the railways and in the coal-fields, and instil tnto their mind that they are not for the revolution but that the revolution is for them.

Similarly the Kisans must also be organised.

3. To start weekly papers in every province to propagate the idea of an independent Indian Republic.

4. To publish booklets and pamphlets with a view to enlightening the public as to the course of events and the current of thoughts as prevalent in the countries outside India.

5. To utilise the influence of the Congress and other public activities as far as possible."

PRIVATE

(a) To establish a secret press and through it to publish such literature which cannot easily be published openly.

(b) To circulate such literature.

(c) To establish branches of this association in every part of the country, district by district.

(d) To collect funds in as many ways as possible.

(e) To send suitable men to foreign countries where they may get military or scientific training so that they may become military or scientific experts to take charge of armies and ammunition factories at the time of open rebellion.

(f) To import arms and ammunitions and also to manufacture them as far as possible, in the country.

(g) To remain in close touch and to cooperate with the Indian revolutionaries outside India.

(h) To get the members of this association enlisted into the present army.

(i) To enlist the sympathy of the public to our cause by occasional retaliatory measures and propaganda and thus create a band of sympathisers."

MEMBERSHIP

"All members shall be recruited by organisers in charge of different districts in every province. Every member must be ready to devote his whole time for the association and to risk his life if necessary.

"He must obey the commands of the district organiser.

IMPLICITY

"He should develop his own initiative and remember that the success of the association depends much on the resourcefulness, the initiative and the sense of duty of its individual members.

"He must behave in a manner that may not prejudice the cause for which this association stands or may not do any harm directly or indirectly to this organisation.

"No member of this association shall belong to any other organisation without the consent of the district organiser.

"No member shall leave his station without informing the district organiser about it.

"Every member must try to avoid being suspected of revolutionary connections by the police or public.

"Every member must remember that his individual behaviour and mistakes might lead to the ruin of the whole organisation.

"No member shall conceal anything from the district organiser as far as his public life is concerned.

"Members who will betray shall be punished with expulsion or death.

" The authority of punishment shall rest entirely with the P. C."

DOCUMENT NO. 2

JUDGMENT

The Hon'ble Sir Louis Stuart, Kt. C. I. E. I. C. S. Chief Justice

The Hon'ble Mr. Justice Muhammed Raza Khan Bahadur.

Between the 28th and 31st of January, 1925 a four page printed pamphlet was circulated secretly by post and by hand in the United Provinces and other parts of India. This pamphlet bore the name of no printing press. The revolutionary : An organ of the Revolutionary party of India. It was called the first number of the first, and bore the date of the Ist January, 1925.

This was the first paragraph :

> Chaos is necessary of the birth of a new star and the birth of life is accompanied by agony and pain. India is also taking a new birth, and is passing through that inevitable phase, when chaos and agony shall play their destined role, when all calculations shall prove futile, when the wise and the mighty shall be bewildered by the simple and the weak, when great empire shall crumble down and new nations shall arise and surprise humanity with the splendour and glory which shall be all its own.

In continuation it was stated that a new power had come into existence in India, that power being the revolutionary movement amongst young men, which inspite of all opposition would eventually triumph. This movement had withstood repression for twenty years. It was now stronger than ever before, and its prospects were brighter. The writer then proceeded to justify the movement on the ground that India was ruled without justification by foreigners whose authority rested on dominion by the sword. The sword of these foreigners was to be met by the sword the Indians.

The writer then proceeded to declare the immediate object of the revolutionary party which was 'to establish a Federal Republic of the united States of India by an organised and armed revolution.' Under this Republic there would be universal manufactures and the shipping industry. The legislature would control the executive. The aims of the revolutionary party were stated to be international rather than national 'and in this respect it follows the foot steps of the great Indian Rishis of the glorious past and of Bolshevik Russia in the modern age. There would be equal rights for all communities, general cooperation and a spiritual recognition of the realities of life.

The writer continues that the time was not ripe for the disclosure of the policy and the programme of the party. The party reserved to itself freedom to associate or not to associate with the Indian Congress. Then follow the words: But this party views all constitutional agitations in the country with contempt and ridicule. After some amplification of this idea came the following passage :

Young Indian : Shake off illusions, face realities with a stout heart, and do not avoid struggles, difficulties and sacrifices. The inevitable is to come. Do not be misguided any more. Peace and tranquillity you cannot have and India's liberty can never be achieved through peaceful and legal means. The following memorable words of a great English author Mr. Robertson may serve to make the wise men of India wiser still.

The movement and programme of reform was mainly the achievment of Irish and protestant leaders to whom British statesmen had revealed the fatal secret that 'England could be bullied but not argued into justice and generosity' (England under the Hanoverians,'-page 197) 'Indian public leaders are still ignorant of this fatal secret or else they are foolishly wise to ignore it.' The writer then proceed to dispute the accuracy of the view that Indians were unable to drive the British out of India by force of arms.'

The pamphlet concluded as follows :

"A few words more about terrorism and anarchism. These two words are playing the most mischievous part in India today. They are being invariably misapplied whenever any reference to the revolutionaries is to be made because it is so very convenient to denounce the revolutionaries under that name. The Indian revolutionaries are neither terrorists nor anarchists. They never aim at spreading anarchy in the land, and therefore, they can never properly be called 'anarchists'. Terrorism is never their object and they cannot becalled 'terrorists'. They do not believe that terrorism for terrorism's sake, although they may at time resort to this method as a very effective means of retaliation. The present Government exists solely because the foreigners have successfully been able to terrorise the Indian people. The Indian people do not love their English masters, they do not want them to be here ; but they do help the Britishers simply because they are terribly afraid of them, and this very fear resists the Indians from extending their helping hands to the 'revolutionaries', not that they do not love them.

"This official terrorism is surely to be met by counter-terrorism. A spirit of utter helplessness pervades every strata of our society and terrorism is an effective means of restoring the proper spirits in the society without which progress will be difficult. Moreoever, the English master and their hired lackeys can never be allowed to do whatever they like, unhampered, unmolested. Every possible difficulty and resistance must be thrown in their way. Terrorism has an international bearing also because the attentions of the enemies of England are at once drawn towards India through the acts of terrorism and revolutionary demonstrations and revolutionaries are hereby able to form an alliance with them, and thus expedite the speedy attainment of India's deliverance. But this revolutionary party has deliberately abstained itself from entering into this terrorist campaign at the present moment even at the greatest provocation in the form of outrages committed on their sisters and mothers by the agents of a foreign government, simply because the party is waiting to deliver the final blow. But when expediency will demand it the party will unhesitatingly enter into a desperate campaign of terrorism, when the life of every officer and the individual who will be helping the foreign rulers in any way will be made intolerable, be he Indian or European, high or low. But even then the party will never forget that terrorism is not their object and they will try incessantly to organise a band of selfless and devoted workers who will devote their best energies, towards the political and social emancipation of their country. They will always remember that the making of nations require the self-sacrifice of thousands of obscure men and women, who care more for the idea of their country than for their own comfort or interest, their own lives and the lives of those whom they love.

VIJAY KUMAR
President, Central Council
The R.P. of I.

Many copies of this pamphlet are proved to have been distributed over districts in the United Provinces between the 28th and the 31st January, 1925. Inspector Master proved that three hundred and six copies were received in eighteen districts in this province and handed over to or recovered by the Government authorities. The recipients were for the most part school masters and school boys. Copies were also distributed in other provinces.

In all cases the source from which these pamphlets had come was not revealed.

Chief Court Judgement—Conspiracy discussed (65) pp.

We find that it is proved overwhelmingly that a conspiracy came into being in the United Provinces in July, 1924 to deprive the King Emperor *of the Sovereignty of British India*, and that the persons who were controlling the conspiracy as the inner circle further conspired to commit dacoities in which fire-arms were intended to be used, in order to obtain funds with which to purchase arms and ammunition, and to carry on revolutionary propaganda. We find that the evidence clearly shows that those persons contemplated that the fire arms should be used in order to enable the dacoities to be committed effectively and with impunity, that they foresaw and realised that murder was probable as likely consequence of those dacoities and that thus it is established that there was within the conspiracy to deprive the King Emperor of his sovereignty of British India, a conspiracy to commit dacoities with murder.

In respect of the meeting at the Vaishya Orphanage at Meerut we find after having heard the arguments of the learned Counsel and considered the evidence for the defence, which has been produced upon the point, that certain members of the revolutionary party among whom were Ram Prasad, Rajendra Nath Lahiri and Suresh Chandra Bhattacharji collected at Meerut in the residential quarters of Vishnu Saran Dublis in the

Meerut Orphanage and there held a secret meeting which was watched by Sub-Inspector Brahma Singh and Pheru Singh whom we find to be reliable witnesses. Their identifications were in each instance supported by their picking out the man identified from a crowd in a jail and repeating identification in Court. The only construction which we can place upon the documentary evidence on this point is that the meeting was pre-arranged meeting of the Revolutionary Society. We find that an attempt was made to mislead by stating that on the 13th September, 1925, the date of the meeting of Committee of the Orphanage whereas no such meeting was in completion and whereas no such meeting was held. We interpret the reference in the intercepted letters sent by Rajendra Nath Lahiri to the unknown person in Calcutta as a request to that person to join this meeting. The letter exhibit P 482 which was in the handwriting of Ram prasad requesting the recipient to attend a meeting at the Orphanage on the 13th September, 1925 of the Shradh ceremony of their grandfather was a summons to this meeting in Meerut. The Shradh ceremony amongst Hindus is a ceremony held usually annually in which surviving male relations offer obligations to the memory of deceased male ancestors. There could have been no such ceremony in which Ram Prasad and the unknown recipient of the letter could have shared and the use of the word Orphanage is very significant.

We shall refer later to the incident of the Meerut meeting in connection with those of the appellants who, we find, participated in it.

JOGESH CHANDRA CHATTERJI
CHIEF COURT

This man as has already been stated, is a resident of Bengal of over thirty years of age. The evidence against him which shows that he was one of the conspirators is that of Banarsi Lal. He is also mentioned by Banwari Lal in his confession. If this evidence is accepted there cannot be the slightest doubt as to the fact that he was a member of the Revolutionary Party. It is corroborated by the fact that both Banwari Lal and Banarsi picked him out of a crowd in jail identification proceedings as the man to whom they referred. This evidence however is not the main evidence against him. The main evidence against him which corroborates the evidence contained in Banarsi Lal's deposition and Banwarilal's confession is the evidence that when he was arrested on the 18th October, 1924, exhibit P. 198 containing an account of the meeting of the Revolutionary Party was found in his possession. This evidence not only strongly corroborates the evidence of the accomplices but in itself would be sufficient for his conviction if believed. It is as follows :

Inspector Muhammad Ismail of the Bengal Criminal Investigation Department has. deposed that he was on duty in the neighbourhood of the Howrah Bridge, Calcutta, on the 18th October, 1924. He saw Jogesh Chandra Chatterji in the precincts of the Howrah Railway Station. He says that he had heard his name before but did not know him before. He considered his behaviour suspicious and followed him over the Howrah Bridge to the junction of Harrison Road and Strand Road. There he apprehended him as a suspect and took him to a shop close to the place of the arrest where he searched him in the presence of two witnesses who were selected at random. Jogesh Chandra Chatterji was made to sit on a bench in front of the shop. While the Inspector was searching his inside pocket Jogesh Chandra Chatterji took a paper from his lower left hand outside pocket and let it fall in the 'takhat' (platform) beneath the bench.

This paper was Exhibit P. 198. We have already given the contents of this paper. If this story is believed, there cannot be the slightest doubt as to the guilt of the appellant. Kabiraj Bhuban Mohan Das, a search witness, was called to prove the discovery of Exhibit P. 198 from the possession of the appellant. He has corroborated Inspector Muhammad Ismail absolutely. In his statement before the special Sessions Judge, the appellant put up the defence that Exhibit P. 198 had not been found in his possession. His case was that the police officers, who had arrested him, had brought this paper with them, and had planted it on him. He called the other search witness Kalidas Ghosh in his defence. He also called two other witnesses to show that on certain dates he could not have been in the United Provinces. He was defended in this court by Mr. N. C. Dutta who confined himself to criticising the evidence for the prosecution. He has been unable to explain how Banarsilal who is a resident of Shahjahanpur and Banwarilal who is a resident of Rae-Bareli could have been in any position to identify Jogesh Chandra Chatterji as they did identify him, if they had not known him before. In respect of the discovery of Exhibit P. 198 Mr. Dutta has been unable to shake the evidence of the prosecution witnesses. Kalidas Ghosh, the witness of the search who was called as a defence witness, has not supported the appellant's statement as it was dropped from the side of appellant opposed to the side on which the witness was standing. Kabiraj Bhuban Mohan Das has stated that he saw the appellant let fall the paper and that he picked it up. His words are, "At the search while the Inspector was searching his pockets Jogesh let fall a paper on the takht on which I was sitting. I picked it up while both I and the inspector tried to do so and I gave it to the Inspector." This was Exhibit P. 198. The appellant stated that when the paper was discovered he protested loudly. Kalidas Ghosh had no recollection of his making any protest. The other two witnesses Prafulla Chandra Chakravarti and Jitendra Bhattacharji do not appear to us to be reliable witness and in no circumstances would their evidence be of great value. The appellant appears to have taken some exception to the fact that a certain witness whose evidence he desired was not called. We find there is no foundation for this objection. A summons was issued for the attendance of this witness. The witness who resided in Calcutta (Medical Certificate was of the Civil Surgeon of Comilla not of Calcutta) sent a medical certificate stating that he was unable to attend and no further steps were taken by the appellant to procure his evidence. The suggestion that Exhibit P. 198 was planted upon the appellant is apart from the evidence a suggestion which can hardly be argued seriously on the date of the appellant's arrest on the 18th October, 1924. Neither the United Provinces Police nor the Bengal Police had any suspicion that there was a specific Revolutionary Party in the United Province with an organisation that had developed as far as the holding of meetings. As has already been noted, the clue afforded by Exhibit P. 198 was not followed up at the time. It is true that Rai Sahib Durga Prasad, Deputy Superintendent of Police in the Criminal Investigation Department, who stated that in July, 1924 there was some sort of a Revolutionary Society and that a man who called himself "Roy"—that is to say the appellant who passed under the name of Roy—was visiting the United Provinces. But he did not communicate his suspicions otherwise than in his confidential diaries to any one until the 19th November, 1924 (a month after the appellant's arrest and the discovery of Exhibit P. 198) when he warned the Superintendent of Police, Shahjahanpur in Exhibit P. 658 of the possibilities of dacoities being committed by Political criminals in the Shahjahanpur district. We believe the evidence of Banarsilal and the statement of Banwarilal and we believe Inspector Muhammad Ismail and Kabiraj Bhuban Mohan Das as to the account which they give to the discovery Exhibit P. 198. We accordingly find that the appellant Jogesh Chandra Chatterji has been rightfully convicted on the charges on which the learned special Sessions Judge convicted him.

DOCUMENT No. 3.

Proceeding of the Council Meeting at Kanpur on 3rd October, 1924, Exhibit 198, in the Kakori Conspiracy Case.

On the 18th October, 1924, Jogesh Chandra Chatterji was arrested in Calcutta as a suspicious character. He was arrested by members of the Calcutta Police force. We shall consider the circumstances of his arrest when we consider his individual case. We note here that we are satisfied that on his arrest a paper (Exhibit P. 198) was found on him. The following was written on this paper in a handwriting unknown :

"A meeting of the P. C. was held on the 3rd October, 1924, in which five among six attended. The following resolutions were passed :

1. Keeping in view the fact that more or less efficiènt representatives acting as or in capacity of district organisers are already posted in the following districts : Banaras, Allahabad, Pratapgarh, Kanpur, Lucknow, Fatehpur, Jaunpur, Etawah, Agra, Aligarh, Jhansi, Hamirpur, Farakkabad, Mainpuri, Mathura, Bulandshahar, Meerut, Delhi, Etah, Bareilly, Pilibhit, Shahjahanpur, Muzaffarnagar.

   The remaining district of these provinces be thus divided among the said organisers so long as sufficient number of efficient men are not available to act as district organiser in each district.

   I. Banaras, Mirzapur, Ghazipur, Ballia, Jaunpur, Azamgarh, Basti, Gorakhpur, Rae-Bareli.

   II. Kanpur. Rae-Bareli, Gorakhpur, Unnao.

   III. Jhansi, Banda.

   IV. Aligarh, Anupsahar.

V. Meerut, Saharanpur, Dehra Dun, Almora, Bijnor, Budaun, Moradabad.

VI. Shahjahanpur, Nainital, Garhwal, Lakhimpur, Sitapur, Hardoi.

VII. As at present there is no member to represent the Fyzabad division consisting of Fyzabad, Bahraich, Gonda, Bara Banki and Sultanpur, it is resolved that suitable member be sent there to take charge of the centre at the earliest opportunity.

2. That at least rupees one hundred (considered to be the least expenditure in case of dire necessity at present) be raised by subscription from members and sympathisers of the following centres :

Banaras, Kanpur, Jhansi, Meerut and Shahjahanpur, the sum being contributed equally by each centre.

(a) That at least a subscription of annas four be realised every month from each member of the Association.

(b) That the above resolution is to be given effect to within the next two months.

3. That the meeting recognises that the total number of its members upto the present time is about one hundred : the following being the total strength in each centre—

Banaras to Jhansi 15 ; Aligarh 12 ; Meerut (not yet received) ; Shahjahanpur 8.

4. That the meeting is of the opinion that the following immediate steps be taken as regards its propaganda through newspapers and magazines which can be utilised by the members of the different centres :
   (A) To set up a campaign against the C. I. D. activities.
   (B) To set up a campaign against the repressive laws and measures.
   (C) To criticise the Congress activities that hinder the work of the Association.
   (D) To preach social revolutionary ideas and Communistic principles.
   (E) To collect stories, episodes and other meterials for publication.
5. That the department of money collection be at present placed under the sole charge of No. 2, 4 and 6 subject to occasional supervision by the P. C. All informations regarding this department from different centres be submitted to the said No. 2, 4 and 6.
6. That instead of 5 departments as mentioned in the General Constitutional rules and regulations only 2 departments be set up at present :
   (a) Propaganda to be guided by Nos. 1, 3 and 5.
   (b) Collection of funds and arms by Nos. 2. 4 & 6.
7. That all the General Constitutional rules and regulations to be enforced to their entirety ex-

cept the 6th resolution which was accepted after amendment for the present.

8. That every possible care be taken as regards the secrecy of the activities of the Association.

That every district organiser should try his best to help the local clubs and associations started with principles which may directly or indirectly promote the causes of revolution and to try to become members of the Congress and take part in its activities whenever advisable putting in view the rules of the Association.

10. That every district organiser should make arrangements to visit neighbouring villages and labour centres with the object of gaining their sympathy.

11. That to provide workers with work it is necessary to divide the district activities into three channels :

    (a) Village works
    (b) Secret works
    (c) Local social functions and activities connected with clubs and associations.

CHAPTER XI

MY STATEMENT BEFORE THE SESSIONS COURT

Q: Do you want to state anything about your arrest in Calcutta ?

A: I was arrested at the junction of the Strand Road and Harrison Road where I had stopped to catch a tram. As soon as I had asked my coolie to hand over my suitcase to me, Inspector Md. Ismail suddenly caught hold of my hands. Sub Inspector Gupta placed his hands round my waist from behind me and Asstt. S. I. Biswas held a photo of mine before my eyes saying in Bengali, "Jogesh Babu, here is your photo." Then and there Md. Ismail felt my pockets and then they took me off eastwards on the footpath of Harrison Road towards Barrabazar Police Station, which was about 200 yards ahead of us. After passing 12-14 shops they suddenly stepped into the dispensary of the witness Bhuban Mohan Das. As soon as we stepped into the shop some person in the shop who was of dark complexion and thin in appearance warned us not to sit on the benches as they were newly painted. After this, this man went away. Then Md. Ismail called a person who was passing by on the road and he was Kalidas Ghosh. Ismail asked him to stand as witness. A little after this Bhuban Mohan Das, who was inside the shop suddenly made a sign to Ismail and the latter who was sitting on the right to me on the bench stood up, went to my left side and picked up a paper which was already lying on the takhat folded up at a little distance from me, I raised an alarm as Ismail said that the paper was found with me. I wanted to see the paper but was not allowed to. Upto this time my personal search had not begun. After this Ismail made me sit on another bench opposite to the former one and began my personal search. All this time the search witness, Kalidas Ghosh was standing. After the search was over the witnesses were requested to sign the search list. Kalidas Ghosh first made the upper note on Exhibit 198 signed by him and then when pressed by the police he added the lower note. At this time the proprietor of the shop was also present there so far as I remember. After this I was taken off to the C.I.D. office Special Branch and then kept in Lalbazar lockup for a week, under section 54 and after this on the 25th October sent to the Presidency Jail under Bengal Ordinance which was promulgated that very day...I came to Banaras in the rainy season of 1923 for a change and remained there during the winter...and went back to Calcutta.

Sarat Bhattacharya was a true witness but Kartik Chatterjee was a false one. I did never know where Kalyan Ashram was.

Q : Why this case against you ?

A : This case has been brought against me as since 1916 I have been a victim of police oppression. I was arrested in 1916 by the C.I.D. who endeavoured to make out a case by extorting a confession from me and they threw me into prison by making false report against me. Contrary to law I was not allowed to make representation to the Government from the Presidency Jail.

As the result of a hunger strike in the summer of 1918 I was transferred to the Rajshahi Central Jail. I then took the earliest opportunity of sending a representation to the Governor General in Council, complaining against the barbarous tortures inflicted on me by the C.I.D. Special Branch, Calcutta. This led to strong comments by the press and this was the reason why I was made a target of oppression in subsequent years. Exhibit D. 48 is an extract of my petition with allegations against the police.

Detenus under D.I.A. (Defence of India Act) were released as a result of Royal Proclamation, but I was not released till September next year as I was in the evil eyes of the police and my release was through Sir Hugh Stephenson, the then Chief Secretary to the Government of Bengal.

In the latter part of July 1920 the D.I.G., C.I.D. Mr. Dixon, came to see me in Rajshahi Jail. In the interview I wanted a chair to be supplied but he refused and went back to Calcutta without any interview. This matter was shortly after published in the Amrita Bazar Patrika with strong editorial comment.

About a fortnight after this Sir Hugh Stephenson came to see me in Rajshahi Jail and as a result of this I was released within a fortnight.

But I had to wait for more than a year to find an opening for the proper direction of my energy by starting a factory at Comilla known as the House of Labourers. My success in this did not give satisfaction to the police; though within a year it was visited by the Chief Chemist, etc.

In the summer of 1923, Mr. Hodson, the then S.P. of Comilla came to see the factory and was shown everything. About a month after this, Mr. Mazumder, Inspector, C.I.D., came to the office and demanded the attendance register from me. I refused this as it involved the prestige of the House and he went away saying that he would come one day with a warrant and take away all the records.

My correspondence was interfered with and the business suffered a good deal as I was the manager. Twice I wrote the Government but was not heeded to. A boy employee was made a police informer and he was turned out of the House. This infuriated the police and that is why I could not return to the House after my return to Calcutta from Banaras.

After my arrest in 1924. the police had grudge

against me as was evidenced by the brutal method of transferring me bare-bodied from Berhampore Jail to Hazaribagh in November, 1925. A censor motion against the Government moved by Mr. J. M. Sengupta was passed by a majority of 8 votes in the then Bengal Legislative Council.

One evening I was called to the jail gate during exercise time. The police asked me to sign a transfer order. I went to the jail office where was the S. P. while I had no clothes on. He did not allow me to go inside to take food and to take my property. I refused to take the journey in the cold without warm clothes, but the police carried me on their shoulders from carriage to carriage and train to train, all the way to Hazaribagh Jail in Bihar. This journey with no clothes on for two winter nights caused me fever on the way. At the Hazaribagh Jail gate my temperature was 102° and later in the night it rose to 105° and for a week I was in jail hospital. This is a specimen of the treatment I received at the hands of the police.

AINUDDIN ABOUT ME IN COMMITTAL ORDERS

"He also came in for a detailed discussion and there is nothing more to be said about him. He was one of those who came from Bengal to establish revolutionary societies in these provinces and exhibit P. 198 is enough to show the leading part he took in this conspiracy. I have no doubt that but for his premature arrest and detention under the Bengal Ordinance, he would have played a still more important part in this Conspiracy."

Under the head-line *Direction from Bengal*, the Special Sessions Judge, Mr. Hamilton states :

"One may in fact state that it was directed from Bengal. Ten accused are Bengalees and two, Jogesh and Kar, are from Dacca. Sanyal was arrested in Bengal and published white leaflets in Bankura. Lahiri was arrested in Dakshineswar House. Bengalees were members who used to come to see Ram Prasad at Shahjahanpur. Lahiri was connected in correspondence with Kali Babu and Kamini Kaka, attended Meerut meeting on 14th September, 1925. (Here the Judge takes Kali Babu and Kamini Kaka to be two persons, but both were the secret party name of martyr Jatindra Nath Das.)

"Jogesh arrived in Calcutta in possession of 198, must have been taking to leaders in Calcutta."

THE SPECIAL SESSION JUDGE ON BANARAS

Banaras appears to have been the centre in the U. P. excepting as regards dacoities.

The yellow leaflets were drafted and redrafted there, the white leaflets were despatched from there to other conspirators for distribution in U. P. Lahiri lived there and Ram Prasad and Banwari used to go to him there, the Sanyal family once lived there ; Jogesh Chatterji stopped for sometime there when he came to the U. P. Mukandilal was arrested there, M. N. Gupta lived there, Raj Kumar Sinha studied there, Ram Kishan Khatri was there from time to time, Ram Nath Pandey lived there, S. N. Sanyal formerly lived there, Suresh Bhattacharjee came from there, S. N. Bakshi who was absconding came from there, Chandra-sekhar Sharma or Azad lived there and Damodar Swarup was a master there,

The Chief Court Judges, Chief Justice Sir Louis Stuart and Justice Khan Bahadur Muhammad Raza' in their judgement on Jogesh Chandra Chatterji said :

"We are satisfied upon the evidence that Jogesh Chandra Chatterji was one of the persons who orginally conceived the idea of the conspiracy and that he was a member of what the rules called 'The Central Council' which operated in Bengal. In these circumstances he must be held responsible for all the very serious offences committed by the conspirators."

SESSIONS JUDGE ON JOGESH CHANDRA CHATTERJI

The recovery of Exhibit p. 198 is sufficient to show that this accused was an important revolutionary, who after working in the U. P.. was bringing back a report to the leaders in Bengal.

Banwarilal, confessing accused, who inentified Jogesh in jail, states that he had met Jogesh in the summer of 1923 in Allahabad and had later been given his name by Lahiri. Some 15 days after that Banwari had brought a copy of ' Bandijiban ' from a hawker, Jogesh spoke to him, asked how he had liked the book and offered him more books.

This gave rise to several other meetings and an invitation to start a branch of the revolutionary society at Pratapgarh.

Again in 1924 Banwari got a letter from Jogesh Chandra from Kanpur and he went and met him there and was introduced by Jogesh to Lahiri and on the anniversary of Jallianwala Bagh Day Jogesh came to Pratapgarh.

Jogesh asserts that he was in Bengal in the summer of 1923 and two witnesses are produced, Prafulla Chakravarty and Jiten Bhattacharjee....That so many partners in this firm should be ex-detenus cannot be a mere coincidence and if some were engaged in revolutionary activities and Jogesh certainly was at a later period, nothing was easier than to mark a man present, although he may not have been....I cannot place reliance on these witnesses.

If there is no corroboration as to the presence of Jogesh in U. P. in the hot weather of 1923, there is as to September or October."

Here the Judge disbelieves the two important defence witnesses and even the Attendance Register of House of Labourers which earned high praises from many eminent men of Bengal like Ramananda

Chatterjee, the editor of the Modern Review and Sir P. C. Roy, the pioneer of modern Chemistry in India. Such were the trials in political cases in British India.

The Judge first disallowed all the names of my defence witnesses, including the name of an eminent businessman-philanthropist, Mahesh Chandra Bhattacharya, the proprietor of M/s M. Bhattacharya & Co. and the prosecution even refused to give the address of their search witness on my arrest in Calcutta in October, 1924. I mean Kalidas Ghose, whom the prosecution would have produced as the prosecution witness. I, therefore, withdrew my defence expressing no confidence in the court. Then some of the witnesses were called including Mahesh Chandra Bhattacharya. He submitted a certificate from the Civil Surgeon of Comilla that due to old age he could undertake the journey only after halting one day in Calcutta and another day at Banaras. But he was not summoned. My witnesses were declared unreliable and so also was the fact of the entry in the Register of the House of Labourers.

The Special Public Prosecutor, Pandit Jagat Narain, totally failed to break search-witness Kalidas Ghose, an employee of the Imperial Bank. But the Judge came to his rescue and put such leading questions that .the Government employee had to say things wanted by the judge.

Regarding my case, both the Sessions Court and

the Chief Court have given too much importance on my identification by approver Banarsilal and the confessing accused Banwarilal. But the fact that my fresh photos were taken by the Bengal C. I. D. men recently in Berhampore Jail, could nowhere be found. I have searched the whole record but it is not there. There were two Englishmen and two Muslims and they were bent upon crushing the revolutionaries at any cost. After our case was over, Ainuddin was made a Khan Sahib which offended him, but it was amended by his English masters, when he was made a Khan Bahadur.

CHIEF COURT ON JOGESH CHANDRA CHATTERJI

I have given what the Magistrate stated about me in his Committal Order. The same was the attitude of the Special Sessions Judge. Let me again refer to what the Chief Court, the title holder Englishman Chief Judge and his title holder Muslim colleague say about me.

Police is supposed to be the custodian of law and order in a country. Their task, of course, is hard and unsmooth ; but if the police also adopts vicious and filthy means to get their work done by hook or crook, it does not serve the purpose of administration. In my case when I was arrested in Calcutta, the search was not made on the spot. I was led to a Kabiraj's dispensary where the assistant of the Kabiraj was a police informer and helper. In the court he was presented as the Kabiraj. Now the question arises if the police indulges in such malpractice, is it not the duty of courts to judge the facts dispassionately and impartially and never to align themselves with any particular side and more definitely with the side of prosecution ? The prosecution is always the stronger side as it possesses adequate means to prepare its side but the defence is always weaker. If the court also becomes direct or indirect helper of the prosecution and tries to let down the defence attempt at every point, there remains no chance for any justice. The independence of judiciary and supremacy of law have got no meaning if the prosecuting and convicting authorities align themselves together. This is what exactly happened in the case under discussion. The committing magistrate was all along for the police and then in Sessions defence was continuously disturbed, interrupted and let down by the court. So many times this act of court reached such disgusting point that we thought it completely useless to produce any defence. When only physical might was to be considered right, there was no place of defence and arguments.

In the British Raj when the sole motive of administrators was to keep the Government running, they adopted all possible treacherous means and ignoble method. It would not be out of point here if I cite a few glaring examples. During the

Kakori trials the committing magistrate and the Sessions Court noticed only those facts which served the purpose of the prosecution. Though Mohammad Ismail of Calcutta Special C. I. D. was on duty at the time of my arrest and he followed me like a shadow, he gave the statement that he had gone to the Railway Station casually and was not on duty there. Though I was arrested on the crossing of Harrison and Strand Road but my search was made in a dispensary of a Kabiraj which was not very near the place of arrest. It was done because the Assistant of the Kabiraj was a police informer and police could get anything done in its favour from him. Another interesting incident that points the conspiracy between the court and prosecution can be seen from the fact that N. C. Dutta was enforced upon me as my defence lawyer. I neither appointed him nor even approved the idea that he should argue for me. Again self-contradiction is evident when it was said that Rai Bahadur Durga Prasad warned the Superintendent of Police of Shahjahanpur of the possibilities of dacoities being committed by political criminals in Shahjahanpur district on the discovery of Exhibit 198, whereas the committing magistrate accused and condemned the Bengal Police for not intimating the U. P. Police the exhibit 198 till the Kakori arrest. These are a few examples of the malpractices of police and the conspiracy of courts with them.

HAND WRITING EXPERT

Reference has already been made to one very important paper, the copy of the proceedings of the meeting of the Provincial Council which was written in my own handwriting and was supposed to have been seized by the Police from my person at the time of my arrest. When I was in Berhampore district Jail, the specimen of my handwriting was taken by the C. I. D. officers. When I gave the specimen of my handwriting I was quite successful in changing the style of my handwriting. I wrote in bold letters and straight style. The result of the change was that when this document was produced in Kakori case, the expert, police and court could not come to any agreed decision. The court wrote about those papers as written by unknown hand. Even the committing magistrate, Syed Ainuddin, got a bit annoyed and said that the papers were discovered from my person and so I must be held responsible.

In law courts where fates of accused are decided and any wrong noting of the judges can give fatal blows to innocent persons, extreme reliance on handwriting experts who are never very correct, may easily lead to a travesty of law. Evidence is the backbone of legal proceedings and if it is relied upon blindly, the real cause of justice can never be served. In the Kakori Case, the expert identified the writing of Ram Prasad Bismil who wrote only one word 'Premkishan', but I wrote two full pages and that could not be ascertained. This one instance shows how far it is correct to rely on the authenticity of experts' opinion. But it is a painful fact that it is always recognised by the law courts.

CHAPTER XII

PERSONS ARRESTED IN KAKORI CASE

1.	Ram Prasad Bismil	of Shahjahanpur	Hanged
2.	Banarasi Lal Kokash	,,	Turned approver & was pardoned
3.	Lal Hargovind	,,	Let off by Sessions
4.	Prem Kishan Khanna	,,	5 years R. I.
5.	Indubhushan Mitra	,,	Turned approver and was pardoned
6.	Roshan Singh	,,	Hanged
7.	Ramdutt Shukla	,,	Let off before trial
8.	Ashfaqullah	,,	Hanged
9.	Birbhadra Tewari	of Kanpur	Let off by lower court
10.	Ramdulare Trivedi	,,	5 years R. I.
11.	Gopi Mohan	,,	Let off
12.	Raj Kumar Sinha	,,	10 years R. I.
13.	Suresh Ch. Bhattacharya	,,	10 years R. I.
14.	Sachindra N. Bakshi	of Banaras	Transportation for life
15.	Seth Damodar Swarup	,,	Bailed off
16.	D. D. Bhattacharya	,,	Let off before trial
17.	Manmatha Nath Gupta	,,	14 years R. I.
18.	Ramnath Pande	,,	5 years R. I.
19.	Indravikram Singh	,,	Let off before trial
20.	Shitla Sahai	of Allahabad	Let off before trial
21.	Bhupendra N. Sanyal	,,	5 years R. I.

22.	Sachindra N. Sanyal	,,	Transportation for life
23.	Chandradhar Janhari	of Agra	Let off before trial
24.	Chandrabhal Janbari	,,	Let off before trial
25.	Shivcharan Lal	,,	Informer (not even arrested)
26.	Babu Ram Verma	of Etah	Let off before trial
27.	Jyoti Shankar Dixit	of Etawah	Let off from lower court
28.	Harnam Sundarlal	of Lucknow	Let off before trial
29.	Sachindra N. Biswas	,,	Let off by the Session
30.	Govinda Charan Kar	,,	Transportation for life
31.	Mohanlal Gautam	of Lahore	Let off before trial
32.	Sarat Chandra Guha	of Bengal	Let off before trial
33.	Jogesh Ch. Chatterji	,,	Transportation for life
34.	Rajendranath Lahiri	,,	Hanged
35.	Mukundilal	of Etawah	Transportation for life
36.	Ram Ratan Shukla	,,	Let off before tria
37.	Vishnu Sharan Dublish	of Meerut	10 years R. I.
38.	Madanlal	,,	Let off before trial
39.	Dhairon Singh	,,	Let off before trial
40.	Kalidas Basu	of Berhampur	Let off before trial
41.	Ram Krishna Khatri	of Chanda	10 years R. I.
42.	Pranabesh Chatterjee	of Jubbalpore	4 years R. I.

43. Banwarilal of Rae-Bareli 4 years R. I.
Chandrasekar Sharma Azad of Banaras could not be arrested.

Sessions Case :
Mr. Hamilton, Special Sessions Judge,
Sessions trial No. 1 of 1926
Decided on 6th April, 1927

Assessors : 1. Mr. Abbus Salem Khan
2. Banwarilal Bhargava
3. Ganu Babu (Jyan Chatterjee)
4. Mohammad Ayub

Age	*Persons Convicted*	*Assessors on Accused*
22.	1. Banwarilal	Unanimous that none participated in dacoity.
26.	2. Prem Kishan Khanna	Not proved against any
18.	3. M. N. Gupta	
37.	4. Roshan Singh	None of the persons
31.	5. Ram Nath Pande	charged.
21.	6. J. C. Chatterji	Admitted the dacoity in pursuance of the conspiracy.
26.	7. P. K. Chatterjee	
26.	8. V. S. Dublish	
28.	9. S. C. Bhattacharjee	No. 1 finds Banwarilal,
33.	10. Mukandilal	M. N. Gupta, J. C.
22.	11. Ram Krishna Khatri	Chatterji, Ram Prasad,
20.	12. R. K. Sinha	Lahiri and Sanyal guilty
21.	13. Ramdulare Trivedi	of conspiracy. Others
29.	15. Ram Prasad Bismil	find Gupta, Ram

30. 15. G. C. Kar
24. 16. R. N. Lahiri
32. 17. S. N. Sanyal
19. 18. B. N. Sanyal

Supplementary Case
22 years 19. Ashfaqullah
20. S. N. Bakshi

Party names :

In a secrct organisation the names of the important members are not used, but each member is given a secret name. These were the secret names of the members :

1. Ram Prasad : Ananda Prakash, Rudra Ram, Paramahans, Master Mahashay and Mohant.
2. Rajendra Nath Lahari ; Nitai, Nitaichand, Nitai Mama, Charu, Jugalkishore, Dixit, Mathura, Mathura Prasad, Jawaharlal Bajpai, K. P. Srivastava.
3. R. K. Khatri : Narendra, Ganga Ram, Govind Prakash.
4. J. C. Chatterji : Roy,' Profulla Chandra Roy, Roy Mahashay.
5. Mukundilal : Maharaj
6. Banwarilal : Tara Singh, Ramanda Singh
7. Ashfaqullah : Kunwarji, Mantana, Wari, Krishan
8. Banarsi : Bawa
9. M. N. Gupta : Nawab, Nawab Sahib
10. Chandrasekhar Azad : Quick Silver

11. S. N. Bakshi : Badri, Kanaiyalal, Bagchi
12. Seth Damodar Swarup : Lalaji
13. G. C. Kar : Chaudhury
14. Indubhusan : Goward

A letter of Ashfaqullah to Banarsilal from Bhopal (translated into English from Urdu), Ex. P. 14 in Kakori Case :

..."You know that I have not a single shell with me to do business. Service means killing of my conscience. You must remember very well that I want to live free and I worship 'freedom' and I am ready to sacrifice my life for a glimpse thereof.

" It would never be for me to have the chain (yoke) of servitude round my neck whoever it may be. I weep for hours when I think of it, but my relations press me that I should take up some service and thus I should serve my old mother. It is right to some extent that this is what our religion commands. But in this way I will have an opportunity to serve the motherland.

" Today if I accept some service in Bhopal Sir Ishrar Hasan Khan Sahib would secure a job at once. My brother asked me to see him and on his slightest recommendations I would get a subedar's post in the military...but then all my schemes would be upset. I donot love my life so that I may hoard money and enjoy but I want to live so that for the attainment of freedom for the country

I may not care in the least even the greatest danger (I care Not) if the world calls me mad or insane. It is my belief and I shall live and die for it.

"This is what I feel...... I have become tired of *wandering aimlessly in the streets of Shahjahanpur...* you know that I have a village, no, no my mother is a Zemindar and that I can get as much land as I require without any difficulty. But I want to do cultivation on my own for which I do not have funds, if you approve of this and take interest therein, lay out money thereon, and let us go and take up our abode there. We will live among our brethern cultivators and will carry on our scheme as well and shall have sufficient money withen a few years. There we would increase our propaganda on a wide scale and would invite our companions to join us. In short if there can be any pious and advantageous work for us, in this world it is cultivation, if you mind to follow it. If you would reply in negative my heart would break. However, you will have to do something or other for your wife and children, then why should we not take to cultivation. Capital is yours, land mine and labour of us both. We too will live like real brothers in the village and after facing bravely the troubles of the world, shall show to the world that what is there in the world that cannot be accomplished by two youths when they have one and the some idea in view and walk on one and the...

"The lands of Nandia and Solpur are extending their hands towards us and their eyes full of love are gazing at us, the poor and the oppressed cultivators are ready to welcome us, so brother do no disappoint these lands and dishearten these cultivators and let me know your opinion. Are you ready for it? If I had money I would have commenced the work and would have made you my partner, but alas: I am penniless and my relations, instead of rendering any help, are pushing me down into the abyss of slavery. They do not realise what cultivation is and the freedom of India depends only on the cultivators. So let us begin cultivation together...

"See how much benefit have Deonarain and Ganga Singh drawn out of cultivation. There will be many to join us after two years and then we will be able to do every-thing else.".....Warsi.

CHAPTER XIII

SHIVCHARANLAL SHARMA'S ROLE IN KAKORI CASE

Shivcharanlal was the younger brother of Ram Charanlal Sharma who was wanted in Kanpur Bolshevik Conspiracy case but could not be prosecuted as he took shelter in French Pondicherry and was kept interned there. In connection with my visit to Pondicherry I have written much about him.

Shivcharan was convicted in the Mainpuri Conspiracy Case of 1918. The conspirators were released on condition that they would give up revolutionary activity. But Chandradhar Jauhari and Shivcharanlal started political work and they were compelled to go to the Jail to serve the sentences passed on them in the Mainpuri Case. Shivcharan was serving his term in the Bareilly jail and was about to be released when I went to meet his brother Ram Charanlal.

Shivcharanlal was the mystery man of Mr. Horton through whom he received many genuine information about the secret revolutionaries. Ram Prasad wrote a letter to Shivcharanlal at his Aligarh address and it fell into the hands of Mr. Horton. Again when Govinda Charan Kar was arrested at Lucknow, a letter was found with him signed by Shivcharanlal. Yet this Shivcharanlal was not an accused in the Kakori Conspiracy Case. Shivcharanlal also attended the Meerut meeting which formed a major part in the Kakori Case. Despite all such evidences against him Shivcharan was not arrested. These raised suspicions in our minds and we soon came to know that Shivcharan had been as a matter of fact arrested but he had entered into a secret understanding wiwh Mr. Horton. From him Mr. Horton came to know of a proposed money action at Kankhal near Hardwar and also of plans to loot postal money in transit in big towns. As a trusted friend of Ram Prasad, a member of the Provincial Council, he knew many important matters of the secret party.

PANDIT RAM PRASAD BISMIL

He was born in 1897. He came from Shahjahanpur. As a boy he was very naughty, used to smoke, rob and do various other mischiefs. But a great son of India brought about a thorough change in him. Satyartha Prakash of Swami Dayanand attracted him very much and he became an Arya Samajist. His father, an orthodox Brahmin could not tolerate this and Ram Prasad had to leave his home. But subsequently his father softened and Ram Prasad came back to the family. He was a lover of firearms and was engaged in smuggling them in the Gwalior State.

During the Lucknow Congress in 1916 his activities in support of Lokmanya Tilak put him in touch with the revolutionaries. Pandit Gendalal

Dixit, the leader of the Mainpuri Conspiracy Case who later died in Delhi, had given him much inspiration. The beginnings of the Mainpuri Conspiracy Case can be traced to the confession of a man who was deputed to collect information about a rich relation of his. The idea was to commit a dacoity in this rich relation's house. But the man gave the information to the police and arrests took place and the Mainpuri Conspiracy started in 1918. Ram Prasad and was wanted in the case charged of revolutionary conspiracy to deprive the King Emperor of his sovereignty over British India.

He had a literary taste and used to write articles. He wrote some booklets and translated others. He wrote good poems. Besides Hindi, Urdu, English he knew Bengali quite well.

After the King's Proclamation his warrant was withdrawn. he came back to Shahjanahpur and started a silk weaving factory for his livelihood.

Ram Prasad was very healthy and good looking. When he was a child, the issue-less Bengali wife of the District Magistrate of Shahjahanpur wanted to adopt him as her child. The parents were agreeable to the proposal, because they had very limited means and the D. M. was wealthy and he had already settled down at Shahjahanpur permanently. But Ram Prasad's grand-mother would not part with her beloved grandchild. When Ram Prasad was under capital sentence and the appeal was being heard, this old lady came to Lucknow and lay prostrate before the Chief Court for several days giving up food and water. After much persuasion, she could be removed.

In 1923, Sachindra Nath Sanyal met Ram Prasad and requested him to work with him afresh. But his efforts were not successful. Early next year I went to Shahjahanpur and persuaded him to join the party and he joined.

His nerves were made of steel. He scarcely had any efficiency in planning things ; but in action he was easily the undaunted master. His command nobody could dare to disobey. When impassioned and angry, he seemed to be the Rudra incarnate. But in normal mood he was very gentle, generous and affectionate.

His life was so much regulated that he never missed the daily physical exercise, took principal meals only once in the midday, did not smoke or chew betel-nuts. With food he did not take any spice. Dal he took rarely ; thick bread, boiled vegetables and ghee was his main food. In the night he took milk and some fruits.

People loved and respected him, because of his well disciplined life and readiness to serve others. For these traits of character, he had an influential circle of friends around him. Added to this was his revolutionary background. Among his ardent admirers were some patriotic and militant youths like Ashfaqullah and Thakur Roshan Singh, the two other Kakori martyrs.

ASHFAQULLAH

This brilliant Muslim youth of Shahjahanpur was the only Muslim in the whole of India to be hanged on the charge of revolutionary conspiracy to deprive the king emperor of his sovereignty over British India.

The militant Muslim instinct inspired him to search for Ram Prasad who, he came to know, was a wanted leader of of the Mainpuri Conspiracy Case. Ram Prasad was in hiding at that time, when he came in the open Ashfaq wanted his revolutionary guidance. He won't give any quarter to a Muslim. But Ashfaq's earnest devotion changed the Pandit's attitude and soon he became Ram Prasad's most trusted lieutenant. Ashfaq was ashamed of the lack of partriotism in his own community. He gave up school and joined the 1921 movement. He once laid himself at the feet of Mahatma Gandhi, but came back disappointed.

He came from a wealthy and educated family many of whom were holding high positions in service but none had anything to do with politics. He had less interest in studies but was an expert in swimming, horse riding and hunting. As a child though he derived immense pleasure from doing mischiefs yet he was very generous. Instances were not unknown when a neighbour got very angry with him for robbing his preserved mangoes in company of other boys and decided to punish him when found out. Once one such man searched the whole neighbourhood for Ashfaq but could not find him. His son was sick, so he had to come back home soon. To his utter surprise he found Ashfaq besides the bed of the sick boy. Ashfaq was nursing the boy. How could he punish him? Ashfaq had a very fine physique. He was tall, broad-shouldered and muscular. When after arrest he was put into the jail he was 185 lbs in weight and there was no sign of fat. Though his shoulders and chest were very broad, his waist was very thin and his legs and arms were very strong and stout.

Syed Ainuddin, the Committing Magistrate, who was a British stooge and an enemy of his countrymen, escorted him from Delhi to Lucknow in a second class compartment. His object as assigned by his British masters was to prevail on Ashfaq as a Muslim and thus get all information from him. So was also the motive of Khan Bahadur Tasadduq Hussain, Deputy S. P. of the Imperial C. I. D. who tried his utmost to inject communalism into the mind of this resolute young revolutionary.

Their arguments were roughly: you are a Muslim, we are also of the same faith. So we are so sorry for you. Why should you spoil your valuable life by being true and faithful to the revolutionary party? Ram Prasad is a Hindu. His object is to establish Hindu Raj in place of the British one. You come from a good and enlightened

Muslim family, why should you join hands with the Kafirs and go against your own faith and against the interest of your own community ? But all these arguments were of no avail. Service to the country had already been accepted by Ashfaq as a firm faith ; he had already divested his mind of stupid and unpatriotic communal feelings. So he replied ; " I am grateful for your good wishes but my ideas are unchangeable. Ram Prasad is not a Hindu to me ; he is a Hindusthani. Not Hindu freedom but Hindustan's freedom is his objective. Had he been inspired by Hindu freedom, even then I would have joined hands with him. If I were to choose between Hindu masters and British masters and if my choice was limited to only these two alternatives, I would have chosen the Hindu masters as after all they would have been Indians." Before this strong and undaunted patriotism their arguments vanished into thin air and they had to retire baffled and humiliated.

Ashfaq escaped arrest on the 26th September 1925, when the police arrested several persons in connection with the Kakori case. When his house was surrounded by the police, he was not at home. He went underground for nearly a year and was arrested at Delhi on 8th December, 1925. He was hanged in Fyzabad jail on the 19th of December, 1927.

Revolutionaries go underground not to escape arrest but to carry on their work. Ashfaq's underground life was beset with dangers and difficulties. Only a determined man like him could stand the strain. Ashfaq was a master in the art of changing his appearance and most of his absconding period he spent in the guise of a Hindu. Due to long and intimate association with Hindu revolutionaries, he was well acquainted with the Hindu mode of living. For a considerable period he had been in the hostel of the Banaras Hindu University ând nobody could suspect him to be a non-Hindu.

Ashfaq had been in Bihar for months as the friend of a Bengali Railway official and the local Muslim Government officer in charge of the area gradually became his most intimate friend. They were frequently going on hunting excursions and naturally Ashfaq the expert hunter earned his great esteem.

He was later living as the guest of the well known patriot late Arjun Lal Sethi of Rajasthan. He found out that the young daughter of his host was very much attracted to him and so he left the place disregarding the earnest request of Sethiji to stay on. But Sethji came to know the reason of Ashaq's sudden departure later when the girl expressed strong inclination to marry him after his arrest. The news of Ashfaq's execution was such a shock to the girl that she fell seriously ill and did not recover.

Ashfaq made up his mind to go abroad. His

object was to go to Russia and for that purpose he wanted first to reach Kabul. For making necessary arrangements he went to Delhi and started preparations,

Here he was living in a Muslim quarter. Nearby was the house of a Muslim engineer. His fine appearance and the story of his good manners was a great attraction for a young daughter of the engineer. One day she sent a letter to him through a maid servant and Ashfaq very politely gave a reply expressing his difficulties. But inspite of this one night the girl herself came to his room. He was taken aback. She proposed to him unhesitatingly but Ashfaq convinced her that their marriage was an impossibility. So the poor girl had to go out disappointed.

Then one day his friend through whom he was trying to go to Kabul betrayed him to the police and he was arrested on the 8th September, 1926.

In the condemned cell he was taking small amount of food and was passing his time in reading and contemplation. Once his mother came to see him and found him to be thin and tears began to trickle down her eyes. Ashfaq told her smilingly 'You think I am getting thin due to the fear of death; not at all. Now I take very light diet. I am deep in thinking. Dietary control helps in the concentration of mind.' This somewhat relieved the pains of the afflicted mother.

He accosted a friend on the last interview that he had with any one 'Well friend, have you come to congratulate me? Yes, tomorrow I am to marry.'

Yes, next morning on the 18th of December, 1927, after bath he wore his own clothes, a special privilege allowed to him, mounted the scaffold and kissed the rope before it was placed round his neck by the hangman.

His last peom uttered before execution meant: "Death is waiting for all. My death is also not unnatural that I should be afraid of it. All things of earth are subject to destruction and *merging in God. I am also obeying that leaving* Fyzabad jail for eternity.'

His last message was that the revolutionaries were not terrorists. Whatever they do, they do it for the country's emancipation. They do not indulge in violence for violences' sake. But how many innocents were killed in cold blood by the rulers at Jalianwala Bagh ? "Let India be free and Indians be happy." He had no regrets. He was proud to be the first Muslim to be hanged for participation in revolutionary activities.

A letter written by Ashfaq from Bhopal to Banarsilal (approver in Kakori case) was an exhibit in the Kakori Case. Nowhere in the case it was mentioned, but this single letter showed what a fine mind and heart Ashfaq possessed. He gave in it a beautiful picture of the life of his dream. In it he described how he wished and every youngman should wish his own development and serve his own country. Selfish motives degrade the individual and discredit the country. This idea he maintained to the last moment of his life. His one reply to all communal appeals was that even if one Muslim betrays the country, it would turnish the community. He could have saved his life easily but he never for a moment thought in terms of his own self.

THAKUR ROSHAN SINGH

Thakur Roshan Singh was born in village Noada in district Shahjahanpur. He had very little academic education, but was very intelligent and efficient in wordly affairs.

He spent his life generally in the village, yet strangely enough, he possessed a fair knowledge of the world at large.

Like Ram Prassad he was also a Arya Samajist, that is to say, he had adopted the reformist cult of Satyartha Prakasha of Swami Dayanand. This must have inspired him to be a revolutionary, though he was actually initiated to the revolutionary movement by Ram Prasad who was his very close friend.

The majority of the village population from where Roshan Singh came were Rajputs. Roshan Singh was also a Rajput. In the remote prosperous village he had sufficient fresh air and varieties of health-giving food, pleasant work and rest. From boyhood he had developed a fine physique by regular exercise and was a leader of the village boys. He was well versed in the art of the use of lathi, sword and gun. He learnt Urdu and Hindi in the village and English in the jail and as a Kakori undertrial he started learning Bengali too.

Though a firm believer in an armed revolution, he joined the non-violent non-cooperation movement led by Mahatma Gandhi in 1921. A patriot could not remain aloof from a national freedom movement whatever might be its form. Roshan had been to various places in connection with his movement and ultimately he was arrested and given 2 years R. I. He was in the Bareilly jail and there he came in touch with many other patriots.

After release he felt disgusted as the non-cooperation movement was withdrawn and also as there was despondency everywhere. He readily accepted Ram Prasad's leadership and became an earnest revolutionary.

Thakur Sahib was a strong man both bodily and mentally. In Lucknow district jail as an under-trial in Kakori Case he used to wrestle with 5 or 6 persons daily as their teacher without getting tired. In the same way during hunger strike he once continued for 16 days without any forced feeding all along doing his normal routine work. He heard the news of his father's death in jail, but remained completely unperturbed.

Unlike the three other Kakori martyrs he was not given capital sentence in the Kakori train dacoity case in which he did not take part, but in another decoity on very weak evidence. We thought that he would get 5 years R. I. in the case and not more than that. Indeed he was given 5 years on the charges of conspiracy but capital sentance in another village decoity. This was a surprise to all. But he took the sentence without the least change in his appearance. He maintained this attitude till the last. As a last measure to save his valuable life his friends persuaded him to submit a mercy petition. But even that went in vain.

Roshan Singh went to the scaffold with the same calmness and shouted 'Bande Mataram' and uttered a sentence in poetic Urdu which meant: "Roshan, realise the greatness of life." Yes, he realised the real greatness of life.

On the 20th of December, 1928, crowds of men were waiting outside the jail for taking his dead body in procession, but all of a sudden the order was given that no procession would be allowed. So his friends did the last rite quietly.

His son who was reading in Gurukul, Brindaban, once came to interview him in the Lucknow jail. The boy had heard wrongly from somebody that his father had given out party secrets to the police. So the boy charged the father with this. Enraged at false charge Thakur Saheb became furious and cried out: "Your father is not ill-born, he is a true Thakur."

RAJENDRA NATH LAHIRI

Rajen Lahiri was born at Bharenga in the Pabna district of Bengal in 1901. His father late Kshitimohan Lahiri, was an ardent patriot and was respected throughout the district for his generosity and services to the people. He was under police surveillance since the Bengal Partition Movement of 1905. The name of the High School of the village still commemorates his memory.

Rajen inherited all the qualities of his father. From his boyhood he was patriotic and was taking part in service of humanity. He came to Benares for his studies.

He came in touch with a revolutionary of Anushilan Samity, named Shyam Chakravarty, who was temporarily at Banaras. A certain boyish act of Rajen Lahiri so much prejudiced the puritan Anushilanite that he told his successor not to take Lahiri in the Party. But Rajen was very eager to do revolutionary work and approached an old ex-revolutionary, who was once connected with Sachindra Nath Sanyal. This gentleman introduced Rajen to Sanyal. When I reached Banaras, Lahiri was much impressed by me and we talked almost daily for hours. Sanyal being alarmed told him many things against Anushilan Samity but nothing against me.

Besides his university studies, Rajen was always keeping himself engaged in various other activities, had connections with clubs, gymnasium and literary activities. He was the honorary Secretary of Bengal Sahitya Parishad of B. H. U. He wrote articles in papers like Bangabani and Sankha. He also wrote a number of articles for 'Agradut', a handwritten monthly journal. He was Secretary of the Health Union. He passed B. A. with history and economics and took up history in M. A.,

Up-to-date bomb making was to be started in U. P. Rajen went to Calcutta for the purpose. He read the news of the Kakori arrests from Dakshineswar Bomb factory where he had just gone. His Banaras house was searched and a warrant was issued for his arrest. The Dakshineswar bomb factory was searched on the 10th November, 1925, and he was given 10 years transportation by the Tribunal.

He was then brought to Lucknow as an accused in the Kakori Cose and kept separate from others in the Central Jail as he was already a long termer. Later he was brought down to the district jail and kept with the other accused in the Kakori case. In the court he never cared to follow anything of the proceedings. He thought that he had done his duty and he was indifferent to the consequences.

He was an out and out revolutionary and revolted against social prejudices and though a Brahmin he threw away the sacred thread. He took pork and beef without the least hesitation: He realised at heart that the social prejudices were great hindrances in the path of progress and they were to be broken off mercilessly. That was the real spirit of a true revolutionary.

He had secret party names, such as Charu, Jawahar, Jugalkisore, etc. It was he who stopped the train in the Kakori action by pulling the chain in a second class compartment. He was dressed in short, shirt and a pugree. He had an attractive figure, broad round face, large eyes with piercing looks like those of Swami Vivekananda.

His last letter ran thus : 'Received news yesterday that the Privy Council Appeal has been dismissed. You have done much to save our life. All efforts having failed it seems that our sacrifice of life is necessary for the country. What is death ? It is life alternate. What is life ? It is nothing but the other aspect of death. Why should then a man be afraid of death, or sorry for it. Death is as sure as the light of sun in the morning. If it is true that history repeats itself, then my firm faith is that our death will not be in vain. My last salutation to all.'

He was hanged on the 17th of December at the Gonda jail. He accepted death quietly with a glorious smile which was visible even in the dead man's lips.

Lahiri did not send any mercy petition.

SACHINDRA NATH SANYAL

In his early youth Sachindra Nath Sanyal independently established Anushilan Samiti at Banaras in 1909. Gradually he came in close touch with important Bengal revolutionaries like Pratul Chandra Ganguli and Rashbehari Bose. During the first World War he along with Girija Babu, the representative of Anushilan Samiti, became lieutenant of Bose and planned for the overthrow of the British Government with the help of the army. In the Banaras conspiracy case Sanyal was given transportation for life and was sent to the Andamans.

He was released in 1920 after Kings Proclamation but again started secret revolutionary activities, first in U. P. and then in Bengal under the Hindustan Republican Association of which he was one of the founders. For issuing a revolutionary leaflet he was sentenced to 2 years R. I. after his arrest in Calcutta in 1925.

These revolutionary leaflets were distributed widely in the country and beyond. Many were seized in different places in U. P. In this connection he was brought as a Kakori under-trial, and although there was no other evidence against him he was given a life sentence as formerly he was a lifer under similar charges.

He developed T. B. in the jail during the Second World War due to extreme mental worries, was released from jail, went to Bhowali T. B. Sanatorium but failed to recover and breathed his last at Gorakhpur early in 1945.

GOVINDA CHARAN KAR

He was an active member of the Anushilan Samity at Dacca from student days. During the first World War he went underground. In this condition the police surrounded him in a place in North Bengal. There was a prolonged fight with the police in which some policemen were wounded and Kar received several bullet shots. He dropped down unconscious in a paddy field. He was arrested and sentenced for 8 years trrnsportation and sent to the Andamans. Three bullets on his chest and hand were not operated out and they remained in his body. He fell seriously ill in the Andaman cellular jail and was released unconditionally in 1920.

After my arrest Kar came to U. P. to maintain the link between Bengal and U. P. On the day of general Kakori arrests he was also arrested at Lucknow and he thought that Shivchrran Lal was responsible for it.

He did not take part in the Kakori Train Dacoity, yet he was falsely implicated in it and given a life sentence.

After his release he was living in Calcutta. Communal Muslims started the campaign of mass killing of Hindus at Dacca. Kar's relations were there. So he went to Dacca by plane but at the aerodrome he was murderously attacked and escaped death calling himself a Muslim, though he received 22 wounds all over the body. He could not fully recover from this and died within a few years. Thus came the end of a brave fighter for the country's freedom.

MUKUNDILAL GUPTA

He comes from a moneyed family of Auraiya, district Etawah. Pandit Gendalal Dixit, the leader of the Mainpuri Conspiracy Case of 1918, was a teacher in this place. Mukundilal came in contact with him and became a full fledged revolutionary. He suffered 6 years R. I. in Mainpuri Conspiracy Case. After release he started a small business at Jhansi. He was recruited to Hindustan Republican Association by Sachindra Nath Bakshi, took part in Kakori Train Dacoity and was given life sentence in Kakori Conspiracy Case. After his release he again plunged himself into the August Movement of 1942 and was given 7 years R. I. This great patriot is passing his old days somehow without anybody to look after him properly.

SACHINDRA NATH BAKSHI

He was one of the early recruits of the Anushilan Samiti at Banaras. His family had a big three-storeyed house at Pataleswar, a locality in the Banaras city and his father was the proprietor and manager of the Ice Factory at Sikrol. Sachindra was a fountain of energy and was busy day and night with the work of the party. For the furtherance of his work he started clubs and associations and his swimming club earned the attraction of the whole city when he first started the 13 mile swimming competition from Chunar to Banaras. He was my right-hand man at Banaras at this time.

When the expansion of the organisation was seriously discussed, he offered himself to go anywhere. Lucknow being the headquarter, a man was required there. I knew Chauduri Khaliquzzaman through Pratul Ganguli. So I introduced Bakshi to him and some others. Bakshi struggled hard but at that time Lucknow was not suitable for our work. I later placed him at Jhansi and he did much solid work there.

He evaded arrest during the Kakori arrests, had a very hard dock workers, life in Bombay and was arrested at Bhagalpur, Bihar, and stood the trial in the supplementary Kakori Conspiracy Case with Ashfaqullah. He was sentenced to transportation for life. His associates at Jhansi, Bhagwandas Mahora and Sadashiva Raghunath Malkapurkar got 14 years R.I. each in what is known as Bhuswal Bomb Case.

VISHNU SARAN DUBLISH

He left his college studies when he was preparing for his B.A. examination in 1921 and joined the non-cooperation movement. When leading a procession he was assaulted by the English head of the district and it created a deep impression on his youthful mind. He was sentenced and was in the Bareilly and Lucknow jails. When he came in contact with Sanyal he turned a very enthusiastic revolutionary and was sentenced to 10 years imprisonment in the Kakori Case. In the Naini Central Jail he was falsely implicated in a jail riot and given life sentence which was reduced to 5 years by the High Court.

He was a heavy smoker and he had to smuggle this contraband article in jail. One day the Governor came to see the Naini jail. In the Circle the Governor stepped into a barrack and wanted to see a prisoner's bed. Colonel Palmer, the Superintendent, pushed open the bed folded in the first berth and cigarettes and bidies came out. The Governor wanted to see the prisoner and it was very interesting when it was found that bed belonged to Dublish. Dublish told the Governor that for a heavy smoker life in the jail was very hard. He requested the Governor to transfer him to the Andamans where prisoners were allowed to smoke. Dublish had a good time in the island as a convict writer.

After release he became an M.L.A. and M.P. for many years. Now he is in bad health in advanced age and yet working as the President of the Meerut Zilla Parisad.

SURESH CHANDRA BHATTACHARJEE

He came from Banaras and was arrested and interned during the First World War. Martyr Ganesh Shankar Vidyarthi took much interest in him and under his guidance he learned Hindi journalism. He was the Hindi teacher in the A.B. School at Kanpur and also edited the 'Vartaman', a Hindi daily when I went to Kanpur in 1924 and lived in the same mess with him at Patkapur.

He took a prominent part in organising the party from 1923. Ramdulare Trivedi, Batukeshwar Dutta, Bijoy Kumar Sinha, Surendranath Pande, etc. were inspired by him. He was the latest Editor of the Hindi Daily 'Pratap'.

RAM KRISHNA KHATRI

He comes from village Chikhli, district Chanda, now in Maharashtra. From boyhood he was attracted by Lokamanya Tilak and Dr. Moonje. But later he became a Sanyasi, and eventually became the Secretary of the Udasi Sampradaya under the name of Govind Prakash. A closer study of life repulsed him, because he saw that barring a few good souls, most men were exploiters of the society under the garb of religion. They were characterless in many ways.

He came in contact with Chandrasekhar Azad and became a member of the Hindustan Republican Association. He was arrested at Poona and given 10 years R.I. in Kakori Case.

Durring my hunger strike in Lucknow jail he left home and came to Lucknow and moved heaven and earth in support of the strike. This was how ultimately he settled down at Lucknow and after my release pressed me to do so which I actually did.

RAJ KUMAR SINHA

He is a lovable person. When he was a B.Sc. student of the Banaras Hindu University, two rifles were recovered from his box and he was arrested at Kanpur. He knew nothing about the Kakori Dacoity but the police managed to give him a sentence of 10 years R.I. He passed his jail life very bravely. He is a great lover of Indian classical music but takes Russian language classes at Kanpur for his livelihood. He now teaches Russian.

MANMATHA NATH GUPTA

He comes from Banaras, was a meritorious student of the Kashi Vidyapith and also was a writer even in his student days. He was also arrested and jailed in early life in 1921.

He was the youngest Kakori accused and had participated in Kakori dacoity and other affairs. He had correspondence with Mahatma Gandhi which was published in 'Young India'.

He was given 14 years R.I. in the Kakori Conspiracy Case, because of his tender age.

In jail he studied much and learnt many foreign languages. He has written dozens of books and has earned a name as a Hindi writer. He is now editing a Hindi paper, a weekly of the Publications Division of the Government of India.

RAMDULARE TRIVEDI

He led a very hard life in boyhood in Bombay after his father's sudden and untimely death. Even as a boy he had to maintain himself, his mother and brother.

In the 1921 movement he was given 6 month's R.I. and fought hard with authorities in the Bareilly jail.

He joined the secret movement through Suresh Battacharya and became intimate with me after my arrival at Kanpur. He was later arrested in the Kakori Case and given 5 years R. I. Police were badly after him even after his release and arrested him once in Dehradun-Kanpur Conspiracy Case and again on suspision that he had killed a boy who was a police informer. He has taken up journalism as his profession. Saheed Ganesh Sankar Vidyarthi had a soft corner for him, because of his patriotism and the dignified way in which he struggled.

PREM KRISAAN KHNNA

His father was a big engineer in Railway Service and he was leading a comfortable life at Shahjahanpur. He came in touch with Ram Prasad Bismil and they became intimate friends. He worked in Delhi.

He had a licenced Mauser pistol and Bismil used it for his revolutionary work, of course, with the knowledge of Khannaji. This led to his arrest in the Kakori Case and he was given 5 years R. I.

He is brave by nature and passed his jail life boldly. After release he started work in the Congress and became an M. L. A. Now he is a member of Parliament.

BHUPENDRANATH SANYAL

He is the youngest brother of Sachindranath Sanyal. He was arrested in Kakori case when he was a B. Sc. student at Allahabad. He was given 5 years R. I.

He is a very good writer and speaker both in Hindi and English. After release he was again sentenced for his speech in a youth conference. Now he is in service.

RAM NATH PANDE

He was the post box of Rajendra Nath Lahiri and was the only son of his widow mother. Due to interception of letters by the police he was detected and arrested in Kakori Case. Though he left his mother alone in distress, he was always cheerful in jail and all efforts of the police to get him on their side failed. Pande was strong both physically and mentally. He was given 2 years R. I.

After release Pande studied Homoepathy and now practises at Banaras as a Homoepathic doctor.

CHAPTER XIV

THE JUDGEMENT AND AFTER

I have given a general idea about the Kakori Case. I shall state here a few words about our defence counsels. We were all greatful to them, because they stood by us when our need was the greatest. We had full faith in Pandit Govind Ballabh Pant and told him that we would not require any other lawyer from outside if he could take the charge. As he could not take the charge because of his other involvements as the leaders of the Swaraj Party, Mr. B. K. Chaudhury had to be brought from Calcutta. Chaudhury made great sacrifices and defended us so nicely that every one of us was highly satisfied. We developed a love and respect for him and tears trickled down his eyes during the occasion of our last parting with him. Every one of us was moved. Shri Mohanlal Saxena and Shri C. B. Gupta also became very intimate with us and they were working for us to the best of their abilities. Shri Daya Shankar Hazela, late Ajit Prasad Agarwal, Mr. Manilal Kothari and R. F. Bahadurji took much interest in our defence.

Particularly Chaudhury, Saxena and Gupta generally used to spend the Sundays with us in the district Jail and used to lunch with us that day and we made special preparations for food. Some of us were good cooks. These meetings and lunches were a source of great pleasure to us during the one and half years' undertrial days in the Lucknow jail.

THE DAY OF JUDGEMENT

I have given an idea of the Kakori drama and at the conclusion let me also describe how the curtain was drawn for the last time. That was really a memorable day for all of us.

All of us got up early in the morning that day, perhaps none had sound sleep in the night. Pandit Ram Prasad Bismil did not have a wink of sleep in the whole night as he was very much upset on the submission of mercy petition by Sanyal. He wrote almost a full length book and got it sent outside. He was upset the very day the thing took place. He had taken me beside the secluded barrack and told me that he saw Sanyal's petition in the office. I could not pacify him. I called Lahiri and we both succeeded in pacifying him somehow. But unhappily his bitterness was expressed through writing against the Bengalees in general. To avoid this bitterness I advised Shri Sanyal to submit his petition after the delivery of the judgment, but unfortunately he did not listen to me. Bismil had this grievance but the way of his expression was unwise.

However, all of us finished our morning duties,

bathing etc. to be ready to start for the Court. At this stage we heard that three cells were being cleaned in the Condemned Cells, just beyond our Ward enclosure. This information created a commotion. We knew that Bismil and Lahiri would be given capital sentence. But none of us could think as to who could be the third person. Some thought that Manmatha Nath who took part in all the overt acts might be the person, and others thought that I had been made the leader of the Conspiracy and I might be the person. None could imagine that it could be Thakur Roshan Singh, who was not only given the capital punishment but was actually hanged.

That morning we were called to the office early. From our barrack we went in a procession to the office. We were fettered inside and as soon as we passed the inner gate we saw the jailor, Rai Sahib Champalal standing there almost overwhelmed with tears. I have spent nearly a quarter of a century in the northern Indian jails but nowhere I have found such a jailor. He was weeping as if he was one us, a very dear friend or relative.

In those days executions of prisoners was a common thing in Lucknow jail, yet I have seen how tears were rolling out from the eyes of this old man during the last interview a prisoner held with his dearest one. He was soft, kind and humane and yet he was a Government title-holder. The peculiarity in him was that unlike other jailors he was not callous. He maintained this trait of his character even in the most dreary life of jail administration, because he possessed a stout heart.

That day also everything took place as usual. For the last one and a half years it was just a part of our routine to go to the Court in a police van, heavily guarded, and then come bock to the jail. That day we were brought all together in the same vehicle. It was also known in the city that judgment in the Kakori Case would be delivered on that day. So just in front of the building where our trail was taking place a huge crowd had assembled. The police was already prepared to face this situation. A considerable number of policemen were on duty and they were smartly dressed and equipped. They made a very big cordon and did not allow the public to come near the building. Only the lawyers were permitted inside the Court. Ram Prasad Bismil was leading and erciting a couplet loudly and we were repeating it. He was singing the inspiring patriotic song of Maulana Hasrat Mohani, the celebrated patriotic poet, which read :

"Sar pharoshi ki tamanna ab hamaray did men hai,
Dekhna hai zor kitna bazuay katil main hai."

(Now our earnest desire is to be beheaded, let us test how much might the hand of the executioner possesses.) We entered the Court room singing this song. The judge had not come by that time. We saw our defence lawyers including late G. B.

Pant standing on one side. We shouted 'Bande Mataram' in the court room. The judge was so much upset and nervous that he came to deliver the judgment after making all arrangements to leave Lucknow. Immediately after delivering the judgement he caught a train for Bombay and from there boarded a ship for London. He did not have that moral courage to live in India any more and left India possibly with a guilty conscience. Only parts of the judgement was read by the judge. Ram Prasad Bismil and Rajendra Nath Lahiri were given capital sentence, as we had apprehended earlier, *but to our surprise the third man* who was given the same sentence was Roshan Singh. He was given only five years' rigorous imprisonment for conspiracy but for participating in dacoity, he was given capital sentence. When the judgement was read, everybody, even our lawyers, were surprised but the Thakur took it very bravely. With his usual coolness and is smiling face, he took my hands in his and stood silently for a while. The Court was adjourned and we were led outside. That day we entered the Court in a grave mood and in a graver mood we left the court after having embraced one another. When it was our turn to board the van the three under capital sentence were separated from us and placed in a different smaller vehicle. Oh, what a painful separation it was !

I stood silently before their car. The three condemned friends, Ram Prasad Bismil, Rajendra

Nath Lahiri and Roshan Singh were so much absorbed in thought that actually they did not turn their eyes to any direction, they did not see anything far or near and yet their eyes were wide open. I stood on the road till the vehicle moved on, yet none of the three looked at me or at any one for that matter. The sudden and abrupt separation from us revealed to them the coming separation from everything of this world and they became sternly pensive.

The small car left that place first and then our van started. Their car was driven through a different route and we did not know where they had been taken. In the jail, we were kept waiting outside the inner gate of the jail. The jail Superintendent was also there and one C. I. D. Inspector who came from Allahabad wanted to have a group photograph of ours. Now we came to know that Bismil, Lahiri and Roshan Singh were also in the same jail, when they were brought from the condemned cells in that yard for their inclusion in the group photograph. And then they were again separated from us and we never met them again. Even today in the Lucknow Jail one big peepal tree reminds me of the smiling faces of these friends who gave their life to erect the foundation of India's freedom. This peepal tree was planted by Thakur Roshan Singh just behind his barrack and he used to water it. One day I asked him how he being an Arya Samajist was worshipping a tree.

He replied humorously that this type of religious show always paid in jail as the other prisoner had regard for it. The tree still stands in pristine calmness, always reminding the sacrifices of my friends hanged on the alter of the freedom of India.

Now it was clear that we all were to be transferred to different jails. Suresh Bhatterjee thought that it would be better if he, myself and Shri Vishnu Saran Dublis could be sent to the Banaras Jail. He talked over this matter to the Deputy jailor. But the I. G. of Prisons consulted the Superintendent of Jail only and the places where we were to be transferred in batches were decided by them. A separate information board for Kakori prisoners was fixed in the I. G.'s office on which the name of every prisoner and the jail where they were to be transferred was written. In a footnote it was written that no Kakori Prisoner would be sent to Banaras Jail.

The instances of bribery were very common in the jail administration. Our Bhattacharjee thought of bribery. He paid Rs. 50/- to the Deputy Jailor who took the money without doing the job he was paid for.

After Colonel Clements, the I. G. of Prisons and Captain Salamatullah, the Superintendent of the Lucknow jail, had decided which batch was to be transferred to which jail, we were sent to different parts of the jail in different batches. A big number of Tongas were brought to the jail gate from the city and also batches of armed police.

Our batch consisted of 3 persons, myself, Govinda Charan Kar and Ramdulare Trivedi. From the jail we were sent to the hospital. After nightfall we were brought to the jail gate. Two batches of prisoners were already outside the jail gate on Tongas and another batch was brought to the inner gate. We came to know here that our friends under capital sentence were the first to be transferred to three different district jails under cross-bar fetters. These district jails were spacialised for condemned prisoners.

The jailor handed over our charge to our escorts and we came to know that we were being transferred to the Fatehgarh Central Prison. We were given a good amount of puris and sweets for our meals on the way. But none of us touched anything. We were not in a mood to take food and there was another serious thing which weighed on our mind.

I have stated that due to hunger strike we were given certain facilities as political prisoners. The Special Sessions Judge during the mediation of the hunger strike had agreed that he would write in his judgement that the dacoities committed by us were for the furtherance of the conspiracy to overthrow His Majesty's Government in India and that the motive was political. The judge did so. We therefore wanted that we should be given special treatement as political prisoners. Our defence counsels had already asked for this.

It was decided between ourselves that in case we were not given special treatment after our conviction, we would start hunger strike from the very day of our sentence. Friends who might be under capital sentence would also resort to hunger strike in their condemned cells. Following this decision we were all on hunger strike from the day the judgement was delivered.

When we were brought to the Raiiway Station we saw some batches of our friends at the Station. All were despatched by the night train. We saw from the distance one of our condemned friends also. We were put into a wait at the Kanpur Station for a long time. Many friends came to meet us. Pandit Balkrishna Sharma was there with two friends. Virbhadra Tewari also came there in khaki. He was holding some post in the Kanpur Municipality. But I was more interested to have a talk with Bijoy Kumar Sinha, the younger brother of Raj Kumar.

He was a member of our Secret party and I had full confidence in him. While Trivedi and Kar Babu were engaged in various discussions with Sharmaji and others I told Bijoy that they should maintain connection with me. We would serve our sentence and they would carry on the work of our mission. I also told him that if our condemned friends were actually hanged, they should try to take me out of the jail so that we could avenge the loss of our friends. I told him that we must retaliate and let it be known to the people of India that the revolutionaries did not take anything lying down. This had special importance for me as Rajendranath Lahiri, one of our friends who got capital punishment, asked me to take revenge if they were hanged. And I considered that to be a sacred duty. At the station I gave Bijoy a secret code and also made him understand how to cipher and decipher the code. Thus a means of communication was established to carry on secret correspondence.

Bijoy told me that I. D. T. (Indian Daily Telegraph) had written a good article on our conviction that day. We got a copy of the paper at the station and read it. But the editorial did not give me satisfaction. The Government was rightly condemned in strong terms for the extraordinary severe sentences passed on us. But the paper also called us misguided youths. This caused us immense pain. We were neither all youths nor were we misguided. Some of us were mature men and we were fully conscious of what we were doing. I could not understand how we could be called misguided youths by the editor of a nationalist paper of Lucknow where under their very eyes the prolonged trial took place. Insults and humiliations were the constant companions of revolutionaries at the hands of the agents of the foreign rulers and revolutionaries did not care the least for that. So long as the country was under slavery the fighters would naturally be treated like that. But when the nationalist Press called them misguided it was very painful.

FATEHGARH CENTRAL JAIL : ONE YEAR

From Kanpur we were brought to Fatehgarh Central Jail and the Superintendent, Dr. Rossair and the Head Jailor, Ganda Singh met us at the jail gate. Dr. Rossair delivered a sermon to us and then left us to the jailor. The jail authorities of course, knew that none of us were new comers to the jail and we each had jail records even prior to the under-trial period in the Lucknow jail. We told them that we were on hunger strike.

Our first protest in this jail was against changing of our clothes. Some convicts were engaged to get our clothes changed. After conviction it was the duty of the Lucknow jail to change our clothes. But the jail officials there were in a hurry to transfer us. So our clothes were not changed there. At the Fatehgarh jail the convicts came to change our clothes. We protested. But the convicts forcibly stripped us naked and attired us with the usual clothings of convicts. We were then separated and kept in three different places.

I was sent to the Casual Circle where there were three prisoners who came from middle class families. Mr. Chaube was an Honorary Magistrate and also a visitor of this jail. He was imprisoned on a charge of murder. The other was Pandit Kalicharan convicted for writing something offensive on the Muslims and third was a Muslim who returned from Persia. At 12 in the night all the prisoners were roused from their sleep and were made to sit in pairs for counting. I refused to leave my bed or to sit in pair. There were threats etc. But I defied everything. I said that was barberous and under no circumstances I would submit to it. I heard later that my other two friends also did the same in their places.

Gradually we became weak due to hunger strike and were removed to the hospital. Kar Babu was still kept separate. Perhaps on the 42nd day late Ganesh Shankar Vidyarthi came to the Jail and persuaded us to give up the strike and promised that they would fight for our cause through the legislature. At first I flatly refused to give up the strike. He then went to the other two friends. They referred him to me and so Vidyarthiji again came to me and said that the other two were depending on me. So at my request the other two were brought to my place and we three discussed the position privately. Some had already given up. We three here and two in Naini Jail, Dublishji and M. N. Gupta were continuing. At the appeal of Vidyarthiji we gave up the strike and Dublishji and Gupta also did so when Vidyarthiji met them.

But the attitude of the Government was revolting. We were so weak yet we were not given anything except the C Class Jail diet. Not even milk was continued. We could not recover our lost health. Then came the order that we would be treated as C Class habituals. This was too much to tolerate. Kar Babu became very angry. My argument was that we submitted to Vidyarthiji, but not to the Government. So we should wait and see what our leaders outside were doing for us. Kar Babu did not agree and restarted the strike.

Jailor Ganda Singh, the brute as he was, oppressed him as much as he could. Kar Babu's condition became critical, We were not allowed to see him but when he reached the critical stage we were allowed to meet him and at our earnest entreaty he gave up the strike.

A clever man as Ganda Singh was, he offered to Ram Dulareji a bait that he would manage to give us some better food on medical ground ; not through the hospital but as a favour. This was a trap to get ourselves entangled in corruption and thereby making us pets of Ganda Singh. We refused to be trapped.

Because of our defiance to obey the orders for midnight counting, the authorities thought it advisable to yield to our pressure and the rule was deleted from the jail Manual.

The Head Jailor, Ganda Singh, a thief of the lower grade, was in great difficulty with us. I call him a low grade thief because he used to sell even jail vegetables and earthen pots made by the convicts in the open market as a daily affair. Local poor women were engaged for this. He had an organisation for his nefarious work both inside and outside the jail. He dominated over the Superintendent and other Jailors, because Col. Clements, the I. G. of Prisons, himself used to get illegal gratification from him. He illegally earned thousands of rupees per month and shared the ill-gotten money with the I. G. But he was always fearful of being detected. He was always afraid that a serious exposer of any vital matter might tumble him down. He tried his utmost to have our cooperation by offering us a little comfort although we were made C Class habituals. But when he was unsucessful he resorted to different methods.

As habituals we had one advantage. The other habitual long termers became our friends and we earned their full confidence. This was advantageous in the jail, because the jail authorities remained fearful of something untoward happening. Our friend Vishnu Saran Dublish was implicated in Naini Jail riot as I stated. So Ganda Singh was afraid of us. Ganda Singh started brutal repressions on some habitual long termers who were very intimate with me. It was in this connection that so many long-termers were transferred to the other jails. There was one Muslim long-termer who was transferred from the Fatehgarh Central Jail and just at the time of his departure from that jail, he told Ganda Singh in his office something against me. As a result Ganda Sing became very vigilant. One headwarder was very helpful to me. He was serving as a link between me and Vijay Kumar. Ganda Singh suspected him. One day it so happened that Mr. Sheo Verma came to the Jail area. Though I had an escape plan but there was no move so far for its execution. Ganda Singh got information of his araival near the jail through the C.I.D. men who were entrusted with this job, and they tried to arrest the man. This incident made Ganda Singh immensely annoyed with me and he fabricated the case that I had received a pistol from outside which was kept hidden somewhere in the jail.

How my comrades outside the jail planned to take me out narrated to me years after by Mr. Surendra Nath Pande who is now working in a manganese mine in Mysore. Bijay Kumar Sinha with whom I was in secret communication from the jail passed on the news of my intention to escape. And Pande hired a house at Hatia, Kanpur, where I would be sheltered after escaping from the Jail.

Pande himself arranged matters, but the plan of my escape was exposed to the Head Jailor through a peculiar way. Two dangerous muslim habitual convicts, both lifers, were being transferred from Fatehgarh to another jail. In the jail gate the Head

Jailor got the news from them that the Head Warder in charge of the Habitual Circle, where I was put up at that time as habitual lifer, was friendly with me.

On this information, Sardar Ganda Singh, the Head Jailor, got the Head Warder's quarter searched. As ill luck would have it, in this search a letter of mine, written to friends outside, was recovered in which there was reference to my escape plan. The Head Warder, a Brahmin, from Kanpur village, was dismissed from service. Pande went to his place saw his mother and wife and offered them help in securing service. The man went to Bombay is search of service, fell ill and died there.

Although it was known that this source was under strong suspicion, yet Mr. Sheo Verma took the risk and went to the jail gate to try to establish a new connection with me. No sooner he reached there he realised that he was being followed by the C.I.D. men. He took the train for Khudlapur and before the train arrived at the station he jumped down from the running train and took shelter with Mr.. Gaya Prasad, who was practising there. The C.I.D. man who followed him in the train from Fatehgarh also jumped down and saw Sheo Verma entering the house of Dr. Gaya Prasad at village Jalalabad, just near the station.

In the early morning hours the house was surrounded by the police, but before the search started both Sheo Verma and Gaya Prasad managed to escape. Later they were both prosecuted in the famous Lahore Conspiracy Case with Sardar Bhagat Singh and others and were given life sentence. My name also appeared prominently in that case for their attempt to take me out from Fatehgarh and Agra jails.

After my transfer to the Agra Jail Pande hired a house at Agra and carried on communications with me. Gradually the Party headquarter was also shifted to Agra and a bomb factory was started there in a separate house where martyr Jatin Das (died in Lahore jail by hunger strike) gave them training in the art of bomb-making.

My transfer was ordered and the police dug up the jail ground at many places in search of the pistol but did not find it. It was just a false accusation and no pistol was brought in by anybody. Ganda Singh wanted to have his own way. After sometime when I was in the Agra jail, I was told by the Head Jailor, C. W. Laig, that Ganda Singh had successfully cashed on that fake case against me as it was due to that he was awarded the title of Sardar Bahadur.

For the head-warder he created an awakward situation by implicating him in a political matter. He got frightened and left the job without any protest and the poor fellow died in Bombay. Only to attract attention of higher authorities he made a mountain out of a mole hill. In fact the I. G. of Prisons was in his hands and the Superintendent of Jail was a new and inexperienced man. He himself fabricated the accusation against me and then without giving me any chance for any clarification before the Superintendent, he got signed from the Superintendent what he wanted and then he called me and transferred me with the highest possible punishment in those circumstances.

According to the Jail Manual the prisoner accused of any jail offence would be put up before the Superintendent on Peshi. The latter would ask for the explanation. Then if the Superintendent was convinced about his offence, he would write it on his History Ticket. I was not put up before the Superintendent, nor was I told dy the Jailor anything of the kind .

And then at the time of my transfer to Agra jail Ganda Singh warned the police men who had to escort me. I was handcuffed, roped, cross bar fettered and then transferred from Fatehgarh jail under a heavy escort of police. I was moving slowly due to cross bar fetters. I was physically put in an Ekka to reach the railway station. At the station every one who saw me was surprised that so many armed men were employed to escort a lean and thin man in chains. We got down at Shikohabad as we had to board another train for Agra. But one overbrige had to be crossed which was not possible for me as I was under cross bar fetters. The police men led me to another platform by crossing the rails. On that platform when we were waiting for the train for Agra, one law student who was going to Agra to appear in final examination got attracted towards me after seeing such heavy armed escorts with me. He asked me whether I was a South Indian. I told him that I was a Bengali but now he should take me to be of U. P. I was domiciled in U. P. He asked about my case. I told him "Kakori Case". As soon as he heard me, he was astonished to see the behaviour of the police. He told the Havildar incharge that he was giving him money and that he should buy sweetmeats and other eatables of my choice and give them to me. The policeman refused. He said that he could not accept money for this purpose. He came to me and told me that though he was given only four annas for my meals, I should not mind and eat whatever I wanted. He said that he would pay for that. I refused this offer with thanks. We reached the Agra jail in the night and for the whole night I was kept under bell chain. Early in the morning when the Head jailor, Mr. Laing, came and asked whether I could speak English. My answer was "yes". He wanted to know the case in which I was convicted. I told him that it was Kakori Case. In the morning that Havildar who escorted me tendered his apology to me. He told me that he was warned by Ganda Singh that I was. a very dangerous man and that some persons would try to make me free on the way ; but he said that he found me a perfect gentleman.

In the train I saw green papers along with my other papers with the Havildar. I took it from the Havildar when the train was in motion and was surprised to read in it that the Superintendent had awarded the highest punishment, namely (1) cellular confinement for three months, (2) bar fetters for indefinite period and (3) exemption from the remission system, for attempt at escape from the jail with the help of firearms and instruments for cutting iron gratings. All this despite the fact that nothing was found even after a thorough search ! All was in the imagination of Ganda Singh for his personal promotion at my cost. This is, however, what I thought at that time. But later I learnt that my friends outside had a plan to take me out of the jail.

AGRA CENTRAL JAIL : ONE YEAR

After spending the night under fetters and bell chain when next morning I was put up before the Superintendent, Major Sheikh, at the jail gate I complained to him about the illegal way of punishing me without even telling me what were the charges. He heard me patiently and said that he was not concerned with what the authorities of other jails did but he gave the assurance that no such thing would be done in his jail. He was quite true to his words and in fact I have never seen such an honest and upright Superintendent in my life. I had full confidence in him and he also had confidence in me.

Col. Clements was a petty man. He was cowardly and as a weak man he was prone to put us in trouble. It would not be quite out of place to mention here that in 1921 when Pandit Motilal Nehru was in the Lucknow Jail, Clements was the Superintendent. Petty man as he was, he wanted to show that as the Superintendent he was somebody in the jail. Panditji was a giant before this pigmy. So only to humour him Panditji used to put one smuggled letter before him every morning as a proof that the Superintendent had no control over his jail.

I was kept under lock and key day and night in a cell in the cellular barrack. Suresh Chandra Bhattacharya and Ram Krishna Khattri were sent to this jail immediately after they were sentenced. They were on good terms with the jail authorities as the authorities had come to know that they were not troublesome in any way. From my cell I established contact with them. Suresh Babu was at times smuggling newspapers and he used to send these to me in the midday when the officials used to be absent.

I received a copy of the Leader of Allahabad in my cell in which appeared an editorial note evidently from the pen of the editor, late C. Y. Chintamoni extolling and welcoming the ceremonial establishment of the Republic in China. Such a strong editorial from a moderate paper was unthinkable. I read it again and again and then returned the paper. It was an open support for armed revolution and implied the condemnation of the non-violent movement of India. So also did Pandit Madan Mohan Malviya. Though moderate in politics, he preferred a revolution. He was in England as a delegate to the Round Table Conference. At that time Sir John Andersons' name was announced as the Governor designate of Bengal. Sir John earned much notoriety as the war time Governor of Ireland in suppressing the liberation movement of Irish people by ruthless means. So Malviyaji directly challenged the then Secretary of State for India questioning if that was the motive behind this appointment in the presence of many Members of Parliament. There were even hot exchange of words.

I remember even today the article written by late C. Y. Chintamani. Who knew then that after getting China free, the revolution would be betrayed ? Who could know then that the communists under Mao after ousting Chiang would become so much expansionist that they would lead a large-scale invasion on India after so much talks of friendship ? Yes, this is the enternal rule of politics : Might is Right. Mao's China has created a big might and they must assert their right over their weak neighbours !

To be lodged in a U. P. jail as a C Class habitual prisoner was a strain on the health of a Bengalee. My weight was reduced to about 100 lbs.

This was because I could not take Chapaties and so I took rice and the rice that was served not at all was eatable. I gave up my food and declared a hunger strike. For three days nobody took any notice of me, though my Kakori Associates became very much perturbed.

On the 4th morning I was put up by the Head Jailor Mr. Laing before the Superintendent for the Peshi. When the Superintendent asked me why I was not taking food I told him that it was not possible for me to take such repulsive food. I was a man from East Bengal. I was not used to eating the sort of rice served to me. So was the case with Dal and these two were my day-to-day diet. I was on fetters and it was difficult to pass my janghia through the fetters when I want to answer nature's call.

The reasonable Superintendent understood my genuine grievances and he knew that without any ailment my weight had been reduced to 100 lbs. from 146 lbs. That was a proof before a doctor. He asked me what minimum things I required. I stated that a changed dal and separately cooked rice can give me relief. For changing clothes I might be allowed a lungi on special grounds. It may be mentioned here that this was given to the Muslim and Sikhs. In this the jailor supported me.

The Superintendent gave written orders that my rice and changed dal be cooked separately in the hospital and he gave me a lungi as a special case and wrote the order on my History Ticket. I gave up hunger strike and thanked the Superintendent and the jailor. From that day we three were getting rice and dal separately cooked for us and it was really a bit tasty. We were getting a little vegetable also from the hospital. Our friends were relieved now.

I had heard that Dublishji had been sent to the Andamans. I wanted to go there. I wrote a letter to Dublishji and received an encouraging reply from him. At this time a demand also came from the Andamans for convict clerks. I gave my name and a casual convict, a Jat, who read up to class VIII also gave his name.

At this time I received a letter from Bijoy Kumar Sinha through Suresh Babu's source. It was very heartening. Then followed a continuous series of correspondence. I informed my friends outside that I had given my name for my transfer to the Andamans. But Bijoy pressed me that I must not go. I agreed and asked for a fever-producing drug named Raskapur. I received this and it was decided that in case I received the transfer order, just before my departure I would take the drug, should get high temperature and thwart all attempts to transfer me. This drug was used by Mr. Satrughna Kumar of the Bareilly shooting case and he ran high temperature and was successful in getting his transfer as a suspected T. B. patient to

Sultanpur Special T. B. Jail. But I did not require to use the drug, because the Andaman authorities rejected my application and accepted that of the Jat.

Though a habitual, I was kept in the Casual Circle as we three were kept in three different places. Suresh Babu was sent to the Habitual Circle and Khatri was kept under the Head Jailor. One black striped man amongst all red-striped men was a striking thing to all. Even the dangerous habituals were on the best of terms with me when I was in the cells. One educated Pathan zamindar of a good family who was a lifer for dacoity told me one Sunday that he would invite more trouble on him. He did not listen to my advice, attacked the Superintendent, received a good thrashing and came back to the cell bleeding profusely and after a week received more than 30 stripes. Another healthy Hindu youth of fine appearance told me a day prior to the annual visit of the I. G. of Prisons that he would assault the Head Jailor during the I. G.'s visit. I entreated him not to do so. But he actually did so and received beatings, stripes and cell life. These showed how much confidence these prisoners had in me.

I was all along having correspondence with my party men through Bijoy. He would write some day that Azad sends his 'namaskar' or on something about Balwant Singh, because that was the name I gave to Bhagat Singh when he came to

Kanpur. Suresh Babu told me one day he had seen some C. I. D. people in the Agra jail with a photo of Bhagat Singh.

Bijoy wanted to know so many things from me about so many persons but never a word was mentioned about Virbhadra Tewari and Tewari was in their full confidence, nay, he was incharge of the U. P. organisation. But we could not rely on him as he was let off by the lower court although there was ample evidence to entangle him in the Kakori Case.

International situation on the North Eastern frontiers was taking a very favourable turn. Amir Amanullah, the king of Afganistan, became pro-Russian under the influence of the Indian revolutionaries, Raja Mahendra Pratap and others. China had already become a single Republic under Chiang. So I was very hopeful about our future.

I advised my friends to establish a line of communication for our secret organisation throughout northern India. At least there must be units established in big railway junctions. The other point I stressed was to try to have communications with Afghanistan and Burma. Later the statement of Kailashpati in the Delhi Conspiracy Case, proved that they did this, as he stated that Badshahgul was given Rs. 2,000 out of Rs. 16,000 looted in the Garodia Bank Dacoity.

I gave them to understand that a political murder was very effective if it served a big public purpose. As examples I mentioned the cases of Kudhiram Bose at Muzaffarpur, Kanailae in the Calcutta jail and the Delhi Bomb outragl on Lord Hardinge. I stated that secret organisations had come into prominence and captured the imagination of the general public by such actions. Saunders murder took place not long after this and my suggestions might have given my friends the idea of retaliation of the murder of Lalaji by the British police officers.

That year (1928) Amir Amanullah became a world figure by his open pro-Russian and anti-British demonstrations. The Amir went on European tour, his main objective was to visit Russia. Britain disliked it and despite.the King of England's personal request he went to Moscow and placed a wreath on Lenin's Mausoleum.

I saw that these developments were golden opportunities for the Indian revolutionaries and I urged upon my friends to get themselves prepared for the utilisation of the situation. They were making every possible efforts. They even changed the name of the party from 'Hindusthan Republican Assòciation' to 'Hindustan Socialist Republican Association' or Army in a Dhlhi meeting. They recruited Badshahgul to the party at this stage. (He is the son of Haji of Turangjai in the no man's land beyond N. W. Frontier Province·)

Not only the Indian revolutionaries but also the nationalists, Hindus and Muslims, were looking forward with high hopes on the developments of the anti-British fronts in Afganistan and China.

Britain was not unaware of this and they carried on a vigorous underground propaganda in Afganistan itself during the absence of Amanullah and succeeded in putting a water carrier named Bachchai Sakko on the gaddi of Afghanistan. A Muslim Head Warder was helping me with all these news and he broke this news to me weeping bitterly. In reality it was a bomb-shell to me- All my hopes were frustrated.

The Simon Commission came facing strong opposition from all parties, including the Moderates. Our friends wanted to blow up the members by bombs on their landing in Bombay. But the bombs they were carrying from Banaras for the purpose exploded in the train at Manmad. The leader was, Manmohan Gupta, the younger brother of Manmatha Nath Gupta of Kakori Case.

Leaders demonstrated against the Commission and led mass demonstration on the visit of the Simon Commission in big cities. Brutal assaults on their persons was the planned policy of the Government. Lala Lajpat Rai was brutally essaulted at Lahore, Nehru and Pant at Lucknow, Rajendra Babu at Patna and Netaji Subhas Bose and J. M. Sen Gupta in Calcutta.

The assault of Lalaji was so severe that he died within a month. He and other big leaders had in the meantime given public statements that time had come when it had to be seriously pondered over whether to change the method of non-violence. Assaults were deeply resented, but Lalaji's death was a death blow to the nation. That was the feeling in every heart. The simultaneous feelings of an impotent anger and failure to retaliate dampened the minds of the Indians into despondency and dejection which over-cast the nation. But this darkness of national frustration was dispelled by one sudden incident. Just after one month of assault on Lalaji, J. P. Saunders, one of the two British police officers who assaulted Lalaji, was shot dead in broad day light on a street of Lahore near the gate of the police station while he was going out of his office.

The news spread like wild fire throughout the length and breadth of the country and a feeling of jubilation was reigning everywhere. Every one felt with pride that we Indians, also knew how to retaliate, how to meet official terrorism with our terrorism and pay them back in their own coin.

No one knew who did it ! but all were convinced that this was the work of the revolutionaries and their prestige raised to a great height. I guessed from the jail that the actors were no other than our friends.

My instruction to my friends was that in case of a second world war I must somehow be taken out by blowing off a portion of the prison wall. This, they assured me, would be done.

I stressed upon my friends the necessity of doing something occasionally to exhibit the might of of the guerilla revolutionaries to the public as a part of our propaganda. I also gave them in writing our methods of committing money actions and murders in a very disciplined way, entrusting different functions to different batches. I instructed that wnen a murder was planned the most experienced and best persons should be on guard and their assistants should do the actual work.

The U. P. Government set up a Jail Enquiry Committee under the Chairmanship of Sir Louis Stewart, the then Chief Judge of the Oudh Chief Court. This Committee had two Indian members and Col. Palmer, the I. G. of Prisons, was its Secretary. This Sir Louis Stewart was a first rate fanatic, and the Congress boycotted and condemned the Enquiry Committee. The Committee visited the Agra Jail also. I was on parade in the casual circle though a habitual convict. They came to that side and passed along without noticing me. When they went to the other parade some of the jail authorities pointed at me. They came to me and told me that I would be called to the jail office. When I was called to the office, I found that instead of asking me anything about my grievances and recording my statement, the Chairman started to talk in a threatening tone and language. He wanted to shout me down. I told him that I never wanted to come before the Committee or to present myself before it. I had no confidence in him and in the Committee as well. The Congress also had no confidence in him and the Commttee under him. It was only due to his request that I went there. If the Committee was not ready to hear me, I would go back as I had no inclination to tell anything to a man in whom I virtually had no faith. I came back. But when the report was submitted by the Committee, it was clearly written there that Mr. Chatterji had no complaint to make before them. I said so many things which were not recorded and then it was falsely presented that since I had no grievance, I did not say anything.

Then one day the Bengal police sent one C. I. D. Inspector to the Agra jail to have elaborate talks with us. The purpose of his visit was not known to me but he called me to the jail office where a jailor was also present all along, and had talks with me for several hours. I repeatedly told him that I had no interest in talking with him and he should not unnecessarily waste his as well as my time. I told him that I was a convict in the U. P. Jail. What business now Bengal C. I. D. had got to disturb me even there ? He said that I originally belonged to Bengal and my records were kept by Bengal police, so he had every right to enquire. He started talking rudely and in a threatening language. I snubbed him. I told him that a slave had nothing to lose but his chains. I was already a habitual and lifer in the jail with bar-fetters on. What more could he inflict upon me. The Government was giving the maximum possible punishment. Then what right the Bengal police had to send its C. I. D. men for giving me pin-pricks ? His face was expressionless and motionless. On the next day he had talks with Sanyal Babu. A few days before this Shri Sanyal came to the Agra jail as he was suspected to be connected with an attempt at escape.

PLAN TO TAKE ME OUT

I informed my friends outside that I would soon be transferred to Lucknow jail. They wanted to take me out on the way. I gave them my consent and informed that they must be equipped with implements for cutting cross-bar fetters, so that my escape may be speedy. They were to keep strict vigit every night, because dangerous prisoners were generally transferred by the night train. Twenty four hours before the transfer, I gave them further news. They had informed me that the action would take place at a spot about 5 miles west of Kanpur.

Their plan was based on my transfer by the train that left Agra at 10 o'clock in the night. Batukeswar Dutta and Rajguru were keeping watch at the station.

To their utter disappointmeut I was escorted to the city station at about 6. It was a mere chance that four guards arrived that day from Lucknow with prisoners and they were to go back. So the police party that was to escort was there and these four men were given my charge. They took charge of me in the afternoon, we all went to the police office and after the formalities they took me at the Railway station. They did not enter the platform, but kept me seated outside under the charge of two guards while the other two went for marketing. I was there for about an hour and looked round, but found nobody. The escorts were not even armed. Two persons with firearms and a cycle could take me away. About half an hour before the depature of the train the two escorts came back and then we went into the platform. About 15 minutes before the train left Batukeswar Dutta and Rajguru came. Just as the train steamed off Dutta made a sign to me. I took that to be a signal that everything was all right.

I did not sleep in the night and was anxiously expecting that the train wood stop suddenly at the appointed place. But nothing happened. The train reached the Kanpur junction and I was locked up in the station office.

What happened has been described in a book recently written by Professor Bhagwandas Mahori of Jhansi who himself participated in this. They had made the preparations only for the train that left at 10 o'clock in the night. But on hearing of my departure by the earlier train they were very much upset. They all went to Kanpur by the next train and wanted to make the attempt near the Ganga Bridge station early in the morning. But this could not be arrenged as the time was very short.

The following persons participated in it: Chandrasekhar Azad, Bhagat Singh, Bijoy Kumar Sinha, Batukeswar Dutt, Rajguru, Sheo Verma, Sadashiv Raghunath Malkapurkar and Bhagwandas Mahore. Rajguru was sent to Kanpur by the same train by which I travelled.

At Kanpur station Azad was pick-pocketted of his purse in which he had all the money and also the motordriving licence. Bhagat Singh was very much distressed at this and asked Mahore to purchase tickets for Agra for all. At this stage they saw me going from the office with heavy chain on my legs towards the Lucknow bound train. They were all very much depressed and when they reached their residence at Agra, Bhagat Singh wept bitterly.

The attempt at escape from the Fatehgarh Central Jail as well as this later one of taking me from the police custody during my transfer from Agra Central Jail to Lucknow Central Prison were two of the main charges in the famous Lahore Conspiracy case against the accused. Sardar Bahadur Ganda Singh, the Head Jailor of Fatehgarh Central Prison, was a prosecution witness to prove the Fatehgarh jail incident against the accused and a jailor and the Superintendent of Agra Central

Prison, Col. Jafra IMS, were prosecution witnesses to prove the second attempt.

The accused gave my name as a defence witness in the Lahore Conspiracy case to disprove the Government allegations. And I would have certainly gone there. But in the meantime during the trial there developed a very serious clash between the Special Tribunal, prosectuion and the accused. As result of this the accused withdrew their defence and the Special Tribunal gave the ex-parte judgement in Jail. It was no longer a public trial. Bhagat Singh, Rajguru and Sukhdev were hanged and their mutilated bodies were burnt in the midnight at a great distance on the bank of the Sutlej. For legalising the ex-parte trial an Ordinance had to be passed by the Governor General of India.

One of the accused, Jatin Das, died in the Lahore Jail. He declared hunger strike, refused to take his food till his demands were fulfilled and died. His dead body was taken from Lahore to Calcutta and millions paid their homage to the departed patriot. Three heroes, who took part in the retaliation of the murder of the national leader, Lajpat Rai, were hanged, mutilated and burnt in the darkness of night and Mahatma Gandhi made a pact with the head of that Government soon after this performance of theirs ! Such is politics ?

LUCKNOW CENTRAL JAIL : ONE YEAR

My friends went back to Agra and I arrived at Lucknow Central Jail on the 18th February, 1929.

Though a habitual 'C' class prisoner, I was lodged in this jail in the European ward cell all alone. To all my protests the Superintendent's only reply used to be that my own friend Sanyal was responsible for this. The Superintendent stated that he was not in favour of my transfer to his jail, but when the I. G. of Prisons pressed him for this he got his permission to keep me alone in the European Ward. The attitude of the Superintendent was distinctly harsh, mainly because Sanyal Babu was involved in an escape plan. Even a habitual convict actually came out of the barrack and made a rope ladder for Sanyal but he did not come out. When the plan was detected the convict was most brutally assaulted and he implicated Sanyal in his statement. This was the reason of the Superintendent's ill treatment.

An Andaman-returned Convict Observer was kept in my ward to keep constant watch on me and this man's behaviour often caused me irritation. He was an uncultured criminal from Hardoi district. I also had the company of two other convicts, one a businessman from Kanpur and another a Pathan from the North West Frontier, who were Head Jailor's Convict Clerks and were very much interested in me. They were daily visiting me at noon time and talked with me for some hours. The Head Jailor and the Warders were under their tip and so they had a free hand in the Head Jailor ward outside the circles.

The man from Kanpur, Babulalji, was very sympathetic and helpful. Through Babulal I established some connections with my friend outside. I received some information through him. Yar Mohommad Khan, the Pathan, was attracted to me for his hunger for knowledge.

The Superintendent kept me alone, but twice or thrice a week he used to visit me in the evening. He used to stand outside and myself inside the cell and we had long talks on various subjects. For my reading materials he arranged with the Aminuddaula Public Library and under his recommendation I was allowed to subscribe the Modern Review. This was a great boon to me. On my release I learned from my cousin that once he saw the editor, late Ramananda Babu and that very day he gave orders that a free copy should be sent to me and I received it regularly till my release in 1937.

The Head Jailor, Mr. Hearne, knew that I was very much dissatisfied with the Superintendent because of segregation and other things. He himself was also in great difficulty because of the curtailment of his private earnings due to the strictness of the Superentendent. So one day he offered to supply a revolver to me if I wanted to kill the Superintendent. So pooar was his knowledge about political prisoners. A political prisoner would never kill a Superintendent on grounds of personal difficulties.

I learnt something about the N. W. Frontier affairs from Yar Mohammad. As an absconder he had come in close touch with Badshagul, who I came to know later, came in contact with our party. He told me that like our Gandhiji they had also a frontier Gandhi. He must have spoken of Khan Abdul Ghaffar Khan. He also spoke of another learned Pathan who was non religious and was married to an English lady. He must have meant Dr. Khan Sahib. Once I talked about escape from the jail. Within a week he smuggled Rs. 200/- for the expenses and told me to arrange the escape. He said after escape our travel upto Rawalpindi would be my risk, but after we crossed the river Attock he would be responsible for my safety. This man remained a few more years in Fyzabad jail and then in Lucknow jail and by that time he turned into a total non believer in religion.

My relations wanted my transfer to a Bengal jail and they even applied for this. The U. P. Government replied that they were ready provided the Bengal Government would accept me. The Bengal Government refused. I complained to Col. Clements, the I. G. of prisons. He said that I was a problem for them, the Andaman authorities would not accept me and the Bengal Government would not accept me either. He then turned to the Superintendent and told him, "Well, Salamatullah, give him Bengal jail diet;" I said that I did not want that and started hunger strike that very day. On the tenth day there was a compromise as due to the martyrdom of Jatin Das the question of classification of political prisoners came up and Nawab of Chhatari, the then Home Member, assured me of better-class treatment.

As a result of taking Bengal jail diet I gained 22 lbs, in weight and after we were classified as 'B' class I was again 146 lbs., the weight I had as an under-trial. This was, therefore, a statistical demonstration of the effect of food on the human body.

Jatin Das sacrificed his life with the deliberate determination that political prisoners must be classified as a special class of prisoners. The Government had to yield to public pressure to a certain extent, but only introduced certain changes in the general rule for all prisoners and nothing for the political prisoners in particular. Though in the Lucknow jail I was the only political prisoner, a dozen non-political prisoners were classfied as 'B' class and they were all sent to Fyzabad Concentration Jail but I was left alone at Lucknow.

Again we Kakori prisoners were given 'B' class, but Jatin Das's own associate of Lahore Conspiracy Case were not at all given 'B' class. Such was the attitude of the alien rule.

CHANDRASEKHAR AZAD'S FIGHT TO DEATH

My transfer from Agra jail was on the 17th February and Azad led the attempt to take me out. Then came the Assembly Bomb Case, the Lahore Conspiracy Case and the martyrdom of Jatin Das. Bhagwandas Mahore and Sadashiv Raghunath Malkapurkar were convicted in Bhushawal Bomb Case. Yet, the leader, Chadrasekhar Azad, survived.

One day came the heart-rending news of the fight to the finish of our dearest friend, the pride of our party, Chandrasekhar Azad. On the 27th of February 1931 morning he was talking to a friend sitting on a bench in a corner of the spacious Alfred Park at Allahabad. He was betrayed and police officer, Notbawer, approached him in a car and shot him on the thigh. At once Azad drew up his pistol and shot his assailant on his arm. Then the fight continued for some time. C. I. D. Inspector Bisweswar Singh's jaw was smashed by a shot from Azad. Long drawn fight was not possible, because the police had come prepared with a big force and Azad fell fighting. It was Azad's strongest determination that he would never step into a jail. He was ever alert for that and told so to friends often. The hero of Kakori, Lahore and Delhi cases at last attained the highest laurels at Allahabad Park. His dead body was promptly cremated by the police and was not given over to his friends or relations.

On his way back from the Karachi Congress my cousin, Paresh Chatterjee, came to interview me. He offered me some money but I said that it was unnecessary. The head jailor's writer, a Bengali, Ghosh, a cheat, told him that I required money for private use and a warder was sent to Paresh by Ghosh without my knowledge. But my Kanpur friend, Babulal, who was a convict clerk of the head jailor and was present in the head jailor's office when Paresh came to interview me, was clever enough to understand Ghosh's game. As soon as he saw the Warder coming, he took the money, from him and gave it to me to my surprise. The Warder's share was given and the rest was kept by me.

One day unexpectedly Rajkumar Sinha's mother and sister came to interview me. Rajkumar, along with Manmathanath Gupta, was on hunger strike for better class treatment following the Lahore hunger strike and Rajkumar was on the point of death. He had just given up the strike at the persuasion of the leaders. They had come from there. I was much pleased to meet them. From them I got much information.

Once late Pratul Chandra Ganguli also come to see me. We were not getting any newspapers and therefore these interviews were the only source of information of the condition outside the walls.

Shri Sachindranath Bakshi was transferred to this jail and after a long time I enjoyed his association. We were both classified as 'B' class: All others were sent to the Fyzabad jail, but we two remained here. We were both on hunger strike as a protest against the discrimination in the diet of Indian and European prisoners and later through compromise with the Superintendent we both took 'C' class diet till the arrival of Col. Palmer, the I. G. of Prisons, who decided the dispute to our satisfaction.

Major Salamatullah was transferred to the Naini Central Jail as Superintendent and Col. Sheikh came to Lucknow in his place.

We again planned to escape. We had contact with outside. One day Shri Satgurudayal Awasthi of Kanpur came outside the main wall of the European ward. Myself and Bakshi were on the big neem tree and through signals we communicated our plan of jumping jail.

Special guards were one day posted and we understood that the matter had leaked out. The I. G. of Prisons visited the jail that day and in the night at 2 A.M. my cell was unlocked by the Chief Head Warder who took me out to the yard. The Head Jailor, Mr. Hearne, was seated in a chair along with the Circle Jailor. Mr. Hearne told me that I was to be transferred at once but he did not reveal the jail where I was to go. I roused Bakshi Babu from sleep, talked to him and gave him some money and accompanied the jailor and others to the gate. I was fettered and then led to the motor van. The whole jail office was active at this dead hour of the night. The Superintendent had brought the order from the I.G.'s office personally in the evening and gave it to the jailor for the execution. The latter got up at 2 A.M. came to the office, brought other officials and warders. Blacksmith and convict clerks were also taken out. The whole jail was astir.

The escorts were all armed men under a Muslim Subedar. The van took the Kanpur Road, and reached Kanpur at day break. Somebody must have seen me and when we were sitting in the train for Agra, Pandit Balkrishna Sharma entered the compartment and asked me how I was being transferred and how the plan of escape failed. I said that I was betrayed from outside. The Subedar became very stern and did not allow me to talk any more. We went up to Tundla junction and even there we were not allowed to talk.

At Agra Fort Station the Superintendent of Police was at the platform with a detachment of armed men. They cordoned me and led me to the motor van. The officers took me to the gate of the very same Agra Central Prison where I spent a full year under different conditions. The Head Jailor, Mr. Gardener, told me later that he had never before received a prisoner in that style.

CHAPTER XV

IN AGRA CENTRAL JAIL AGAIN : Three and Half Years

I arrived at Agra Jail on the first of August 1931. Rajkumar Sinha and Ram Krishna Khatri were there in the European Ward. Khatri was transferred to Lucknow that very afternoon. We only enjoyed each other's company for a few hours.

Rajkumar was very pleased to have me as a companion. Through his letters his mother, sister and brother came to know of my arrival. His brother, Bijoy Kumar Sinha, was in Rajahmundry jail from where he wrote a letter envying his brother's luck to have me with him. His sister then started correspondence with me from Karachi. She wrote lengthy letters dealing with various matters.

My former sojourn in this jail was only for a year, but that had been very eventful. I, a habitual 'C' class prisoner under heavy fetters and heavy sentence, lived then with the hardened long-term criminals and earned the full confidence of my jail mates. I defied the Bengal C. I. D. Inspector, the Chief Judge of Oudh Chief Court and even the jail authorities on moral grounds. But this time, though under the same sentence, I was a privileged prisoner in a better class, living aloof from others in a separate spacious European Ward. This meant only monotony and no romance. Formerly I was in constant touch with the active members of the party. Now that was a thing of the past. Chandrasekhar Azad, Bhagat Singh and Rajguru were already in the rank of martyred national heroes and others like Bijoy and Batukeswar were struggling hard as long-termer 'C' class in South Indian Jails, about to be transferred to Andamans.

About 500 Bengal detenus were sent to Deoli Detention Camp, 71 miles from the city of Ajmer. Convicts were sent from U.P. jails to serve them. Two of them belonging to Aligarh district came back to Agra jail on their way to be released. From them we came to know that there had been a lathi-charge in the camp. The news was conveyed to Satyendranath Mitra, who gave the news in the Hindustan Times and also put a short notice question before the Assembly. The reply was not satisfactory. But immediately after this the Home Member personally went there for enquiry and the Commander was transferred and a new Commander was given the charge.

Sachindranath Bakshi, whom I had left in Lucknow jail was transferred to Agra jail and Rajkumar Sinha was sent to Lucknow. Now Khatri and Sinha, sentenced to 10 years each, were in Lucknow jail and myself and Bakshi, the two lifers were in Agra Central jail. Shaukat Usmani also was brought to this jail after his conviction in the Meerut Conspiracy Case. He had very serious differences with his comrades in the Meerut case, because when he started a hunger strike, as a protest against the misbehaviour of a C.I.D. Inspector, nobody supported him and consequently he felt humiliated. He was kept in a separate jail as an under-trial in that case and after conviction all were sent to Allahabad Jail, but he alone was sent to Agra Central Jail. He was very resentful and depressed, and pressed me for an escape plan with the object of going to Moscow with me. I was not enthused and suddenly one day he was *transferred to the district jail.*

Mahavir Banga of Allabahad was in a cell here on his sentence of two years rigorous imprisonment under the Arms Act. Also Sudama Prasad of the Shahjahanpur Bomb Case came with a conviction but later he was let off through the efforts of Devnarain Bharati.

I had nothing with which to occupy myself. So I took gardening in right earnest. There were big plots of land in front and on one side of my ward. At the back was the jail garden. Flower gardens were already in the front yard, started by my friends, and I made some improvements. I started vegetable gardening along one side first and it was gradually extended to the back. I read books on this topic and learned the theories of gardening but I picked up much more from the prisoners who had life-long practical knowledge of gardening. To get their help was ordinarily difficult in jail but as I was a privileged prisoner, I could manage it. Butter, sugar, eggs and loaf helped me a good deal. The warders, convict officials and prisoners were helpful to me due to these delicacies. The jailor or the Superintendent came came occasionally and the jail used to remain practically in the hands of the warders and convict officials. I was also regarded as an experienced person in jail affairs. Throughout the day I used to keep myself engaged in gardening and produced very nice flowers and vegetables. I composed a good quality manure and found that ashes applied in the compost and around the stem were the remedy against insects. In this my products were the finest. The jailor used to take the headwarder in charge of the garden to my place and showed my products and put him to task for bad results in the his garden. How could the poor warder compete with me ? He was working for his living with forced labour. He had to extort money from the convicts. He had to satisfy the jailor and other officials providing them with a fixed supply. The quality vegetables were only needed for officials. The jailor knew the reality but he took the warder to task only as a general way of stimulating work. But for me, how to dispose of my garden products was a problem. Readily edible produce, such as carrot, beans, watermelons, etc. were taken away by warders but nobody wanted green vegetables. Myself and our cook could take very little.

AGRA CONSPIRACY MEN

Some boys of local prosperous families were involved in the Agra Conspiracy Case and detained at the jail. We managed to meet them privately but officially they were not allowed to mix with us. They were given heavy sentences and transported elsewhere.

Bhupen Sanyal came here with a fresh sentence after his release from the Kakori conviction. This time he was given 18 months R. I. for a seditious speech in a Youth Conference at Mathura. But soon he was transferred to another jail.

DEATH OF MY COUSIN SAILESH CHANDRA CHATTERJEE

The most painful news of my life in jail was received here. Bakshi and myself had just finished our midday meals. The Chief Head-warder was coming towards our yard with some papers. He handed over one telegram to me. I read it and was just on the verge of collapsing. Bakshi snatched it from me and I came to myself and then read it carefully. The first shock was so sudden and so terrible that it seemed to me as if I had lost all contact with the earth and my hand with the paper was shaking. The telegram was to our Jail Superintendent from the Commandant of Deoli

Detention Camp. The message was: "Inform Jogesh Chatterji that his brother Sailesh Chatterjee died of sudden fever yesterday morning." Sailesh was my cousin who was hardly two years old when I went to jail in 1916. On my return from jail he became very intimate with me. He used to eat with me and sleep with me and he felt uncomfortable in my absence. He had such a loving nature that everybody was irresistably endeared by him. Health, beauty, intelligence and energy he possessed amply. Naturally he became a very active member of the party. He was thrown into prison before he completed even his seventeenth year, when he was preparing for his Intermediate examination in Science. He was in Hijli Detention Camp where two detenus were shot dead by the guards, and there was a countrywide agitation over this. From there he appeared in B.A. examination and passed with distinction. Then he was transferred to Deoli Camp. He had an attack of high fever and was removed to the hospital. He was there alone and a Dr. Khan gave him an intravenous quinine injection of 10 c.c. He died, rather the doctor killed him. Later I came to know that my father, too, died the same day in East Bengal.

Even then I wrote to my aunt that I suspected some evil hand in the death of Sailesh. This was in 1933 and eight years later in 1941 I came to know the matter in detail from the compounder who was present at the time of my cousin's death. I was then in the jail hospital. The compounder was going to his quarters after his duty was over. He stopped beside my bed and we had talks about the camp. He began narrating some old stories of of the place. He told of an incident when Bengal detenus were there and an episode happened resulting in the death of a brilliant youth. He said that Dr. Khan was solely responsible for that death. He said that he had been present at the time and objected to the administration of 10 c. c. quinine to a person in such high fever,—when the temperature was as high as 1040 ; but the doctor went ahead and the tragedy took place. The compounder had no idea that the youth he was talking about was my own cousin. When I told him this, he was very much afraid that he might lose his job if I attempted an agitation after eight years which would be ineffective and futile.

The Divisional Commissioner came on a visit one afternoon. After some talks on literature, he asked us if we needed anything. I said that he might do one thing for us. If he tried, we might he able to get books from the Missionary College Library. He promised to support my request but asked me to write it. Accordingly I wrote to the Principal of the Missionary College through the Commissioner that though the College Library was not meant for outsiders, theirs was a missionary institution and we were prisoners in jail ;

he might supply us a few such books as could be spared. I would suggest the subject and he would select the books. He was good enough to agree to my proposal and sent 10 books in the first month. It was a great boon to us. We read the books voraciously and sent them back in time and received the second instalment the next month. We returned the books duly. We asked for more books but none were received. We complained but no one paid any heed. The College authorities sent reminders but no reply was given. At the end of the third month the Principal wrote a strong personal letter to the Superintendent and he came to us. We complained of the lack of attention to so straight forward a request as these books.

ADMINISTRATION OF AGRA JAIL

As a man Col. Jafri was not bad. But he had no personality of his own and no integrity. He always depended on his subordinates against whom he could never think of talking any step even for the most gross misconduct. He would never dare to hear any of the prisoners. So the jail under him was a veritable hell. One Andaman returned Muslim of hardened character was incharge of cells. He was at liberty to do whatever he liked. So a reign of terror prevailed there. He was daily beating prisoners mercilessly. He extorted money from prisoners. Any youngster he could have as his boy for homosexuality. Even our complaint to the Superintendent against this act was futile. But at last the prisoners themselves took revenge. He was given glass powder with Halwa (a sweet dish) and he died in the hospital under excrutiating pain asking for God's mercy for his mis-deeds. The jail authorities did not know the cause of his pain but I knew, as the man who administered it told me what he had done. Such was the confidence of other convicts in me.

The Aligarh Muslim died but his role was taken up by a Brahmin of Mainpuri. This Brahmin, as a newcomer, had received brutal beatings from the Muslim and he complained to me very bitterly. But soon after the Muslim's death be became the jailor's pet and started doing the very same thing. It is not the person but the system which is responsible for all this. A radical change is necessary for social development, no matter whether it is in jail or outside.

Inside the jail wall there is a society of men under the same administration. The highly paid Superintendent is assisted by an army of low paid men. From amongst the prisoners also there are men on privileged position through whom others are kept in check. Force is the main factor. If the top is slack, then the whole jail is slack. Every officer's object is to. earn something extra. The result is that Government properties are looted freely and the prisoners are atrociously and ruthlessly oppressed. That was the condition of the Agra Jail during the three years that I spent there as a 'B' class prisoner.

But quite different was the position during the time of Col. Seikh who was honest and upright to the core. The officials were terribly afraid of him, corruption was much reduced and prisoners were much better off. Looting of Government property was reduced.

Col. Seikh had the determination to stop illicit smuggling of articles in jail but Col. Clements, the I. G. of Prisons, told him that it was impossible. Seikh had to agree after a period of experimenting. In Lucknow jail Hearne studied the weak points in Seikh and befooled him by various devices. Hearne used to allow the rich relatives of the prisoners interview in his bungalow and received a good amount of money from them. Seikh had no knowledge of it. One day while convicts were in the jailor's bungalow, a warder of the gate guard, Alam Ali, gave the whistle of alarm. The Superintendent's bungalow was at a distance. So the daring iailor asked Alam Ali to allow the prisoners to get in. But Alam Ali warned him with loaded gun not to come near. In the meantime Jailor's men placed a ladder on the outer wall and jumped into the jail. One very fatty tradesman failed to do so and remained out. But the jailor with the assistance of others managed to show in the counting of prisoners that everything was alright. The poor warder was dismissed for giving false alarm. Long after this Seikh came to know the truth and on his admonition the trader himself made the confession. So Alam Ali was reinstated and promoted as a head-warder. But even then no step could be taken against the Anglo-Indian jailor.

Even Salamatullah, a strict disciplinarian could not bring Hearne under his control. No doubt Hearne felt his pressure and was uncomfortable, as much of his income was reduced. He openly revolted at times in the presence of subordinates and Salamatullah had to yield, because he knew that in an open tussle Hearne would be backed by the Government. Hearne belonged to the rulers' race and that was his strength. Clements could never support Salamatullah against Hearne. Every white skinned man had the superiority complex. Clements looked upon us, the political prisoners, as his personal enemies. He ill treated us deliberately and was afraid of us. He told me after our conviction that we should forget now that we were Kakori men. It was because of his suggestion that we were classified as habituals after the hunger strike. I made it a point since then to be indifferent towards him. My grave indifference made him so much afraid of me that when he came on a visit he dragged two warder guards in front when he noticed that I was inside the weaving factory. This attracted so much notice from the habitual long-termers that they discussed this amongst themselves after he left the factory.

HUNGER STRIKE AT AGRA 1934
(11-7-'34 to 29-11-'34)

The Lahore Conspiracy Case was an offshoot of the Kakori Case. A struggle for special treatment of political prisoners in jail was taken up by the Lahore Case undertrials. Jatin Das, who was the link between Bengal and the rest of northern India after the arrest of Sanyal and myself, reluctantly resorted to hunger strike with others. He was at the beginning averse to it, because he knew the Government attitude in Kakori prisoners' cases. But when he joined it he was fully conscious of the dangerous consequences. His determination was either to mend the Government attitude or end himself. He proved true to it by ending himself.

Owing to strong public pressure the Government promised to do something. But the matter ended in duplicity. No special class was given to political prisoners but prisoners in general were classified into three divisions, 'A' 'B' and 'C'. As the result of this 95%of the political prisoners were classified as 'C'; about 3 or 4 percent were classed as 'B' and less then 1 percent as 'A'. This was an instrument to break the solidarity of political prisoners. The stereotyped policy of 'divide and rule' was introduced in jail. We the Kakori prisoners got 'B' class. But this Government attitude oppressed us too much.

The Kakori prisoners were given 'B' class the very first day classification was introduced in U. P.

jails, but they were neither sent to the Concentration Jail at Fyzabad nor allowed mutual associations. They were kept alone or in twos. Against this Manindra Nath Banerjee resorted to hunger strike in Fatehgarh Central Prison and ultimately died. Banerjee was given 10 years R. I. for shooting Rai Bahadur Jitendra Nath Banerjee, Dy. S. P., C. I. D. While firing he shouted 'Revenge of Kakori'.

The news gave us a shock. For three days we thought and thought. Are we to die one by one in this way? No, not at all. If we are to die we must do so with a loud protest. We gave notice to the Government through the Superintendent that (i) all political prisoners must be formed into a special class and given better class treatment; (ii) they must be given daily newspapers and other reading facilities; (iii) they must be accommodated in Association barracks and given opportunities for games and exercise. So I started my historic and grim hunger strike,—the hardest one of my life, in early July 1934 along with Sachin Bakshi, in Agra Central Jail. Bakshi developed dysentery during the strike and had to drop out on the 45th day at my request. His aged father was brought down from Banaras and sought my assistance which I readily gave. I was now alone and felt relieved as now I was free of any other responsibility.

From the 55th day I gave up water as well. The I. G. of Prisons, Lt. Col. Palmer, had already told me that I might die and his Government wouldn't care. So I wrote to him that as an honourable Englishman he might keep his word by giving orders to the Superintendent of the Jail not to give me even water through my nose. The Superintendent saw that I was losing weight at the rate of one lb. per day for not taking water and this was very dangerous at this stage. So he was giving me one lb. of water along with the pint of liquids that he was feeding me through my nose. I redoubled my struggle when this water-feeding started. The first day I gave a blow to the junior doctor when he was twisting my left hand during the feeding. The Superintendent realised that this doctor was my enemy. So from the next day this junior doctor was ordered to look after my health and the senior doctor since then used to visit me only once during the force feeding with the Superintendent. The junior doctor once taunted me saying that he had met many hunger strikers in jail and like them I would continue about a month or so and then would give it up.

It was a grim competition. The authorities were determined to keep me alive and I was determined to bring about a crisis. Government attitude was well known to me and so I started with good preparations. Even before I gave notice of the strike I kept four big feathers cleaned and sterilized underneath my bed.

Every morning the Superintendent used to come

to my cell with a retinue of performers and went away leaving me along after the food. I used to take out a feather and vomit out the liquid with its help, into the bed pan. But the system would absorb a good portion of the food within 5 or 10 minutes.

One day the Chief Head Warder, a muslim commissioned ex-serviceman of the Punjab, saw the sweeper washing the bed-pan in which there was a big amount of vomitted food materials and reported the matter to the Superintendent, Lt. Col. Jafri. He came out in the afternoon with the jailor, the doctors and others and made a thorough search and the four feathers were discovered and taken away. The whole night I felt uneasy and disturbed in mind. If I fail to vomit, they would be able to keep me alive for an indefinite period and the troubles and tortures would continue. But to my great pleasure the next morning I vomitted down the same portion of food as I was doing so long with the help of the feathers. More than a month's continuous practice had already made the system helpful for this. So in spite of the regular and substantial feeds my weight was going down steadily.

The condition was so much alarming that on the 68th day the European District Magistrate came to see me and talked with me for nearly an hour and half. The trend of the talk clearly indicated that he was seeking a way out. I made the Government and the Jail Superintendent, too, responsible for this desperate step of mine. The Government must recognise political prisoners as a special class of prisoners and the jail authorities too, must be made to feel that we are not ordinary criminals,—these were my demands. I was a determined man on the death bed and the examples of Jatin Das and Mani Banerjee were before me. I, therefore, spoke to this Englishman as an Indian patriot who was speaking to a representative of our exploiter though I was in no way impolite to him.

The next day came the Commissioner of the Division. He, too, was an Englishman. He categorically asked me if I would go to the Andamans. This was significant. Because once in the past I had volunteered to go to the Andamans as an English knowing Clerk. I told the Commissioner that I was quite ready to go to the Andamans, provided that my standard of living would continue to be the same as a 'B' class prisoner and that I was on hunger strike for the cause of all political prisoners. I told him categorically that I stood by my demands. They might get rid of me by sending me to the Andamans, but that would not solve the problem. This proposal of mine was no solution of their problem and he went away rather puzzled.

The very next day Pandit Srikrishna Dutt Paliwal, Balkrishna Sharma, Prem Krishna Khanna and other gentlemen came to see me. Without even asking me anything first, Paliwalji delivered a speech in English that on behalf of the public they want that I should surrender as the alien Government would not meet my demand and allow me to die as others have died. The country could not afford to lose me. He also assured me that a big reform was to come and that the Congress would come into power in a couple of years and it would then get us out of jail. When he stopped Sharmaji, in the like manner, delivered a fine short speech. In the meantime Khanna was very much upset and began to weep when he felt that my hands and legs were tied down to the bed. I was covered upto the neck with a bed sheet and the ends of the sheet were carefully fastened to the bed with big safety pins. I was kept in this condition for months by the Jail Superindendent on the ground that I might otherwise commit suicide. I had spoken to the D. M. that this allegation of the Superintendent was absolutely groundless because, as a veteran revolutionary, I hated the idea of suicide.

The hunger strike lingered on and I continued to suffer terrible pain day in and day out for nearly another two and half months.

But there was fortunately a big change in my favour. The Junior Doctor who was my enemy so long suddenly became a fast friend. He overheard the talk that I had with the D. M. In the afternoon he came to me alone and declared that he was my friend and would render all possible help to me. On my enquiry he gave the reason that he overheard the talk and he never before believed that an Indian prisoner could talk on equal terms with an English D. M. Since then he used to give me all secret information regarding my affairs and used to go to Paliwalji and the editor of a local daily to acquaint them with the latest news regarding my health. There was also a warder, who took a keen interest in me purely on patriotic grounds and took the risk of coming to the back of my cell. On hearing his tap on the wall I used to be attentive and exchanged words slowly and quickly. So although absolutely alone in my bed, counting the days of life in excruciating pain, I had three sure friends : the sweeper, the warder and the doctor, to console me.

The Chief Head Warder again saw one day the bedpan being cleared by the sweeper in the drain in which the vomitted materials were being washed away. He again reported to the Superintendent. This time the order was that over and above my fastened hands legs, a thick newar rope be fastened round my chest in such a way that I had to lie down on my back and could not stir. I was kept in this way for one hour after forced feeding and then the Senior Doctor used to come and unfasten the rope. This was because after the feed a man can vomit within half an hour and after that liquid is absorbed by the body. But to my delight even in this prostrate condition a considerable quantity of food came out and dropped down on my chest soiling the cloth. The Superintendent could do nothing to prevent this and hence from the next day after the feed while roping me up with the bed they placed a big towel on my chest and it was taken away by the Doctor when he came to unfasten me.

There was no natural motion and hunger strikers generally do not have natural motions. I never had a natural motion in any of my hunger strikes. This was a problem this time with the Superintendent. From the beginning I refused to take enema. This was a veritable struggle between myself and the jail authorities. My task was to get rid of these tortures as soon as I could either through an honourable compromise or through an early death. A number of people used to overpower me, clutching hold of my hands, legs and the head and the compounder used to sit on my body. The junior doctor used to hold the head steady and the senior doctor used to help the Superintendent, in thrusting the long tube inside the nostril. The tube was soft and made slippery by dipping in glycerine before passing it through the nose. Daily I struggled hard and got completely exhausted and the pound of water that they poured into the stomach caused me a terrible pain for nearly an hour when I used to make water. My body was reduced to a mere skeleton, only the loose skin remaining on it. My intestines also shrinked and hence the big amount of water along with the liquid feed gave me so much pain. But at the same time this water helped me a good deal in vomitting out the liquid and water too. So the process of reduction continued slowly but surely.

I was given feeds for 6 days every week and on the seventh day a big quantity of castor oil emulsion was given in the stomach through the nostril. That day no feed was possible. In the beginning I was getting a motion after the administration of this castor oil, but with the passage of time I was getting physically exhausted and was losing proportionately the power of regular motion. At an advanced stage I was getting a motion the next day or the day after or even the third day and no feed was possible as long as the castor oil was there. The smell was nauseating and the pain too very acute.

At long last this very thing brought about the crisis. The Superintendent gave me castor oil emulsion feed for three consecutive days but there was no motion. He was alarmed. He consulted the Civil Surgeon and perhaps the other doctor friends and then for another three days consecutively he gave me a drug called Cascara. Yet there was no motion. My pain was simply unbearable and the condition became frightful for myself as well as the jail authorities. The Superintendent reported that I could never survive more than a fortnight. For a week I could not have a wink of sleep and was restless. Even today the very memory of that gives me a shudder. The inhuman police tortures of 1916 was nothing compared to this pain I was suffering. The hallowed memory of my dearest comrade Jatin Das was constantly in my mind and the Government's refusal to fulfil the public demand for a special class for the political prisoners was inspiring me. Young Mani Banerjee's martyrdom at Fatehgarh jail was the fresh stimulant with which I started the Strike. I tried to forget all pain absorbing myself in these thoughts and felt refreshed and relieved.

Within more than five and half months my weight was reduced from 138 lbs. to 76 lbs. only. The organs inside were working alright though feebly. Sense organs were rather keen. A slight sound anywhere would stir me up and even the chirping of small birds distubred me a good deal. In fact in my own mind I had taken leave of the world. The doctors used to examine my heart very often. Their idea was, as my doctor told me, that one day suddenly my heart would fail. But before that my pain would be unbearable for a day or two. I told him that I would put up with that patiently.

At this stage I heard that the I. G. of Prisons was to visit the jail. Preparations were going on very vigorously, because the notice was very short. One morning the doctor friends gave me the information that the Governor had suddenly come to Agra and was staying in the Circuit House and the Jail Superintendent had been there in the night. He thought that it had something to do with my hunger-strike.

In the morning two chairs were placed in my cell and the doctor informed me that this was done under the orders of the I. G. of Prisons, Lt. Col. Salamatullah, who would come to see me. He came at about 11 A. M. after hurriedly finishing his round of jail and sat near me for full two hours, accompanied by the Jail Superintendent. He tried to persuade me to give up the strike. As the first Indian I. G. of Prisons he had come authorised to meet most of my demands. But he was not ready to come to definite terms. I told him that after an exhaustive struggle the situation was now under my control. The Government policy of keeping me alive indefinitely was now shaken off and I controlled the reins. Therefore I could not give up the strike unless I was assured of the future. It was not a personal matter at all. He told me again and again that he had come fully authorised and could therefore say that most of my grievances would be removed. He requested me again and again to take one last chance and I only said in reply that the matter required clarification, otherwise I might again be placed in the same terrible plight. At last I agreed to take the chance once again giving him the warning that the strike would surely be restarted if the matter was not decided satisfactorily and he would be held responsible. He agreed and I called off the strike by taking a little milk. He also promised me that I would be transferred to Naini Jail.

Later I realised that I did this because when a man hangs between life and death, the life-saving instinct prevails on him. It was certainly weakness on my part to give up the strike without any clear and definite understanding.

The doctor friend came to me shortly after the departure of the I. G. of Prisons. He had earlier given me the information that in the evening the Superintendent had been to the Governor. Now he gave me the information that the Governor came to Agra accompanied by the I. G. of Civil Hospitals, the outgoing I. G. of Prisons, Lt. Col. Palmer, and the incoming I. G. of Prisons, Lt. Col. Salamatullah and Major Bhandari I. M. S. Our Jail Superintendent met them in the Circuit House with the records of my case and all the doctors were agreed on the report of the Superintendent that my case was really beyond their control and my death was inevitable. So they decided that I would be released unconditionally and kept in the Thomson Hospital for treatment. But Lt. Col. Salamatullah volunteered to make the last effort to see if I could be persuaded to give up the strike.

I was under the sentence of transportation for life in a dangerous case. In this respect my unconditional release would have been a big thing for me no doubt. But the cause for which I suffered would not have gained anything as a result of my release. In this sense my conditional calling off of the strike was better, because by giving up the strike I did not give up the case. And really I had to restart it at Lucknow the next year as the Government's attitude was callous and even deceitful.

Gradually I recovered my health satisfactorily. The first few days were very critical. A man must be very careful and must restrain himself strictly till he reaches the normal condition. A slight wrong step at this stage may prove dangerous. I was an expert on this due to my long practice as a hunger striker. Gandhiji also considered himself to be expert on fasting. But compared to him my practice and sufferings were hundred times more. Gandhiji had been on strike utmost for 3 weeks at a time but I had been for months and months. He was never given a forced feeding.

So many revolutionary prisoners have died in India, the Andamans and Burma by hunger strikes. Parallel occurrences can hardly be found in other countries. Mac Swiny is the single example in Europe. Old Russian revolutionaries were once on hunger strike in Cara prison in Siberia. It continued for a little over a week. Some leading women revolutionaries in the female jail which was at a distance of about seven miles from the Cara

Prison were also on hunger strikes. But they could not continue and had to give up. The reaction of this frustration was so intense that later some of these men and women committed suicide by taking opium. Death by hunger strike is still continuing in the Indian Union under the Congress rule as a protest against the administrative policy.

A few days after I gave up the strike the mother of Rajkumar Sinha came to see me at about 10 A. M. I was lying on a mat in the sun and my convict cook was massaging mustard oil on my body. The jailor and the mother sat on the two chairs. Though a skeleton I could even walk a little, but at my first attempts I dropped down several times. I mildly complained to Rajkumar's mother that I did not get proper stimulating nourishment. I asked my cook to show her what rotten fruits I was given. Then I told her that I asked for fish and fish was actually brought for me and shown to me, but when the Superintendent saw this he told them not to give me that. Of course, he had no evil intention, he thought it would be harmful. Rajkumar's mother said that it would have been better if she could cook for me.

Her report in the press that I was not getting proper nourishment produced a good result. I started getting good things.

My doctor friend was anxious, because of the rapidity of my heart-beats but when he talked to the Superintendent, Col. Jafri, he stated that it was quite natural. My heart-beat was fast, he said, due to the rapidity of recovery and for this reason the pulse of children work very rapidly.

I was all alone and I pressed for association. The result was may transfer to Lucknow jail again.

CHAPTER XVI

TRANSFERRED TO LUCKNOW CENTRAL PRISON

I was soon transferred to Lucknow Central Jail where I met again Rajkumar Sinha and Ram Krishna Khatri. Lt. Col. Sheikh was the Superintendent. I recovered my lost health rapidly in their pleasant association. My heart which had sunk down alarmingly during the strike now became normal. But as a result of the hunger strike my lever was permanently damaged and the nerve system weakened.

Ram Krishna Khatri and Raj Kumar Sinha had made the small European Ward a nice place. Beautiful flower beds were developed and they also planted some big crotons. The atmosphere was very pleasant. Time was passing well.

They both had served their terms of 10 years and the time of their release was approaching. Rajkumar's release was more important. He and his brother were in jail and the mother was alone at Kanpur. At last the pleasant day arrived and Raj Kumar and Khatri were released from jail. Kashi Ram and Haldhar Bajpai came in their place. Haldhar Bajpai came from Banaras Central Jail.

Famous Bengal revolutionary of Anushilan Samiti, Sitanath De, had come to Banaras and approached late Acharya Narendra Deva for shelter. Acharyaji, the Principal of the Kashi Vidyapith, gave the charge to a student of the Vidyapith. Sitanath De thought that he was betrayed to the police. He met Haldhar Bajpai in Banaras jail and told him that his object in coming to U. P. was to take me out from jail. But he was arrested even before he could try to contact me. This message was brought by Haldhar Bajpai.

Sachindra Nath Sanyal was also transferred to Lucknow Jail. I met Sanyal after many years. Although we met at Agra casually, exchange of ideas was not possible there. Here I realised the difference in ideas between us. He persuaded me to the best of his ability not to restart hunger strike. But I was determined. When he fully realised my grim determination he gave up arguing. I told him that I knew that the Government would not pay any heed and my death was absolutely sure and yet the strike had to be resorted to. Jatin Das had sacrificed himself and let me also follow the same path. I wanted nothing but death.

Gradually I realised that I have been befooled by the I. G. of Prisons and the Government. In Lucknow jail personally I was given an association of four persons and in place of a weekly paper a biweekly was given. My demand was not at all personal. So this could not give me the least satisfaction, rather it exasperated me to further action. So I sent an application wherein I put my grievances and the I. G. of Prisons came personally to see me; but his sweet words could not at all convince me. I now saw that another hunger strike was inevitable. In the meantime Khatri and Sinha had gone out after serving their long 10 years' terms. Through them and through other souces the news was sent out that I was serious on this. Pressure was put on me from outside that such a step at this time would be very dangerous and hence should not be resorted to. Sachindranath Sanyal was transferred to Lucknow surely with this purpose. He was constantly dissuading me from my determination. But no amount of argument or pressure could slacken my firm stand. At last I gave the Government one month's ultimatum.

HUNGER STRIKE AGAIN

Sanyal realised the gravity and told me that India was going to lose an honest revolutionary. The I. G. of Prisons and the U. P. Government knew now that it was a greater problem before them than that of Agra. On the completion of the month I started the Hunger strike in October 1935. This time because it was a real fast unto death the demands were also placed before the authorities in a crystal clear manner. They were:

(1) All political prisoners are to be classified as one class and given better class treatment.

(2) Daily newspapers are to be supplied at State expense.

(3) All political prisoners are to be kept in concentration jail and be given facilities for games, reading and writing and accommodation in association barracks.

(4) All political prisoners kept in Andaman must be repatriated to the Indian jails.

On the sixth day I was removed to hospital cell. I parted from my associates with the idea of parting for good. I was absolutely prepared for that. None had the least idea that I would survive. The only problem in my mind was how to hasten the end. The very idea of hunger strike was a terror to me yet I had to resort to it.

The circumstances here were more favourable in the sense that the Superintendent was not doing anything himself. He left everything to the Muslim senior doctor who was also callous and gave false reports to the Superintendent. The doctor came to me seldom and depended on the compounder. And the junior doctor was in touch with the revolutionaries as a student and hence he was sympathetic to me.

One day one person came from Kanpur and had a talk with me. He said that they were not giving anything to the Press and trying their utmost to come to some settlement with the Government by private negotiations. I only told him that the matter was not so easy.

On the sixth day Pandit Jagadamba Prasad Hitaisi was allowed to meet me in jail hospital, but Surendranath Pande and Maulana Hasrat Mohani had to remain outside the jail gate as they were not allowed to meet me.

On the 23rd day the Home Members, Sir Maharaj Singh came. He said that a daily paper was a most reasonable thing and and this could be given; but concentration of all political prisoners into one jail was simply impossible. I refused to enter into any discussion and said that my demands were there in the application and the Government would either concede them or allow me to die peacefully. He sympathetically felt the temperature of my forehead with his hand and then went away telling the Superintendent to keep me warm.

I was struggling on for more than a month. I was given a big feed in the hospital and I was afraid. But I vomitted out much of it the very first day and nobody kept any watch on me. I gave up water as well. But some water out of the feed was absorbed by the body. The doctor gave the false report always that I took water. I, however, felt very thirsty all along.

There was no news about my strike in any newspaper. Ram Krishna Khatri, who had gone home in Central Provinces after release from this jail, was astonished not to see any news in any paper. Khatri came to Lucknow and Swami Kumaranand joined him. At their instance the Pratap of Kanpur came out with the news for the first time in bold headline and thus gave the start to propaganda. Then the cause was taken up by all other leaders including the President of the Indian National Congress, Babu Rajendra Prasad and the U. P. Congress President Rafi Ahmed Kidwai. A countrywide vigorous propaganda was carried on and a Day was observed. I was in day to day correspondence with Khatri and received cuttings of various papers daily. The sweeper helped me in this. Daily I was also receiving telegrams from leaders, of course, persuading me to give up the strike as the country had taken up my cause. Yet I did not believe that this time there could be any compromise with the authorities. So in the midst of all this I was trying hard for an early end of myself. My weight was going down alright. What worried me was the thought of the continuance of my sufferings. From the beginning I had worked out a set plan from an early end. I never put a drop of water into my mouth. As a result after about a hundred days my gums began to bleed. An intolerable bad odour was constantly coming out of the mouth from the beginning only for this reason. This pyorreah in the gum would emit dangerous poison and this would go into the stomach and .poison the intestines and thus my death will be hastened. On hearing this the Superintendent persuaded me very seriously to save my fine set of teeth from immediate ruination. Though an eccentrically strict man he told me that the Government was ready to concede my main demands and he was sure that I won't require to end myself. The Government was on the move and I should not live the rest of my life without teeth. I could disbelieve any other official but not Lt. Col. Sheikh, the Superintendent whom I knew thoroughly for so many years. I have not seen such a fanatically honest man in jail in my 24 years of jail life in different provices of northern India. It was now clear to me that a compromise move was ahead on behalf of the Government. So I agreed to get my gum and teeth treated. He sent for the doctor and gave detailed instruction and himself attended the first course. My teeth were saved with slight permanent damages.

Within a week after this one morning Rafi Ahmed Kidwai, Mohanlal Saksena, Balkrishna Sharma and Ram Krishna Khatri came to interview me. They said that Maharaj Singh had sent for them and given them the clear understanding that they would concentrate all politicals into one jail, grant daily newspapers, keep the political prisoners in association barrack and give them facilities for reading writing and sports. But as regards the two other demands namely, to treat all politicals as a special class and repatriation of Andaman prisoners to Indian jails, the U. P. Government would strongly write to the Government of India for an early settlement. It may be mentioned here that before Maharaj Singh sent for the four leaders, it was announced through the press that Maharaj Singh had gone to Simla for consultations with the Central Government regarding some problems of U. P. It was also hinted by the press that the hunger strike in jail was one of the problems. It was decided that some member would put a question in the Council and the Home Member would give the reply that the Government would look into the case after Chatterji gave up the hunger strike.

The point of dispute was that I wanted a time limit for the fulfilment of the two main points. This was decided to be a year and a half. They then left and came back after five days with the question and answer in the Council and I terminated the strike in their presence on the 111th day.

My hunger strike was terminated in January. Lucknow was busy at that time for the next session of the Indian National Congress (1936) under the Presidentship of Jawaharlal Nehru. When after the hunger strike was over and I was fit to travel, my transfer took place to Naini Jail.

We were four in number. The guards were on friendly terms with me on our way, because as a result of the victory in my hunger strike, sympathies of many Indian elements among the Government servants were with us.

That is the reason why our escort in charge told me while we were standing outside the Allahabad Station waiting for transport to Naini, that Jawaharlal Nehru was at the station and we might meet him if we liked. Nehru was coming out of the platform when our guard told him about us. Nehru came to us and told us that he had come to the station to see off Dr. B. C. Roy and we could also have met Dr. Roy had it been known a little before. I regretted this loss and thanked Nehru for meeting us. He enquired about our well-being and left and we left for Naini Jail.

The year and half was to be completed on the 31st August, 1937 and the Congress Ministry was formed in U. P. in June 1937 and our defence counsel Govind Ballav Pant, became the Chief Minister and Rafi Ahmed Kidwai the Home Minister in charge of jail. In July I made an application to the Chief Minister to the effect that on the 31st August a year and half would be completed and hence from the 1st of September I would be free to restart the hunger strike if the two demands were not fulfilled. A copy was also sent to the Hon'ble Home Minister. We, the Kakori prisoners were released on the 24th August and on the 28th night I met Kidwai at the residence of Acharya Narendra Deva and the first question he asked me was, 'Mr. Chatterji, when are you going to restart the hunger strike ?

CONGRESS WORKING COMMITTEE RESOLUTION

Shortly after the formation of ministries in the provinces a meeting of the Congress Working

Committee was held at Wardha. It passed a resolution to the effect that political prisoners should be treated as a special class. The resolution was moved by Babu Rajendra Prasad and my name was mentioned in it. It stated that the Committee accepted the demand put forward by me (Jogesh Chatterjee) for the treatment of political prisoners in jail as a standard demand. They, therefore, directed that such rules be framed in those provinces where Congress ministries were established and that in other provinces, too, the attempt should be made for the formulation of such rules.

Gopinath Srivastava, the then Parliamentary Secretary to the Ministry of Jail in U. P. drafted rules on that line and one day showed them to me. I pointed out to him that I had objection to one paragraph in which it was stated that the political prisoners would be kept in association barracks but such prisoners sentenced on a charge of violence could be lodged in cells. He insisted that this demarcation should be there but I told him that if somehow I reach jail on a charge involving violence I would challenge this. After this he changed the paragraph and placed it before me and I thanked him. But these rules were not adopted by the U. P. Government. In fact in the whole counrty only one province adopted the rules, and it was the Central Province.

I have stated how unexpectedly the hunger

strike was terminated through the mediation of four leaders whose help the Home Member, Maharaj Singh, sought. The Government attitude was changed only because of the great public pressure started by two persons and then taken up by the entire country. It has been mentioned how Ram Krishna Khatri compelled the Kanpur leaders to come in the open in support of the cause taken up by me. The next person to take up my cause was Shri Rafi Ahmed Kidwai. As President of the U.P. P.C.C. he took it up vigorously and it was Kidwai who persuaded the then President of the Indian National Congress Babu Rajendra Prasad to take up our cause. Honest and sincere patriot as he was, he gave it much importance. He telegraphed and wrote to many leaders. Pandit Balkrishna Sharma read out to me the long letter he wrote about me. Bengal took up my cause very seriously. Akhil Chandra Datta, Shri Prakash and others sent wires and letters to me in jail. Meetings and demonstrations were held particularly in U.P. and Bengal.

My strong determination to die and the people's determination to save me were the two factors which compelled the Government to yield. Jatin Das had created the field and that experience, and again my historic hunger strike a year ago in Agra jail, made the Government shaky which at last gave way.

There had been so many hunger strikes by

many determined persons but the Government had not softened a little. But this time they conceded the main demands even when I was alive. This was a new thing in the whole history of hunger strike in Indian jails. What Sir Maharaj Singh thought impossible on the 23rd day of my hunger strike was conceded by his Government on the 111th day of my strike. That was not gained by me but by my countrymen who stood solidly behind the demands.

Political prisoners were not ordinary criminals especially in a dependency. They were national soldiers fighting the nation's war against foreign domination. The exploiting foreigners were always ready to crush them. They changed only when the outburst of public opinion compelled them to do so. So really my triumph was the victory of the people over the foreign Government.

European criminals were getting special class treatment only because they were European, that is to say, of the ruling race. But Indian fighters for freedom were treated as worst criminals because they were people of the subject race. Political prisoners had to fight against that in Indian jails and in the Andamans. So they fought while they were at large and again they fought when they were in jail. Constant fighting was the lot of these fighters for freedom.

ONE YEAR IN NAINI CENTRAL JAIL IN FEMALE WARD

I have stated how we reached Naini Jail. So far as I remember, we three were transferred together from Lucknow Jail, Kashiram, Haldhar Bajpai and myself. Sheo Singh, a communist, joined us on the way. We were kept in the female ward which was vacated for us, all female convicts having been transferred elsewhere. A deputy jailor, Mr. Abdul Jalil, a graduate of Aligarh University was specially deputed to look after us.

We were having regular interviews on Sundays. The mother of Manindra Banerjee used to come almost every Sunday. She was living at Allahabad at the time. One day Rafi Ahmed Kidwai came to see me. He apologised for coming after long time but I told him that they were to work hard for the country's cause and we were Royal Prisoners now under the safe custody of the rulers and hence required not much care from our own men. They have done their duty when we were in difficulty.

The female ward of the Naini Central Jail was the concentration jail for the political prisoners. We were all kept here in big association barracks, were getting books and newspapers and for exercise badminton and volley-ball were given. Some of us were having interviews on every Sunday. In a way we were now in direct touch with the world outside the jail walls. Now it was possible for us to have concentrated studies in various subjects and regular classes were started. The British Indian bureaucracy were not ready to concede these amenities to us. This little change was brought about after years of hard and strenuous fights in which many valuable lives were lost. For this special treatment of political prisoners we had to suffer so much during undertrial stage and even after conviction. Yet we got something only as a temporary patch work.

MINISTRY BY CONGRESS AND AFTER

After the Congress Ministry was formed in U. P. in 1937 the release of political prisoners was the general public demand. The Ministry was in a difficult position on this issue. They were ready to do things but the British Governor was reluctant. At this stage Sachin Bakshi started hunger strike, demanding release. This forced the hands of the Governor. Sir R. S. Pandit and Dr. K. N. Katju came to interview us all on two different dates and tried to know our mind. Then there was direct tussle between the Governor and the Ministry in which the Ministry had to threaten resignation as a result of which the Governor submitted. Sachin Bakshi was released on parole and we, the most dangerous Kakori prisoners, were let off.

CHAPTER XVII

RELEASE AND DEMONSTRATIONS

The people of U. P. were jubilant over this success of theirs. Despite the strict directive of Nehru that there should not be any demonstration and despite the drizzling rains the whole day, thousands gathered before the Naini Jail on hearing the news of the release of Kakori prisoners. We were brought to Allahabad in a procession and there was a public meeting at Purushottam Das Park that evening. The next day we were given receptions in the Ward Congress Committees and from 3 P. M. till dusk we were in the Anand Bhawan with Jawaharlal Nehru. For two and a half hours we were closeted with Nehru in a hall on the first floor and his sister, Mrs. Vijay Lakshmi Pandit, was sitting by his side all along. Nehru gave us a discourse on the international and national situation and urged upon us the necessity of working for the national liberation. We were quite agreeable to work with the Congress for the common cause. Then we came downstairs and there was a grand tea party to which all the notable Congress leaders of Allahabad were invited.

NEHRU AND PANT

In the meantime telephonic talks were going on between Nehru and Pant, the Chief Minister. The people of Kanpur and Lucknow, too, were preparing for our reception but these two leaders were nervous about it. Their apprehension was that if too much importance was given to us, the revolutionaries, their absolute leadership might be in jeopardy in the long run. Nehru phoned to Balkrishna Sarma, the President of City Congress Committee at Kanpur that there should be no demonstration. Sharmaji said that there would be a big demonstration even without the Congress participating in it. Congress and Sharmaji himself would only be condemned by the public. So he and the Congress could not keep aloof in such a matter. Pant sent for him ; but he sent a friend and himself remained at Kanpur to receive us.

The Kanpur demonstration was unique in the whole history of Kanpur. The whole city welcomed the released men with open arms. Balkrishnaji himself led the crowd at the Railway Station and he was with them every where. The procession and the meeting at parade grounds was huge. More than a lakh of people attended the meeting. Next day the reception in the morning by Ward Congress Committees, the reception by the Municipal Board, the Congress Workers' meeting at the Tilak Hall and the labour meeting at Goaltuli were of the same type as of the previous day. The Governor was upset at this. The second day he went to Kanpur and sent for the Congress leaders at the Circuit House, and asked them if a revolution was going to take place. The leaders impreesed on him that there was no question of any revolution. The people were jubilant that their demand was fulfilled and that big change had been ushered into existence along with the establishment of Congress Ministry. Lucknow, too, did not lag behind in the demonstrations. Huge crowds waited at the Railway station under the leadership of C. B. Gupta, the then President of City Congress Committee. Here, too, the procession and the meeting at Aminuddaula Park were unexpectedly big. I use the word 'unexpectedly' because Lucknow city is traditionally backward in politics. The meeting at Chowk the next day was also very big, though it was spoiled by heavy showers of rain. The University students of Lucknow gave us a very hearty welcome the next day. The gathering was fairly big.

KANPUR OR LUCKNOW

Kanpur was my old field of work. Suresh Babu was still there. Bhagat Singh, Ganesh Shankar Vidyarthi had been great martyrs and their memory was fresh with us. Kanpur had supplied the life-blood in Kakori and Lahore cases after Banaras. Kanpur political prisoners were still rotting in Naini Jail. Our old friends and sympathisers were there and the general demand was that I should start afresh from Kanpur. That was also my choice. But Khatri won't allow me to leave

Lucknow. And he did so much for me during the hunger strike. Mohanlal Saksena and C. B. Gupta the two Kakori defence counsels, were at Lucknow occupying public position and both of them offered hearty cooperation. Lucknow was also the provincial headquarter. Acharya Narendra Deva was the President of the Provincial Congress Committee and Seth Damodar Swarup, our old friend, was the General Secretary. So I decided to stay on at Luckhow. One difficulty was there. That was the attitude of Govind Ballabh Pant, the Premier. Though he too was our defence counsel in Kakori Case, he was looking on us with suspicion. He wanted us to be docile and moderate, but this we could not do. The radical difference was this that he wanted a compromising attitude towards the power that-be, but we preferred a fighting mood. Pant's attitude towards the revolutionaries continued to remain unchanged till his death, It may be mentioned here that as the Union Home Minister he ordered that the files maintained by the British Government in India on the revolutionaries and now deposited with the different Government Archives should not normally be shown even to the research scholar. He is also reported to have given the fantastic argument that perusal of such documents may lead to an increase of subversive activities.

PROPAGANDA TOUR FOR RELEASE OF POLITICALS

After so much ovations and demonstrations when we entered into the actual field of work we encountered great difficulties. People and even youths were praising us from a distance but they were not ready to come forward and join hands in our revolutionary activities. The Congress was the common platform and we also like others started work through Congress. A separate move seemed to be very difficult. The first thing we did was to try for the release of the political prisoners who were still in Naini Jail. For this propaganda the Provincial Congress Committee sent a circular to the districts that they might organise a tour of ex-Kakori men in their districts. Invitations came from almost all districts and programme was chalked out. Sachin Bakshi, Ram Krishna Khatri and myself covered the first round of the tour of the Eastern Districts.

The Congress High Command was alarmed at this. Acharyaji and Sethji were accused by the Congress bosses for allowing the circular and the programme. Acharyaji felt embarrassed. Sethji had signed the circular and he had given us a room in the P.C.C. office to live in.

When we were touring the Eastern Districts on behalf of the U.P.P.C.C Nehru and Pant were busy in counteracting our growing influence in the public. Through their influence Mahatma

Gandhi wrote an article in which he stated that according to his opinion the demonstrations on the release of Kakori prisoners was a political mistake. This writing by Gandhiji was painful to us and the general public also could not apreciate it. The proof was that in spite of this writing our tour in Western districts was a grand success. M. N. Roy was to preside over a Youth Conference at Dehra Dun. But at the eleventh hour he fell ill and wired to the Reception Committee to get me in his place. So K. K. Sinha saw me at Lucknow and with my consent gave the news to the Press, The conference was a grand success. There I received the invitation to preside over a conference in Delhi for the release of political prisoners. From Dehra Dun we started the tour of Western districts. Great enthusiasm of the people was witnessed everywhere. We were holding three or four meetings in different parts of the district and at night a meeting was being held in the district headquarters town. The programme terminated in the district of Meerut where almost all the Kakori prisoners were gathered at the residence of ex-Kakori prisoner Vishnu Saran Dublish. The programme lasted for four days and we covered the whole district in different batches.

Just after we had finished the tour of Eastern districts and came to Lucknow I had a meeting with Shri Krishnadat Paliwal, who was staying with Pant. He was summoned by Pant to take charge of the Rural Development Scheme of U. P. Government. Paliwal was taking his meals and we were talking. Pant entered the room and finding me there accused me straight of delivering objectionable speeches. He particularly mentioned my Gorakhpur speech. I told him politely that the C. I. D. reports were not correct and that all the prominent Congress leaders of the district were present in the meeting and he might know the reality from them. Then Pant told Paliwal that the District Magistrate would be in charge of their respective districts, of the R. D. work. At this Paliwal became wild in portest. Pant silently consented.

When we were at Meerut Pant and Kidwai were also there one day and the former invited us to tea at his place. After tea he took myself and Sanyal aside and his first sentence was, "You people are creating a lot of trouble for us." He spoke in this strain and wanted an understanding. This was not possible. We could enter into an understanding easily with Pant but no understanding could be arrived at with the Britishers and Pant wanted that. This difference between us was fundamental.

It was a question of belief and faith. We had this difference throughout our career. We had been in the Congress from 1920 to the transfer of power in 1947. But it was possible only because the Congress then was not a party but a common anti-British platform. Gandhiji was the dominating figure but his ideas and principles were different from those of ours. So at times there were open or tacit conflict of ideas. While a life Kakori prisoner in the European Ward of Lucknow Jail I chanced to receive a statement of Gandhiji in which he went so far as to say that revolutionaries of India were as much enemies of the country as the alien rulers. I was so much upset that nearly for a week I was quite restless. I saw clearly that though we differed so much with Gandhiji yet we had a respect for him ; but it was clear that he himself had no respect for us.

This trend of his mind and those of the Congress High Command were evidenced on various occasions. The whole country was vocal in demonstrations and lamentations over the martyrdom of Jatin Das by hunger strike in Lahore Central Jail but Gandhiji remained absolutely silent over this great historical event. Netaji Subhas and other eminent Indian patriots urged upon him the necessity of saving the life of Bhagat Singh and his other two comrades by incorporating that demand in the Gandhi-Irwin Pact. But Gandhi was not ready to go so far and the Government executed these patriots just on the eve of the Karachi Session of the Congress. A section of the public, therefore, staged a demonstration and showed him black flags at Karachi.

The attitudes of Nehru and Pandit became

apathetic to ex-Kakori men as soon as they saw that they were hostile to the Government even after the reforms. Nehru did two more things during that period. When ex-Kakori men were arrested in Delhi defying the unjustifiable and humiliating orders of the Chief Commissioner, somebody put up a resolution in their support in the Provincial Political Conference at Harduaganj (U.P.). Nehru himself opposed it stating that by defying the orders without the permission of the Congress they had committed an offence and disciplinary action should be taken against such violations. Men like Mohan Lal Saksena and Acharya Narendra Deva were also made to oppose it ; as Acharyaji himself told me later that he did not like it but Nehru forced him to stand up. There was another occasion in January 1938. Nehru declared before the P.C.C. meeting that the representatives of the districts of Meerut and Muzaffarnagar (which were just transferred from Delhi to U.P. Congress Province) should elect one person who would be taken in the Provincial Executive. After the P.C.C. meeting was over, the representatives of the two districts met and unanimously elected ex-Kakori prisoner Vishnu Saran Dublish. The next day before the session Nehru told Dublishji that he should resign as he was involved in a dangerous case and if such a man was taken in the P.C.C. executive the Governor would resent it. Dublish did not resign. He was the district leader of the Congress and a legislator.

NEHRU ON AZAD

Nehru in his autobiography has remarked about the revolutionaries that they were fascists in ideas. He had very scanty knowledge of the revolutionaries. From an interview with Chanrasekhar Azad, the martyr, he jumped to this conclusion. There was not the least justification for him to make such a remark about persons who had created history in this slave country by shedding their blood drop by drop on the scaffold, in the solitary cells of the Andamans, in various Indian jails of different provinces and by facing bullets.

Nehru was in Lucknow district jail once with the revolutionary prisoners. They questioned him on this. His reply was that he had very little personal knowledge about the revolutionaries, but he had been in Naini jail once with Sachin Sanyal and from his talks with Sanyal he had the impression that he was fascistic in ideas. This showed his natural apathy for the revolutionaries and this also gives the clue why he subtly condemned the revolutionaries in his autobiography.

When Nehru started criticising the revolutionaries adversely he was openly questioned as to why he himself gave a tea party in Anand Bhavan to the released Kakori prisoners. As a reply to this, he gave a public statement that there was no party. Some of the prisoners were known to him, they came to his place and he gave them tea. The readers are only to judge whether the function was like that or it was an attempt at belittling it.

THE COMMUNISTS AND YASHPAL

I knew that our release was not far off. Various ideas about our future stand occupied my mind. I came to jail about 13 years ago and in jail I had very little connection with the outside world. Amongst our own men I totally differed with the ideas of Sanyal. Others seemed to be on the right track. But we were not certain as to what stand we should take. For myself much depended on our Bengal comrades. I had been with them in Bengal jail at the beginning but I knew nothing about the latest developments. There seemed to be three factors in our favour, the Communists, the Congress Socialists and the Royists. From the jail the Communists seemed to be the nearest. So I had greater sympathy with them and read their literature eagerly. Amongst others Yashpal seemed to be inclined towards them mainly on one ground as he told me that they had vast resources at their disposal. He spoke particularly of the North West Frontier where the Communists were spending big amount of money and this he said was within his knowledge.

On our release Z. A. Ahmed and Sajjad Zaheer took a prominent part in our processions and meetings. After tea at Anand Bhawan Sajjad Zaheer made the proposal to me that if I liked he would take me to R. D. Bharadwaj, who, according to him, was underground at the time. I consulted Khatri about this and he said that it was not a fact that Bharadwaj was exactly absconding. He was often seen in the open. I at once saw that they thought that I was a romantic person of the old revolutionary school and they planned their romance only to capitivate my imagination. I did not express my willingness to meet him and they did not insist. The next morning Sajjad Zaheer again met us at the Railway Station when we were leaving for Kanpur and he brought his mother, Lady Wazir Hussain, and we were introduced to her.

Sometimes after this, after our tour of eastern districts, Bakshi, Khatri and myself along with others were going to Naini jail to interview the political prisoners for whose release we were on the propaganda tour of the province. On the way M. N. Gupta met us and gave us the information that a statement was going to the press that the political prisoners of Naini Jail were against the the propaganda demonstration of the released Kakori men and that Z. A. Ahmed was doing this through Yashpal. In the interview we applied for seeing all, and all except Yashpal came. It was stated that Yashpal had an interview with Shiv Singh, a Communist, the previous day and hence was not entitled to an interview with us. We asked them all if they had any objection to our propaganda work. They supported our move strongly and wholeheartedly. From jail we went straight to the A. I. C. C. office to meet Z. A. Ahmed. Shiv Singh told us that the papers given to him by Yashpal were with Ahmed who was absent. We, however, found him out as we were going out by the back door of the house. He was there with Lohia and Ashraf. At our insistence Ahmed gave us the original statement of Yashpal and also some 25 typed copies. Only one copy was given over to the A. P. I. who, it was learned over the phone, had sent a copy to Calcutta. A wire was at once sent to Calcutta not to publish it and we burned down all the copies and the original. Yet at Lucknow next morning we read the news in the morning papers. We at once issued a statement to the press contradicting it over the signature of all of us and it, too, was published in the papers the next morning. This incident left a very bad impression on my mind and I lost faith in the Communists' sincerity of purpose.

Long after when I joined the Congress Socialist Party, I narrated this story to Minoo Masani. At that time though they knew that Ahmed and Sajjad Zaheer were leaders of the Communist Party they allowed both to be on the National Executive of the C. S. P. Masani asked me if I would be ready to give this in writing that they both tried to recruit me to the Communist Party on my release so that they might be expelled on that ground. I was ready to give that in writing but the party leadership was so weak that they dared not do it for years, though they knew the facts.

DELHI ARRESTS

After the U. P. tour, we reached Delhi on the morning of the 2nd December 1937. Prior to this during our Meerut Programme Bimal Prasad Jain asked me at Hapur as to what I would do if any restriction was placed on the occasion of the Delhi Conference. "It shall be defied," was my simple reply. In the public meeting at Meerut which we addressed on the 1st evening many C. I. D. men of Delhi were seen. The next morning as soon as the Frontier Mail reached Delhi we saw a number of policemen on the platform but nobody on behalf of the Reception Committee. Later we learned that the police did not allow them to come. They served an order on behalf of the Chief Commissioner of Delhi on five of us that we must quit Delhi within six hours and must not take part in any meeting or procession. After this they allowed the Reception Committee men to enter the platform. After formal reception, garlanding, etc., I sat on the decorated carriage. But the Delhi leaders were in an awkward position. They did not like that their invited guests be arrested, but we had no other alternative than to defy the order and court arrest. It was settled between ourselves that my friends would defy the order by joining procession and I would court arrest when Manmatha Nath Gupta, Ram Krishna Khatri and Ram Dulare Trivedi were arrested while leading the procession one after another. I entered the pandal through the famale gate and took my seat on the dias unnoticed by anybody when the inaugural speech was being delivered by Munshi Ahmed Deen. As soon as he finished I went to the mike, was duly garlanded and started speaking. Within a few minutes the police caught hold of me and there was a wild scene for a minute. With the permission of the police men, I requested the audience to be peaceful and then left with the police men. Pandit Parmanand then volunteered as the President and delivered his speech and he, too, was arrested and later jailed. Only Sachin Sanyal did not court arrest. Parmanand was given 6 weeks R. I. and all others four months, R. I. each. The Conference itself was very successful. The release of political prisoner was a general demand throughout the country. The object of the Conference was to demonstrate this at the capital. So the general public were enthusiastic and 16 gates were made on the route of our proposed procession. The entry of the pandal was not free. The fee was Rs. 1 to Rs. 25/- Yet at the time of my arrest about 5, 000 men were within the pandal. A huge crowd was waiting outside and cheered me as the police car took me away. The pandal was made upon to the public after my arrest and it was a huge gathering. I had come out of jail after full 13 years. How could I obey the orders of the Delhi Chief Commissioner and leave Delhi without any procession or meeting ? Neither could we obtain permits from the Congress at that time. Yet Nehru announced in the Harduaganj Conference that it was an act of indiscipline on our part to defy the order without the permission of the Congress.

We were bailed out and soon I was in Lucknow Medical College Hospital with an an attack of double pneumonia. In this condition a Muslim C.I.D. Inspector served an order of the Bengal Muslim League Government externing me from that province, the province of my birth.

Between my discharge form the hospital and entering Delhi jail there was a stormy meeting of the U.P. P.C.C. at Lucknow in January 1938. In this meeting two different views clashed. M. N. Roy supported one side and I differed with him. Socialist and non-socialist question was there. Roy, Paliwal and others supported the candidature of Mohanlal Saksena for the provincial presidentship and we, ourselves, Acharya Narendra Deva and C. B. Gupta supported Sampurnanand. At the instance of Nehru Sampurnanand's name was withdrawn and our position was compromised.

Then I went to Delhi jail for 4 months and

met the other friends inside. I met there B.K. Dutta, the associate of Bhagat Singh, who was close to me at Kanpur when he was a student there.

I marked that Dutt had undergone a psychological change. The terrible suffering in the jails of India and Andamans had told on his mind. A very honest and sincere youth as he was, he frankly expressed this to me. This is why he could not stick to politics after his release. Prolonged and endless sufferings at times unnerve a man.

One day Akhil Chandra Datta, the then Deputy President of the Central Legislative Assembly, came to see me in jail with his wife. They were our leaders at Comilla. I told him that there was no justification on the part of the Bengal Government to serve an externment order against me. U.P. was now my home, yet I should have the right of visiting Bengal on occasions. My old mother and other friends were there and I was not meeting them for nearly 15 years. He promised that he would try to do whatever was possible. After a few days a C.I.D. Inspector interviewed me and asked for an answer of the Bengal Government's query as to what I would do in Bengal. My reply was that I would not remain there permanently but would go there from time to time. The same man came again later and gave me the notice that the Bengal Government was pleased to cancel the externment order. I conveyed this happy news to all and gave thanks to Akhil Babu through Mohanlal Saksena, M.L.A. (Central) who came to interview me.

MOTHER'S ILLNESS : IN BENGAL FOR FEW DAYS

Suddenly there was a telegram from Subhas Chandra Bose to Asaf Ali that my mother was seriously ill and the latter should try to get my premature release through the Chief Commissioner so that I may see her in her death bed. The news was published in Delhi papers with bold head-lines. The Chief Head Warder and the Deputy Jailor told me that I might be let off as I had only 14 days more to end the term of my sentence. I was actually released that morning so suddenly that even the C.I.D, Inspector who was to meet me inside the jail met me near the Delhi Gate while I was going to the city in a tonga. I was under close watch up to my home in East Bengal. A number of friends attended the Howrah Station to receive me but my rail ticket was via Bandel and Naihati. So they went away disappointed. At Bandel junction I enquired about my train from a youth who later told me that he was on a token hunger strike during my hunger strike in Lucknow jail and he accompanied me upto the Naihati Junction.

My mother had an attack of paralysis and she

was unconscious. For four days and nights I sat by her bed but she never regained consciousness even for a moment. On the fourth day a retired Civil Surgeon of a neighbouring village came to see her. He said that the illness would linger on indefinitely. I was to return to U. P. as I was to preside over a Conference in Unnao district. At that time the All India Kisan Conference was being held at Comilla, the place where I had spent the whole of my youth.

AT COMILLA FOR FOUR DAYS

I therefore went to Comilla to meet my friends as also the political workers who had gathered there. Naturally I was given a good reception at the station. The next day I presided over a meeting at the town hall in which Jaiprakas Narain spoke on Socialism. I also spoke before the Kisan Conference according to arrangement made by Kamini Kumar Datta, the Chairman of the Reception Committee and Bankim Mukherjee.

My cousin, Paresh Chandra Chatterjee, his family and myself planned to go to his tea garden for a pleasure trip next night. But in the morning at about 11 A. M. an Inspector of Calcutta C. I. D. accompanied by four other men came from Calcutta and served me an order of externment from Bengal. I was also given to understand that these men would follow me till I leave Bengal. Akhil Babu very much resented this attitude of the Bengal

Government. I went home for a few hours and sat by my mother, who was still unconscious and then left her and the place of my birth never to see them again.

At Comilla I had an important talk with Jai Prakash Narain. Bengal friends were already moving with him. J. P. invited me to come to Sonepur where shortly the Congress Socialists were to hold a summer school of politics.

When I reached Sealdah station at Calcutta many friends came to see me. There were a number of C. I. D. men besides the 5 who were shadowing me from Comilla. They insisted that I must catch a certain train at Howrah as the order was to quit Bengal at the earliest. My contention was that I would catch the train I liked. It appeared to be certain that I would again have to go to jail in Bengal. However, my friend Gopal Chatterjee, an employee of the Calcutta Corporation, took me to his residence. I was ill at that time. A doctor was called. My temperature was 102^0 and the doctor certified that I was unfit to travel for a week. I thus got an opportunity to stay on in Calcutta and during these days met many notable friends, including our party leaders who were at large. More important leaders were yet in jail.

I later come to know that there was a move in Calcutta to give me a reception not on behalf of our party only but by the revolutionaries in general. After the stiffest fight with the Government most of them were now released from detention and they were in Calcutta. A group of leading persons among them approached the B. P. P. C. for this but they refused to comply on the ground that Gandhiji had written in the Harijan that demonstration on our release was a political mistake. Thereupon a brisk preparation was started on behalf of the revolutionaries to give me such a reception as was not given even to Gandhiji in Calcutta. At that stage it was possible because the revolutionaries felt that they should all stand united. Bhupendra Kumar Dutta conveyed that idea to me from jail through Suresh Das. His message was that I should not take any decision without consulting with other revolutionaries. That was really a matter to be taken into consideration very seriously. But I had a great difficulty in this. The question of ideology was now a very big factor. A big section of revolutionaries had definitely been inspired by the ideology of Marxism. They were uncompromising on this. One section of them had been with the Communist Party of India and others seriously differed with it. My old colleagues and friends were ardent Marxist-Leninists but they differed with the latest move of the Third International under Moscow's leadership. My own inclination was also towards Marxist-Leninists. About Bhupen Datta and his friends I came to know that they were not in favour of socialism.

I have already stated that my Bengal friends

were already very close to the Congress Socialists and hence here in U.P. our representative comrade Keshav Prasad Sharma was even living with Acharya Narendra Deva, the leader of C.S.P. Acharyaji was also a supporter of the revolutionaries all along. He was at the same time a strong Marxist. So for my differences with M. N. Roy I was attracted towards Acharji.

CHAPTER XVIII

MOVE TO JOIN C. S. P.

Under the circumstances the clear question before us was whether to stand as a separate revolutionary Socialist Party or to work through some other party that was nearest to our ideology. To start a separate party was not an easy affair for us. As revolutionaries we were the worst sufferers in the hands of the foreign exploiters whom we gave the mortal challenge. When we were in jail all our worries of life were over. But as soon as we stepped out of the jail all the problems of food, clothes and shelter overwhelmed us as we had already burned our boat after becoming a revolutionary. I remember a letter written by Probodh Das Gupta's mother when he was in Rajshahi jail. In this letter she expressed how happy she was to learn that her son, a dangerous escapee from the police lock up at Dallanda House, and from the Gauhati fight with the police, was arrested and lodged in the jail. Das Gupta took Potassium Cyanide at the time of his arrest and escaped death only because the poison was spoiled by long exposure. How were we to get money to run a party? For a public party well-known personalities, money and other resources are required. But we had none. So there seemed to be no other alternative before us than to join some existing party. After discarding the Royists and Communists, the Congress Socialists were the only alternative left before us.

Myself, Keshav Prasad Sharma and Tridib Kumar Chaudhury met Jay Praksh Narain at Sonepur in this mood and atmosphere. We had a four days, talk. J. P. convincingly assured us that the C. S. P. stood clearly and difinitely for Marxism. Just like us, the revolutionaries, the C. S. P. had no faith in Gandhism or non-violence and it too like us believed in the attainment of independence through an armed revolution. He also appealed to us not to start a separate party but to join hands with them and thus make the C. S. P. a real All India Revolutionary Socialist Party. He also suggested that I should have further talks with Acharyaji and then take the decision. Acharyaji also said the very same thing and urged upon us the necessity of joining the party at the earliest. Then we took the final decision with this understanding that for a certain period we would keep our existence separate and then merge.

At that time the Congress Socialist Party was tremendously forceful in U.P. Important Congressmen of the province, including the two big leaders, Sampurnanand and C. B. Gupta were within its fold under the leadership of Acharya Narendra Deva. The over-all position was not too bad, but organisationally the C.S.P. was very weak and Communists were engaged with a plan to capture it. Ahmed and Sajjad Zaheer were already in the National Executive of the C. S. P. At Lucknow the meetings of the Party were being held in their houses. In the districts, too, their workers were being pushed forward. The local leaders were not realising it and were helpful in this plan. Sajjad Zaheer was a member of the Scrutiny Committee along with Acharyaji and Seth Damodar Swarup. The latter too were not even fully conscious of the happenings though they knew by that time that the communists had already captured their entire organisations in some areas of South India. J. P. had reported to us this fact during our conversations at Sonepur.

It was, therefore, the first task of Comrade Keshav Prasad Sharma and myself to drive out the communists from the organisation. At Unnao and Aligarh the communists had entrenched themselves strongly. At our instance, by a majority decision the Scrutiny Committee scratched the names of the communists from the membership of the C. S. P. By this way we became unpopular with the communists but Acharyaji appreciated our work and he openly expressed that he depended much on us for the U. P. organisation.

The next political happening of all India importance was the decision of Subhas Chandra Bose, the then President of the Indian National Congress, to contest the presidential election for the second time against the wishes of Gandhiji and the High Command, who had set up Dr Pattabhi Sitaramayya as their candidate. The general situation of the world at the time was a bit tense. Besides Soviet Russia, a third force was rising rapidly. A world war was in the offing. Anglo-American politicians were rather alarmed. The Congress High Command under Gandhiji's leadership was on a rightist compromising mood and Gandhism due to its presuppositions could think of nothing but compromise. The world youth movement was very strong at the time and Bose was an idol of the Indian youths. Bose, therefore, gave the Congress High Command a challenge.

At our request Acharya Narendra Deva issued a fine statement to the press supporting the candidature of Bose. In U. P., besides the Congress Socialists, Rafi Ahmed Kidwai was also supporting Bose. We took up the task very seriously. Lala Sankar Lal of Delhi was the election-in-charge of Subhas Chandra Bose. He wrote to me at Lucknow that the ministerial group was very strong in U. P. and they were holding the majority. Therefore, it should be our task to see that least number of votes were cast against Bose. I wrote back to him in reply that how wrong his notion was would only be realized by him when he saw the result.

Acharya Narendra Deva's statement in support of Bose was published widely in U. P. in all local languages, besides English. This made the people conscious about the general position and after that an organisational attempt was necessary to reach the P. C. C. voters. For this Vishnu Saran Dublish was looking after Meerut area, Thakar Malkan Singh looked after Aligarh area, Seth Damodar Swaroop took charge of Bareilly area and I toured thirteen districts. Mohan Lal Gautam and Keshav Prasad Sharma looked after most of the eastern districts. Thus we carried on a vigorous propaganda in favour of Bose. Our strong associate, a leader of the former All Bengal Students movement, Amarendra Nath Roy, a former Anushilanite and founder of C. S. P. in Bengal, was at Lucknow as our most trusted helper. Acharyaji had full faith in him and so also Bose.

Because of the adverse report of Lala Shankar Lal, Bose was very worried about U. P. He, therefore, sent the revolutionary veteran, Birendranath Chatterjee, to Lucknow. Amar Roy made him to understand that things were going smoothly and further activities from Bengal might disturb the situation. Biren Chatterjee quietly went back and reported to Bose accordingly. But it seemed that Bose was not very satisfied, because Biren Chatterjee, though a veteran revolutionary of the Anushilan Samiti, was not much educated. So again Bose sent Dhiren Mukherjee, a brilliant graduate of Allahabad University, an ex-Anushilanite, to Lucknow. Amar Roy gave him to understand everything in details and he was thoroughly convinced that things were going on very satisfactorily in U. P. and Bose was also satisfied.

We were realising that the move was gaining momentum through the enthusiastic youths everywhere. I myself had a whirlwind tour of many districts of U.P. with this purpose and the response every where was good. When votes were counted in the P.C.C. meeting at Lucknow, Bose secured 84 votes more than his rival. In all he got 199 votes more and hence U.P.'s contribution was not negligibile. In the morning next day I received a lengthy telegram of congratulations from Lala Shankar Lal from Delhi.

TRIPURI CONGRESS

The Congress High Command was really upset at the victory of Bose and Gandhiji himself came out with the statement that Dr. Pattabhi's defeat was his own defeat. The High Command had made up their mind that at Tripuri Bose must be crushed at any cost. Sardar Patel and Rajagopalcharya were the main figures in this nefarious design. We shall come to this later. Let us see what was going on in U.P. before Tripuri.

Bose had realised the importance of U.P. and hence Lala Shankar Lal's secretary, Hukam Singh, came to Lucknow. He naturally approached Rafi Saheb. But now the situation was such that he could not accept this offer. Hukam Singh then approached C. B. Gupta but he, too, was not ready to accept it, because he was afraid of staking his position in the Congress. Then he came to me and I readily agreed to do whatever was possible. When C.B. Gupta came to know this, he cautioned me. I told him that even if the High Command took disciplinary action against me, my role as a revolutionary would continue. Gupta was satisfied with my reply and I carried on my work to the best of my ability.

The orthodox Congressmen were not in our favour but younger enthusiasts were ready to support Bose at Tripuri. Following the former statement of Acharyaji the C.S.P. men were all in his favour. The orthodox Congress circles were alarmed at our activities. They were also active against Bose following the statement of Gandhiji that Pattabhi's defeat was his defeat.

With such background the session of the Congress at Tripuri was held. We reached there with Acharya Narendra Deva. The reception Committee men wanted to take Acharyaji to the leaders' camp but he refused. Acharyaji and others stayed at the station and I hurriedly hired a family quarter in his name and we went there. It was near the Bank of Narbada. On one side was the camp of Swami Sahajanand and on the other was the camp of Jai Prakash Narayan. We all went to take a bath in the river and on our return could not find Acharyaji. Shiv Prasad Gupta, the great patriot of Banaras, had personally come and forced Acharyaji to go to the leaders' camp with him. This was the first assault on us by the High Command. Had Acharyaji been with us we could have free consultations with him ; but there was no free access into the leaders' camp which was at a great distance from our quarter.

A brisk and vigorous compaign was going on in the delegates' camp and everywhere against the President, Subhas Bose. Sardar Patel and Rajagopalacharya were freely doing this till late hours in the night. As a result the majority of A.I.C.C. members were already against Bose. But they failed to assess definitely if the majority of the delegates were in their favour. Bose was running high temperature and his condition was critical, yet the propaganda was carried on by responsible persons that Bose was not ill at all. The news of his illness was only to attract sympathy for him.

I pressed Acharyaji to do something here in support of Bose as he did at Lucknow. He said that his difficulty was that Bose was not putting forward any proposal. For this I requested him to pay a visit to him even if it was only to see him as he was ill. He saw Bose that evening but there was no proposal from the latter. I then realised my own mistake. I should have informed Bose about this after I had a talk with Acharyaji. I repented this later. So the High Command was successful in their propaganda and we failed.

In the open session a resolution was put forward by M. S. Aney that the power vested in the delegates be given to the members of the A.I.C.C. This was opposed by the majority of the delegates from Bengal and U. P. Others remained neutral. Maulana Azad counted the votes and declared that it was passed. We challenged it and wanted a division. They were not ready for that. But we insisted and walked to the passage in front of the dias. Nehru wanted to hoodwink us by saying that a disturbance by 200 Bengalees would not be able to disturb the Congress Session. This remark was resented by all. Neither the demonstrators were only 200, nor were they all Bengalees. The majority of U. P. delegates were there. At this stage J. P. came down from the dias and finding me in the crowd asked me why we were doing this. I counter-questioned him if he supported the Aney Resolution. His reply was in the negative. On his further question as to what could we do I said angrily that we would break the dias and finish the Congress and then go away. The thing was that I was attending the Congress after a lapse of 14 years, as I was in jail. It was a democratic platform of the nation and from this platform an arbitrary action was simply revolting to us. The resolution, too, did not come through the Subjects Committee as was the usual rule. J. P. then asked me in an angry mood that there were about 3,000 delegates in this gathering of nearly a lakh and half men, and how could a division be taken? I said in reply that an announcement might be made that after the other business was over the delegates should go to the Delegates Pandal when the division would be taken. He then left for the dias but before he reached there the resolution was withdrawn. We then sat quietly in our respective delegates' blocks.

All were astonished that night to hear from Nehru the report of the Civil Surgeon of Jabbalpur that Bose was running temperature of 104° and that it was essential that he should be removed to hospital in the city, otherwise his life was in danger and also that despite this report Bose was not ready to go to the hospital.

The next morning there was a very unpleasant scene in the President's camp. Due to the deliberte negligence and inattention, Sarat Bose, the elder brother of Subhas Bose, got his articles in a taxi for quitting the Congress and going back to Calcutta. Govind Das, the Chairman of the Reception Committee, was himself responsible for this. This was resented even by the volunteers on duty. So they stopped the car of Rajendra Prasad and reported the matter to him. He approached Govind Das and prevented Sarat Bose from going back. A number of brand new cars with drivers were given free by the Ford Motor Co. for use. But the Congress President was only given a second-hand car.

Sardar Patel did another act full of designs for this Session. They knew that they would do many improper things there ; so Gandhiji was kept engaged at Rajkot in a Satyagraha movement. The got up movement consequently was a total failure.

In the morning after the open session J.P. came to our quarters and took myself and Keshava Prasad Sharma aside and stated that C.S.P. and C.P.I. leaders had discussed the Pant Resolution and decided that they both would remain neutral. The Pant Resolution was like the Aney Resolution for the A.I.C.C. to vest the authority of the elected President in Gandhiji. To agree to this was to make the election of President null and void. I was mad with rage and told J. P. that I had a suggestion to make. He asked for it eagerly and I said that there should be a resolution placed before the Congress on our behalf that so long as Gandhiji was alive he should be given the absolute authority of the Congress and there should be no plenary session of the Congress during his life-time. J.P's face became red and he went away without uttering a word.

The Pant Resolution was to be moved in the Delegates' Pandal at 8 A.M. I waited for Acharyaji at the leaders' entrance and asked for his opinion on it as soon as he alighted from his car. He said that he could not take part in the meeting due to his health and the decision was communicated to him by J.P. at 7-30 A.M. Under the circumstances, he thought the decision was correct. I then entered the Pandal, a thorughly dejected man and sat aloof at a distance. My colleagues C. B. Gupta, Bishambhar Dayal Tripathi, Seth Damodar Swarup, Mohanlal Gautam and Algurai Shastri asked me to come near them again and again. When I came they asked if I would resign from the party as a protest. I readily agreed and Tripathi at once made the draft which was signed by us except Gautam and Algurai and then handed over the same to J. P. just before he was to speak. The next morning the news of our resignation was published in all the dailies.

That evening I left Tripuri out of disgust. But J. P. called a meeting of the C. S. P. men the next morning and accused me of disruptive activities. This was objected to by many and J. P. had to withdraw his words. Naturally on such a vital question compromise was not at all justifiable. Compromise unfortunately again had been the role of this party as the Socialist Party even at the Delhi Session of A. I. C. C. on the Communal Division of India. There again by opposing the move the party could stand as a great force with the backing of the masses of India of diverse shades of opinion. But here again they were neutral. Naturally, therefore, intelligent people took this Party to be a junior partner of the Congress. And they preferred Congress to this Party in the general election of 1952.

LUCKNOW MEETING

After our return to Lucknow Acharyaji asked us how to rejuvenate the Party. A meeting of the district representatives was called at Lucknow and there my suggestion was accepted that the provincial organisation would be run strictly democratically. For this a provincial conference would be held shortly. Myself and Sethji then withdrew our resignation.

At Tripuri we resigned as a protest against the wrong stand but yet did not go the length of voting against the Pant Resolution. That would have been an open defiance. We only kept aloof from the wrong act. The Party was, however, so immobile that the proposed U. P. conference could not be actually held. And in September came the great event of the Second World War.

SECOND WORLD WAR

We had very definitely worked for a revolution during the First World War. I was only a student then in one corner of the vast country. But later through failure we learned a good deal. The opportunity was grand but we were immature and inexperienced. We could not properly utilise the great material resources, native and foreign, that were at our disposal. The history taught us that a war opens up unthinkable avenues for the working out a revolution. A dependency like India under the mighty British rule could not shake off the shackles on her own in normal days. Foreign help was essential for such a change. In normal times, no foreign power could help us. The international law itself was a great barrier. But during a war in which Britain was involved, her enemies would give us the utmost help only if we were in a position to accept and avail it and use it for the guerilla method of warfare for the seizure of power.

Second World War was our second chance. The country was now much advanced politically. The consciousness of the evils of an alien rule was widespread because of the mass movements under the leadership of Gandhiji and the Congress. But this was also a great handicap. The clash of ideas and ideologies was a great deterrent to the tremendous forces that were let loose in the country. The Congress under Gandhiji preached non-violence and the revolutionaries were for an armed revolution. In between were the Communists who wanted to make a capital out of both. Sometimes they would be anti-Congress and pro-revolutionary and on other occasions they would be anti-revolutionary and pro-Congress. Their strength lay in the fact that people took them to be representatives of Moscow and Moscow was the great progressive force. The revolutionaries rose through struggle from the soil and hence they were indigenous and were always with the nationalist movement while the Communists were always anti-national and pro-Russian. So one section of the people wanted them whole-heartedly but the vast majority disliked them with equal vehemence. These were the ground why we could not properly avail of the opportuniny of the Second World War, too.

WARDHA

As soon as the war started I approached Acharyaji and proposed that we must at the earliest come in touch with some anti-British power. He understood that I meant Japan. He said that Japan was a fascist power and we were socialist. If we established contact with them we would go down in the eyes of our countrymen. I was mortally disappointed at this and realised my helpless position. We had no separate organisation of ours. Hence the way of our separate move was barred. The leaders, who assured us that they were really for an armed revolution like ourselves, were now taking shelter under theoretical socialism. When the path to an armed revolution was open how could we sit on the fence, I could not understand and was, much worried. However, after a tour of Banaras and adjacent places Acharyaji told us that much material would be available for a vigorous propaganda work. That was some consolation.

The Congress announced that the Working Committee and the A.I.C.C. meetings would be held at Wardha early in October. About ten days prior to this the C.S.P. also was to hold a meeting of the National Executive at Lucknow. J.P. came to Lucknow earlier and he himself proposed that a War council would be formed and a secret organisation would be run with its headquarters at Lucknow. He proposed the formation of a War Council with Acharya Narendra Deva, Pratul Ganguli, myself and himself as its members. He also stated that Acharyaji and Ganguli would court arrest but he and myself would go underground. This was somewhat heartening for me. Japanese help would be sought automatically with immense precautionary measures. Arms would be the first requirement and then money and other things would naturally follow. I was confident that an immense force would be created, before which the Congress would remain as Gandhian impotent onlooker. The entire youth would rally round us and the masses too would be inspired through them. The Gandhians would be confined to their Ashrams of Khaddar organisatien. They won't be able to inspire anybody except the too wise.

But at Wardha the C.S.P. and J.P. surrendered to Gandhism and decided that they would only participate in the movement if it was started by Gandhiji and would not start any separate movement. This was a death-blow to us. We returned from Wardha completely disappointed.

DR. HEDGEWARE AT NAGPUR

On our way back I went to see Dr. Hedgeware the founder of the R. S. S. organisation with Maharaj. Sri Trailokya Nath Chakravarty, under whom Dr. Hedgeware was working as a member of the secret Anushilan Samiti when he was a student in the Calcutta National Medical College. He said that he gave physical training to youths without any designed political objective, because in that case the work of the organisation could not be carried on. But if during the war period we could do anything then their men, about 44,000 in number at that time, he thought, would be helpful to us. The Doctor passed away in the next summer and his organisation did not come forward during the August Movement of 1942, although some individuals did.

CONGRESS STAND

Empowered by the Government of India Act of 1935, the Congress had established ministries in most of the provinces. But these were withdrawn on the ground that Britain had involved India in the World War without consulting the people of India whom the Congress represented. This was a big non-cooperation step. But after that the Congress became quite inactive. On the one hand, no help was to be rendered for the war efforts and on the other hand it was decided that there should also be no embarrassment to the Britishers. People of the country wanted that something must be done at this time because England's difficulty was their opportunity. But the Congress and the C.S.P. remained inactive.

RAMGARH : SEPARATION FROM C.S.P.

The Ramgarh Session of the Congress in March 1940 was therefore very dull. Subhas Bose was by now a Congress rebel. had orHeg anised a Conference at Ramgarh during this session styled as Anti-compromise Conference. People were more interested in it than they were in the Congress. Bose was given a big reception at the Railway Station. The Congress High Comand asked Acharya Narendra Deva to speak at the Congress when Bose arrived at the Railway Station. They knew that none else could hold the audience and prevent the Congress members from joining the reception to Bose. This gives us inkling of the role of the C.S.P. which because of its woolly headed policies and half-hearted moves failed to bring about a radical change in the country's political life. When Subhas Bose had been at Lucknow as the President of the Congress in 1938 he met the C.S.P. leaders at the residence of Minister Sampurananand. Before the gathering Bose said: "I am thinking of joining the C.S.P." Sri Mohanlal Gautam, the U.P. secretary of the party, at once stood up and requested Bose to take the decision soon so that the Party might be strengthened. But thanks to C.S.P's sentimental weakness for Gandhian leadership, it failed to go the whole hog with Bose. So Bose formed the Forward Bloc, not as party but as a platform, only because there was no other alternative before him. He wanted to drag us into it, but we had firm faith in an ideology and we were unable to follow that loose path. We were definite that the objective must be crystal clear and the programme too must be commensurate with it. We had full sympathy with Bose but could not join hands with him only because of this fact. He, too, appreciated this.

L. K. SHARMA AND BOSE'S MOVE

Since the outbreak of the war Bose decided to establish eontact with Japan and wanted to send Lala Shankar Lal to Japan with the help of a revolutionary of U. P., L. K. Sharma. Sharma had his pass port and other travel documents with him. I sent him to our Calcutta leaders with the request that some responsible person should be sent to Japan with him. It was proposed that I should go to Japan. But I thought that the news of my going to Japan would be known to the British government and that it would be impossible for me to come back to India. Work in India was more vital during the war than contact with Japan. But we wished we could establish some contact with that country. No other power could help us. Moreover, Rashbehari Bose was there and he would have certainly helped. But the Bengal leaders of our party did not accept my proposals.

L. K. Sharma met me at Ramgarh Congress and told me that he had very important matters to discuss with me and I must not not leave Ramgarh without meeting him. But I forgot to ask him where he was putting up. Later we searched for him but could not find him anywhere. Then there was heavy rain and we left Ramgarh with great difficulty. When I came to know long after that Sharma and Lalaji had left for Japan, I understood, why he told me not to leave Ramgarh without meeting him.

CHAPTER XIX

FORMATION OF R. S. P. AT RAMGARH

We were very eager to do something. We were not only disappointed but disgusted too with the C. S. P. and I have stated why we did not join hands with Bose. The alternative before us was to form a new party of our own based on the ideas of Karl Marx and Lenin for the emancipation of the masses through a revolution and then bring-about a new social order in which exploitation of man by man was to be a thing of the past.

With this object in view a meeting was held in a big tent of a friend, Vir Raghav Achariar, who was then the Senior Vice-Chairman of the Manbhum District Board. Revolutionaries of different provinces gathered there and the decision was taken after prolonged discussion that a new party of the Indian Marxist revolutionaries be formed and this party be named the Revolutionary Socialist Party which would very clearly convey the ideas for which it was brought into being. A Committee was formed there for giving a proper shape to the Party and making a draft constitution and programme. I was elected as its convener.

It was war time and the formation of a revolutionary party with the veteran and tried revolutionaries was an eye-sore to the administration. They were not to sit idle and allow this party to proceed with its work smoothly. They set their machinery in motion against these revolutionaries and within a short time most of the leading persons were rounded up and thrown into prison, of course, without any trial. So the committee could not even hold its first meeting. Bengal, however, proceeded with the organisational work promptly.

C. S. P. POSITION

In Bengal the revolutionary organisation was very old and it had province-wide ramifications. It was not so in U. P. Here there was a complete break down after the activities during the First World War and Sanyal and myself had to start anew. Again after the Kakori releases when we joined the C. S. P. our number was very limited. We devoted our energy to form the C. S. P. as a left organisation within the congress platform. For this at Ramgarh Comrade Keshav Sharma was not in favour of leaving C. S. P. But my two years' experience with it convinced me that C. S. P. could never become a real left socialist party. Therefore, ultimately we would be nowhere. Hence it was better for us to separate with whatever small force we could command. C. S. P. was not a party of democratic centralism, but a party of leaders holding divergent views and having no proper democratic connection with the rank and file. The leaders had positions in the Congress and hence they were born leaders in C. S. P. and it did not matter whether they were Marxist Socialists or not. They financed the party through dubious and even at times questionable means and the rank and file had no voice over them. The ranks were either to remain in the party silently or quit.

A SOURCE FOR JAPANESE CONTACT

So after Ramgarh our position in U.P. was not very strong but we were quite sure that in no time the energetic and enthusiastic youths would rally round us. An atmosphere had to be created for that somehow. I was known to the political workers and youths of U.P. but to start an organisation material resources were necessary. In this we were lacking badly. The old method of forcible collection of money could not be followed. I was much worried.

At this time I got a chance. A junior officer of Japanese foreign office was learning Urdu at Lucknow. He promised that he would help me to establish contact with the Japanese Consul-General at Simla and could get forged Indian currency notes from Japan through Thailand. At this time also came Comrade Tridib Chaudhury from Bengal and gave me the good news that Subhas Bose wanted to do something serious and he could not entirely rely on his loose F.B. organisation. Bose at this time received a list of some 30 persons of his F.B. some of whom were secretly in touch with the C.I.D. He was, therefore, trying to amalgamate the better elements of F.B. with R.S.P. Bose himself sent Tridib Chaudhury to me for that purpose. He was also sent by Bose to the North Western Frontier Province.

THE ARRESTS

This scheme of Bose remained unfulfilled as shortly after this he was himself jailed. I was eagerly expecting some news from Simla but was one day suddenly arrested and sent to jail as a detenu. Four days later Keshav Sharma also reached the jail and I suspected a man to have betrayed us. Sharma was arrested in his house, yet he would not believe that he was betrayed by him. This man was very eager to work with us. But I was reluctant to take him in full confidence. I told Sharma to have details about his antecedents from Banaras where he was a student of the Hindu University. He later assured me that the man was very reliable. In a day or two came Seth Damodar Swarup to the jail. He told us positively that he was the man who had got him arrested. Now Sharma also was convinced of it. That man later became an officer of the C.I.D.

I did my utmost to avoid arrest. Though we had formed the R.S.P. at Ramgarh and I was its convenor, yet I tried to keep the outward form as mild as possible. We were having a Satyagraha parade in a park at Lucknow in which all the members of the City Congress Executive, including C.B. Gupta, were on parade. The police dramatically came there in a lorry, and took me away to my residence and searched everything but nothing objectionable was found. I was then living in the same house with Mohan Lal Gautam, M.L.A., the U.P. Secretary of C.S.P., who later became a Congress Minister. He was present during the search and police men were polite to me. From the Kotwali I was taken to jail late in the night and I was so well-known in the Lucknow District Jail that no personal search was made there and I was lodged in the hospital barrack for the night.

IN JAIL AGAIN, MAY 1940

Everything was familiar to me in Lucknow jail. We were here as Kakori under-trials. For hours in the night I could not have any sleep. The memories of old friends haunted me and the chain of thoughts kept me awake.

In the morning I was sent to the Civil Ward where the old Lahore Case comrades were still there to welcome me. This was the place where I was lodged when I entered this jail 15 years ago for the first time. On many occasions we had been there to interview the Lahore Case friends and spent hours during the Congress Ministry. This time I was the first person in the province to be arrested on provincial warrant.

We all were detained under War Ordinance yet we were not given all those concessions which the convicts were getting. Many other detenus in other jails were given only ordinary 'C' class diet. This was intolerable. So, as a protest, myself and Keshava Sharma started hunger strike. After a week the same old Superintendent of Agra jail hunger strike days, Lt. Col. Jafri, tried to give me a nasal feed. He tried his best but failed totally.

He fed me in Agra jail in my longest hunger strike of 142 days through one nostril. A year after this another inexperienced doctor did the same thing for 111 days in the Lucknow Central Prison. Because of all this there was a permanent sore inside my nose and blood often oozed out even now after decades. Medical treatment proved ineffective to cure this and it has now become my life's companion. Because of this sore forced feeding was impossible. This made the authorities a bit nervous. They did not like public agitation on this especially during the days of the frightful war. Babu Purshottamdas Tandon interfered in the matter on the 10th day and at his request we abandoned the strike. As a result all detenus were given better class.

The Lahore Case prisoners were brought down to Lucknow jall on their repatriation from the Andamans. They belonged to U.P. and hence were allowed by the Congress Ministry to be lodged here and were given 'B' class. The Punjab Government at first were not agreeable to this but when U.P. refused to keep the political prisoners in 'C' class, they had to give their consent, as otherwise they would have been sent back to the Punjab and this they did not like at all. When the three Ootacamund Bank Robbery Case lifer repatriates from the Andamans were released from Lahore, they were sent to Delhi under police escort. Such was the attitude of the Punjab Government. Even in Congress ministry there were differences of attitudes. Rajagopal Acharya as the Premier of Madras did not even recognise the revolutionaries as politicals.

During the war the British Government at first was as strong on the Communists as they were on the revolutionaries. Two communist absconders, beside others, were also arrested at Lucknow and put up with us. One of them, Mazumdar, is now a lecturer in the Lucknow University and the other was Ajoy Kumar Ghosh of Kanpur. But the most difficult position was that of B. K. Mukherjee, M.L.A. He had a big family and had no connection whatever with revolutionary politics and yet he was brought to the jail. However, he was soon released from Fatehgarh Jail.

TRANSFERRED TO DEOLI DETENTION CAMP IN AJMER

In the latter part of 1940 a concentration camp was started at Deoli in Ajmer. Detenus from all over India except Bengal were lodged there. We were also brought down to Deoli Camp from different jails of U. P. by batches. When Dr. Z. A. Ahmed of C. P. I. met me at Deoli he congratulated me for the timely hunger strike at Lucknow jail, as otherwise many would have been in 'C' class. In fact due to this all the detenus of U. P. were put in 'A' class in Deoli camp, thought most of the Punjab and Bihar detenus of eminence were given 'B' class.

C. I. D. officials of various provinces were in charge of the camp under a European army officer. The fencing was made of double line of barbed wires covered with mats under the guard of armed sentries all round. The internal management was left to the detenus themselves under official control. Separate enclosures were there for each camp, but we all could meet in the morning and evening in an enclosure set apart for games and exercises, at fixed times when they were kept open. A hospital camp also was there at a distance, as also separate punishment cells.

Two classes of political prisoners were its inmates, communists and the revolutionaries. The former were in the majority. For management of affairs a camp committee was formed which was recognised by the authorities. Internal differences were there, yet the committee was all along working satisfactorily. But we had to have separate kitchens as the two groups refused to dine together. This possibly was a reflection of our Hindu collective subconscious instinct where segregation of differing people at dinners is very often recognised as the norm. To the Indians dining together very often signifies many deeper cultural traits than can be seen on the surface.

The first meeting of the prisoners was held under the presidentship of Master Mota Singh for the formation of the camp committee. Dr. Z. A. Ahmed spoke as to how the communists would conduct themselves ; they would spend their time mainly in studies and would not like fights with the authorities and particularly deprecated hunger strikes in jail. I strongly supported hunger strike as the only weapon in confined life and also said that we must continue our fight even in jail. There were police agents amongst us through whom the reports of the meeting reached the authorities.

Our only connection with the outside world was through the newspapers, books, letters and interviews. But this was much curtailed because of very strict censor on letters and interviews were ther in such a God forsaken place.

It was war time and the comumunists were sure of Germany's victory as Soviet Russia was on friendly terms with them. Their leaders preached openly that Red Army was such a mighty force that it could conquer the world easily, but, of course, they were not aggressive. Then when the table turned and German army marched on Russia, men like Master Mota Singh became enthusiastic and thereby became an object of attack by the communists, who wanted to remove him from the camp committee.

We observed 'Bhagat Singh and Azad day but the communists did not participate, as it was, according to them, against their principle. But we participated in their Lenin day ceremony and October Revolution Day. On a Lenin day comrade B.T. Randive in the presence of all invitees of the other camp enunciated their policy stating that they did not recognise the existence of any other party in India except the Communist Party not even the Congress he declared emphatically.

We were once in a fighting mood with the authorities and the committee was to decide as to what was to be done. Sachin Sanyal suggested hunger strike but prompt came the retort from Randive "We cannot do that, that's the Gandhian method." Not long after that on another occasion the C.P.I. pleaded before the committee that only hunger strike should be resorted to and nothing else. When Randive's former remark was referred to Dr. Ahmed said "That was Randive's personal opinion."

My cousin Sailesh Chatterjee, was killed by one, Dr. Khan, when he was a detenue here in 1933. This time, therefore, when one of us, Satrughna Kumar of Dehra Dun, was down with high fever we wanted that one of us should accompany him to the hospital as an attendant. He refused to go alone and the authorities wanted to take him anyhow. The military Superintendent came fully prepared to take him by force. He put a big number of extra armed guards all round the fencing and an equal number were placed inside. A fight seemed to be inevitable. The communists were not only aloof, but some of them also jeered at us. But the situation was saved by Master Mota Singh. He followed Satrughna Kumar's stretcher feigning to be a sickman. Neither the doctor nor the Superintendent dared to stop him.

A show is not perfect without a clown and we had a veritable clown in Mobarak Mazdoor, who would stand half-naked before the Superintendent with some portion of his body painted black. He was even sent to the solitary cells as a punishment but he remained unchanged even there.

Jay Prakash Narayan arranged to smuggle some letters outside through a source. He asked me if I would like to send some letters outside to somebody. I said to him that he might send first some unimportant things just to test the source. But he did not pay any heed to my caution. The man did not do the job and J.P. got it back after a long time. Then when his wife came to interview him, he tried to pass on a bundle of papers to her. But the C.I.D. officer, a sub-inspector from Bengal, caught him red-handed and he, Master Mota Singh and Munshi Ahmed Deen were punished. J.P.'s letter was, long after, given to the press by the Government of India. This was done when everything was prepared for a general hunger strike in all the three camps.

What happened was this. The Government was very much upset on the preparations of general hunger strike with a demand to redress 18 grievances. N.M. Joshi came to see us on this but no way out was found out. Though tmqeoot plains were common they were represented to him differently by the two different sets of detenus communists and non-communists. The communist draft was prepared by them and presented to Joshi by comrade Mahmuduzzaffar and the one of non-communists was written by J.P. and presented by me. The authorities wanted to take advantage of this difference by publishing the J.P. letter through the press before the strike started. The letter had many adverse remarks about the C.P.I. and their men. They, therefore, naturally thought that this letter would further embitter the relationship between the two groups and as a consequence the strike move would fail.

The morning the letter was published J.P. was taken to the office and then the newspapers were sent to the camp. Only when J.P. assured the Superintendent that there would be no quarrel or assault on him he was sent back to the camp from the office on his own responsibilty.

Joshi on his return to Bombay submitted a report to Mahatma Gandhi and also issued a press statement in which, strangely enough, he placed our last point as the first, as if repatriation to respective provinces was our main demand. Later on we realised that the object of the C.P.I. in starting the hunger strike was repatriation and nothing else. But that was not the aim of others. That is why during the strike when N.M. Joshi came for negotiations they gave up the strike on the understanding that they would be repatriated ; but others who were serious, continued for more than a month. When Joshi saw me alone he told me that the C.C. of C.P.I. had urged upon their comrades to give up the strike.

Allow me to digress a little. Martyr Bhagat Singh's two brothers, Kulbir Singh and Kultar Singh, used to chat with me every evening before the lock-up time. I thought that this was because their brother was associate of mine. But one day Kulbir Singh told me very sentimentally taking me aside that their illustrious brother had told them in the condemned cell in Lahore jail that if they would like to work in the political field and if I would be alive till then, they should work according to my direction and then they would not be misled. My relation with Sardar Bhagat Singh was very deep no doubt, but I could not think of so implicit a faith in me on behalf of this brilliant youth, who came to me at Kanpur at the age of 17 and lived under my guidance only for a couple of months.

This sentiment of the great martyr Sardar Bhagat Singh was manifest into later documents, as well. Veteran revolutionary leader, Pratul Chandra Ganguli, wrote a letter from Calcutta to my Lusknow address on 9-2-52 in which he wrote "Bhagat Singh had spoken many things about you. He had the greatest regard for you. As a revolutionary leader, his confidence and regard for you was above anybody else." Professor Bhagwandas Mahore of Bhusawal Bomb Case, who was a close associate of Sardar Bhagat Singh, and participated in the attempt to take me out while I was being transferred from Agra to Lucknow jail, writes "When we all came back to Agra (after the failure of the attempt) Bhagat Singh on entry to the house wept bitterly, although all the way (from Kanpur to Agra) he restrained himself in such a way that nobody could say seeing him on the way that he was so much mortified."

Comrade Batliwala of Bombay was in Hijli Detention Camp in Bengal. That camp was dominated hy the Revolutionary Socialists, who were confirmed Marxist-Leninists. Naturally Batliwalla was much impressed by them. When he was transferred to Deoli Camp he wanted to talk to me. We were known to each other as leading members of the Congress Socialist Party. But when he came to my place to deliver the message of the Hijli camp the C. P. I. leaders felt nervous. We had hardly started the talk when he was taken away on the plea of an urgent call by the Communist leaders.

Just on the eve of the general hunger strike Dange, Ranadive and Batliwala were separated from us and kept in another segregated camp. When they were going away I invited them to tea in our kitchen. On that occasion the sentiments that Batliwala expressed for me regarding the fight with the authorities, was not liked by the other two. They were dead silent. Ultimately Batliwala could not accomodate himself in the Party and left politics foor good.

Shortly after our arrival at Deoli there was a swing towards the C. P. I. and most of the Congress Socialists and Red Communists joined the C. P. I. ceremoniously in which the camp committee members were invited. Speeches were delivered by the leaders of the new entrants extolling the C. P. I. to the best of their ability. But again after the arrival of J. P., most of the C. S. P. men in the same way came back to the C. S. P.

HUNGER STRIKE AND RELEASE

I was well-known in the country as a hunger striker due to my prolonged hunger strikes several times during my previous life sentence as a leader of the famous Kakori Case. Much propaganda was was carried on in the papers about this hunger strike even before this was actually started. I was already an aged man now and as a result of the strike I was gowing down rather rapidly. Attempts were made by the doctors four times to give me nasal feeding forcibly. They not only failed in it, but profuse bleeding continued for hours as a result of the attempt. Friends were alarmed and all were agitated. The news reached the camp and strong protests were made to the Superintendent when he came for his round. In the afternoon J. P. and A. K. Ghosh were sent to the hospital for the enquiry. I had just explained the position to J. P., when the doctor-in-charge, an Anglo-Indian I. M. D., came there. When he admitted to J. P. that attempts were made to feed me 4 times and 4 times they had failed and that he thought that my condition was such that I might even die in a week, then he said that as a doctor he should report the position to the authorities. A doctor is not supposed to torture a patient. As I had told J. P. that if another attempt was made on me then I would physically resist it and others in the ward also promised to help me. J. P. also requested his party leaders of the Punjab, a professor and an M.L.A., who were in the adjoining room, to come to my help, should there be a fight.

Next morning a Punjabi doctor came and told

me that he would remove me to the operation room of the hospital and then make an attempt. My comrades on either side of my bed sprang up from their beds and told the doctor that my body won't be removed before they were dead. Undoubtedly the object of the doctor was to torture me there in the lonely place and thereby get my mouth opened. But the talk of the previous evening and the threat of my friends that morning acted as a brake against the evil intention of the doctor and he went away disappointed. That day the doctor-in-charge submitted his report to the Superintendent that my condition was critical and I might die in a week or so.

RELEASE FROM DEOLI CAMP

On the 17th day of the hunger strike the Superintendent came to the hospital very early at 8 A.M. and stop'ed near my bed and told me "There is a good news for you. You are released unconditionally." I said. "I am in the midst of a fight and I cannot leave the field without any decision." "This is Govt. of India order" he said. "And I cannot detain you." He then said that N. M. Joshi was expected that day. On that I argued that if he came with some understanding then there might be some compromise and in that case the strike might also be called off. Then no question will remain of my release. Of course it was not possible for him in the face of the Govt. order. I was carried to the camp and thence to a room, meant for the officers, in the military hospital. I was to be there as a free man till I was fit to undertake travel.

Here is an extract from "Pioneer" on my release.

GOVERNMENT OF INDIA COMMUNIQUE ON UNCONDITIONAL RELEASE FROM DEOLI CAMP

Pioneer, Friday, November 7, 1941.

Unconditional Release of Jogesh Chandra Chatterji. New Delhi, November 6,

Yesterday afternoon, November 5, the Government of India received information that the health of Jogesh Chandra Chatterji, one of the security prisoners, who is on hunger strike at Deoli, was detoriorating owing to the fact that, for certain physical reasons, it was impossible to administer food by artifiicial means, states a press communique.

In these peculiar circumstances, the Government of India, after consulting the Government of the United Provinces by whose order he had been detained under Defence Rule 26, informed the Superintendent, Deoli, late last night that Jogesh Chandra Chatterji was to be released unconditionally forthwith.

Sachindranath Sanyal was in the hospital as a positive T.B. case and he expected release as he tol pme that the Superintendent had recommended strongiy for that. But instead he was sent to special T.B. Jail at Sultanpur. At my earnest request Acharya Narendra Devaji made vigorous effort for his release and he was released only to die after another year's struggle.

After my release the Government of India issued a communique to the press regarding the precarious condition of my health, which alarmed my Luckhow friends and Sri C. B. Gupta, sent Ram Lakhan Benipuri to escort me back to Lucknow. Dr. Mukherji of Ajmer accompanied Benipuri in a car and on the 5th day I was brought to Ajmer. On the 6th morning when the train steamed into the Lucknow station Sri Gupta was astonished to find me standing on the door of the compartment. He had already phoned to the Medical College to keep the ambulance car ready to carry me home from the station.

Before I conclude this chapter, I should refer to the unity talks between the C.S.P. and the R.S.P. in the Deoli Camp. Under J.P.'s initiative unity talks were carried on for 3 days between the C.S.P. and the R.S.P. On their behalf were J.P., Seth Damodar Swarup, Mohanlal Gautam and Munshi Ahmed Deen, and on our behalf were myself, Keshava Prasad Sharma and Sushil Bhattacharya. There was complete agreement on all points but it was broken up abruptly on the fourth day when the question of a new name of the party was raised. J.P. could only concede that had Subhas

Bose also agreed to join with his Forward Bloc. Bose was then in Europe.

J.P. was in jail early in 1940 before the Ramgarh Session of the Congress. So he did not know that at Ramgarh we had formed the R.S.P. In Hazaribagh jail he wrote a thesis for a new party of leftists and named it R.S.P. He also sent a lengthy private letter to Subhas Bose through a released political prisoner. Later on he came to know that we had already formed R.S.P. On his release he went to Calcutta and had lengthy talks with Subhas Bose and Pratul Ganguli separately. On his arrival at Deoli Camp he narrated to me and Keshava Prasad Sharma the substance of the talks.

BACK TO LUCKNOW

The worst period of my life was at Lucknow. Physically I was very weak due to hunger strike. Economically also I was in a bad shape. On hearing of my release my sister came to Lucknow. I rented a house and came into it but had no money to pull on. I was so much sorrounded by the C. I. D. men that I could not move about freely. The C. I. D. people approached the owner of the house and he was so much afraid that I had to leave it and go to another place.

I took a loan of Rs. 100/- from C. B. Gupta and started a laundry. At that time my brother also came. This laundry helped me much at the time. Though the income was small but I was successful to avoid C.I.D. vigilance. Finding me engaged they lessened their attention and thereby I got an opportunity to proceed on with my life's mission I mean, the underground work.

I came out of jail in November, 1941 and one painful tragedy happend the next month just when the Japanese attack on the far East was in the offing. A Bengal revolutionary of our party Jiten Moulick came to Lucknow as an absconder and took shelter in "Sangharsh" office in Model Houses. Ramakanta Shastri, the editor, brought him to me in a dark night to see if he was a genuine man. I was convinced that he was a valued comrade. My sister served him food but he could not take even half the quantity. I expressed my surprise at it because he appeared to be a stout and healthy youth. The next day I heard that he was down with high fever which turned out to be typhoid. He was betrayed and in this condition he was taken to the police station and thence to jail. The inevitable result was that he breathed his last in two days on the 15th or 16th of December 1941. I gave him assurance about my sympathy and support but I could not come to his help in his direst need. This feeling I cannot forget even at this distant date. The news of his death was conveyed to the "Sangharsh" office through the Arya Samaj, whose men had taken out the dead boy for cremation. I received the news in the night when everything was over. He came from village Madhyapara in Vikrampur in the district of Dacca, Bengal. Later I came to know that he was sent to Lucknow by the party to establish contact with me. He also had told me so.

CHAPTER XX

NEW SITUATION ON JAPANESE VICTORIES

Japanese thumping victories and their triumphant march towards India's borders, smashing and crushing the British forces, created a great stir in India. Prior to this there was no life in India. C. P. I.'s move was to cooperate with the British government since German army marched against Soviet Russia. Their leader P. C. Joshi had an interview with the then Home Secy. Mr. Reginald Maxwell and the comrades came out of jail. Gandhiji had started preaching through the press that he would start his movement after the war was over. But the new situation created by Japan reversed the position altogether. The British prestige in the east was brought down to the lowest point. A new hope was generated in our country. Churchill was compelled to send Cripps Mission to pacify India at this most critical hour. Nehru was ready to accept it but Gandhiji's wishes prevailed at the eleventh hour and the Mission failed.

Rafi Ahmed Kidwai, the ex-Home Minister was living in Room No. 6 of the Councillors Residence. I was living very near him and was spending hours daily in his room. Many people came daily from various places to meet. As I could not move about due to C.I.D. vigilance, his house was the best meeting place for me.

One morning myself and Rafi Saheb were strolling in the lawn. He was in a pensive mood. Suddenly he halted, turned to me and said "Jogesh Babu, the communists have gone over to the Government side, the Congress is dead and if you people, who have fought heroically against the British Government, are also to be inactive, then what's the future of India? For a moment I was dumbfounded and then I looked at him and said "This is war time and all my friends are in jail. Yet I shall try to mobilise the youth of the country. Can I bank on your support?" To this he gave an emphatic assent and he was quite true to his words.

I had just left for Farrukhabad by the morning train for Kanpur. After about an hour Rafi Saheb got the information that I was under warrant of arrest. He sent Durgaji and Ram Krishna Khatri to Kanpur by the next train to convey the information and I went underground. Rafi Saheb was arrested and thrown into prison shortly after this when no other eminent Congress leader was under arrest. The political Adviser to the Govt. hard-pressed by the press representatives told them that his early arrest was due to his association with me.

1942 MOVEMENT

My secret movement in U. P. was not an easy affair. Yet I came in contact with a good number of revolutionary youths of this province and contacted youths of Bengal and Bihar too. These youths played a very big part in the August Movement of 1942. My plan then was, as I stated to many eminent persons, that we should keep ourselves prepared to rise in revolt and join forces with the I. N. A. as soon they marched into India.

I invited two Bengal comrades at Muzaffarpur and instructed them to make all possible efforts to establish contact with the I. N. A. through Chittagong and Cox's Bazar and through Assam, if possible.

I had contacted youths from Banaras and Saharanpur, but before I could get them organized and activised properly, the premature 1942 August rising took place. Congress leaders throughout the country were arrested immediately after they passed the resolution to launch a movement at Bombay A. I. C. C. meeting on 8-8-42.

Angry people carried on Hartal for 3 days, 9th, 10th and 11th of August, for they knew not what to do in the absence of any programme. The programme was ultimately issued on the 11th night through a B. B. C. broadcast by Mr. Amery, the Secretary of State for India. America and Russia were the war allies of Great Britain. They were upset by the arrests in their war base in India.

A reply was essèntial on behalf of British Govt. So Mr. Amery stated point by point that the Congress wanted to oust them from India by various acts of sabotage. The programme of Amery became the Congress programme and it was worked out by the infuriated people in every nook and corner of the country. But all that was done in a week was an accomplished revolution. It could not succeed because it was a spontaneous reaction without any preparation or organization. The country sustained immense losses in wealth and the sufferings ard sacrifices of the people were limitless due to Governmental repressions.

All this was in vain as the time was not opportune. If we could organise such activities when the I. N. A. knocked at the doors of India, we certainly would have registered success. Had I.N.A. marched from outside and the rising of the people inside been simultaneous, millions of Indians in the army would have made a common cause with the two forces. In that case the few lakhs of British and American forces could have been forced to surrender. The march to Delhi from the eastern border of India would have been accompolished in a gigantic scale. Not only Britishers would have brought to their knees but their allies, the war profiteers and black-marketeers, could have never escaped the wrath of the serging masses of men fired with the spirit of sublime patriotism. Elimination of the British vested interests of every type was inevitable and that would have been real freedom earned by the people by their combined efforts. In a word, national enthusiasm would have built a nation, politically, economically and socially.

That chance we lost due to the conflict of ideas in the country—I mean, Revolutionism and Gandhism. During the First World War the only force to fight freedom battle was the nascent force of revolution inside the country. An effort was made to fight the British government with the help of German arms. But during the Second World War the fighting forces had divided allegiances, on the basis of violence and non-violence. Though the country was much advanced politically and the people were much more conscious, yet due to this difference in faith we could not avail of the great opportunity offered to us by the I. N. A. movement backed by Japan. The I. N. A. had no Gandhian influence and so was 1942 movement inside India. But no joint effort was possible between the two.

ETAH JAIL TRIAL

I was arrested at Soron in the district of Etah along with Thakur Mukund Singh of Sahranpur, Puttoo Singh Chauhan, Ram Larete Pande of Mainpuri and Govardhan Singh of Badaun. The trial was held under the special Courts Ordinance inside the jail for attempt at murder of a police sub-inspector and Arms Act. I was given

10 years R.I. and Govardhan Singh 3 years under Arms Act and others were detained in jail.

The district Magistrate, Mr. G. M. Lobo Probhu, I. C. S. came to see us in jail. I told him that trumped.up charges had been brought against us by the police. He promised justice and fairness The next week he awarded the policemen and witnesses of our case rewards in a Durbar held in the Police Lines. Then again for believing that the C.I.D. report in the case was true, two sub-inspectors of Soron were kept in the police lines. under suspension. The D.M. was the supreme authority in the district and he even told my defence counsel, Pandit Girija Shanker Chaturvedi,. " Chatterji may be a dangerous man and he may even be detained in jail. But I do not want that any body should be falsely implicated in my district." But I.C.S. sense of justice ended only by paying lip service to it.

After this everybody thought that the case would be withdrawn. But suddenly at this stage, the Governor, Sir Malcolm Haily, came to Kasganj and had an hour's talk with the D.M. The atmosphere changed and we were sentenced. Pandit Girija Shankar happened to be present at Lucknow on the day of my release 4 years later and he told me at my residence before a gathering that the Governor pressed the D.M. saying that I was an enemy of the state and hence not only the case should be proceeded against me but I deserved capital punishment.

On the 7th January 1943, I submitted a written statement before the Court, which shows the condition of my mind at the time. See Appendix.

LUCKNOW BARABANKI CONSPIRACY CASE

Govardhan and I were sent to the concentration jail of B Class revolutionaries at the District Jail as Lucknow-Barabanki Conspiracy case was started with myself as the chief accused and I was given 7 years R.I. after a protracted trial. In this case members of R.S.P., H.S.R.A and C.S.P. were involved. The Judge. Mr. K.R. Damle, I.C.S. gave uniform sentence to all. Three letters sent privately by Jharkhande Rai from jail, all of which contained my name and some literature left by me at my residence were kept in an absconders' house at Lucknow. These were seized by the police. They were sufficient to entangle myself and Rai in the case. So Rai got the sentence only for these letters.

The police tried to prove a province-wide conspiracy with myself as the head. But the Govt. did not allow this. So three different cases were instituted, the Lucknow case, the Gorakhpur Conspiracy case with Shri Shibban Lal Saksena and Agra Conspiracy case with Pandit Shri Ram Sharma as the leaders. Another case was to be started at Banaras. But when the Agra case failed in the High Court it was dropped.

I have spent my whole life in the company of

youths. During the Kakori case I was above 30 and faced trial with a big batch of enthusiastic youths. In this case, after the lapse of two decades the very same thing was repeated at Lucknow. Though a bit gray-haired I was taken to Lucknow court daily under fetters with a batch of patriotic youths. We sang and raised slogans as of old.

Lucknow case men were given 'B' class and were in Revolutionary Ward. Lahore case old friends were also there and Shibbanlal Saksena and others were brought from different districts. Life was pleasant and fruitful. Time was passing in studies and discussions. Generally due to confined life petty affairs often give birth to bitterness. But here petty things were not allowed to come between us.

For some time we had the company of K. Rama Rao, the editor of the National Herald. Some Congress leaders were also brought into the jail.

Stories began to pour in from different jails about the inhuman and brutal treatment of 1942 movement prisoners. The news of the treatment of C class revolutionaries in the Gaddha barrack of the Bareilly concentration jail was quite disturbing. Even cattles were not treated like that. They were the finest patriotic youths of the province. A robust youth of Ghazipur, Umashankar Upadhyaya, who came from a wealthy family was some times at Lucknow jail and I was much impressed by him. This brilliant youth was so much tortured to death when he was unconscious with high temperature.

(Hunger Strike on 16-1-46 to 6-2-46. See my Note Book marked Appendix. For appendix first application to the adviser of the Governor on 25/27-7-45)

These painful and inhuman torture upon the best elements of the country was unbearable. We all were much disturbed. I sent an application to the Government against all this requesting immediate redress of our grievances. I sent reminders but for 6 months there was no response. This was intolerable. I thought and at last came to a decision. I quietly submitted an application to the authorities giving an ultimatum of one month, on the completion of which I was to resort to hunger strike unto death, unless the grievances were removed. After I handed over my ultimatum to the authorities I divulged the news to my comrades. At this their anger was beyond limit. They discussed this and sent Rai to me to charge me with the betrayal of party principles and discipline. I was quite prepared for it. I asked Rai if they would have allowed me to submit it, had it been shown to them before being sent. He naturally replied in the negative pressing on the point that they would have also joined the strike. I said that was the reason why I did not show it to them. Mass hunger strike was usually ineffective. Hence it should be done by one and I was the best man for this owing to my past history. Their duty as comrades should be to carry on vigorous propaganda which was essential for the success of it. They submitted to my reasoning and I started the strike fully prepared.

Ráma Rao, did a great service to our cause by publishing the news of the strike prominently on the front page. My demands, etc. were given in a different column in detail and the second editorial of the National Herald of the day was on this subject. The grievance was genuine and I had nothing personal in it, because I was already a privileged prisoner in 'B' class. My past life and death struggles by prolonged hunger strikes were already known to all those interested in politics. Therefore this time the politically conscious Indians took up the cause very strongly. My health was deteriorating very fast. Within a few days I was passing through a crisis as I developed extreme biliousness.

My privileges as a superior class prisoner were partially withdrawn. The authorities refused to supply me with any newspaper. This was a hard-earned right during our Kakori conviction. In protest I stopped drinking water and refused to take any medicine. As soon as biliousness created a crisis I was allowed newspapers. Piles troubles disappeared on the administration of medicine. Nasal feeding was impossible and hence I was passing through a crisis again after two weeks. Press was active in distributing the day to day report on my health. Public agitation was going on vigorously, particularly in Bengal. Powerful papers wrote strong editorial notes. Meetings were held in Calcutta daily.

At this stage Sarat Bose wired to Pandit Nehru to try to settle the matter somehow. Nehru telephoned from Allahabad to C. B. Gupta at Lucknow and asked him to meet me in jail and try to ascertain how it could be terminated. Gupta met me in jail hospital cell. I gave him a cold reception, to which the jailor asked if I knew him. I thought that he had come to ask me to give up the strike unconditionally. He, however, wanted to know that minimum satisfaction I would demand in order to call off the strike.

Nehru reached Lucknow next morning, 6-2-46, and after a discussion with him Gupta went to the Adviser to the Governor. The Adviser was not ready to concede my minimum demands. Yet Nehru sent him to me with a two page letter in his handwriting giving me hope and advising me to give up the strike.* I was in a very difficult position. To accept this was as much difficult as reject it. Gupta tried to persuade me for nearly two hours but I could not be convinced. He went to our barrack, had a discussion with other friends and then came to me with four of them. They discussed the

* See Appendix.

matter with me and I had to agree to give up the strike. Nehru's long statement was published in all papers next morning in support of the cause for which I had to resort to the strike.

In the meanwhile we collected as much materials as we could, on the 1942 movement. We all read them aud then we held a serious debate. Our discussions continued for nearly a month though we were meeting daily for some hours. I used to preside over these meetings. The Lahore Case comrades, Sheo Varma, Jaydev Kapur and Dr. Gaya Prasad also joined our discussion at the beginning but later they backed out. They had joined the Communist Party when they were in the Andamans. It was not possible for them to participate because their party was not only not with the 42 movement and the I. N. A., but they worked against these in complete cooperation with the British Government. Their General Secretary, P. C. Joshi, wrote two signed articles in their party organ 'People's War' wherein he wrote that "Subhas was a traitor" and went to the extent of writing that if Bose set his feet on Indian soil, he and his party would welcome him with bullets.

SHAHEED RAJ NARAIN MISHRA

The most outstanding event in this jail was the arrival of comrade Raj Narain Mishra of Bhikampur, in Lakhimpur Kheri. He was put into a condemned cell under capital sentence. The socialist comrades, who were with us in the Lucknow-Barabanki Case claimed him to be a member of their party. Though I knew that he and the batch with him was with me and one of them, Makhan Lal, was with me till one day prior to my arrest, yet he was with the Socialist at the time when he was in the Central Jail at Lucknow.

Mishra came to know that I was in that jail and sent me a small slip of paper full of noble sentiments. This slip revealed to all what was in his mind. He naturally wondered how I was not communicating with him, being the leader of the Party with which he was connected through me. But soon we established regular correspondence. I requested him to write his life sketch in the correspondence. And this was done. Under my instructions comrade Rai used to copy out these letters in his note book. This was published after our release in a book form as the life story of Shaheed Raj Narain Mishra.

In the course of my long revolutionary life many of my associates and friends have met their ends by police or military bullets and by the hangman's rope. I heard and read the stories of heroic martyrs facing gallows fearlessly inspired by the glory of the great cause. In Raj Narain I saw another example of this. He behaved, as if, the very facing of the gallows was the biggest ceremony of his life. As the end of his life came nearer and nearer, he became more and more cheerful.

When after our last interview with him we were returning one of us was shedding tears. He chastised him from inside his cell "Why shed tears? Be brave and go away laughing."

In the afternoon the clinking sound of fetters attracted my attention towards the jail gate from the gate of our ward. I thought that somebody was being escorted to the gate, because from such a distance I could not recognize the person. "Dada, call them all" were the shouts of Raj Narain. He stopped and I ran inside our ward and called every body. But he was not there. We all waited eagerly for a very long time. Then we saw him returning to his cell. He took his last leave from us all.

Next morning only his slogans were heard, loudest and distinct. Then in a twinkling of an eye everything was over. Raj Narain, so lovely and lively, was only a name. His dead body was taken out by a group of patriots and consigned to flames on the bank of the Ganges at Kanpur.

He came from a poor family and was a victim of social oppressions, conscious and unconscious, by the wealthier sections. So the ideas of socialism were very appealing to him. He, therefore, advocated, economic and social freedom and thought that they were not of lesser importance than political freedom. In his last letters from the condemned cells to his brothers and to us he gave out his ideas clearly. According to him, a revolution was necessary and after that the common man must have economic and social rights, otherwise freedom would be meaningless.

People suggested that after his execution his young wife and the small child and another in the mother's womb be sent to the Ashram of Gandhiji at Sevagram. The idea was very unpleasant to him and he wrote to us that this must not be done, because he did not believe in Gandhian Utopia. His daughter, Devaki, was married but became a widow and now earns her living as a teacher. His son, Banarsi, is a student. His wife now gets a meagre pension of Rs. 45/- per month, much less than what a domestic servant earns.

As an absconder he did not hesitate to suffer imprisonment in Madhya Pradesh and in Delhi with an assumed name. And in Midnapore in Bengal he served the afflicted people as a worker of the Marwari Relief Committee. But there too, Raj Narain, the revolutionary socialist, differed seriously with their policy and left the work utterly disgusted.

His life story from his own pen is a piece of valuable treasure. But to day in independent but corrupt India nobody cares to read a book like that. Today we may forget him but he served his beloved country with the last drop of his blood in his own way and helped in bringing about the political change. He was the only man in U. P. to be hanged in the August Movement in 1942.

CONGRESS GOVERNMENT AGAIN AND RELEASE

Congress formed Government in U. P. on the 1st of April, 1946 and the whole atmosphere was changed. On the 4th day Rafi Saheb came to meet us in jail. I suggested immediate concentration of political prisoners in regional jails as special class and then release them. But he said that would not be necessary if they were released promptly. He did that. C. B Gupta also met us in jail one day. Then on the 17th our turn also came and we were released.

The news of my impending release was published in the papers for some days. One day the Secretary of the City Congress Committee came to the jail gate to receive me and take me to their office. Though not like what happened after the Kakori release, this time too there was enthusiasm and general jubilition on our release and a gathering of more than 10,000 received us in the meeting at Amin-Uddaula Park.

CHAPTER XXI

MY RELEASE AND AFTER

I was released from Lucknow Jail on 17th April, 1946, that is, on the seventeenth day of the formation of the Congress Ministry in U.P. Immediately after my release two important friends, namely, Satish Sirkar and Jatin Chakravarty came to meet me at Lucknow from Bengal and they pressed me to issue a statement to the press as the General Secretary of the Revolutionary Socialist Party. They insisted that I was elected the Secretary of R.S.P. at the time of its formation at Ramgarh. Those were war times and Government could not tolerate a separate party of revolutionaries. The Government adopted all measures of oppression and all the leading members of the party were put in jail. Thus the proper functioning of the R.S.P. could not become possible in the absence of the leading members. But now all of them were released and so the party out to function properly with its old Secretary, elected at Ramgarh. I was released from the jail only two days back, so I did not want to take any step so hastily. I wanted to study the situation in the country for a short while before issuing any statement to the press.

CONVENTION IN DELHI

Those of my friends who were released earlier thought of holding the first party convention in Delhi, the capital city. The idea was good but to make the arrangement was not an easy affair. This much was in my fovour in Delhi that I was arrested there in 1937 as the President of a conference and jailed. Therefore my name was popular. So I agreed to this proposal of Comrade Keshava Prasad Sharma. Yet I sent Satyendranath Banerjee to arrange everything.

In the mean time I was busy in my tour programe. Meetings were being held and purses were also being presented in certain meetings. Fresh party organisation required resources.

A revolutionary prisoner is in a difficult position just on his release from jail. In jail he has nothing to think of, he gets essential necessaries of life at state expense. But on release he has to arrange shelter, food and clothing. These were serious problems. I still remember how after release I purchased some material somehow and asked the tailor to make some clothes for me. But I had nothing in my pocket to pay him. Jatin Chakravarty realised this and paid the money. For such persons to start an organisation was not an easy affair.

Yet we did form an organisation within a very short time. Revolutionaries were strong people and they were not afraid of suffering for the cause.

Such men were to gather in Delhi in a convention. The idea had to be realised. Our friends with their scanty resources started the preparation. Satyen Banerjee failed to get any accommodation for the delegates. He was very much worried.

I was on three days' tour at Allahabad. Satish Sarkar and Jatin Chakrvarty came to Allahabad. I was asked by Satyen to go to Delhi at the earliest. I had to cut short my stay at Allahabad and go to Delhi with Sarkar. By the morning of the next day I secured two places for our delegates. The Conference at Gandhi Ground, Chandni Chowk, was a grand success. Through this conference we were established as a party in northern India. On their return to their places, the delegates of the Conference engaged themselves heart and soul for the ramifications of the organisation, the Revolutionary Socialist Party.

The historic Delhi Convention was held on the 11th 12th and 13th of May, 1946 and after that the organisational Work of the R.S.P. proceeded briskly, because for the first time the revolutionaries found themselves as an organised public body with the clear objective of getting socialism established through a revolutionary fight.

As a Congress Socialist in 1938-39 I was working mainly in the peasant and labour field. In 1939 I was Secretary of the U.P. Kisan Sabha and also a member of the A.I.K.S. A huge Kisan Conference was held at Gaya in 1939 under the

Presidentship of Acharya Narendra Deva. This was organised by Swami Sahajanand, an eminent Kishan leader of India. In the A.I.K.S. meeting I had a heated controversy with comrade Muzaffar Ahmed, the veteran Communist leader. The fun was that though we were very old acquaintances, after a lapse of many years we did not recognise each other. At the end late Bankim Mukherjee got us freshly introduced.

During the war period the All India Kisan Sabha was practically monopolised by the Communists, because they alone were in the field having decided to cooperate with the Government whereas all other parties were in a fighting mood and their leaders were in jail.

Babu Purshottam Das Tandon, one of the founders of the Kishan Organisation, called a Kisan Conference in Bombay and requested me to go. There was also the A.I.C.C. meeting in Bombay. On that occasion in the Conference held in Jinnah Hall, the All India Kisan Sangha was formed with Tandonji as President and Swami Sahajanand as General Secretary. On Tandonji's proposal I was elected a Vice-President. A five-member committee was formed for drafting a constitution and I was one of the members of this committee.

The Revolutionary Socialist Party was essentially a mass party and therefore it concentrated its activities mainly on the Kisans and labours.

In the labour front we were working through the All India Trade Union Congress. Jatin Chakravarty was working in Bengal with the help of Mrinal Kanti Bose. In U.P. we were working in sugar labour and other unions. In Bihar our trade union activity registered considerable success under the leadership of Shri Ranen Roy.

When the Revolutionary Socialist Party was formed, all the veteren leaders of the Anushilan Samiti were there. Anushilan leaders, Trailokya nath Chakravarty, late Pratul Chandra Ganguli, Ramesh Acharya, Rabindra Mohan Sen and others who had spent their whole lives in revolutionary fight for freedom, participated. But unfortunately the younger elements in jail in Bengal started a propaganda group-campaign against the veterans that they were not up to date in their ideas.

This fissiparous attitude of the second grade leaders in Bengal was ruinous for the party. The veterans were brilliant guerilla fighters and they had earned public respect through their life-long sufferings and sacrifices. To suppress them meant nothing but suppressing the very movement of the revolutionaries.

In a planned way the younger element suppressed the elders, but somebody was necessary at least to be called as their leader only to show that the party was not leaderless. My name was well-known as a revolutionary fighter and I was outside Bengal. So it was a part of their plan to catch hold of me to fill up the gap of their want of an All India leader. This motive was in their mind and therefore Satish Sarkar and Jatin Chakravarty ran to Lucknow immediately after my release and pressed me hard to make a statement as the General Secretary of the Revolutionary Socialist Party.

I wanted to study the situation and then come to some decision. But after giving the statement my hands and feet were bound down to their design as I realised gradually. But there was no way out. My entry to Bengal was banned by the Muslim League Ministry of Bengal and I met old Anushilan leaders from time to time outside Bengal. I made a last attempt to meet the Anushilan veterans at Deoghar in Bihar and to pursuade them to work for the party.

Ramesh Acharya was living at Deoghar. At my request Purnananda Das Gupta arranged a meeting there. Trailokyanath Chakravarty, Pratual Ganguli and others came together with some leaders of the second grade. Satish Sarkar as spokesman of the latter took up such an attitude that it was clear that they were not to go with the veterans. I rebuked him but it was in vain. They went back to Calcutta and I came to Rameshda's residence with other leaders. Here I told them that I was sent to U.P. as the representative of the Anushilan, that is, as their representative, and without them I would feel very uncomfortable. In fact I felt their absence in the party much, but I was helpless.

We accepted Marxism and Leninism as our line and elders did not disagree. So there was no fundamental difference. Then in the last analysis the idea came to some one's mind that it might be the question of position in the party which was the root cause of rift. The hunger for power, before even the acquirement of real power was, basically a weakness which had retarded our progress even during the days when we were fighting against the British Government.

1946 was one of the most stormy years in the history of freedom struggle of India. One of the most glaring and sensational happenings of this year was the I. N. A. trials. When the news about I. N. A. affairs reached the Indian masses through the enthusiasm of the Indian press, a deep sympathy and reverence among the masses for the I. N. A. people was the outcome. It became a symbol of national feeling and direct fight between British Government in India and the Indian People. At the time of such a national upsurge the trial of I. N. A. men took place in the historic Red Fort. The Congress party also became aware of this nation wide sympathy and support for I. N. A. and thus the top Congress leaders could not remain indifferent to it. Bhula Bhai Desai, a member of the Congress Committee and one of the most prominent lawyers of India took the responsibility of chief defence lawyer. Even Pandit Jawaharlal Nehru attended the proceedings of the Court as one of the defence Counsels. The entire British bureaucracy was trying its best to inflict heavy punishments on I. N. A. heroes and India stood united to defend them.

In Calcutta disturbances started. The students movement took place very vehemently. On the way of their march to Dalhousie Square several rounds of firing were ordered. One Hindu and one Muslim student were shot dead. Consequently, disturbances spread throughout the entire city. Military vehicles, American and British, were burnt and destroyed. The military and police also could not remain untouched. The naval power which consisted of very efficient and highly technically equipped men revolted against the Government in Bombay. The British Government ordered the Air Force to bombard the naval unit, but the air force men refused to comply. Now the Government was in a great perplexity. The edifice of British imperialism seemed to be crumbling down before the eyes of those who had nurtured it. Rift within the bureaucracy and disobedience in the armed forces were such factors which could bring the functioning of the British administrative machinery to a standstill. The second world war gave such a crushing blow to England that her entire economy was shattered into pieces. She was not left with enough resources to suppress growing Indian national discontent. The only probable solution which the White Hall could think, was to compromise with Indian wishes and agree to the demand for freedom.

* * * *

Britain was compelled to think more deeply about the situation in India. Lord Wavell, the Governor General, was busy with plans. The Labour Government sent the Cabinet Mission and they placed their plan. Prior to that was the Simla Conference at Simla but which had failed as Mr. Jinnah insisted on implementation of Pakistan Resolution. This weakened the nationalist Muslims and Jinnah became dominant.

The Cabinet Mission announced a scheme of Union of India, formation of the Constituent Assembly and an Interim Government at the Centre.

* * * *

The Second Convention of the Party was held at Muzaffarpur, Bihar. A strong section was for severing all connections with the Congress but the majority was not in favour. All this happened before the transfer of power.

PRELUDE TO PARTITION

With freedom almost within the reach, the gereral election of 1946 was fought with a remarkable enthusiasm on two platforms viz, the Congress and the Muslim League, backed primarily by the nationalists and the average muslim population respectively. An Interim Coalition Government was formed and for the first time in the known history of India power was transferred across a table over a piece of paper with the British masters on one side and the Congress and Muslim League leaders on the other side to accept the power in divided India within the Commonwealth.

Right from the days of Lahore Congress resolution of 1930 the Congress stood firmly for complete (and unconditional) Independence and also against the division of the country on communal basis ; but the British plan to transfer power within the Commonwealth and also on the principle of divided India was accepted by the power greedy popular leaders of the Congress.

After the formation of the Interim Coalition Government, the muslims started a communal riot in Calcutta, on 16 August, 1946, which gradually spread to different parts of India. Thus, the entire political atmosphere of the country was vitiated with communal feelings. In these circumstances, the British Government found an opportunity to divide the country on communal basis. They removed the Governor General, Lord Wavell, who was not in favour of partition. He was replaced by Lord Mountbatten. Lord Mountbatten with all his military zeal and deplomatic tact began fishing in the troubled water of India for partition. The way in which he manipulated the partition, throws a pathetic light on the personality, character and integrity of the Congress leaders.

My Entry into Bengal after the transfer of Power :

I have stated earlier that the Muslim League Ministry in Bengal had all along banned my entry into Bengal. But after the transfer of power, Dr. Prafulla Chandra Ghosh formed the Congress Ministry in West Bengal on the 15th of August, 1947. This opened the way of my entry into Bengal.

I was invited on behalf of the Jatin Das Memorial Committee to attend the martyr's anniversary on the 13th September, 1947. The Secretary, Satish Sarkar, came to Kanpur and I gave him detailed instructions. I wrote to sympathetic Bengal leaders and received their welcome replies. I asked to raise a purse on the occasion and Sarkar in his telegram from Calcutta stated "fund assured." But the Bengal unit of the party did not allow this as I came to know on arrival at Calcutta. Satish Sarkar felt so much humiliated that after this he took very little interest in the party affairs. I was also shocked at the attitude of the Bengal unit. Purses I received in U. P. were utilised for the All India and U.P. Party, but Bengal took up a strange stand. Later on they explained that they were to raise a fund for a press. On that occasion the popular feeling was so much in our favour that they could easily raise a purse of Rs. 50,000 and out of that money they also could establish a press. The incident pained me because it indicated an evil intention.

Bengal leaders and the press welcomed me with an open heart. On that day, the 12th September, 1947, all the educational institutions of Calcutta from the University to primary schools were given half holiday to receive me at Howrah Station in the afternoon. Although the train was three hours late, some 25,000 people were present there when the train steamed in. I was taken to the residence of Kiran Das from where I went to my cousin Paresh Chandra Chatterjee's place. He kept at my disposal a new car and a driver with as much coupon for petrol as could be required. This was a great help in my very heavy 13 days' programme.

On the 13th September the morning programme was at the burning ghat at Keoratala, where Jatin Das was cremated. Many prominent revolutionaries and Congress leaders were present there. In the evening was the public meeting at Hazra Park. The well known revolutionary leader Dr. Jadugopal Mukherjee presided. The park was overcrowded.

I was given a public reception in the University Institute. The President of BPCC, Shri S. M. Ghose presided. The hall was rather overpacked. The meeting of the university was a grander one. The Vice-Chancellor Dr. Banerjee presided. The students heard me with great attention. Next I addressed the girl students of the Bethune College.

At the invitation of the All India Radio I also gave a talk on Hindu Muslim unity.

There was a big procession and meeting in Beliaghata. One volunteer organisation of Howrah arranged a procession and a meeting. Meetings and processions also were held at Chinsura, Howrah and other places.

I addressed party members in our party office at Sealdah. I had interviews with important persons like the Chief Minister Dr. P. C. Ghosh, A. C. Dutta, Suhrawardy, Mazumdar of Ananda Bazar Patrika and Hindustan Standard and also T. K. Ghosh of the Amrita Bazar Patrika.

The last very big meeting was held at Kanchrapara which was organised by the Railway workers. They had fixed up a date and Dr. Banerjee, the Labour Minister, was also to go according to official programme. The workers wanted me to be there alone. So the date of my visit was changed. The next day I was to leave for Lucknow. So it was decided that I would dine with Heramba Bhattacharya, the proprietor of M/s. M. Bhattacharya & Co. His car waited at Sealdah station for two hours from 8 to 10 p. m. but I could not come. I was very much delayed at Kancharapara. Such a big number of persons had gathered that it was difficult to take me to the hall when the procession stopped near it. The ground was overpacked with men. The organisers realised that it was impossible to hold the meeting either in the hall or on the ground in front. The workers within an hour and half erected a dias and fitted electric lights and then the huge meeting was held there. So I returned to Calcutta very late in the night and I had to dine with Heramba Babu the next evening on my way to Howrah station.

All these thirteen days, demonstrations clearly showed what a feeling the people of Bengal had for the revolutionary fighters for freedom. Bengal politics was ever dominated by the revolutionaries. Netaji was himself a revolutionary and C. R. Das and J. M. Sen Gupta had mainly to depend on the support of the revolutionaries. Revolutionaries thus dominated the Congress.

TRANSFER OF POWER

Though it seems a very short time that the struggle for freedom started in the early part of the present century and not before long, India was declared independent but this short period in the history of India was full of events and commotions. It may seem to be a short period in terms of sacrifice for the motherland, will to face the brutal tortures inflicted upon patriots and the socio-political upheaval of the country, this was definitely one of the most glorious periods in the history of India. How did we achieve independence and what were the factors that contributed towards it are controversial matters. Once success is achieved, interpretations differ.

As it is generally taught to the present generation, who do not have any first hand knowledge of the actual struggle, that only Congress non-violent movement brought independence to this country, it is, in my personal opinion, a grave distortion of historical fact.

It is an undisputed fact that the Congress movement, led by Gandhiji was one of the decisive factors. But we must not forget that there were other factors which contributed towards the awakening of national consciousness among Indians. The daring exploits of the revolutionaries, the patriotic writings of the literatteures, the sacrifice of countless unknown people, the intellectual integrity of some intellectuals and many more things made what India is to-day. International politics also played its vital role in the drama which cannot be ignored altogether.

After the second world war two great powers came into being, viz., USA and USSR both growing rapidly in industry, commerce and science and having divergent political and social ideologies. Even during the second world war Churchill cautioned the British people against the growing power of the Communist World.

The world was to be consolidated into two ideological groups, viz. Communists and non-communists. In this ideological war, USA took the leadership of the West and Britain was reduced to a second class power. Britain with her vast colonisation monopolised the largest part of the world market. The orthodox Marxist saw an impending clash between the expanding capitalism of U.S.A. and the moribund economy of U. K. But faced with the growing menace of world communism the Western powers were not in a position to afford an inner rift between themselves. And in this tussle, U. K. which was now a comparatively weaker power than the USA, was bound to yield her interest. She yielded and adopted a general policy of liberation of colonies.

United States since the the very beginning of its history is a champion of freedom and not colonisation. They had also suffered British colonialism and its bitter experience were preserved in their memory. So United States ideologically also ridiculed the idea of imperialism and was particularly interested in the liberation of Asian and African countries.

The second block in the world politics, that is, the Communist bloc was very conscious of the importance of Asian and African countries. They knew that inner discontent in these countries had reached up to the brim and revolution was brewing everywhere. If Russia could simply provide the necessary ignition, the explosion would definitely go out of control of the western imperialists. The Communist bloc was waiting anxiouly for the maturity of situation when they could exploit it successfully. Now it was for the Western powers to choose whether they should retain their subjection of Asian and African countries and give them chance to explode with the direct and indirect help and sympathy of communist bloc or liberate them honourably and try to win the heart of the subject races with sympathy, goodwill and commercialisation. The latter path was more prudent and they adopted it. Unable to win over the Afro-Asian people to its side Communism consolidated its forces in China, Russia and many of the East European countries. Ruthless suppression of the Hungarian revolt followed.

CHAPTER XXII

PARTITION AND AFTER

Within five weeks of the transfer of power ceremony in 1947 the Revolutionary Socialist Party walked out of the Congress. Gradually an uneasy atmosphere began to be felt within the Congress and Sardar Patel decided to reorganise the party under one flag, one name and one leadership. So long the Congress was a common platform of many political opinions. The Congress Socialist Party was also squeezed out of the Congress.

REFUGEE REHABILITATION

The minority communities of the West Pakistan after a serious loss of lives and property came out rapidly and the Central Government of India, took prompt action to rehabilitate them.

But the refugees from East Pakistan were the worst suffers. For many years they were not recognised as refugees and were kept in crowded camps on doles. These prolonged inhuman habitations totally deprived them of human good qualities and capacity to work.

West Bengal Government had no sympathy for them and money sanctioned for them was mostly misused. Fifteen lakhs of them were settled in West Bengal without any Government help.

When their lives became absolutely intolerable in East Pakistan, there were mass migrations defying our Government's wrong restrictions put on them there. They came almost naked and were immediately sent to most backward and undeveloped areas in different parts of the country, where no proper rehabilitations were arranged.

These unfortunates left everything in Pakistan but were not given any compensation, whereas refugees from West Pakistan came with their valuable things, got vast evacuee properties left by muslims, and over and above that got compensation of rupees 300 crores, all their claims having been accepted without any enquiry.

Thus the Hindus of East Pakistan, who suffered much for freedom's fight, received no sympathetic treatment from the rulers of Independent India.

CHAPTER XXIII

CONFERENCE OF INDIAN REVOLUTIONARIES IN DECEMBER, 1958.

As the Convenor, I called a conference of Indian revolutionaries in Delhi which was held in the Parade Ground on the 13th and 14th December, 1958 under the Presidentship of the veteran revolutionary, Dr. Bhupendra Nath Dutta, younger brother of Swami Vivekananda. About 400 delegates from all over India, including Barindra Kumar Ghosh, younger brother of Sri Aurobindo, Baba Sohan Singh Bhakna, the founder President of the Ghadar Party in America, Dr. Khankhoje (Ghadar Party), Dr. Bhagwan Singh (Ghadar Party), Dr. V. V. Athalye of Satara Conspiracy case (1910) attended the conference. Delegates were ledged in the former Delhi District jail.

Pandit Govindballabh Pant inaugurated it and the Prime Minister, Pandit Jawaharlal Nehru, invited the delegates at his residence.

It was a unique thing after 11 years of independence. The Secretary of the Congress Party in Parliament invited the delegates to the Parliament House and entertained them with tea and the Delhi Pradesh Congress Committee gave them a tea party in the Constitution Club.

The chairman of the Reception Committee was

Lala Hanumant Sahai, the veteran revolutionary of Delhi who was sentenced to 7 years' imprisonment in the famous Hardinge Bomb Conspiracy case, along with Master Amirchand, Avadbehari, Balmukand, and Basanta Kumar Biswas, who were all hanged in the case.

When in the open conference Mr. Manindra Nath Naik of Chanderanagore stood up to move a memorial resolution on the great Indian revolutionary, late Rashbehari Bose, I introduced him to the audience saying that he was the maker of that bomb which was thrown on the Viceroy Lord Hardinge, the audience hailed him with prolonged cheers and clapping.

The conference passed only one resolution that a history of the contribution of revolutionaries in the freedom movement of India be compiled and memorials to revolutionary martyrs be erected.

For the memorial the Delhi jail was proposed to be preserved. Accordingly I wrote a letter to the Prime Minister. His reply was that because the jail was to be the Maulana Azad National Medical College only a plaque would be put up on the spot where stood the gallows. I was directed to approach the Home Minister. We met him several times. At last he formed a committee under the chairmanship of Mr. Datar, Minister in the Ministry of Home Affairs and Mr. A. D. Pandit, Chief Commissioner of Delhi, Mr. Sehgal, Jt. Secretary, Home and Mr. Sharma, Senior Architect were the official members and Dr. Yudhvir Singh and myself were non-official members.

After about half an hour's discussion Mr. Pandit suggested that because the jail was going to be a medical college no public memorial could be preserved in it. So he proposed that the memorial be erected in front of the jail gate. I welcomed the idea. Sehgal asked about the cost and Pandit Stated that it would be about two to three lakhs.

Asked by Mr. Datar I submitted a plan with a sketch, a plaster model and a rough estimate of about two lakhs prepared by the famous artist, Ashit Kumar Haldar.

How much anti-revolutionary the Congress Government was, was conclusively proved when after all this the Home Ministry under Pandit Pant flatly refused to do anything.

I later prepared a book on this conference named 'Indian Revolutionaries in Conference' in which about 50 photos of revolutionary martyrs have been given and the correspondence I had with Mr. Datar on this subject has been published. Two photoes in this book, which are today of very great historical importance—one photo of the spot were the Hardinge Bomb case martyrs were hanged, the other photo is of the condemed cells of that jail where the martyrs passed their last days. These two historic things today exist only in these two photoes in that book.

Congress Government will someday go but this

book will remain to commemmorate the martyrs, who laid down their lives as heroic Indian fighters for freedom. Delhi will remember Master Amirchand and India will pay her homage to this son of Delhi. In the book I have tried to preserve the memories of many a revolutionary who, thanks to the apathy of the Congress Government, have already been relegated into partial oblivion. Master Amirchand is one such patriot.

Master Amirchand was not an ordinary citizen of Delhi, but was a foremost publicman of this historic city. One instance, as mentioned elsewhere, will show what he was. He was running a weekly in Delhi called "Akash". The editor was Pandit Ram Chandra Bhardwaj of North West Frontier Provinces. Under vernacular Press Act all the papers of the type were stopped by the Government. Amirchand was not much sorry for his own paper. But the *Swarajya* of Allahabad was the prestige paper, of which 3 editors were transported to the Andamans. Amirchand decided to continue the paper and collected money for it and sent the editor of his own paper to Allahabad to restart the *Swarajya*. Rashbehari Bose had no difficulty in picking up such a fiery person as his revolutionary accomplice.

British Government erected four memorials on Lord Hardinge in Delhi, namely, the Hardinge Library, the Hardinge Hospital, the Hardinge Bridge and the Hardinge Avenue. But the independent

Government of India would not erect memorial to Hurdinge Bomb conspiracy case martyrs, who were hanged.

The memorials of only Congress men erected by the Congress Government are note creating much inspiration in the people. Inspite of tonnes and tonnes of propaganda publicity, morale of the people are going down.. The Congress' attitude towards the revolutionaries was well-known to us. But it became crystal clear to us on the very day on which we achieved our independence. Two days before the 15th of August, 1947, the day of transfer of power to Indian hands, there was a meeting of the Lucknow City Congress Committee. In that meeting I proposed that on the 15th morning we should assemble at Aminuddaula Park and march to the Residency with the Indian national flag and hoist that flag on the Residency building in place of the British flag that was flying there since its British occupation after the Sepoy Mutiny in 1857.

The idea appeared to be welcome to all. But Shri C. B. Gupta, the President of the Committee, remarked, "Why on that very day? It may be done later." This clearly indicated the trend of mind of the Congress leaders regarding the transfer of power.

On the 15th August, 1947 it was crystal clear that the Congress was not to bring about the least change in the tradition established by the foreign rulers. The Congress simply wanted to imitate them in letter and spirit.

Mrs. Sarojini Naidu that day assumed charge as the Governor of U.P. A tea party was announced in the Government House in the evening. I was invited there as a member of the City Congress Committee.

In the afternoon my friend, Govinda Charan Kar, a Kakori lifer, came to my place and after tea we went to Aminabad to see how people were observing the day. We found that the freedom fighters of Congress had gathered there and were preparing vigorously to go to the Government House in a torch-light procession.

When they started myself and Govind Kar followed them to encourage them in their enthusiasm. But when they reached the gate they were not allowed to go in. Kar pushed open the gate in defying mood challenging the sentries. On hearing the shouts some City Congress members came near the gate and requested me to get in. But I refused. The demonstrators stayed there for nearly half an hour and then returned cursing the Congress leaders.

Conscious people understood from that very day that power came not for the masses but for a few leaders only.

After the transfer of power, how my entry into Bengal was welcomed by the people on the occasion of the Jatin Das anniversary has been narrated. But the Congress attitude towards the revolutionary fighters for freedom was distinctly apathetic. This was because they knew that power transfer took place as the direct result of the grim direct-action fight of the revolutionaries. That glaring fact must be wiped out from the memory of the people by somehow pushing these fighters into oblivion and preaching outright that the Congress did everything.

We were also realising this, and, therefore, in the first week of October, 1947, we in our R. S. P. C. C. meeting at Gopalganj in Bihar took the decision to leave the Congress which was announced by me, as the General Secretary of the Party. This received wide publicity.

I was moving heaven and earth for strengthening the Party, but the thought that our veteran leaders were not with us always haunted me. The new leadership of the party treated the veteran very shabbily. Let me cite only one instance of this treatment.

Once I was in our Bengal Office in Calcutta, when Pratul Chandra Ganguli came to see me, the Bengal Secretary, Makhan Paul, kept him waiting for nearly an hour. He was about to go back out of disgust when I was brought before him. I apologised to him but was very much ashamed at heart.

The third all-party conference was held at Basti in U. P. Till then the R. S. P. was gaining strength in U. P. But later on my own friends developed internal clique and thereby ruined the Party in U.P. An important section left the party and ultimately joined the C. P. I.

U. P. R. S. P. was the creation of my life-long service and when my own lieutenants brought about its ruination I was very much shocked and told the party leadership that I should be relieved of the secretaryship of the party. But yet I was rather compelled to linger on for another three years and ultimately left the party quietly announcing before the Steering Committee meeting in New Delhi that they should elect somebody else as their General Secretary in their all party conference in Bombay, which was about to be held by the end of 1953.

For six long years after we stood against the ruling Congress Party, I, as R. S. P. leader, had one single objective in my mind and that was to create a united front of leftists to stand as a rival to the Congress. We stood by Swami Sahajanand and three years later responded readily to the call of late Sarat Chandra Bose. But unfortunately no real unity could be achieved.

So I left politics out of disgust and spent a year in the hills and jungles of Orissa. The Congress passed the Avadi Resolution in 1955 and I could see a ray of hope. Urged by some friends I met Pandit Jawaharlal Nehru and through him rejoined the Congress. But gradually I have been disillusioned of the charm of Socialism of the Congress variety.

As a revolutionary, I was never a believer in compromise, because I was convinced that it would degrade that nation. But I could never dream that whatever patriotic spirit we could acquire in the course of our fight for freedom in fifty years would be totally lost only within 18 years of independence. Within such a short time our national character has been so thoroughly degraded that today we have become a nation of self-seekers. Today neither the administration nor the Congress organisation has strong foundation among the people. Only top leadership is there, and that, too, not free from popular distrust.

How this nation is to rise again, that question alone is disturbing the mind of all honest and right-thinking Indians.

I have not the least doubt that a section of the youths of the country would again rise and form the vanguard of revolution and bring about the much-desired change in the atmosphere. The sooner that happens the better it would be for this accursed land of ours. I would very eargerly wait for the day before I breathe my last.

Appendix

APPENDIX I

BANDIJIBAN PART III—BY SACHINDRANATH SANYAL

After the draft of my book was completed I received a copy of the latest edition of Bandijiban of Late Mr. Sachindra Nath Sanyal in which the publisher, Mr. Banarsidas Chaturvedi has added a posthumous third to the original two parts published by the author himself in the third decade of the present century.

On perusal I find that this has put me in an awkward position, because it is full of distortions of facts and uncalled for attacks on his former co-workers, particularly the Anusilan Samiti and its reputed leaders, with whom he had worked all through his career as a revolutionary (strange, he contradicts his own opinion expressed in Bandijiban Parts I and II).

Chaturvediji has overlooked one important fact that Mr. Sanyal wrote these articles in Hindi weekly Pratap of Kanpur after his release from the Kakori case when he had no connection with any political organisation and was passing through hard days with his family. That his object of writing was earning money and at the same time to belittle his old co-workers who were still active in the organisation, only to please some interested person.

I shall not deal with the matter in details, because my object is not to criticise his writings at this distant time, more than twenty years after his death, but only to touch upon a few points, so that his writings now published in the form of a book by a distinguished publisher may not go unchallenged.

I have ignored the gross misrepresentation of facts by another author, Shri Arun Chandra Guha, M. P., in his history of revolutionary movement published in the *Amrit Bazar Patrika* of Calcutta. I was deputed to U. P. by the Anushilan Samiti but Guha says that I had differences with the Samiti and for that reason I came to work in U. P., although Mr. Sanyal wrote two decades ago that I came deputed by the Samiti. In the Kakori-trial also it was clear that Anushilan Samiti deputed me.

to U. P. Guha has not cared to know the real facts. His history about Girija Babu is simply ridiculous. The man had died in Agra Central Jail within a few years after his sentence in Banaras Conspiracy Case in 1915. Yet Mr. Guha writes that he has been released and he has given up the revolutionary line of work.

Mr. Sanyal's thesis is different. He asserts that he was a man of very superior quality, but others were mere pigmies before him. He states that after his release from the Andamans he created a gigantic organisation in U. P. and Punjab before he left U. P. in 1924. But in the big Kakori Conspiracy Case his name came nowhere even once, although his recruit Banwarilal became a confessing accused in the case and through his confession the Kakori dacoity itself was established.

Was he again a vigorous revolutionary in U. P. on release as he states ?

My answer to this question is an emphatic No. On his release from the Andamans (convicted in Banaras Conspiracy Case for life) he had not the least desire to restart the secret revolutionary work. His own writings and actions are glaring proofs of that. Mr. Barin Ghosh openly declared on release that they had 'given up revolution for good', but Mr. Sanyal did not do so openly. But he told so to his intimate friends in Calcutta. He started brick-making business in Bengal and he married. When this business failed he took up railway service in Bengal. This petty service of Rs. 50/- p. m., he thought was insufficient. So, he approached C. R. Das and S. N. Haldar. Haldar was then the President of the Jamshedpur Labour Union. The latter made him a paid office secretary of the Union on Rs. 150/- per month. These had nothing to do with secret revolutionary work. Even after his arrival in U. P. in later part of 1922, he tried for a railway job through a European C. I. D. official. When he failed in this and also came to know that Anushilan Samiti was already active in U. P. only then his attention was drawn to the secret revolutionary work. I have stated how he came in contact with Rajen Lahiri, an abandoned Anushilan recruit, through Dr. Suren Mukherjee and also received a revolver through him, although he himself was not at all active.

I have already stated that on his release in 1920 Sanyal had no idea of restarting secret revolutionary organisation. Facts prove that and he said so to Pratul Chandra Ganguli. Ganguli stated this to me and for this reason he did not give me any letter of introduction to Sanyal when I was leaving Bengal for U. P, in 1923.

The *assertions, as I stated, of* Sanyal *that* he carried on a vigorous work in U. P. after his release from the Andamans are vulgar exaggerations and are not supported by facts. In fact, he did nothing between the years of 1920 to 1922. He states that Banwarilal was his first recruit at Allahabad. Banwari stated in Kakori case before the court that he came in touch with the party in the summer of 1923. Sanyal writes on page 255 that Lahiri was a B. A. student. This, too, cannot be earlier than 1923.

HOW WAS SANYAL RELEASED FROM THE ANDAMANS ?

It is true that Sanyal did not give any direct undertaking for his release from the Andamans. But from his own writing it appears that he indirectly gave some understanding to B. C. Chatterjee (page 226) for which Chatterjee told him in clear terms that he should work on the line of reforms and should give up secret revolutionary work, as he gave him to understand in his letter from the Andamans. Certainly, with this idea in mind he told his old friends that he would not work on secret revolutionary line and again with this idea in mind till 1922 he tried to get himself established economically.

Sanyal's arguments that he was released but Savarkar was not released because, there was strong agitation in Bengal but no such thing happened in Maharashtra. This does not hold good at all because Sanyal, a lifer of U. P., was released but Trailokya Nath Chakravarty of Bengal, who was transported for 15 years was not released and many others, like Amrita Hazra etc. were not released.

WAS THE MAJORITY OF BENGAL REVOLUTIONARIES IN FAVOUR OF REFORMS ?

On page 229 Sanyal writes that the majority of Bengal revolutionaries were in favour of working out the Montagu-

Chemsford reforms, whereas Gandhiji was for its rejection. That can only mean that the revolutionaries became more moderate that even Gandhiji and the Congress. Such a thing never happened. Revolutionaries were never believers of reformism at any stage of their freedom struggle. In the same paragraph he states that the released revolutionaries did not take any decision. He says so because he had no connection whatever with the revolutionaries at this time as he gave up revolutionary politics and that must be the reason for this incorrect statement. He again makes a wrong statement that C. R. Das was not in favour of Gandhiji Had he the least connection with Bengal politics of the time, he would not have been so very ignorant of the fact that on the eve of the Nagpur session in December. 1920 Bengal Congress passed a resolution to oppose Gandhiji at Nagpur, but Das surrendred to Gandhiji at Nagpur contrary to the Bengal resolution.

HOW SANYAL CAME IN TOUCH WITH RASHBEHARI BOSE ?

Sanyal writes on page 231 : "During my travels I accidentally came in touch with the Chandernagore party". Then he states, "I came in touch with Chandernagore group through some members of the Dacca Samity" (that is, Dacca Anushilan Samiti). He does not even tell the real fact that it was Pratul Chandra Ganguli, the leader of the Dacca Anushilan Samiti, who introduced him to Rashbehari Bose, along with Srish Ghose, and others of Chandernagore. Ganguli himself has written about this in his articles in the Prabasi (Bengali monthly) shortly before his death.

Sanyal is almost silent about Girija Babu, his Anushilan colleague in U. P. He does not say a word about Girija Babu (Nagendranath Datta) who worked with Rashbehari in Northern India as the representative of the Anushilan Samiti and who was given 7 years' rigorous imprisonment in Banaras Conspiracy case as his co-accussed. Rashbehari Bose, however, has given equal importance to Girija Babu as one of his two most trusted lieutenants, who took leave of him together at the Calcutta port when he was leaving for Japan under the assumed name of P. N. Tagore. Bose gave a detailed description about this in an article in Prabartak (Bengali monthly). There he clearly stated that the expenses of his journey were borne by the Anushilan Samiti. Certainly, it was done through Girija Babu, the Anushilan leader, whom I had the honour of meeting at Comilla about this time when he gave us the bad news of Punjab, (i. e. failures of Army rising plan on 21st February, 1915).

Sanyal states on page 241 : "After my return from the Andamans, the Dacca Samiti leaders did not show the spirit of co-operation with me." How was it possible when he stated to them that he would not work in secret revolutionary movement. Anushilan Samiti was deeply engaged in this work and it had nothing to do with persons who were not interested in such work.

Sanyal condemns Pulin Behari Das for his lack of any ability ; but the Seditien Committee speaks very highly of Das' ability as an organiser and states that he organised 500 Committees within the course of two years in East and North Bengal. He condemns all outstanding leaders of the Anushilan Samiti. He even acuses Rashbehari Bose for not being a man of much learning. Why then the learned man made him his leader ? These writings clearly show that at that time Sanyal was a thoroughly frustrated man.

While Anushilanites were vigorously active in politics, Sanyal was quite aloof from politics. Later he was rather compelled by force of circumstances to restart secret work after meeting various reverses. He hankered after leadership and when it was conceded by Trailokyanath Chakravarty, be started work vigorously with his headquarter in Calcutta (1924). But after arrest he dropped down like anything. In Bankura Court, Mr. Mills, the Deputy Commissinor of the C. I. D. privately offered to him that he would be in a good place and be given a good allowance to live with his family, provided he accepted the responsibility of the "Revolutionary" leaflet before the court. Sanyal was ready to accept it, as he told me in Lucknow jail, but Jatin Das and also S. N. Halder, his defence counsel pressed him not to do so. They opposed it particularly on political ground. Public leaders stated that the "Revolutionary" leaflets were distributed by agent provocateurs. So, if it was accepted by a prominent revolutionary the stand of the leaders would be falsified. And that is why Das and Haldar dissuaded Sanyal from accepting the offer.

Because Sanyal evinced weakness in his talks with the jail authorities during our under-trial period when the Kakori case was in the sessions court one day in a meeting in jail he was forbidden to act as our representative before the jail authorities and my name was prosposed instead. And I have already stated elsewhere how his m rcy petition to Mr. Horton before the delivery of judgement, upset Ram Parsad Bismil and made him furious,

After release from Kakori case we were both living at Lucknow very near to each other, but Sanyal did not like to have anything to do with me. Once Dhiren Mukherjee, who is now holding a very high position in a private business firm in Calcutta, came to Lucknow. He took me with him to Sanyal's residence. Sanyal disliked it so much that Mukherjee told me when we came out that he realised that he made a mistake in taking me there with him.

Frustration must be the root cause of this sort of behaviour. He had no touch with the 1921 movement, yet he very adversely criticises the activities of his old Anushilan associates regarding this movement on the basis of what he heard from the men of opposite groups. During the movement the Anushilan men on the one hand were very active in Congress work as is evidenced by the facts that important Anushilan leaders were also office-bearers of Congress Committees, for example, Narendra Mohan Sen was the Secretary of the Dacca Congress Committee and Purnananda Das Gupta was the Assistant Secretary ; Prabhas Lahiri was the Secretary of Rajshahi Congress Committee and Atindra Mohan Roy was the Secretary of Tippera Congress Committee etc. and on the other hand they were also running the Bharat Sevak Sangha, which enabled them to reestablish their own Anushilan Samiti in Bengal. Through this source they were also in a position to establish a press in Calcutta under the name of Calcutta Printing Works of which Naren Bhattacharya was the Manager and a weekly party organ, 'Sankha' was started with Nalini Kishore Guha as the editor.

Sanyal states on page 244 of his book that other groups of revolutionaries were divided into small units but the Anushilan Samiti was very strong. Perhaps for that very reason he abuses the Anushilan leadership without giving proper grounds. He makes the allegation that Pulin Bihari Das gave a list of some of his associates to the authorities stating that they were again starting secret revolutionary activities. He alleges that this was the cause how Das was separated from the Dacca Samiti. This allegation is absolutely without any foundation. I am in a position to assert this, because at that time I came to Calcutta from Comilla and was staying at 93, Mechuabazar Street with Pulin Das. Das wanted everybody to obey his orders without any question as of old, but we asserted that was not possible under the changed circumstances. We must argue and discuss matters properly and then proceed according to agreed programmes. Pulin Das differed with his followers on this point very seriously and we all parted company and agreed to differ and he was left alone. But all the same we all had regard for him as a great personality and respected him till the last, When after independence I was allowed to enter Bengal I took the first opportunity of meeting him at his residence. He was highly pleased and entertained us with sweets. Again on his passing away I offered wreaths as the General Secretary of the Revolutionary Socialist Party and on behalf of Pratul Ganguli. Biren Chatterjee, Rabindra Mohan Sen Gupta and myself carried the bier on our shoulders from the Upper Circular Road to the Nimtala Ghat.

Sanyal writes on page 245 that due to non-violent movement of Gandhiji the revolutionary movement suffered a great set back. This may be true for others, who gave up their own efforts for secret revolutionary activities ; but it was not so for the Anushilan Samiti, because they carried on the revolutionary work along with the open Congress activities. Many others merged themselves with the Congress movement but Anushilan Samiti did not do that. It took full advantage of the open movement to strengthen itself for the secret revolutionary movement.

Sanyal states in one place that he left Jamshedpur after Gandhiji was arrested and sentenced, but in another place he states that he came to Allahabad in 1921. This is absolutely wrong. He states that he met Satish Sinha at Banaras. This is also wrong. He never met Satish. He might have met his elder brother Kshetra Sinha, who was at Banaras only temporarily. Sanyal states that Satish Sinha worked in Bihar. This also shows that he meant Kshetra Sinha, but not Satish Sinha, becausa Kshetra Sinha was once in charge of Bihar, not Satish Sinha.

Sanyal states that after 1920 no representative of Anushilan was in U.P. or Northern India. This is also wrong It shows his ignorance. Two students were already sent by the Anushilan to the Hindu Unniversity. Shyam Chakravarty also came to Banaras long before Sanyal came from Jamshedpur. Shyam Chakravarty was the man who laid the foundation of Anushilan at Banaras city in 1922. Satish took charge from Shyam Chakravarty. Sanyal was not in U.P. till then, although he says that he was the first to start work in U.P. (after 1st World War). In reality, Sanyal started work not long before my arrival.

Sanyal has gone to any length in abusing and disreputing the Anushilan Samiti and its accredited leaders. He not only calls Pulin Bihari Das, the builder of the Dacca Anushilan Samiti, a worthless person but also pictures the general leadership as a group of ignorant fools, implying thereby that he himself was the ablest and the wisest man.

After his release from Kakori case in 1937, Sanyal finding himself alone without any support from any quarter, found pleasure only in abusing his own old colleagues. He cites an example and states that they read of Bertrand Russel but knew nothing of Dr. Sunyat Sen, although even when we were students at Comilla we discussed Sunyat Sen in our secret party meetings. The fact is that Sanyal had no rigid and disciplined training as a revolutionary as we had in East Bengal. Sanyal makes another sweeping remark that the Anushilanites showed no interest in studies during detention This showed only his ignorance and nothing else. I have described our life in Rajshahi Central Jail as Regulation III State Prisoners where we were engaged in very deep studies. Sanyal had no direct knowledge of this, because he did not live as a detenu, yet he writes these imaginary things as an expression of an utterly frustrated mind. Whatever he heard from the anti-Anushilan men he has believed to be the gospel truth.

The real fact is that there is a vast difference between Sanyal, the revolutionary worker and Sanyal the lonely frustrated man. His failure and consequent frustration made him almost mad with rage and this anger he has expressed through the pages of the Hindi *Pratap* of Kanpur. These articles should not have come out as the third part of Bandijiban. Sanyal himself did not do it so long as he was alive.

Pulin Bihari Das, Narendra Mohan Sen and Pratul Chandra Ganguli were not ordinary persons in the revolutionary history of Bengal. The publisher should have given some thought before the book was published. I challenge the publisher to rectify the things he published about Bhagat Singh at Kanpur. I assert that Bhagat Singh was not working at Kanpur before my arrival. He came to me and lived with me at Patkapur mess of Suresh Bhattacharya. Awasthi and Bhattacharya are still alive and are at Kanpur and they can bear me out.

Sanyal accuses Anushilan leaders that they sent men to Banaras without consultation with him. I have shown that he was neither in U.P. nor in revolutionary work when Anushilan sent me at Banaras. It is an absurd accusation and such a thing can be stated either by a man of unbalanced mind or by a man with some bad motive. When Anushilan workers started work at Banaras, Sanyal had no intention of doing secret revolutionary work. Even on arrival in U.P. at first he tried for a service and after failing to secure one more he started secret work. It is again quite false that I was sent to U.P. at his suggestion that some abler man be sent there. It was at first decided that I should take up the party work in Bombay. About six months later when it was necessary to send a man to U.P., Ganguli's assistant, Ashit Bhattacharya suggested my name and it was readily accepted by him.

Sanyal writes so much about workers from different districts when he had only two main active workers for whom he hired a house at Allahabad and himself lived with them there for some time. They were Banwarilal and Chhedalal. Both of them betrayed the party after arrest.

On page 278, Sanyal states that he established 25/30 revolutionary centres in U.P. early in 1923. This is absolutely without any foundation.

Sanyal writes that after the Delhi Session of the Congress I met him at Allahabad several times. I did not not meet him after the Delhi Session because long before that the amalgamation talk through Ramesh Chaudhury had failed. I met him before that and not after the Delhi Session.

Sanyal writes on page 382 that upto that time (1924) Pratul Ganguli had no knowledge of the principles of communism. Ganguli read and discussed a good deal of socialism and communism in Rajshahi Jail in 1918-19 whereas Sanyal learnt these things from Satya Bhakta and Kutubuddin in 1923 as he himself writes after his return from Jamshedpur.

Rashbihari Bose's first impression about Sanyal is very interesting. Rashbihari found Sanyal to be a man of very restless habit and so he remarked "Will it not be dangerous to mix with this man? He seems to be very restless. I am working in the army. Who knows that he will not do some wrong thing?" And because of his restless habit he named him 'Lattoo' (a top).

In 1924, after the amalgamation when he took charge of U.P. and left for Bengal with his family he told me frankly that he was afraid of the jails of U.P, and Punjab. Bengal jail was tolerable. For the sake of safety he went straight to French Chandernagore but failing to get accommodation there he had to come to Calcutta.

APPENDIX—II

STATEMENT OF S. BHAGAT SINGH AND B. K. DUTT

Pioneer of June 8, 1929.

Delhi, June 6, 1929. Assembly Bomb Case ; Statement of Sardar Bhagat Singh and B. K. Dutt.

The following Statement was made by the accused in the Assembly Bomb Case, Delhi on Thursday, before Mr. Leonard Middleton, Sessions Judge :

"We stand charged with serious offences, and at this stage we explain our conduct. The following questions arise :

(1) Were the bombs thrown into the Chamber, and if so why ?

(2) Is the charge as framed by the lower court correct or otherwise ?

"To the first half of the first question our reply is in the affirmative, but some of the so-called "eye-witness" have perjured themselves and since we are not denying our liability to that extent and such as it is let our statement be judged for what it is worth. By way of illustration we may point out that the evidence of Sergeon Terry regarding the seizure of the pistol from one of us is a deliberate falsehood for neither of us had a pistol at the time we gave ourselves up. Other witnesses who deposed to having seen bombs thrown by us have not scrupled to tell lies patent on the face of them. It has its own moral for those who aim at judicial purity and fairplay. At the same time we acknowledge the fairness of the Public Prosecutor and the judicial attitude of the Court so far.

"In our reply to the next half of the first question we are constrained to go into some detail to offer a full and frank explanation of our motive and circumstances leading up to what has now become a historic event. When we were told by some police officers who visited us in jail that Lord Irwin in his address to the joint session of the two Houses, after the event in question, described it as an attack directed against no individual but against an institution itself we readily recognized that the true significance of the incident had been correctly appreciated. We are next to none in our love of humanity and so far from having any malice against any individual we hold human life sacred beyond words. We are neither perpetrators of dastardly outrages and therefore a disgrace to the country as the pseudo-socialist Diwan Chamanlal is reported to have described us, nor are we "Lunatics" as the "Tribune" of Lahore and some others would have it believed. We humbly claim to be no more than serious students of history and conditions of our country and human aspirations and we despise hypocrisy.

MISCHIEVOUS INSTITUTION

"Our practical protest was against an institution which since its birth has eminently helped to display not only its far reaching power for mischief. The more we have pondered the more deeply we have been convinced it exists only to demonstrate to the world India's humiliation and helplessness and it symbolises the overriding domination of an irresponsible and autocratic rule. Time and again national demand has been pressed by the peoples' representatives only to find the waste-paper basket as its final destination. Solemn resolutions passed by the House have been contemptnously trampled under foot on the floor of the so-called Indian Parliament. Resolutions regarding the repeal of repressive and arbitrary measures have been treated with sublime contempt and Governments' measures and proposals rejected as unacceptable by elected members have been restored by a stroke of the pen. In brief, inspite of the earnest endeavours we have utterly failed to find any justification for the existence of an institution which despite all the pomp and splendour organised with the hard-earned money of the sweating millions of India is only a hollow show and a mischievous make-believe.

HELPLESS SUBJECTION

"Also have we failed to comprehend the mentality of public leaders who help squander public time and money on so manifestly a stage managed exhibition of India's helpless subjection We have been ruminating upon all this as also upon the wholesale arrests of leaders of the labour movement when the introduction of the Trade Disputes Bill brought us into the Assembly to watch its progress and the course of the debate only served to confirm our conviction that the labouring millions of India had nothing to expect from an institution that stood as a menacing monument to the strangling power of exploiters and the serfdom of the helpless labourers.

"Finally the result of what we considered an inhuman and barbarous measure was hurled on the devoted heads of representatives of an entire country and the starving and struggling millions were deprived of their primary right and sole means of improving their economic welfare. None who has felt like us for the dumb driven drudges of labour could possibly witness this spectacle with equanimity. None whose heart bleeds for those who have given their life blood in silence to the building up of the economic structure of the exploiter of whom Government happens to be the biggest in this country repress the cry of a soul agonising anguish which is so ruthless a blow wrung out of our hearts.

WORDS OF MR. S. R. DAS

"Consequently bearing in mind the words of the late Mr. S. R Das, once Law Member of the Governor-General's Executive Council, which appeared in the famous letter he had addressed to his son to the effect that the bomb was necessary to awaken England from her dreams, we dropped the bombs on the floor of the Assembly Chamber to register our protest on behalf of those who had no other means left to give expression to their heart-rending agony. Our sole purpose was "to make the deaf hear" and to give the heedless a timely warning. Others have as keenly felt as we have done and from under the seeming stillness of the sea of Indian humanity a veritable storm is about to break out. We have only hoisted a danger-signal to warn those who are speeding along without heeding the grave dangers ahead. We have only marked the end of the era of utopian non-violence of whose futility the rising generation has been convinced beyond the shadow of a doubt.

"Out of our sincerest goodwill to and love of humanity

have we adopted this method of warning to present untold sufferings which we, like millions of others, clearly foresee.

"We have used the expression 'utopian non-violence' in the foregoing para which requires some explanation. Force when agressively applied is violence, and is, therefore, morally unjustifiable, but when it is used in furtherance of a legitimate cause it has its moral justification. Elimination of force at all costs is utopian, and the new movement which has arisen in the country, and of which we have given a warning, is inspired by ideals which guided Guru Govind Singh and Shivaji; Kamal Pasha and Reja Khan; Washington and Garibaldi; Lafayettee and Lenin. As both the alien government and Indian public leaders appeared to have shut their eyes and closed their ears against the existence and voice of this movement we felt it our duty to sound a warning where it could not be unheard.

EXTENT OF INTENTION

"We have so far dealt with the motive behind the incident in question, and now we must define the extent of our intention. It cannot be again said that we bore no personal grudge or malice against any one of those who received slight injuries or against any other person in the Assembly. On the contrary we repeat that we hold human lives sacred beyond words and would better lay down our own lives in the service of humanity than injure any one else. Unlike the mercenary soldiers of imperialist armies, who are disciplined to kill without compunction, we respect and, in so far as it lies in us, attempt to save human life. And still we admit having deliberately thrown bombs into the Assembly Chamber. Facts, however, speak for themselves and the intention should be judged from the result of the action without drawing upon hypothetical circumstances and presumptions. Despite the evidence of the Government experts, the bombs that were thrown in the Assembly Chamber resulted in slight damage to any empty bench and few slight abrasions in less than half-dozen cases. While the Government's scientist ascribed this result to a miracle we see nothing but a precisely scientific process in it all. Firstly, the two bombs exploded in vacant spaces within wooden barriers of desks and benches ; secondly, even those who were within even two feet of the explosion, for instance, Mr. P. R. Rau, Mr. Shankar Rao and Sir George Schuster were not hurt or only slightly scratched.

"Bombs of the capacity deposed to by the Government expert (though his estimate being imaginary exaggerated) loaded with an effective charge of chlorate and sensitive picrate would have smashed the barriers and laid many low within some yards of the explosion. Again had they been loaded with some other high explosive with a charge of destructive pellets or darts they would have sufficed to wipe out the majority of the members of the Legislative Assembly. Still, again, we could have flung them into the official box chockful of people of note, finally we could have ambushed Sir John Simon whose luckless Commission was loathed by all responsible people and who was sitting in the President's gallery at the time. All this, however, was beyond our intention, and the bombs did no more than they were designed to do and the miracle consisted of no more than the deliberate aim.

A HISTORICAL LESSON

"We then deliberately offered ourselves to bear the penalty for what we had done, and to let the imperialist exploiters know that insignificant units the nation cannot be crushed. We wanted to emphasise the historical lesson that letters de cachets and Bastilles could not crush the revolutionary movement in France. Gallows and Siberian Mines could not extinguish the Russian revolution. Can Ordinances and Safety bills snuff out the flame of freedom in India ? Conspiracy cases, trumped up or discovered, and the incarceration of all young men who cherish the vision of a greater ideal cannot check the march of revolution. But timely warning, if not unheeded, can help to prevent the loss of life and general suffering. We took it upon ourselves to provide this warning and our duty is done.

WHAT IS REVOLUTION

"Bhagat Singh was asked in the lower court as to what we meant by the word "Revolution". In answer to that question,

I would say that revolution does not necessarily involve sanguinary strife nor is there any place in it an individual vendetta. It is not the cult of the bomb and the pistol. By revolution we mean that the present order of things, which is based on manifest injustice, must change Producers or labourers, inspite of being a most necessary element of society, are robbed by the exploiters of the fruits of their labour and deprived of their elementary right. On the one hand the peasant who grows corn for all starves with his family ; the weaver who supplies the world market with textile fabrics cannot find enough to cover his own and his childrens' bodies ; masons, smiths and carpenters who rear magnificent palaces live and perish in the slums ; and, on the other hand capitalist exploiters, parasites of society, squander millions on their whims These terrible inequalities and forced disparity of chances are heading to world chaos. This state of affairs, cannot last, and it is obvious that the present order of society is merry making on the brick of a volcano, and innocent children of the exploiters no less than millions of the exploited are walking on the edge of a dangerous precipice.

RADICAL CHANGE

"The whole edifice of this civilization if not saved in time shall crumble. Radical change, therefore, is necessary, and it is the duty of those who realise this is re-organise society on a socialistic basis. Unless this is done and exploitation of man by man and of nation by nation, which goes masquerading as imperialism, is brought to an end, the sufferings and carnage with which humanity is threatened today cannot be prevented, and all talk of ending wars and ushering an era of universal peace is undisguised hypocrisy. By revolution we mean the ultimate establishment of an order of society which may not be threatened by such a breakdown, and in which the sovereignty of the proletariat should be recognised and as a result of which a world federation should redeem humanity from the bondage of capitalism and the misery of imperial wars.

A FAIR WARNING

"This is our ideal and with this ideology for our inspiration we have given a fair and loud enough warning. If, however, it goes unheeded and the present system of government continues to be an impediment in the way of the natural forces that are welling up, a grim struggle must ensure involving the over-throw of all obstacles and the establishment of the dictatorship of the proletariat to pave the way for the consummation of the ideal of revolution. Revolution is the inalienable right of mankind. Freedom is an imperishable birthright of all. The labourer is the real sustainer of society.

Sovereignty of the people is the ultimate destiny of the workers for these ideals and for this faith we shall welcome any suffering to which we may be condemned. To the altar of this revolution we have brought our youth as incense, for no sacrifice is too great for so magnificent a cause. We are content. We await the advent of revolution Long Live Revolution.

———

APPENDIX—III

STATEMENTS

Statement of Jogesh Chandra Chatterji (tried under Special Courts Ordinance) before Special Judge Hari Shankar Vidyarthi, in Etah Jail under Sec. 307 I.P.C., 19F Arms Act and 38 D.I.R. on 7-1-43.

Case No. 84 of 1942. King Emperor Vs—Jogesh Chandra Chatterjee & Others.

I am an old revolutionary, and, as such, am undoubtedly, avowed enemy of the British Indian Bureaucracy under Churchillian Imperialism. Against this system I have fought tooth and nail all through my life and suffered agonies of untold and unbearable pains and humiliations along with hundreds and thousands of patriotic countrymen. I have spent long 19 years inside British prisons for the crime of intense patriotism, some times with the show of a trial and mostly even without that. In my experience, the difference between the so called democratic Imperialism and Nazism or Fascism is that the former kills a man, inch by inch, by years of slow torture, whereas the latter frees him from all worldly pain by the prompt use of a sharp bullet. So, there is nothing to be chosen between the two. Both are machines of ruthless repression and oppression for the terrorised masses of men throughout the world. Therefore the revolutionary in every land tries to get rid of them both in order to bring about real peace and happiness in every home through the establishment of a Socialist World Society for which two great world figures, Marx and Lenin, devoted their whole life and energy, Lenin's Russia, the realised dream of Marx, which was the only hope of the whole depressed world, has suffered terribly under unworthy Stalin, who, foolishly enough, has saved, for the time being, the Churchillian empire even at the cost of that great Russia. After three years of terrific war, Asia and Africa are still groaning under the heavy and unnatural burden of imperialist pressure. That very pressure I am feeling in my tiny heart, day in and day out. sitting in the remote Female Ward of this jail, far removed from all human touch. As a piece of war propaganda President Roosevelt may speak of globe-freedom but such high sounding words from the lips of an imperialist politician has no no meaning at all. For has he not said, in the same breath, France will be given back all her Imperial possessions ? Give freedom and imperial possessions may be contradictory terms to a logician,—a mere school teacher, but what does he know of imperial politics,—the subjects reserved for Roosevelts and Churchills for be-fooling the credulous world ? Ask General Smuts about India's freedom and prompt will come out the answer from this imperial hireling that it was England's domestic affair. England is the master and India his mistress. So the master will decide how the mistress is to conduct herself. This position has to be changed, whatever be the cost. The British Indian machine of repression may grind into dust any number of pigmies like me with ease today, but by constant grinding even the strongest machine is sure to wear out, following the eternal processess of time and existence, and the day is not far off when the whole structure is going to tumble down like a house of cards.

2, Such a consummation was quite visible in Indian politics when, after the Japanese were well-established on the eastern border of India, the Germans were about to march on Iran through the Caucasus. But finding British imperialism in peril their American cousins, unfortunately for world peace and justice, came to their rescue. At the prospecting advent of the two great Fascist powers at the Eastern and Western gates of India the masses of the country, as I then observed, were not at all afraid. In fact they seemed to realise that because of the internally-present clash of vital permanent interests of these two white and coloured nations of Europe and Asia (viz., Germany and Japan) Indian freedom was assuredly a foregone conclusion after the removal of British Imperialism from this country through the help of these two great powers, adversely interested to the British and also to themselves. But now as the result of the new turn of events. we poor Indians, deprived as we are, have only one last hope and that is, the extreme weakening and permanent exhaustion of the white aggressive races in the present concentrated theatres of warfare in north Africa. China, Dr. Sun Yat Sen's great China, our neighbour and brother for ever, is today a tool of our enemy, Mr. Churchill and his friend Roosevelt because of foolish stand of Chiang-kai-sekh, the tyrant, who after gaining power through the help of Soviet Russia and the Chinese masses, turned on them both and started a bloody internecine struggle and deliberately paved the way for Japanese aggression and has now ultimately become an instrument in the hands of imperialist England and America. At present the politically conscious masses of India only look upon the Indian National Army, beyond the eastern border of India as the best possible hope of the country if it escapes the injudicious menace by the foolish Chinese tools of white imperialism in Asia. The internal struggle for Indian independence against British imperialism, is however making a great headway. This is all our own and therefore our greatest hope.

3. One word about the psychological position of a revolutionary mind, and I shall enter into the case direct. When a self-respecting Indian youth of generous emotions sees amidst the imperial grandeur of a great city like Calcutta a poor bare-bodied skeleton pick up food particles from the dustbin in order to keep his body and soul together he is set thinking about the root cause of this object of human degradation and poverty amidst overflowing plenty. He thinks, thinks and thinks hard, and tries to find out the cause of such a phenomenon of human misery. The thought haunts him day and night so much that he becomes mad with it Ultimately he identifies himself with that skeleton and vows solemnly that he would stake his all in order to make such a thing impossible in human society. Dutt, Dadabhai and Digby tell him that a slave country like India cannot remove the root cause of her poverty unless she is free and independent. Hence arises the great craving for freedom as first and necessary background for all reform and endeavour. Rousseau, Mazzini, Dr. Sun and Lenin —all tell the same tale. Pain, agony and humiliations are inevitable phases of this priceless treasure. Dearest friends and relations die in great agony, in jail, as victims of police bullet and from the hangman's rope. Thousands suffer all this

silently and patiently with the great dream in their imagination that everything will ultimately be crowned with success at last one day when every one will feel that he is in an atmosphere of freedom, peace and happiness and no one is exploiting his neighbour, every one is well-fed well-clothed and well housed through dignified labour and life is no more a burden but a pleasant thing to live, aspire and enjoy, and peoples of nations both great and small, world over, are at peace and par.

4. Centuries of slavery cannot be removed by democratic reformism under the alien patronages, it requires a drastic revolutionary change. Reforms cannot bring about true freedom. Centuries of imperialistic rule has accumulated heaps of rots in the system for safegarding the imperialists at the cost of the masses. Princely order, idle landlordism, big capitalism, top heavy services, slave-producing educational institutions, communal, racia land caste frictions, immasculation of the masses by withholding and denying the use of arms, heavy taxation and hundreds of such other things cannot be got rid of through democratic reformism under any, however liberal, protection ; but they can only be profitably and effectively removed from the body politic under a strong but temporary military dictatorship. But the dictator and his associates must be those who have completely identified themselves with the cause of the toiling masses.

5. So far as to why I am standing this trial before the court today, and now to the case itself. If the court thinks that as the part and parcel of the administration it is its duty to punish its enemy at any cost, then I shall suffer silently and patiently any punishment your honour may be pleased to inflict on me. But if, on the other hand the court thinks, as is expected, that he would deliver judgement after scrutinising the correctness or otherwise of the evidence produced, keeping always in view that only justice and fairness be done to the parties concerned, then I would say with all the emphasis I can command that the entire story of Mr. Dataram & Co. is a great fabrication from top to bottom, every item and each sentence of it being far removed from the truth. One of the several hirelings of Dataram of the socalled public of Soron

is a professional bad character, and as such had been in jail. I am not exposing him on purpose. He knew me as an inmate in jail. It was through his information that Dataram earned the credit of arresting me. He has not mentioned this in his report. A clever man as he is, he has made out a very good case for the reward and promotion of himself and his entire staff so that nobody should have any grievance against him or a reason to state the profitless truth and has at the same time succeeded to put me, an enemy of the state, his paymaster, in the worst position. Hence the story that I fired at them taking out a revolver from my jhola and also that Govardhan Singh drew out his imaginary revolver from the imaginery Jhola, is a fabrication. In fact I was all alone and nobody was with me. It was later planted on me and I learn that the revolvers can be easily had for plantation in Soron circle. I will most earnestly request you not as the judge receiving and recording evidence technically but as a gentleman anxious to find out the truth and do justice, to make a personal enquiry into the matter whether actually a fire was shot or I was invited into the Thana and then arrested when I was proceeding to the railway station.

6. A public enquiry would mostly be futile, because the public of Soron are so much terrorised by Soron police and their lathi armed and loose-roped hirelings that they do not dare speak the truth publicly in the days of ordinance and unlimited police power, specially after Balbhadra and Phoolchand have been arrested under the D. I. R. for no other fault but helping my defence. But the public may still speak the truth in private.

7. In fact I was that day going from Kasganj to Bareilly and on the way went to Soron to see the historical Kund there. One man mentioned above, there recognised me and carried the news to the Thana and when after seeing the Kund while proceeding to the railway station for catching the afternoon train, I reached in front of the police station I was told to go inside, There the S. I. Dataram was sitting on a chair in the plain dress. Sitting on the bench in front when I told him my name he seemed to be very much delighted and told a constable to take me to the lockup. My

Jhola with a Dhoti, a shirt and a napkin was left on the table. I had no revolver or ammunition; Before locking me up they also took away my fountain pen, the wearing Dhoti, Korta, wrapper, my purse with about Rs. 20/-in it and also my high powered spectacles, leaving me only on a banian and an underwear. I protested against this sort of behaviour of leaving me almost naked but in vain. Some outsiders were then brought in front of the lock up and myself and some 5 other people who had been arrested by this time from amongst the pilgrim crowds of Soron, were shown to them. Some two hours after our arrest Dataram and Tilakram made their appearance for the first time in front of us in uniform. Even at this time Dataram refused to give me back my spectacles, dhoti korta, This was the first time that I saw Tilakram. The latter on this second round gave me my spectacles, dhoti and korta but no other articles, neither they made any search list nor was there any witness present as is customary nor was I asked to sign on any prepared search list. Such was Dataram's treatment even after our arrest.

8. In the police lock up I learned that Govardhan Singh and Ram Larete Pande were arrested on suspicion when proceeding to or arriving at the railway station, independently; another Bengali, Haripada Sarkar, a mechanic in Nagaria Nuly Sugar Mills was arrested at the Railway station. Two persons, Puttoo Singh and Mukand Singh, were also locked up with us after their arrest from inside the Jaleswarwali Dharamshala at Soron. Two other men were also arrested but were, later, let off And the next morning only 6 of us were sent to Etah Jail in open akhas by Tilakram and we met Dataram in the police lorry some 5 miles off from Etah and in this van we were conducted to the jail gate.

9. While in jail one day one of us, Mr. Puttoo Singh was taken out by the police and was only sent back to the jail the next day after about 20 hours. The next day Pandit Ramlarete Pande was also requisitioned to be sent out. We all, including Mr. Pande, protested against this sort of procedure in writing to the D.M. and Puttoo Singh submitted a written protest and complaint against the misbehaviour of the police. After this 5 high officials of the C.I.D. from

different districts also came and saw us all in jail one by one. Their purpose was to observe our features etc. minutely so that we could be easily identified in some case or cases. We petitioned to D.M. against this. One of these described himself to be the inspector from Aligarh and actually one man was brought down from Aligarh to identify us in connection with the bomb outrage and murder there. But fortunately he could not identify anybody.

10. One afternoon the S,D.O. of Aligarh, Mr. Kola, ordered all 6 of us to stand for identification along with 30 other ordinary undertrial villagers, all uncultured rustic people, hence having no affinity or similarity in appearance or dress with us We wanted men of our own class and standard in society for mixing up in the parade and hence we refused. I then wanted that my counsel should be present. But at first he argued with me against it, but when we refused it was decided in the presence of our counsel that the identification parade would take place the next day and Congress prisoners would be mixed up with us. This was done the next day but no man could identify any of us.

11. These are the bare facts and if you are convinced as the result of your own personal enquiry that a fire was actually shot at the time of the arrest or that I had a revolver or that I was arrested by Dataram anywhere outside the railway station, then I should be given the maximum punishment, but, if on the other hand, you are convinced that no fire took place and that I was invited into the police station and then arrested without any resistence or demur on my part and a revolver was planted on me, then not only I should be let off but also Dataram and the party, including the four so called members of the public mentioned in the First Information Report, should be ordered to be prosecuted for bringing of a false charge against innocent men. It is certainly not the first time in the history of the police administration in this country for unscrupulous police people to implicate innocent men falsely and try to get King's police medal.

12. It is a well known fact that the executive authorities have distributed prizes and rewards not only to the whole staff of Soron police for arresting us but also to three other men or

the so called public, but in fact professional hirelings of Soron Police ; these three men are also prosecution witnesses. When a case is subjidice it tantamounts to encouraging and bribing them for giving false evidence by the administrative authorities. In this particular case this is also an indirect way of terrorising the public not to tell the truth against the fabricated story put forward by the local police. This official terrorisation has further taken a different shape in my case in as much as a Deputy Collector, Mr. Makhanlal Kola, went so far as to threaten my defence counsel, Pandit Girijashankar Chaturvedi, by saying that so long he was a Hindusabhite but now had started playing with fire etc. meeting, thereby, that by defending a revolutionary he was taking the risk of being victimised by the executive.

13. I did hot ask any police man to resign.

14. I state the above facts before you in the hope that you being the head of the judiaiary in the district , as distinct from the executive, will not be prejudiced against me but shall try to arrive at the honest truth and deliver judgement accordingly.

15. I have committed no offence ; but if the thought and working for the good of my countrymen Hindu, Muslim, Christian and all, including all species of Govt., satellites and officials, not excluding even our lost Indian policemen and all the future generations, be a crime, then let me be the first criminal in the land. Otherwise, in equity, justice, fact and fairness I claim an acquittal.

LONG LIVE REVOLUTION
Jogesh Chandra Chatterji
7th January, 1943.

APPENDIX—IV

LUCKNOW BARA BANKI CONSPIRACY CASE 1943-44

In the Court of K. R. Damle Esqr. I. C. S., Addl. Session Judge, Lucknow.

STATEMENT OF JOGESH CHANDRA CHATTERJI

1. My experiences of judicial trials of revolutionaries in this land of my birth are quite bitter. My Etah trial is only a year old. The judge there, a greyhaired and venerable looking European, knew quite well at heart that I was the victim of a concocted case ; that the prosecution story was a cock and bull one ; that the witnesses were not at all independent ; that very important witnesses were not put up in the witness box ; that the main witnessness also were rewarded and again both the S. Is were suspended before the trial began, yet he passed a sentence on me. Again in order to guard against the sentence being set aside by the High Court in revision he applied a subterfuge by forwarding the papers etc. to the High Court without giving any information of it either to me or to my defence counsel, the natural consequence of which was that in reply to my application for personal attendance I was forthwith informed that my case had already been disposed of, of course, ex-parte. It has been revealed here through the Moharrir of Sadar Malkhana, Etah, P. W. Eizaz Hussein that the Special Judge, long after the trial, on the 13th of May, 1943, after Calcutta and Bombay High Courts had declared Special Courts Ordinance ultra vires and the judgement of the Federal Court to the same effect was about to be passed, got 7 spent up cartridges destroyed. This is a clever way of concealing a piece of evidence which shattered the case against me there. For, 3 out of these 7 cartridges, were alleged to be the same, which were in the chamber of the revolver with which I was said to have shot at S. I. Dataram. These cartridges did not all fire vide my petition dated 14. 1. 1943 and also the note of my Etah counsel. Had these 3 cartridges been amongst the

Exhibits, it could have been seen that the hammer had struck the shells but the gunpowder did not catch fire. And subsequently it would have been seen clearly that I could not have shot at Mr. Dataram with such a cartridge. The hammer mark on the shell also might have shown that the said cartridge was not fired from this revolver.

2. Seriously and emphatically I complained about the false charge brought against me by the police to the D. M. of Etah, when he visited the Jail shortly after my entry into it as an undertrial prisoner. He assured me of justice and fairness. The next week or so, he rewarded the witnesses in a special Darbar in the police lines ; and a week or two later the C. I. D. report, of course out of jealousy to the Soron police but not for my good, that the case was false, must have convinced the D. M. of the truthfulness of my complaint, and the two S. I s were suspended. Pressu e from the above must have silenced him later on, when the S. I. s. were reinstated and I was sentenced, thus baffling his assurance of justice and fairness.

3. It will not be out-of-place to mention here that constable Lalaram of Soron and also Shiv Singh told me when escorting us to Lucknow from Etah that they gave in writing to the D. I. G. of Police during the enquiry that the case against us was false and got up and that the S. I. Dataram had a row with his wife for bringing the false accusation against national workers. And they also told that they heard that the S. P. of Etah had recommended that Mr. Dataram be promoted to inspectorship and given the King's Police Medal. And K. S. Nasir Ali Khan told in the lower court, after his evidence was over that he himself got the two S. I. S. of Soron suspended for concocting the case against me.

4. My feeling has again been cruelly outraged here in the enquiry stage. The Magistrate, Mr. Laiq Ali Khan, repeatedly declared in the court, before everybody present, that there was no case against 3, naming myself, Mr. Jharkhande Rai and C. B. Shukla. He even urged that these cases should be argued before him. A date was accordingly fixed when the P. I. was to put forward the prosecution case. I was to argue my case and Mr. Sukla's case was to be argued by his counsel.

Tents and furnitures etc. were, in the mean time, removed from the Jail compound ; and on the appointed day—a Sunday, the Magistrate presented himself with his staff and 3 or 4 C. I. D. officials into our B Class ward and ordered me to proceed on with my arguments. Mr. Shukla's counsel and men had, therefore, to go back disappointed. While passing the Commital Orders, the Magistrate said that he wanted to release 3, but was forced to commit all. Not only is there no mention of the above facts in his C. Orders but he has also made these 3 men solely responsible for the whole case of conspiracy. Was not this a trick or strategy, to help the prosecution by knowing the defence points in advance in the weak case ? This very magistrate has shown in the well-known B. S. Singha case that he was a great friend of the police and hence scathing remarks were made about him by Dr. K. N. Katju while arguing the case before the sessions judge of Lucknow. He occupies a fine bangalow in the heart of the city, the provincial head-quarter, very near the Zenana Park. Let the enemies of the state go to dogs, he must enjoy this beautiful and happy earth. This is why last year the Hon'ble Judges of the Lahore and Bombay High Courts passed strictures against magistrates remarking that they were under the thumb of the police. On February 9, 1944, in the Central Assembly, in support of Mr. Kazmi's adjournment motion to censure the Govt. of India for the "reign of terror" in the provinces arising from the misapplication of the D. I R. Mr. Frank Anthony is reported to have "commented on the fusion of Judicial and executive functions and declared that the Magistracy in India was nauseatingly servile and characterised by a complete lack of independence. Some magistrates have, told him that they were virtually subordinate to the police and were against their better judgement, provoked to convict persons, whom they would otherwise have acquitted." This report wos quoted by the Modern Review of Calcutta of March, 1944 on page 70.

5. I know at least one political case of these provinces in which 3 persons coming from respectable middle class educated families were falsely implicated in a shooting case at Bareilly and were sentenced to transportation for life. The accused did not know who shot the police constable ; and, in fact, two

of them had never before been to the city of Bareilly, just as I myself have not yet seen the place from where I am alleged to have fired at Dataram, yet they had to serve their full term of sentence. One habitual long-term convict in Fatehgarh Central Jail, Buddhan Khan of Shahjahanpur, told me once in the course of a talk about his adventures that one night while returning from the village side to the town, a constable of Bareilly on watch duty challenged them. They shot him down and went away. He also told me that some Congressmen, he heard, were wrongly sentenced for this. Buddhan Khan belonged to a dangerous gang of criminals, who were responsible for many heinous crimes, including murders. His elder brother, along with 20 others, was hanged in Bombay. In that case, he said, out of 22 men all were hanged except himself, who was sent to the lunatic asylum as a youth of unsound mind.

6. But quite different was the attitude of the then Bengal Government at least in one case that I know. One person, Mr. Ashutosh Lahiri, was given 8 years' transportation in a political decoity case. When he had served nearly half of his sentence in the Andamans, the authorities came to know that he was wrongly sentenced. Orders for his release were issued immediately. A leading parliamentarian, Lord Ronaldshay, was the Governor of Bengal at the time, not an I.C.S. man, as in U. P. Lahiri is now an important leader of the Hindumahasabha.

7. It is not unknown to the citizens of Lucknow how the accued in the Kakori conspiracy Case were dealt with by the chief judge of the Oudh Chief Court, Sir Luis Stuart. But one fact is not known to the General Public that Mr. S. N. Bakhsi of the case had complained to him, when he visited jail as the Chairman of the U. P. Jails Inquiry Committee that the former was assaulted by Mr. Ladlie, the Jailer, who figured in the National Herald case, and who was the superintendent of the Kanpur jail, of which Ramharab complains so bitterly. To know the result of his complaint Bakhsi purchased a copy of the Report, but only to find the fact whitewashed clean, saying that Bakhsi made no complaint.

8. For the above grounds I have very little faith in the British court of justice. A fair and just trial is only possible in an atmosphere of freedom. It is fultile to expect justice and fairness under an autocratic and oppressive alien rule, which naturally had to depend on the police. Even the judiciary cannot be altogether free from this evil influence. Certainly there are individual stalwarts, who enjoy the respect of the public ; but there are also judges, like the gentleman at Etah or the late Chief Judge of the Oudh Chief Court, against whom even the Oudh Bar Association had to do the unpleasant duty of passing a resolution in condemnation.

9. I am suffering for the cause of my country. So before I touch upon the case I should add a few words on the political situation as the dweller of the Pain-abode or as the jail is called by the prisoners, gets very little chance of it from inside the high walls. If we analyse the current affairs we find that the Muslim League and C. P. I. are making a big capital out of the disturbed condition. Mr. Jinnah has established League ministries in 5 provinces and is going to get himself installed in Pakistan, leaving Hindustan, which is the Kafiristan to him now. And Comrade P. C. Joshi, coming out of his hiding place, has shaken hands with Sir Reginald Maxwell and consquently having a good time. Both have made an unholy alliance against the stupid nationalists, Messrs. Gandhi, Subhas and Jaiprakash to the great satisfaction of Messrs. Churchill, Amery & Co., who badly require such help at this critical hour of their empire in order to damn the disturbing trio. Both have many things in common, both thrive on official smiles, talk big and derive their lifeblood from the presence of the militant nationalist movement ; and both are antinational, in as much as they live in India and think in terms of Mecca and Moscow.

10. Joshi's shout of Muslim self determination, national Government and release of leaders, is only a cloak for the consolidation of the party position against the strong opposition due to their antinational war stand. Jinnah's Pakistan and Joshi's Muslim self determination slogans without first gaining national independence, may, before long, materialise into a new Hindustan in the Middle, with two Pakistan wings on either

side, east and west ; and, of course, with Britishers as the guide of both. Moscow is not to interfere in Britain's domestic affairs and the budding Arab Federation may help the western Pakistan ; but the eastern one will certainly feel isolated and helpless.

11. I shall, however, be failing in my duty if I do not draw a marked distinction between the two. Mr. Jinnah's stand is not religious at all. It is purely a devise of political exploitation of the religious sentiments of the ignorant Muslim masses by a few big clever self-seekers. Are not 3 muslim knights the chief ministers out of the 5 League ministries ? And, have not lakhs and lakhs of Bengal Muslims died inch by inch of starvation under Sir Nizimuddin, while Ispahanies were helped to profiteer and fatten ? Jinnah has revealed himself at last the other day stating to the representative of the News Chronicle that he wanted Britain to divide India and stay thus belying his former slogan "divide and quit" Why a League minister of Sindh is mentioned in connection with the diabolical murder plot of the Muslim ex-premier, Mr. Allahbox, who was first ousted from that position by all fague-Briton clique, because of his staunch nationalist stand ? A Muslim Peer Pagaro, a detenu in British prison, is suddenly hanged one day without a public trial. Jinnàh does not raise a finger of protest against this horrid occurence, but readily extends the hand to the British to grab the huge looted treasure of the Peer's castle for the League. So he is simply for loaves and fishes for a fat few. This might have exasperated the Muslim youth to attempt on the life of Jinnah and this again can explain the find of more than 2000 letters and telegrams, which the Khaksar Muslims had addressed to him, by the police from his residence, entreating him to be patriotic enough to come to terms with the Congress. But Joshi stands for a lofty principle, which is also the very breath of my life, though I entertain nothing but hatred for his present anti-national move. Disruption of national forces will not ultimately help Jinnah, Joshi or any other Indian, exept our enemy. Too much Leagism is bound to land force to Hindusabha and the result will be the weakening of the Congress, thus benefiting the third party. A slave India cannot but be against war-efforts, as it

means winning the war by England at the cost of men and materials of India for the perpetuation of British supremacy here. Churchill is not to liquidate the empire and hence must remain here as the master and exploiter, not as friend and helper.

12. President Roosevelt could easily declare the independence of the Philipinoes after Japan had already given them full independent status ; but premier Churchill is not ready to concede that to the Burmese even by a word of the mouth. Unlike Mr. U. Saw, Dr. Ba Maw, was a wellknown anti Japanese, but today he seems to be highly satisfied with the attitude of the Japanese, who have made Burma practically an independent country. Of course Japan did not do this quite willingly but circumstances compelled them this eventuality. Whatever be the reason, it is now an accomplished fact. Burmese people must, therefore, be as much grateful to the Japanese as they are hateful to the Britishers. Dr. Ba Maw, the anti-Japanese, is today the head of the independent Burmese Govt. but the Indian pronounced anti-Japanese and even pro-British, Pandit Nehru. is languishing in British prison, whereas the British fascist leader Sir Oswald Mosley is out.

13. The Viceroy, Lord Wavell, the follower of Lord Linlithgo, demands unconditional surrender of the Indian National Congress and wants to rule this country by the Military, the Police and the officials, ignoring the people and their representatives, though it is said to be the result of his report that Malaya, Singapore and Burma were lost due to the anti-British feeling of the local populations, and hence was the need of pacification in India, that prompted Churchill to send the Cripps Mission in India. But now it seems that the Russian virtories over the Germans on the one hand and the throwing in of lakhs and lakhs of Indians, Chinese and African soldiers at the eastern theatre with vast equipments, had again emboldened this imperialist soldier politician to change his front. Again his imperlialistic mind has started imagining that in our adversity lies their property ; and, therefore, we must not be given the least chance to prosper. The more people die of starvation, nakedness and preventible diseases. the more soldiers, sappers

and miners and other war workers they will have at the cheapest rate ; and more young girls will fill up the brothels for the enjoyment of these men, just as today there are 30,000 young Bengali girls in the brothels out of its last year's 2 lakhs of destitute from the neighbouring places.

14. Responsible national leaders and courageous workers all are in jail, where their treatment is as cruel and inhuman as possible ; the entire press of the country is severely gagged and the people are terrified ; expressions and feelings through the public platform is strictly prohibited ; the essential requirements of the people are unobtainable ; no work except war work ; forcible collection of war funds under various pretexts and devices ; collective fines and general ordinance rule are felt by the people very bitterly though they cannot give vent to their indignation. A despondent man generally becomes hopeless and inactive until he turns desperate. In my jail out of every 8 men 1 is a convicted soldier and there is one Congress worker, whose property worth several thousand has been looted and burned in 1942 ; and, on the 26th August, 1943 his young wife of 7 months pregency has been taken away by the police under arrest and she is still untraced.

15. This is the stage when a little ray of hope from any quarter may easily turn people to it desperately, just as a sinking man catches at a straw. Who can say what is to happen tomorrow ? May not the suppressed feeling turn suddenly on the oppressor at the least chance ? There appears to be something like this in the atmosphere. Subhas Bose is there on the eastern boder with an army of 3 lakhs of trained Indians. An additional 10 lakhs of Indian civilians are entirely and wholeheartedly with him. And, besides the independent Burmese, millions of people of the "Co-prosperity sphere of East Asia" are his active supporters.

16. How can the Indians remain unaffected under such circumstances ? They have, no doubt, heard that the Japanese were bad ; but they know Subhas and also that Burma is today independent, and people are not starving there. Will not, therefore, people compare the Britons side by side with the Japanese ? Will not they sav within themselves that the

Japanese may be bad, but certainly they cannot be so bad as our present masters ?

17. Of course, our masters think it an impossibility now, otherwise they could not have played with the lives of millions of human beings as they are doing here today. The very day that Lord Wavell assumed the responsibility of the Viceroyalty of India, Subhas Bose formed his provisional Independent Govt. of India at Singapore. Was it a mere chance coincidence ? An one-eyed man is regarded as inauspicious by the superstitious messes, and, in fact, Wavell, a great general though he is, has not gained anything anywhere in this war. He only yielded grounds to Marshall Rommel in north Africa, and again he gave away the valuable Far Eastern possessions of the empire to the Japanese. So people are saying everywhere he will lose India, too.

18. The problems of China and India are not identical. In China tha Japanese are hateful aggressers ; but here the Japanese are helping Bose, not for any good sentiments towards India but to check the fearful threat of their annihilation, to guard against the Allies' move of invading Japan from India via Burma, and China. Bose is the trusted leader of the people with a brilliant career as a sufferer for a great cause involving not merely the interests but the very existence of millions and millions of men. It is, therefore, wrong to compare Bose with Wang-Ching Wei. Moreover, Gen. Smut's remarkable picture of the post-war world provides no room for China or France as world power. Herein lies the strength of Bose's stand.

19. I am an Indian revolutionary ; therefore, I am a natural enemy of Churchill. I am a socialist ; therefore, my interest clashes with that of Roosevelt. The cause of Socialism can never advance if the economic resources of India and China are shared by England and America, depriving the people of the soil. Indians will have to stand against this, regardless of the consequences. No falling back till the goal is reached, Last year I was heavily sentenced in a district where all the heads,—the D. M., the S. P., the judge and the C. S. were Indians, on a purely false charge brought by the local police. But this time the prosecutor is the expert C.I.D.,

the place is Lucknow, in Oudh, the head quarter of the local Govt. Here again, though I had not the least connection with this case, it has been arranged by the police in a convincing way. And if, inspite of so many challenging materials, the high police officials are relied on, then there could be no way out for me.

20. I shall only speak a word more before I resume my seat. A great friend of the police like Laiq Ali Khan is the magistrate, great helpers of the police like Ibrar Hussein and Atiq Ahmen are on the jail staff and again the court is held in Jail, where no lawyers of note, no pressman, no member of the public, not even any friend or relation of the accused attend Police gets a free hand in everything ; accused are shown to the witnesses by various well-devised strategical means and they go to the length of getting published in news papers false and exaggerated reports of the case against the accused. To get the cases inside jail from the court they assault the accused in the court compound most brutally, against which the Oudh Bar Association had to record a resolution as a protest. Laiq Ali Khan at last extorts the points of defence to be given over to the prosecution. After all this, much hope is not left of getting justice and fairness.

21. Inspite of the evidence on oath of K. S. Nasir Ali Khan, Dy. S.P., C.I.D. and contrary to Ramhark's tutored statement that I was an organiser or provincial secretary of the H.S.R.A., I declare here most solemnly, giving it out as the word of honour of an honest revolutionary that I have never in my life been even a member of this body. Let it be a news to the C.I.D. and to the court and through the court to the Govt. and also to the public. A vigorous but vain attempt has been made by the prosecution to show that the H.S.R.A. and the R.S.P.I. are one and the same thing. The C.I.D. are no doubt powerful ; and they can prove a dark night to be the broad day in their court ; but, yet, I maintain that they are not so powerful as to alter a historical fact.

22. The much-advertised Jaiprakash Narayan letter, published by the Government of India on the 16th of October, 1941, is a strong documentary evidence to bear me out, to prove convincingly and even conclusively that R.S.P.I. and

H.S.R.A. are two different organisations, run side by side, as rivals. Each and every detenu of Deoli camp knows this and also of Fatehgarh Central Prison, the special jail, where revolutionary detenus of the province are concentrated. Examined from this point of view, it will be clearly seen by any impartial man that I had or could have, nothing to do with it.

23. The Revolutionary Socialist Party of India is not at all a secret body but a public Marxist Leninist organisation, the object of which is to establish a world socialist society, after first making India a socialist independent state, as a preliminary. In Bengal it is a declared public organisation ; but in the U P. the declaration could not be made as the adherents were arrested and jailed before there was any time and oppertunity for this. Prior to that the members were working through the Congress Socialist Party without keeping any connection, whatever, with any other organisation, secret or open, of course exept the 3 mass basic organisations, the Indian National Congress, the Kisan Sabha and the Trade Union.

24. As a revolutionary socialist I am believer in the masses ; and that is why my line of work was very clear and definite. In the latest election I was elected Vice President of the Lucknow City Congress Committee, a member of the U. P. S. C. and President of the Lucknow Municipal Workers Union and also I was before the beginning of the War an organising secretary of the U. P. Kisan Sabha, and a member of the All India Kisan Council.

25. My past history of being in jail as a political suspect since 1916, figuring in Kakori and Lahore cases and the Externment Order against my entry into my own province, not relaxed to this day etc. were already prejudicial materials against me. This really is the reason why a false case was made out at Etah ; and again I have been dragged into this serious case on such flimsy ground.

26. One outstanding fact, however, will certainly strike any man going through the evidence against me in this case that there are two approvers in the two connected cases who are said to have travelled far and wide but have nothing positive to link me with the case ; and there are also a good many prosecution

witness, who came from Lucknow and its neighbourhood and I was a strictly watched resident of this city ; but nobody (including the C. I. D. watch men) has seen me associating with any of the accused. And the prosecution case is that I was the provincial secretary of the Organisation, which is alleged to be responsible for both the cases. If not criminal association, at least association of some kind should have been there. This single fact, apart from nothing to do with this case. The alleged find of the papers in the Mahabubganj house can never be free from suspicion, particularly as the police are not ready to divulge who was their informant. The way the Khan Saheb secures so sure a news of the house previously, the way the accused are secured and dealt with and the search witnesses speak in vital matters, are not at all normal and convincing

27. My humble submission is that before accepting the prosecution case against me your honour and the gentlemen of the jury and the assessors will have to take into consideration at least the following few points, besides many other things :—

(1) Not proving my association with other accused in the case though I was the most closely watched man in the city.

(2) The coded note book of Soron, Exh. 142, gives 3 addresses of Lucknow men but none of this is least connected with this case.

(3) The alleged Rai's letter, Exh. 99, speaks of great monitary difficulty in May or early June, 1942. This could not be the case had I been connected with Sahajanwa men, who are alleged to have looted about Rs. 10,000 shortly before this.

(4) A day or two prior to the search, Nasir Khan's privileged informant gives him the news of Mahabubganj house. Could he not himself plant things in the house before giving the information ?

(5) One single political party could never go under two different names simultaneouslg as H.S.R.A. and R S.P.I. while even in jail they they are two different rival groups.

28. I have been heavily sentenced unfairly in a false case at Etah, of which the appeal is before the High Court ;

and that is again the basis of second heavy charge case. Therefore, there is no other alternative than to submit to the inhuman forces of an oppressive foreign tyranny. I have spent 20 years of my adult life in jail and now I am old man and the rest of my days I shall pass without any feeling of discomfort knowing, as I do, this to be an inevitable phase before this tyranny is finally and fully overcome.

29. Our countrymen must live as human beings. Normal opportunity must be open to them. The task of the administration is only to facilitate this. Exploitation of man by man, is a crime against humanity ; and it is a greater crime for one nation to dominate over and exploit another nation. To suffer wrongs meekly is also a crime, as it leads to degradation and ruination. Punishment can never deter true patriots from their duty. Individuals are even crushed ; but the urge remains and will remain until India attains freedom and independence for her huge masses of men. She can no more remain satisfied as hewers of wood and drawers of water, or die of hunger and malnutrition-diseases enmass as today.

30. To suffer for a noble cause is the proud privilege of a revolutionary. I have suffered much in the past, I am suffering at present and I shall suffer as long as I know that I shall never be afraid of suffering so long as the cause is noble and great. So help me, Mother India. Long live Revolution.

Made on 22nd April, 1944
Jogesh Chandra Chatterjee
24-4-1844

APPENDIX V

MY LETTER TO THE ADVISER TO THE GOVERNOR OF U. P. FROM LUCKNOW JAIL ON 25/27-7-1945.

To the Hon'ble Adviser, Jail Deptt., to His Excellency the Governor of U. P., Lucknow.

Sir, I beg to state that years ago, following the tragic death of a B class revolutionary prisoner in Fatehgarh Central Jail in 1934, I, then as a Kakori case lifer, had submitted before the Government that political prisioners be treated as a special class, and as such they be given—

1. Superior class treatment, which includes better food and clothings.
2. Daily newspapers and other facilities for indoor and outdoor games.
3. Living accommodation in Association barracks in a concentration Jail etc.

And to get them fulfilled I had staked my very life thrice subsequently, besides the last one in Deoli Detention Camp, by resorting to hunger strike once in Agra Central Jail in 1934 for 142 days and again in Lucknow Central Prison in 1935-36 for 111 days. During the last occasion the then Home Member to the Government, Kunwar Sir Maharaj Singh, early in 1936 had sent for some public gentlemen, Mr. Rafi Ahmed Kidwai and others, and through their mediation brought about a settlement of the serious matter by concentrating all political prisoners of the province in the Central Prison at Naini, where all the facilities asked for were very kindly and generously conceded to.

These petty demands of mine were later on endorsed by the Congress Working Committee and the Congress ministries were, thereafter. directed to frame rules on the line. Rules, I know, were framed in the provinces; but unfortunately were not given effect to any where except in the Central Provinces.

The result was that not only convicts but even political detenus were being treated as ordinary C class convicts as regards their food. This was stopped in 1940, but was again revived particularly after the 1942 mevement. The repercussion of outside repression were terribly reflected inside the jail; and I think the worst sufferers of this are the C class revolutionary prisoners confined in the Gaddha Barrack of Bareilley District Jail.

The tortures, legal or illegal, which the prisoners of Bareilley Gaddha Barrack had to undergo, are simply shocking. Stories of brutal whippings, Jail "Fall-ins", solitary cells, fetters, uneatable food. denial of interviews with dearest and nearest ones, denial of books, tearing to pieces of letters and various other mental and physical indignities and unbearable sufferings that we have heard from our comrades, who have come from that jail, had already made us very unhappy. This was why Prof Shibbanlal Saxena, M.L.A. on 17-5-45 put forward a forceful statement on these points before the City Magistrate of Lucknow as to how these 89 unfortunate and helpless persons were passing their long days, months and years since 1941 in great misery, agony and humiliation. The two latest arrivals here have described before us how callously and inhumanly the authorities allowed the two bright and young patriots to meet their end quite uncared for, as if they were two stray dogs.

Comrade Umashankar Upadhyaya of Ghazipur, a life transportation convict in Sahajanwa Train Dacoity case, was a healthy and stout person when leaving this jail last year. He was down with unremitting fever for days and developed pnneumonia, yet was not even removed to the hospital and on the 9th day when his case was quite serious the Head Warder, neither the doctor nor the compounder, tried to take him to the hospital, dragged by two convict overseers and this revolting and brutal attitude was only stopped when his friends stood in the way. Only then a stretcher was brought and he was removed to the hospital and kept in a cell without any attendant, though the case was serious and it was not an infectious case. There, in the next night he fell down from his bed and remained so for a long time before it was detected and he was removed. The next day he was sent to the General Hospital almost in a senseless condition only to die there the next night. The case of Udai Singh of Almora, a convict of August Movement of 1942, was no better. Down with cholera, the poor man died the next night in his barrack and only the deadbody was removed to the jail hospital.

Mr. C. W. Laig, who was once left unconcious in a drain at Bareilley after a heavy thrashing by some bad characters whose men were being tortured by him as the jailor of Bareilley Central Prison and whose name is well known to the politicals due to the most inhuman treatment of politicals in Lucknow Camp Jail and Chunar Fort and more recent wanton shooting and assaults etc: on the non-political Bengal detenus in Allahabad District Jail, is the Superintendent of the Bareilley District Jail. It is said that he finds pleasure in maltreating the politicals there. At times even as a matter of course he pokes a person with his baton as if he is not even a human being. Naturally it originated on such an affair, when he used his baton on one, Hari Pratap Tiwari of Sahajanwa and Lucknow cases, and who is here with us now. Two have already died there, one has lost his mental balance and most of them are suffering from various ailments. If things continue as such anything may happen to any man any day.

Hundreds of long termers are passing their terrible days, particularly in the central jails, of the August Movement of 1942. The Viceroy's recent broadcast in which he appealed to the political Indians to "forgive and forget" cannot be appreciated if it is not followed by practical action. If the political prisoners are not released immediately, then at least they may certainly expect a prompt and definite change for the better in their treatment in jail.

It is, therefore, my humble and earnest request to you that the revolutionary C class prisoners of Bareilley District Jail (of Gaddha Barrack) be immediately removed to a special concentration jail of revolutionary prisoners of the province, like the one at Naini in 1936, where they can get the above mentioned treatment, namely, 1. Superior Class treatment which includes better food and clothing ; 2. daily newspapers and other facilities for reading and writing ; 3. facilities for indoor and outdoor games ; and 4. living accommodation in association barrack in a concentration jail etc. and all the politicals convicted of offence in connection with the 1942 movement be also similarly treated.

As a person who has spent nearly 24 years in different jails of northern India I would like to point out to you that some Superintendents of U.P. Jails, because of their harem ideas, have created unhealthy enclosures which are exceptionally harmful in a tropical country like India. Politicals be immediately removed from such cells and cell-enclosures purely on medical ground. In this connection, as examples, I may cite the cases of the two central jails of these provinces, besides Bareilley and here. 1. Cell No. 22 of Lucknow Central Jail was formerly a line of cells with a veranda in front, but it has been divided into some blocks with enclosures in front covered by high walls leaving very little passage for proper ventilation. Cell No. 21 was formerly a barrack. This was first transformed into cell by a partition wall. These cells were themselves unhealthy as there was no proper cross ventilation. And later on, these cells have been made into so many blocks enclosed with high walls. these are the dungeons in which politicals, convicted and C class detenus on punishment, have to boil in heat in hot summer months.

2. The European Ward of Agra Central Jail had no surrounding walls so long as it was meant for the Europeans. But now that Indian politicals are lodged in it, it has been enclosed with walls all round, even the entrance gate being blocked by a separate wall at a distance, leaving very little space inside over for a walk. So also narrow cell blocks have been separated from cells No. 35, 36 with high walls all round. Circles have also cells for the politicals.

3. The surrounding wall of our ward here also has just been raised by about 7 ft., thus blocking the passage of air. And such is the case with the revolutionary ward of Bareilley District Jail where the very ward, Gaddha Barrack as it is called, is about 7 ft. below the ground level of the rest of the jail.

In fine, I would like to add that one effect of the Simla Conference is that there has been a distinct change of attitude between the governors and the governed and this has emboldened me to come forward with this long-felt grievance of the politicals in general and therefore, I fervently hope you will very kindly give this that amount of importance with which it is being written. Belated justice is better than denial of justice.

Thanking you in anticipation and expecting an early reply.

I have the honour to be,
Sir,
Yours faithfully,
Jogesh Chandra Chatterji.

Dated, Lucknow District
Jail, 25th July, 1945.

APPENDIX VI

ONE MONTH'S ULTIMATUM

To

The Hon'ble Advisor, Jail, to the Governor of U. P,
Through the Superintendent, District Jail, Lucknow.

Sir,

I beg to remind you that I submitted a lengthy note to you on 27. 7. 1945 re. the treatment of political prisoners in U. P. Jails, suggesting that all politicals be treated as a special class and they be kept in association barracks and facilities be given for games and reading and writing.

Since then there has been a considerable agitation in the the country in general over this question and there have been hunger strikes in Jails and even death and strikes are on even now.

As regards our own case here we are also facing a good deal of trouble over our letters and particularly interviews, the only two sources through which a prisoner is in touch with the world outside the high walls.

Before the August Movement of 1942, relations and friends could interview the revolutionary prisoners of this ward with the permission of the Jail Superintendent as usual. But in 1942 during the movement, the authority was transferred to the District Magistrate as also was the case with the detenus in those years. The order was, however, withdrawn in 1944 and usual course was restored everywhere except perhaps. in this jail, where it still persists. I petitioned to the D. M. of Lucknow last year for permission for interviews with my relations ; but he has not cared to give any reply though I made repeated personal requests to the D. M. and the A.D.M. on their visits. The result is that last year my brother had to go back from the jail gate and so was the case with a cousin of mine recently. I have patiently waited for years without any interview. But now I am feeling so much aggrieved that the very life seems to be a burden to me. The right of an interview is a basic concession granted to a good conduct prisoner. To deny this by an arbitrary and artificial means is a wanton torture to his very human sentiment.

Under the circumstances, I hope that I shall not be driven to desperation and my most humble submission is that you will be good enough to redress the genuine grievances satisfactorily within utmost another month from now.

Thanking you in anticipation and expecting an early reply.

I am
Jogesh Chandra Chatterji

Dated District Jail,
Lucknow,
December 16,1945.

APPENDIX VII

THE STRIKE NOTICE TO THE JAIL SUPERINTENDENT

To

The Superintendent, District Jail, Lucknow.

Sir,

I beg to lay before you that it is nearly six months that following the general gesture "forgive and forget" of the Viceroy I put forward the proposition before the local Government that political prisoners be formed into a single Special Class, and as such they be given :

1. Superior class treatment which includes better food and clothing.
2. Facilities for indoor and outdoor games, and
3. Daily newspaper and other facilities for reading and writing, and
4. Living accommodation in association barrack in a concentration jail etc.

But the wooden heart of 'Steel Frame' could not be softened. During these months hunger strikes have taken place almost in every central jail, and Dewan Singh, the stout youth of Almora, has died in Bareilley Jail as a result of this. In the mean time there has been a tremendous agitation in the country over the treatment and trial of the I. N. A. prisoners. The leaders of INA have at long last been let off the very day that they were sentenced to transportion for life. I have only raised the question of the treatment, and not the release, of the political prisioners, though in the face of INA release, these releases are certainly overdue.

Nobody knows the hollowness more of the August rebellion trials than myself. Even the District Magistrate himself of Etah was not ready to try me on a fictitious charge ; but the Governor, Sir Maurice Hallet, prevailed on him personally going over there and I received a heavy sentence. Not content with that, they, later made me the provincial leader of the

Lucknow-Barabanki Conspiracy Case, though after I was already clapped in jail, and where members of different organisations were herded together in a common conspiracy. Some were tried before the same judge previously, as members of Hindustan Socialist Republican Association ; two were office-bearers of the Congress Socialist Party whereas I was founder-member of the Revolutionary Socialist Party of India. The poor tutored approver boy thrice changed the front during the course of the trial, and yet we were given sentences all right. Thus in ripe old age I was again made to undergo the same indignities, insults and humiliations at Lucknow, as in the days of the Kakori Conspiracy Case two decades ago. The court recorded my statement for two days in the so-called open trial, but not a word of it was allowed to be published in the papers.

Old memories hunt me and goad me to action. Many of my intimate friends from Bengal to the Punjub, including four martyrs of the Kakori Case who were here, have been victims of police bullets and the hangman's rope in the part ; and comrade Raj Narayan Mishra's memory is only a year old. I cannot forget his parting message and also that two of his brothers are serving life sentences as C class prisoners in Lucknow and Fatehgarh Central Prisons. My own compatriot of Kakori case, Mr. Mukundilal Gupta, who was in B Class for 8 years then. is now in C class in Fatehgarh Jail at this advanced age of 60 with a sentence of 7 year Rigorous Imprisonment. After so much whippings and illegal tortures many of my revolutionary friends all brilliant youths, are still in the Gaddha Barrack of Bareilley District Jail in C class.

The recently framed otherwise good rules of the North West Frontier province Government for the politicals are marred by the odious clause "provided that the offence does not involve violence." Such a clause bars all the August movement prisoners from being designated as political and hence must be eliminated.

The other objectionable tendency is the segregation of certain important prisoners from the rest of his kind. As examples of this may be cited the case of Mr. Shibbanlal Saksena from here to Naini Jail 'Kuttaghar' segretation ward, Mr. Chandra Bhusan Tewari from Lucknow Central to

Gorakhpur Jail and Mr Madanmohon Upadhyaya from Almora to Meerut jail, Mr. Devakinandan Dixit to Fyzabad from Lucknow Central Jail

These are some of the grounds which have compelled me to take the grim decision, though really I simply shudder at the very idea of it, as so often I had been on the verge of death after protracted agonising sufferings. I had given one month's ultimatum on 16. 12 45 for a reply, but unfortunately no reply has so far been received. So I am on hunger strike since this morning with the determination that either the grievances will be redressed or the fast will continue upto death.

I am,
Jogesh Chandra Chatterji
Dated Lucknow District Jail,
16th January. 1946.

APPENDIX VIII

A note for the militant youths on the day I started strike

(This is from my note book in jail in the hand writing of a comrade, who is now a Government servant.)

If we cast a glance at the Independence Movement of the country of recent times a few outstanding features cannot but strike our vision , here in these provinces, as also in the country at large. Every one knew that a second world war was coming rather fast. So the Congress accepted ministries in 1937 with the Working Committee's mandate that they would not work out the constitution, but would only try to prepare the country, through their instrumentality, for attaining independence, taking advantage of that war situation. We all know how the ministries as also the forces guiding them, forgot all about it, the mandate remaining only in the blue book. Professions were not put into practice.

In the U.P. the Kakori men on their release started a vigorous propaganda for this ; but they were not only discouraged but even condemned by Pantji and Nehruji, and even they prevailed on Gandhiji to write an adverse note in the 'Harijan'. In their adversity during the Kakori trial they stood by them. Pantji himself led the defence and after a decade, as the Premier, got them released fighting with the Governor. Pandit Nehru gave them a party at the Anand Bhawan on their release and again minimised it by a public statement, condemned them at Harduaganj Conference for their defiance of the orders of the Chief Commissioner of Delhi and courting arrest and imprisonment. One of them was duly elected to the Council of U.P. P C C., but Nehruji requested him to withdraw on the ground that such a dangerous revolutionary should not be in the Provincial Congress executive immediately on release. But we find many Kakori prisoners in jail even now as detenus and convicts.

Subhas Chandra Bose took up an extreme attitude. So every efforts were made to corner and crush him. Even prior to this he was disabled, through a legal flaw, from getting a big sum left by V.J. Patel for national public work. Shortly before the August Movement of 1942 he was condemned by the Congress leaders everywhere. Nehruji castigated him in strong terms standing in the very heart of Bengal where even then the people were solidly behind Bose. Now, of course, under the changed circumstances, Nehruji also has changed and become greatest advocate of Netaji Bose and his I.N.A. Now he has realised that Bose was a patriot, the bravest leader and the supreme organiser, because well aware of all these condemnations Netaji had organised a Nehru brigade also. So Nehruji had lost faith in his colleague but later had confidence in Bose as a great countryman of his. Netaji had the respect and faith in his countrymen, so the INA men reposed unreserved confidence in him and were ever ready to sacrifice life and all at his command, and thousands have done so already,

When actually the war started Mahatmaji came out with the astounding statement that "the country was not prepared". Due to public pressure and also to give a pressure to the British Government, the ministries were promptly given up, but no other step was taken for about a year. Then following the non-embrassment policy towards the Government was the childish and farcical 'individual satyagraha' and its natural extinction within another year due to sheer exhaustion. About this time, that is, by the end of 1941, Gandhiji started the propaganda that a fight would be given after the war. Consequently the prestige of the Congress at this time had gone down very low. But the magnificent Japanese victories brought a new life in the country. The masses were stirred everywhere throughout the country. Finding the Japanese invasion inevitable and even imminent, the Cripps offer came but the leaders also were heartened by this time. So the offer was rejected and the Quit India move was given. The movement was gaining tremendous momentum, as everybody thought that the Britishers being crushed everywhere, would not be able to resist ; the capitalists stood by the leaders as by this time their war-profitering had reached a certain points of satiety and they saw that in case of a successful invasion the bourgeois leadership would be of immense help to them and after success Netaji would be the real leader and he would naturally have to seek the help of Gandhiji. Sardar Patel and Rajendra Babu were very active, but Nehruji hesitant. But the sudden and wholesale arrest of leaders, without giving any programme beforehand, gave the masses the oportunity to make the disorganised and spontaneous attempt of a grand revolution. On release Gandhiji threw these revolutionaries overboard as he was being badly cornered by the Britishers since the decline of the Axis forces; but Nehruji saved the situation by taking up the cause of the rebels in his characteristic straight forward way and thus today the country is pulsating with a new life over again. Today even the Indian Stalinists are observing the I.N.A. Day.

The forces ushered into existence through the great attempt of revolution is a big problem before the leaders. They are, therefore, busy in devising means of harnessing them and keeping them under their own safe custody. The country is under foreign domination, the worst type of feudal system is present here, the capitalists, who have amassed immense sums through black-marketing and war-profiteering, are now making new efforts of further strengthening their position by entering into fresh alliances with the British and American capitalists. The revolutionary masses are not so blind as not to realise this. So they are being attracted to socialist economy as the only remedy. The leaders have, therefore, brought into being a high sounding socialistic worded manifesto to throw dust into the eyes of the masses and at the same time are busy with a gigantic move of monopolising all power for themselves and crushing the real revolutionary forces mercilessly. Hence the preaching all round of the efficiency of one party, one leader and one programme,—the programme of the Charkha and the bulluck cart. The Congress is the organisation of the masses, hence there is no need of maintaining any separate body of the Kisans or the mazdoors. This is why Gandhiji says that Marxism is obsolete. Nehruji, the well-known advocate of progressive socialism for the last 15 years, stated the other day before the students at

Panta that Socialism and Marxism are foreign imported ideas and not suited to India. Sarat Bose, who call himself the elder brother of Forward Bloc and condemns the fascist methods of Chiang, prefering those of Mao and his comrades, preached in a recent Calcutta meeting the great tradition and history of India. Are we only to derive inspiration from our past greatness and not to look to the world out side ? This is a dangerous propaganda in the middle of the twentieth century, when science and the means of communication have changed the face of the earth altogether ? Our leaders are almost all foreign-educated persons. See the subtle move that 'Bande Mataram' the traditional Congress slogan may not be replaced by 'Jai Hind'.

The Calcutta students observed the I. N. A. Day and the police bullets freely rained on those unarmed youths. But the Congress leaders were conspicuous by their absence at the terrible stage. The Congress President was also misinformed about the facts by his compatriots ; so he issued an adverse note from his Vindhyachal retreat. Later on the Maulana Saheb (Azad) had to rectify his position by praising the heroic stand of the students and accusing the leaders for their non-cooperation at the critical stage

Bapuji's inner voice says that Netaji Bose was alive and hiding and this gives him a good chance of condemning once more the method Bose followed. After so much I. N. A. propaganda in the country it was necessary, particularly when the negotiation of a compromise with the British Government was proceeding apace. Alas, had Netaji been alive no amount of propaganda for one partycould dislodge the lively leftist-socialist forces within the Congress. Under his magnetic leadership these forces could easily combine and bring about the country's INDEPEN-DENCE and at the same time the feudalism and the capitalism would have vanished in no time. Not Ram Raj. but real Peoples Raj through a true socialist economy would have ushered in. A good-worded manifesto is nothing unless there be real force of the people behind it for its practical realisation. Only the leftist bodies are that force. They were tne rebels of 1942 ; but they were not for a moment disloyal to the

Indian National Congress. The revolutionary socialist forces were the only hope of our future and hence they must be preserved at any cost for the proper guidance of the oppressed and the down-trodden.

The 1942 movement prisoners, as also the incarcerated INA men, were the real essence of the revolutionary force. Therefore, they must be in association in jail in order to keep them fit ; better food, clothing and games were necessary for their physical wellbeing and news papers and other facilities for reading and writing were essential for their mental development.

These fundamental necessities must be within easy reach of each and every political prisoner, whatever be the nature of his offence, that is to say whether it involves violence or non-violence. So the clause in the Fronter Government rules "provided that the offence does not involve violence" must be eliminated. During the recent hunger strikes of politicals the provincial secretaries of the Congress, Messrs K. D. Malviya and Lal Bahadur Shastri, have urged that they be only allowed to supplement their food through friends outside. This is entirely wrong both in principle and also from the practical point of view. The local Government's soothing balm of keeping some in association and others in segregation or allowing the newspapers from the detenu neighbours are meagre palliatives. A thorough change of outlook must be brought about.

I have taken up their cause, because the cause is great and I am also the fittest person for this. I have fought all though my life for the oppressed, in every field under all circumstances. I have lived practically the whole of my adult life in jail and banishment and from a privileged position I have ever fought for the politicals from inside prison several times risking my life. Even now I am a privileged prisoner. Now the country has advanced much and I have also grown grey. Let this be my last fight inside prison for the revolutionary prisoners of the country. If I do not succeed alive, let me attain it by my death. My natural death is not far off. Many fine and stout youths have died, let another old man be added to the number. But the object has to be attained.

For that is my appeal to the students and the militant youths of the land. They have shown their metal and the whole country is proud of them. I, therefore, want that they should take up this great cause in right earnestness. The success or failure will be in vain unless the demand be made a national one and unless every nook and corner of this vast country is vibrated with the sound of this essential demand of the rebel revolutionaries, who have left their hearth and home and all personal comforts for making their land of birth free and independent, to make it independent of any foreign domination and also free from all oppressive elements within itself.

This is a noble undertaking and hence the generous and noble youths are to back it with the greatest possible efforts, not for any person or party, creed or community, but for the real selvation of our common country and the common people. Jai Hind.

(Jogesh Chandra Chatterji)

Dated Lucknow District Jail,
January 16, 1946.

APPENDIX IX

SOME LETTERS

To Pandit Bishwambhar Dayal Tripathi of Unnao from District Jail, Lucknow

...Now-a-days my mind is restless because of the situation out side.

After a brilliant activity and immense sufferings and sacrifices by the leftist forces of the country today they seem to stand on the threshold of a great crisis. This is taxing my brain too much these days and hence I am approaching you with the serious question that requires to be solved satisfactorily before it is too late,

What was the great 1942 movement and who actually fought it? The first statement of Gandhiji on the starting of the war was that the country was not prepared for a fight, then was the suspension of provincial ministries but no other action ; after about 10 months the farcical individual satyagraha and Gandhiji's statement that if Nehru and Bhabe carry on with the satyagraha, it would he successful. Congress was quite inactive when Japan gained the grand victories at our very door and, thereby, reduced the British prestige to zero. To save the position at this critical stage came the Cripps offer. Gandhiji and others thought that I.N.A. would successfully march into India and people would fraternise with them. Hence there was no need of compromise and the offer was rejected. After that Gandhiji was honour-bound to launch the movement.

Patel prepared his province for a 'short and swift victory in a week'. Rajendra Babu goaded Bihar zamindars to action. Other High Commanders, including Nehru, did nothing. Patel had influenced the mill owners, So on the arrest of the leaders the move was there. The first 3 days there was only Hartal. But after this Bose and L. S. Amery's hints gave the ignition to the already combustible India. Spontaneously the people brought about a revolution In it the Gandhian

Charkhawalas played a very insignificant part. what did your Sadakat Ashram do ? Were they not spending a huge amount of money every year ?) Ahmedabad and Jamshedpur strikes were only due to the millowners, who wanted to make a capital out of the new position after the inevitable fall of the Britishers. Only in the N.W. Frontier Khan Saheb gave a big Gandhite move ; but it was suppressed swiftly and brutally.

Every one knows that the brilliant activities were done by the militant youths of the country, drawing inspiration for the field work of the C.S.P., the F.B., R.S.P. etc. Bose's heroic and historic activities outside India was a unique one which gave the greatest inspiration to his countrymen. JP after his escape, tried promptly to line up with the great men of Bose. We have ample proof of this through his pamphlets etc. for which, like Bose, he was also called 'traitor' by the Indian Stalinists. Particularly for this I have supported Bose's stand in my written statement before the Etah Court on 7.1.43. and again before the Lucknow court on 22nd and 24th of April, 1944.

What do we find today ? Those people, who were out to crush Bose are praising him loudly, of course, not forgetting at the same time, to show him pity on his brilliant patriotic but wrong move. How in a subtle way they are exploiting the terrible sufferings of the masses. They are now determined to make their position unassailable, they are out to bring the true revolutionaries who fought the war of 1942, with their all, to their knees. All the leftist-socialist organisations must be liquidated and brought under one leader, one flag and one organisation. The dictator Patel, who crushed Bose, when the C.S.P. fearfully stood aloof, is now raising the hatchet on the C.S.P. and with it, of course, all others, of its kind. He is said to have already told so to Acharya Narendra Deva at Poona.

Like the Labour Party of England, the Congress executive of India also will form the executive of the British Viceroy. They will be the virtual dictators of India with the help of India's finance-capital. They will also guide the socio-politico-economic affairs,

It is really a turning point in the history of India and the greatest menace to the real militant socialist forces of the country. Therefore, it is incumbent on them to make a swift and frantic effort to get themselves organised against it. An immediate merger of these forces into a most formidable one is the need of the hour. At least those, who have so many things common in them may easily combine, say the C S P, the F B and the R S P.

For this they require to have regotiations and talks amongst themselves, as also with responsible persons of other groups. This is not less important than the ensuring elections and, therefore, must be carried on very earnestly and promptly.

In the meantime the decision of the High Command must be deferred as long as possible on the very reasonable plea of the release of other leaders and workers on the one hand and the election of new Congress executives on the other. The 5 year old executives have no right to decide this, leaving out those, who suffered in 1942.

The F B was not a party originally, but was platform. But at Nagpur it took the shape of party under Bose's leadership and declared socialism as its object. After the departure of Bose, this was again reiterated in Delhi by the FB Conference. On release Mr. Ruikar also stated that it was a socialist body.

Jaiprakash Babu wrote to Bose from Hazaribagh jail, in substance, that he was wrong and Bose was right. He had prolonged talks separately with Bose and Ganguli in Calcutta for three days. In his captured letter from Deoli (published by Government of India) he says they cannot do in Bengal without the cooperation of the RSP. Again after his escape from Hazaribagh jail he completely agreed with the move of Bose outside, as expressed through pamphlets etc.

In these circumstances, the need of the hour seems to be to strengthen these groups by a merger. Only then can there be a strong socialist body in the country, strong enough to with stand the onslaught of the reactionary Gandhian pressure on the one hand and the more dangerous and more vigorous C.P.I. on the other.

A complete merger at this time is not an easy affair, particularly because of the prestige gained by the C.S.P. inside through the activities of J.P. and F.B, through Bose outside.

But I am sure that a deep impassionedt hinking will convince the leaders and the thoughtful workers that my humble suggestion is of immense value. Separately, for their very existence. they will be mere lackeys of the Congress High Command ; and, therefore, the more progressive and militant of them will gradually swell the number of the C P.I., whose signboard is more attractive. In the case of a merger, this (new party) can easily be the best socialist left wing of the Congress, vigorously preparing the country for the next successful revolution, through the Student, Labour and Kisan Congresses ; and also by establishing contact with the military on technical lines. The survivors of the INA will naturally r. lly round this and their expert knowledge will be a boon to us in this most important work. A revolution without the army on our side is a day dream.

Now, therefore, there are two alternatives before the leftists, either to get themselves liquidated or to resist the mischievous move of Patel, sternly and stubbornly ; and if the struggle is nct successful inside the Congress, then even to go outside and form a formidable socialist party.

Indeed a serious problem is facing the leftists. The key of the Congress is really in the hands of the once Kisan leader of Bardoli, I mean, Sardar Patel, who stands today entrenched behind the financial magnates of Bombay. In case if the leftists succumb to him, then India may turn into a second China and this Chiang of Bombay, may once again give the Indian masses a blood bath in the shape of a grim internecine struggle between the Congress and the C.P.I. Because, in the absence of any leftist-socialist group in the Gandhian Congress, or even outside of it, the militant youths, and through them, a good number of the masses, will naturally go over to the C.P.I. Our unhappy country need not have that terrible experience after so much sufferings at a time when good days are clearly visible ahead.

Therefore my earnest appeal to you, and through you to all progressive leftwing congressmen, to form a strong socialist party within the Congress, or even outside of it. Today to me individually, this seems to be the only way of harnessing and leading the militant youths of the country to its cherished goal. They, and they alone, will be able to deliver goods, not the meek khaddarwalas, however widespread their organisational ramifications.

The need of the time is to carry on with brisk and vigorous negotiations between the responsible released leaders and workers. After attaining a certain amount of success in private talks, an informal conference may be held. This conference may set up a constitution making committee to draft a constitution and also a clear and forceful manifesto. Then a general conference may be called with a sustained propaganda, and this conference may ultimately give out a constitution and the manifesto with a spectacular demonstration. After this the High Command will dare not ask anybody to wind up any lively organization.

For the present, time should be taken on the plea of release of other important persons, as also for the Congress executive elections, the current body being pre-1942, that is 5 years old.

This is my individual opinion ; I am not in touch with my own men, the most important of whom are in jail like myself.

Jogesh Chandra Chatterji
Dt. 18-9 1945. District Jail, Lucknow,

I wrote three Letters to leaders from Lucknow Jail as suggestions that after release there should be an attempt to stand jointly as a leftist force. The letters were of the similar ideas. Letter to Acharya Narendra Deva was dated 16-9-45, shortly after his release. The letter to Pandit Vishwambhar Dayal Tripathi was dated 18-9-45 and third one to Shri Sarat Chandra Bose was dated 30-9-45, Letters were sent from jail through private sources and the last one was on the release of Bose, sent to him privately through Shri Tripathi.

APPENDIX—X

Letter of Pandit Jawaharlal Nehru to Jogesh Chandra Chatterji through C. B. Gupta for calling off the hunger strike on 6-2-46.

Dear Jogesh Chatterji,

Chandra Bhanu Gupta has told me of his interview with you. We are naturally anxious that you should not endanger your life and we are also convinced that the treatment of many political prisoners has been and is bad and even the ordinary facilities are denied them. Personally I think, and many others are of the same opinion that at the present moment specially hunger strikes on these issues are unfortunate. Big changes are in the air, or, in the alternative, a conflict. Naturally it must be function of any popular government to put an end to these questions by release of political prisoners. If for a temporary period some continue they must have all facilities. That is the definite policy of the Congress, often repeated, and our own people will see to it that it is carried out.

About present conditions, Gupta and others are trying their best to get them changed for the better. As for newspapers, I am suggesting that Government be told that we shall gladly pay for them if they agree to supply them. Other matters, too, should be and will be pressed. But for the moment the decision does not rest with us. I hope that you will not persist in the hunger strike and thus endanger your life or at any rate ruin your health. We have to keep ourselves fit for future work. Therefore I trust you will give up the hunger strike.

Lucknow
6-2-46

Yours sincerely.
Jawaharlal Nehru.

APPENDIX—XI

ON HUNGER STRIKE

JOGESH CHATTERJI GIVES UP FAST

PIONEER, FEBRUARY 7, 1946.

Mr. Jogesh Chandra Chatterji, who had been on hunger strike for the last 22 days in the Lucknow District Jail, broke his fast on Wednesday in the presence of Mr. C. B. Gupta, President of Lucknow City Congress Committee, who, it is understood earlier, conveyed to Mr. Chatterji the wishes of Pandit Jawaharlal Nehru, Pandit Govind Ballabh Pant and Acharya Narendra Deva that he should give up the fast.

Mr. Chatterji is reported to have lost more than 26 lbs. in weight.

MR. GUPTA'S STATEMENT

Mr. C. B. Gupta in a press statement says, Mr. Jogesh Chandra Chatterji has broken his fast at 3 O'clock in my presence 'after three hours' pursuation, and after I had communicated to him the wishes of our great leaders, Pandit Jawharlal Nehru, Acharya Narendra Deva and Pandit Govind Ballabh Pant. It was a difficult task to convince him about the properiety of giving up his fast ; but ultimately I made him agree on the definite assurance that public opinion will assert itself, and the new era, that is soon to follow, will bring about a situation which will force popular governments to take up the cause of the political prisoners.

I hope the present Government, especially its Adviser in the Home Department, will immediately pass orders in relation to matters which I had discussed with him this morning before going to Mr. Chatterji, and thus set things right during the interim period in between the coming of popular Governments. He will also consider the advisability of transferring the 'C' class prisoners concentrated in the District Jail, Bareilly, to a place more congenial.

Mr. Chatterji has communicated through me to all comrades, who had gone on a sympathetic hunger strike in the various jails of the province to give up their hunger strike and act up to the advice of our leaders. I whole-heartedly endorse this advice of Mr. Chatterji and request the various superintendents of jails in the province immediately to communicate this desire of Mr, Chatterji to them.

PIONEER, FEBRUARY 7, 1946

B. P. C. C. urged Release

Calcutta, February 5, 1946

The Executive Committee of the Bengal Provincial Congress Committee in a resolution passed today expressed grave concern at the continued hunger strike and consequent deterioration in the condition of Mr. Jogesh Chandra Chatterji, and other political prisoners confined in Lucknow, Bareilly and Fatehgrah jails. A. P. I.

PANDIT JAWHARLAL NEHRU ON JOGESH CHATTERJI'S HUNGER STRIKE

National Herald, February 8, 1964

I am glad to hear that Srijut Jogesh Chandra Chatterji has ended his hunger strike. As I have often said I dislike hunger strike. Perhaps on a very special occasion when there is no other remedy left a hunger strike may be justified said Pandit Jawaharlal Nehru in an interview to the Associated Press of India.

Pandit Nehru added : "But this weapon is too mighty to be used except for those very special occasions. A tendency to indulge in it otherwise is unfortunate. I realise, however, that the lot of political prisoners and more specially long term prisoners, has been a terribly hard one. Some of them have spent greater part of their lives in prison. Jogesh Chatterji has, I believe, spent 25 years already in prison.

"Manifestly, from any human standard, the normal conveniences for a sane physicial and mental life should be provided to them. It is bad enough for vital young men to be kept in prison for all their young lives and a system of government which has to function in this way is a failure. But in any event they should be treated as human beings with bodies and minds which require care and nourishment. Mental nourishment is even more important than physical. None of us dare judge the actions of a person who had to undergo the agony of long years in prison with all physical and mental consequences that it brings.

"There is so much talk now of changes in the Government and of Indian independence being near. Surely, the present Governmental authorities might show some appreciation of the changes that are bound to come soon. They should at least provide healthy quarters for the prisoners to live in, books and news papers and writing materials and request interviews. If they grudge the money for books and newspapers, we shall provide the funds. In particular there are many complaints of living conditions of 'C' class political prisoners in the Bareilly District jail. It is a small matter which can easily be remedied without any expense or trouble."

APPENDIX XII

NEHRU'S VIEWS ON BHAGAT SINGH IN AUTOBIOGRAPHY, Page 174-75-76

"It was this sense of national humilitation (as felt by Lalaji) that weighed on the mind of India and when Lalaji's death came soon after inevitably it was connected with the assault, and sorrow itself gave pride of place to anger and indignation. It is well to appreciate this for only so can we have some understanding of subsequent events, of the phenomenon of Bhagat Singh and of his sudden and amazing popularity in North India. It is very easy and very fatuous to condemn persons or acts without seeking to understand the springs of action, the causes that underlie them. Bhagat Singh was not previously well-known : he did not become popular because of an act of violence, an act of terrorism Terroriss have flourished in India, off and on for nearly thirty years, and at no time, except in the early days in Bengal, did any of them attain a fraction of that popularity which came to Bhagat Singh. This is a patent fact which cannot be denied ; it has to be admitted. And another fact which is equally obvious, is that terrorism, inspite of occasional recrudescenee, has no longer any real appeal for the youth of India. Fifteen years' stress on non-violence has changed the whole background in India, and made the masses much more indifferent to, and even hostile to the idea of terrorism as a method of political action. Even the classes from which the terrorists are usually drawn, the lower middle classes and intelligentsia, have been powerfully affected by the Congress propaganda against method of violence. Their active and impatient elements, who think in terms of revolutionary action, also realise fully now that revolution does not come through terrorism, and that terrorism is an outworn and profitless method which comes in the way of real revolutionary action. Terrorism is a dying thing in India and elsewere, not because of Government coercion which can only suppress and bottle up, not eradicate, but because of basic causes and world events. Terrorism usually represents the infancy of a revolutionary urge in a country. That stage passes, and with it passes terrorism as an important phenomenon. Occasional outbursts may continue because of local causes or stage and no doubt even the occasional outbursts will gradually die out. But this does not mean that all people in India have ceased to believe in individual violence and terrorism but many, no doubt, still think that a time may come when organised violent methods may be necessary in other countries, that is today an academic issue, which time alone will put to the test ; it has nothing to do with terroristic method."

"Bhagat Singh thus did not become popular because of his acts of terrorism, but because he seemed to vindicate for the moment, the honour of Lala Lajpat Rai, and through him of the nation. He became a symbol ; the act was forgotten, the symbol remained, and within a few months each town and village of the Punjab, and to a lesser extent in the rest of northern India, resounded with his name. Innumberable songs grew up about him, and the popularity that the man achieved was something amazing."

NEHRU ON CHANDRASEKHAR AZAD

I remember a curious incident about that time, which gave an insight into the mind of the torrorist group in India. This took place soon after my discharge from prison, either a little before father's death or a few days after. A stranger came to see me at our house, and I was told that he was Chandrasekhar Azad. I had never seen him before, but I had heard of him ten years earlier, when he had non-cooperated from school and gone to prison during the N. C. C. movement in 1921. A boy of 15 or so then, he had been flogged in prison for some breach of jail discipline. Later he had drifted towards the terrorists, and he became one of their prominent men in north India. All this I had heard vaguely, and I had taken no interest in these rumours. I was surprised, therefore, to see him. He had been induced to visit me because of the general expectation (owing to our release) that some negotitations between the Government and the Congress were likely. He wanted to know if, in case of a settlement, his group of people, would have a peace. Would they still be considered, and treated, as outlaws, hunted out from place to place, with a price on their heads, and the prospect of the gallows ever before them ? Or was there a possibility of their being allowed to pursue peacefully vocations ? He told me that as far as he was concerned, as well as many of his associates, they were convinced now, that purely terrorist methods were futile and did no good. He was not, however, prepared to believe that India would gain her freedom wholly by peaceful methods. He thought that some time in future a violent conflict might take place, but this would not be terrorism. He ruled out terrorism as such so far as the question of Indian freedom was concerned But then, he added, what was to do when no chance was given him to settle down, as was being founded all the time ? Many of the terroristic acts that had occurred recently, according to him, were purely in self-defence.

I was glad to learn from Azad, and I had confirmation of this subsequently, that the belief in terrorism was dying down. a group notion, indeed, it had practically gone, and individual and sporadic cases were probably due, to some special reason, act or reprisal or individual aberration, and not a general idea. This did not mean, of course, that the old terrorism or their new associates had become converts to non-violence or admirers of British rule. But they did not think in terms of terrorism as they used to. Many of them it seems to me, have definitely the fascist mentality.

I tried to explain to Chandrasekhar Azad what my philosophy of political action was, and tried to convert him to my view point. But I had no answer to his basic question. What was he to do now ? Nothing was likely to happen that would bring him, or his like, any reliet of peace. All I could suggest was that he should use his influence to prevent the occurrence of terrorist acts in the future, for these could only injure the larger cause as well as his own group.

Two or three weeks later, while the Gandhi-Irwin talks were going on, I heard at Delhi that Chandrasekhar Azad had been shot down and killed by the police in Allahabad. He was recognised in the day time in a park and was surrounded by a large police force. He tried to defend himself from behind a tree; there was quite a shooting-match and he injured one or two police men before he was shot down.

Jawaharlal Nehru, An autobiography
Page 261-62

AND THE FOLLOWING APPEARS AT PAGES 10 TO 14 OF THE RECENT PUBLICATION STYLED "THE UNTOLD STORY" BY B. M. KAUL.

"My second assignment came a few days later. I was to deliver a parcel to a mendicant in the Old Fort. This, was done, at the dead of night, without knowing who the recipient was, what I carried or its purpose as is often the case in such hush-hush missions.

"Sir John Simon had come to India as Chairman of a Commission for reporting how desirable it was to establish or restrict self-government in India. There was deep resentment against this Commission throughout the country. It was thought to be a contrivance on the part of the British Government to retard our self-rule. Black flags bearing 'Go Back Simon' confronted him wherever he went. When he came to Delhi, I did the same to him, as a mark of protest. We had a field day (nearly a hundred thousand people from all walks of life having assembled for the occasion) and gave a hot reception to this unwelcome visitor.

"I often visited the Legislative Assembly and heard stirring speeches by stalwarts like Pandit Motilal Nehru, Madan Mohan Malviya and Mohammad Ali Jinnah. One day, I had gone to attend a debate on what was called the Public Safety Bill which the British were trying to push through the House and under which they could detain anyone without trial indefinitely. Public galleries were packed on that exciting day. I remember Pandit Motilal Nehru warming up in the House and saying : 'I am not one of those who shiver in their shoes at the name of.........'Soon after, there was a commotion in the House. Two young men, sitting next to me, whom I did not know, suddenly sprang up to their feet. One of them pulled out a bundle of leaflets from under his coat and threw it in all directions. These leaflets carried the caption 'To make the deaf hear.........motto of the French Revolution', and, in a flash, two bombs had been hurled in quick succession by Bhagat Singh and B. K. Dutt which exploded on the floor of the House creating a resounding blast. Pandemonium was let loose and people ran helter-skelter. A fat and frightened nominated member crawled under a bench to save his skin. Another one ran towards a lavatory. Only two leaders kept standing like rock : Vithal Bhai Patel and Pandit Motilal Nehru. The latter shouted at members of his party : *Are bhai, bhagtey kiyon ho ! Yeh to koi apne hi admi malum hote hain* (Look chums, why are you bolting away ? They—the bomb-thrower and his companion—look like our own men).

"I along with many people was detained on suspision. Bhagat Singh and B. K. Dutt, however, surrendered to the police, lest some innocent persons should be apprehended. As these two revolutionaries were being removed in police custody to a lock-up from the Assembly Chamber, they shouted 'Inqilab Zindabad' (Long Live Revolution) and walked fearlessly past the crowds like two tigers. I looked at them with pride. The bomb they had thrown shook Indians throughout the country.

"I heard that recently Lala Lajpat Rai, the redoubtable leader of Punjab, had lost his life as a result of a blow inflicted by Saunders, a British Police Officer, during the course of a baton charge on a nationalist procession led by him. This infuriated many people, including Bhagat Singh, a member of the Revolutionary Party, who daringly shot Saunders dead opposite the Police Headquarters. He had taken an eye for an eye. Bhagat Singh had absconded till he appeared in the incident described above.

"Bhagat Singh and B. K. Dutt were tried and sentenced to death and transportation of life respectively. I heard from a reliable source when I was on my way to a bonfire of British goods that Bhagat Singh, an idol of the nation by now, was to be hanged in the District jail at Lahore that day. I was emotionally aroused on hearing this news and went to a vantage point from where I could see the walls of the jail behind which Bhagat Singh stood ready to die.

"In reverential silence, I shared the sorrow of the whole nation. I heard an eye witness account, later, of how unflinchingly he had faced his doom. Two others besides Bhagat Singh, Raj Guru and Sukh Dev, were being hanged that day for loving their country. When Bhagat Singh's turn came, he was given a mask, to cover his face, before he went up to the gallows He threw it away scornfully and advanced, his chin up, and with a steady and unfaltering step, solemnly kissed his gallows, saying he was lucky to be laying down his life for his country; he then bade good-bye to the Indian jailor, doctor and magistrate, who stood there as silent witnesses. He was hanged, with his eyes breathing fire and with revolution on his lips. The handful of Indian officials present at the time hung their heads in sorrow and in shame for hanging a patriotic compatriot.

"The British had not allowed Bhagat Singh's body to be handed over to his next-of-kin, fearing that it would incite the masses. It is alleged that his charred corpse was left on the dry bed of the river Sutlej where it was found by the locals the next morning. It was then brought down to Lahore where the people seemed to run 'amuck' at the sight of their idol's remains. I was among the multitude of a quarter million people who followed the remains of this martyr to the cremation ground to pay their last homage. The whole country sobbed for their hero.

"(Thirtysix years later, I heard that the renowned patriot B. K. Dutt was lying seriously ill in the Medical Institute, Delhi, and went there to find out how he was on 11 February 1965. I had never set my eyes on him since 1929. When I told him I had seen him on the day he and Bhagat Singh threw the bombs in the Legislative Assembly many years ago, his eyes brightened up. He told me he had been a member of the Revolutionary Party since he was about 17 and never imagined he would hit the headlines one day. He and Bhagat Singh had volunteered for a job, the grave consequence of which they fully realized. They were glad to have offered their lives in the service of their country. He told me that it was not until Bhagat Singh and he had courted arrest that they were apprehended. They did this lest unnecessary reprisals were inflicted upon innocent Indians. Dutt was released a few years later due to ill health but was arrested again in 1942. Due to continuous sufferings in and out of jail his health cracked up. He had been very ill in the last few months. He said Gulzarilal Nanda had now brought him here for medical attention. Talking of Bhagat Singh, he said the latter was informed by the authorities about five o'clock one evening that he was to be hanged a few hours later. Bhagat Singh and two other revolutionaries, Raj Guru and Sukh Dev, then walked fearlessly to their gallows and gave their lives for their country with great courage and pride. He went on to say that their bodies were cremated by government the same day on the dry bed of river Sutlej and left there mercilessly half-charred, as I have described earlier.

"I was moved beyond words to see this great revolutionary, now lying broken in body and shattered in health. There was fire in his eyes and his spirit was undaunted even today. I told him I was honoured to meet one whose deeds in 1929 had stirred me and I was inspired to hear how he had kept challenging his destiny to this day. In bidding farewell, I wished him the best of luck and asked him to let me know if there was any little thing I could do for him. With tears in his eyes and sadness in his voice, he replied : 'There is nothing I want from anyone.'

"Ironically, despite all the tributes everyone paid to him on his death in July 1965, Dutt whose bravery had hastened our freedom, once had to earn his livelihood, even after 1947, by having to start a bakery and running a bus service.)"

NOTE : The two comments on two of India's greatest revolutionaries by the Prime Minister of India have great historical significance. They reveal the mind of a man who enjoyed the fruits of the revolutionaries' sacrifices. Bhagat Singh's popularity was no doubt amazing, but it was not sudden. It was not by way of a reaction to Lalaji's death. Even Gandhiji had to take note of his popularity and he was compelled by force of public opinion to appeal to the Viceroy for saving his life. Bhagat Singh became popular because he had successfully organised an act which finds place as one of the brightest events in the history of Indian revolution. Saunders was killed not because he was guilty of causing Lalaji's death, but because he became a symbol of oppression for the British Government. Starting from the Muzaffarpur bomb intended for Kingsford such symbols had been made targets for the revolutionary movement. This was nothing new in India, it is one of the important techniques in the revolutionary history of the world.

Pandit Nehru's comment—that fifteen years of stress on non-violence had changed the whole background in India and made masses much more indifferent to and even hostile to the idea of terrorism as a method of political action—is one which is far-from the truth. Non-violence as a political campaign started in 1920. In 1930 with the Armoury Raid in Chittagong an organised revolutionary movement spread all over India and swept the country for nearly three years. The British Government did not attach much importance to the ten years of non-violence movement, but they trembled in their shoes at the revolutionary upsurge. This was conclusively demonstrated when the British Government feared to appoint a fourth European magistrate for the district of Midnapore after the successive murders of three district magistrates there. The fourth one appointed was a Bengali.

No revolutionary movement has the same intensity for all times. Ups and downs must be there and the entire phase is taken as an integrated whole. This is true for revolutionary movements all over the world. The Indian revolution started in 1930, gradually died down after 1932, after raising for three years in full fury. There was then a lull in the revolutionary activity and non-violence again found a new vista. It continued to hold the field for another ten years. Again in 1942 the Quit India movement started by the leaders of the non-violence gospel took a revolutionary turn and again the British Government found themselves in an extremely awkward position. The Quit India was soon followed by the I.N.A. in 1944 and both together may be called one integrated revolutionary movement of a longer duration. The revolutionary upsurge took place almost exactly every ten years. It started in 1906, second phase was 1915-17, third phase in 1930-32 and the last phase in 1942-45 and it was the last phase along with the cumulative weight of the other phases that forced the British to Quit India. The political inconsistency of Nehru is conclusively demonstrated by the fact that he had donned the Barrister's gown to defend those very revolutionaries whose leader Subhas Chandra Bose was condemned by him as a Japanese Quisling. He did so because he was clever enough to distinguish the magnitude and intensity of popularity between his own non-violent followers and the revolutionaries.

ERRATA

Page:	Line:	Corret:	Incorrect:
31	22 & 23	Lord Hardinge was etc... and the orderly died.	Lord and Lady Hardinge were etc. ...and the Mahout died.
45	28	addition	additoon
108	10	post-graduate	post ra duate
111	17	one	on
116	23	known of international	known interna-tional
119	11	befell	befall
121	16	once in the Dacca Jail	once the Dacca Jail
141	7	Association	Assciation
169	1	the teak wood	the teak
186	16	others	other
191	30 & 31	Dasaswamedh was the centre	Dasaswamedh was centre
192	31	war	wear
196	15	always	alwas
196	19	came	come
214	15 & 16	who was living	who living
215	30	X	IX
215	30	party by me were	party were
226	25	Manilal	Manial
241	3	backed	baeked
249	4	hang	hand
281	23	against	againts
297	8	flanked	fanked
323	15	the	they

346	5	for the birth	of the birth
346	28	sword of the Indians	sword the Indians
376	5 (3)	Lala	Lal
377	3 (23)	Janahari	Janhari
377	22 (36)	trial	tria
378	18	21	31
378	19	31	21
385	10	Ram Prasad was	Ram Prasad and was
407	20	5 years	2 years
411	7	back	bock
411	19	reciting	erciting
412	20	and smiling face	and is smiling face
415	13	waiting room	wait
422	11	arrival	araival
424	20	Laing	Laig
425	14	by	dy
434	3	outrage	outragt
442	1	Jafri	Jafra
457	13	104	1040
458	21	taking any step	talking any step
465	2	me alone after the feed	me along after the food
466	29	and another gentle-man	and other gentlemen
468	13	although	a though
468	18	cleaned	cleared
469	17	catch-	clutch-
479	6	sources	souces
490	7	undertrial	undertria
490	18	Sri R. S. Pandit	Sir R. S. Pandit
505	4	arrest after Manmatha	arrest when Manmatha
506	2	open	upon
512	8	Achariyaji	Acharji

530	8	He had organised a conference	had or Heg anised a conference
541	27	were rare in such	were ther in such
550	29	told me	tol pme
553	29	dead body	dead boy
558	12	sufferings and sacrifices	sufferings ard sacrifices
563	1	tortured that he was	tortured to death when he was
571	20	ought to function	out to function
577	28 & 29	Congress Working Committee	Congress Committee
iv (appendix)	3	moderate than even	moderate that even
vii (")	26	and Pratul Ganguli	and on behalf of Pratul Ganguli
ix (")	31	one he started	one more he started
xvi („)	21	this is to re-organise	this is re-organise
xxv („)	12	meaning	meeting
xxvi („)	8	Indian	European
xxvi („)	31	did not at all fire	did not all fire.
xxxiv („)	10	masses	messes
Liii. („)	15	Frontier Government	Fronter Government
Lvii („)	17	was a platform	was platform
Lxii („)	19	February 8, 1946	February 8, 1964
Lxv („)	23	terrorist	torrorist